S0-ADE-071

WITHDRAWN

Mad
Seasons

Karra Porter   The Story of the First Women's
Professional Basketball League, 1978–1981

University of Nebraska Press • Lincoln & London

Publication of this volume was assisted by
the Virginia Faulkner Fund, established
in memory of Virginia Faulkner, editor in
chief of the University of Nebraska Press.

Library of Congress
Cataloging-in-Publication Data
Porter, Karra.
Mad seasons : the story of the first
Women's Professional Basketball
League, 1978–1981 / Karra Porter.
p. cm.
Includes bibliographical references and index.
ISBN-13: 978-0-8032-8789-1 (pbk. : alk. paper)
ISBN-10: 0-8032-8789-5 (pbk. : alk. paper)
1. Women's Professional Basketball League—
History.   2. Basketball for women—United
States—History.   3. Women basketball play-
ers—United States—History.   I. Title.
GV885.515.W66P67 2006
796.323'8—dc22
2005026399

Contents

Illustrations

Preface

"I have to ask you a question," Bill Byrne said as we sat in a hotel lobby near his home in Ohio. "Who was Joe Carr? You don't know, do you?"

No, I didn't.

"Joe Carr was the first commissioner in the NFL," he said. "Everybody forgets—believe me, everybody forgets unless people like you are writing books."

And that's why I wrote this book. The Women's Professional Basketball League has been erased from history. As both a sports and history buff, I find it disturbing. Without understanding the past, how can players, owners, and fans appreciate what they have now? A three-hour layover in an airport doesn't sound so bad to women who used to drag themselves into a gym after an all-day bus ride, play a 48-minute game in a 55-degree arena, then turn around and ride back again to save hotel costs.

And where are the great intergenerational debates that rage in men's basketball? We might not know whether Wilt Chamberlain would have schooled Shaquille O'Neal, but we've certainly heard it argued often enough. Would Rosie Walker, indeed, "break Lisa Leslie in half"? Most of us could not refute this contention of St. Louis Streak coach Larry Gillman, because so few are aware of the first generation of professional women's basketball players. (My take, by the way: WBL MVP Walker might have twisted WNBA MVP Leslie into a pretzel, but Leslie can go inside or out, and Walker never strayed more than four feet from the basket. Each of them would score 32 points, but Walker would muscle her way in for more rebounds.)

People like Gillman, who can still recount the strengths and weaknesses of virtually any WBL player put to him, are a rare source of such fun speculation. "If you took Rosie Walker, Althea Gwyn, [Nancy] Lieberman, [Ann] Meyers, [Carol] Blazejowski, and [Liz] Silcott—those six, they would kick anybody's butt in this league right now," he says, then adds, "Molly [Bolin] should have been in that group too." It's an intriguing, if not audacious, claim that begs to be tossed around. It's my kind of conjecture.

But I hadn't even heard of the WBL until a few years ago, when I leafed through a piece of basketball memorabilia that turned out to be a media guide from a women's professional league—*twenty years ago*? That was a shock; I had always assumed the first pro league was the American Basketball League (ABL), which tipped off in 1996, a year before the Women's National Basketball Association (WNBA).

When an Ohio man named Bill Byrne decided to start a professional women's basketball league in 1978, the idea—some might say the nerve— was almost inconceivable. The *men's* pro league was on shaky ground at the time. (One of my favorite headlines of that era is from a 1979 *New York Post* article: "O'Brien denies NBA is kaput.") Women had been playing full court for less than a decade, and many prospects for a women's league hadn't been able to play high school ball, let alone hope for an athletic scholarship to college. I am still amazed at the man's audacity—or vision, depending on one's perspective.

I am even more amazed that no one has written about the Women's Professional Basketball League before. The WBL lasted three full seasons, longer than any women's league except the WNBA. It had scandal, conflict, humor, bitterness, pride, and even murder. The players happily struggled for little or no pay under conditions that today's players could not imagine, all for love of the game.

In interviewing nearly one hundred people involved with the WBL, I was struck by the recurring theme that, regardless of the league's problems a quarter century ago, it is now a source of accomplishment. Susan Summons, whose New England Gulls went on strike after months of nonpayment, puts it well: "When we look at history, there was never a great event before there was a great struggle. I am proud that we are part of history, and I feel just as proud that we were a part of the struggle."

While I am likewise proud to chronicle both the WBL's history and its struggles, one disadvantage of being the first to do so is the impossibility of completely covering any one subject while keeping the work manageable. In my view, each chapter in *Mad Seasons* could sustain its own book. I also had to sacrifice individual team histories and playoff accounts that were nearly as long as the main text.

Finally, a style note: Many WBL personnel married or changed their names after their time in the league. For ease of reference, I have generally used the names by which they were known at the time.

Acknowledgments

This book would not have been possible without the dozens of WBL players, owners, and staffers willing to be interviewed, whose names are interspersed throughout the text. In addition, a vast amount of information about the WBL would have remained buried if former commissioner and Chicago Hustle co-owner Sherwin Fischer hadn't let me camp in his supply room for a week rifling through his copies of league records.

WBL founder Bill Byrne was also generous with his time, allowing me to delve into old memories for two days in Ohio. Another extended interview was with league "midwife" Karen Logan, who, I learned after putting the word out for her all over the country, turned out to live only thirty-five miles from me in Utah.

(Incidentally, one of the worst moments in this project was when a secretary who was transcribing interview tapes for me after hours "lost" several tapes after she was terminated by my firm, causing those people who gave their time to be underrepresented in the book.)

I am also indebted to many people for sharing their scrapbooks and other memorabilia, including Jo-Ellen Bistromowitz Mesa, Molly (Bolin) Kazmer, Patti Bucklew, Jean Cione, Chris Critelli, Jimmy Damon, Tom Davis, Jan Doleschal, Doris Draving, Liz Galloway McQuitter, Lynda Gehrke Phillip, Bertha Hardy, Cardie Hicks, Bill Himmelman, Sue Hlavacek, Barb Hostert, Jill Hutchison, John Katzler, Marguerite Keeley, Candace Klinzing, Larry Kozlicki, Rod Lein, Karen Logan, Cindy Lundberg, Charlie McCabe, Kate McEnroe, Michelle McKenzie, Muisette McKinney, Mariah Burton Nelson,

Anita Ortega, Darla Plice, John Robert Scott, Ione Shadduck, Lynnette Sjoquist, Sylvia Sweeney, and Ethel "Poco" White.

The Iowa Women's Archive went above and beyond my expectations in helping with the Cornets, and I owe a big favor now to my sister Kelly Porter Hull and niece Elizabeth Hull, who made the long trip to the University of Kansas library for days on end after I played the desperate-sister card. I'm also grateful to Connie Barney for hundreds of hours of transcription and revision work, and to my mother Betty Porter, who swore she didn't mind using her entire vacation and more to proofread, check cites, and handle other tedious but critical stuff.

Mad Seasons

Prologue Birth of a League

COLUMBUS, OHIO 1977
Bill Byrne left his office and drove to a local sports bar, where he ran across half a dozen friends seated around a table. An idea had been germinating in Byrne's head for some time, and tonight seemed as good as any to mention it. "I'll spring it on these guys," he decided. "They're all jocks."

A couple of drinks later, Byrne opened the conversation. "What do you think of women's pro basketball?" he asked. Not much, as it turned out, but Byrne persisted. Did they know how many colleges now had women's basketball teams? How many scholarships were now being offered to women? Byrne knew.

In 1971 fewer than three hundred thousand girls in the United States competed in interscholastic athletics, only 7 percent of all participants. Eleven states had no girls' programs at all. By the 1976–77 school year, that figure had grown to 28 percent, and participation by women at the college level had tripled. More than eight hundred colleges now sponsored women's basketball teams, a number expected to double in the next few years.

It didn't take a genius to see that big action was coming to women's sports, Byrne figured. He had seen the signs with his own eyes, as he drove past schoolyards with young girls playing basketball under the 100-degree sun. Crowds were growing for Amateur Athletic Union (AAU), high school, and collegiate women's basketball games—five hundred here, fifteen hundred there—and some women's teams were drawing better than a minor league football team that he operated. "What the hell is happening here?" he mused.

The six men in an Ohio bar remained unimpressed. "Well, I'm going to do a women's pro basketball league," he declared. His friends laughed, and Byrne stood up, more determined than angry. "I can do this," he insisted. Byrne walked out of the bar shortly before midnight, thinking about his friends' derision. No, he was not an idiot, he decided, and, no, he had not lost his mind, but anything that could arouse that much negativity must have potential. The next morning, Byrne called his staff together and announced the formation of the Women's Professional Basketball League.

This was not the first time that friends had heard Bill Byrne enthusing about some unconventional sports venture. Since graduating from Ohio State University sixteen years earlier, William J. Byrne had gone from operating a sporting goods store to the presidency of the semi-pro football team Columbus Bucks. In 1974 he became director of player personnel for the Chicago Fire, a franchise in the short-lived World Football League.

Shortly after that venture, Byrne founded two more entities: the National Scouting Association, which provided player information to the National Football League and other sports leagues, and the American Professional Slo-Pitch League. "In the 1950s, I was known as a hustler. In the '60s, I was a promoter. In the '70s, I was an entrepreneur," he says. The difference? "I just paid my bills in the '70s."

Byrne was, by all accounts, a salesman—which was not always a compliment. "I think you either loved him or you hated him," says Kate McEnroe, director of public relations for the WBL in its first season. "He was absolutely an entrepreneur and I liked him, but I also understood that he was demanding and, I think, a little before his time. He talked big, and I think he dreamt big, and his vision of the league is what the WNBA is today. He might have stretched the truth at times, but part of it was to keep enthusiasm up and running."

Lynn Arturi, a WBL player who also worked in the league office, puts it a little more bluntly. "I have to say that sometimes I thought of him as the flim flam man," she says, "a guy who would talk you out of your last dollar. He was good with people. He was a likeable guy, but you always had a sense that you were talking to someone that was trying to get the most out of you and might take advantage of you."

Joining Byrne's new venture were some key staffers from the slo-pitch league. Byrne's right-hand man was David S. Almstead, a business major from Ohio Wesleyan who sold insurance to help put himself through college. Byrne met Almstead when the young man tried out for a kicker position with the Fire. Driving away from the field, Byrne saw one of the hopefuls walking along the road and offered a lift back to the hotel. No, thanks, Almstead declined pleasantly, he'd like to walk. "It was five miles!" Byrne exclaims. He liked Almstead's gumption, and when Byrne needed help with a professional softball league, he gave Almstead the job. Byrne now tapped Almstead again to help run his new basketball league.

Another, less enthusiastic transplant from slo-pitch was Tim Koelble, a former sportswriter who handled public relations for the softball league. Koelble was not high on the notion of women's professional sports, Byrne says. "He hated women. *Hated* them," at least when it came to athletics. "It was a trial for Tim," he recalls. "There's women's women and there's men's men. He was a man's man." Nonetheless, Koelble agreed to take on communications duties for the new venture.

When Koelble transferred to management of the wbl's Dayton franchise, Byrne replaced him with twenty-four-year-old Kate McEnroe, a University of Colorado graduate he had met when she wrote a freelance article about the wbl. McEnroe was interested in sports but hadn't had many opportunities at her high school ("Competitive sports there was cheerleading"). "I felt like it was important for women to learn how to compete and have that team experience," she says of her wbl days. "I also felt to some degree that if we could make this successful, generations behind us wouldn't have to work so hard and have to prove themselves."

Although the league's official title was the Women's Professional Basketball League, Byrne dropped the *P* to keep the moniker three letters long. "nfl, nba, wbl, end of story," he figured. "If they can do it, we can do it." (Some newspapers, however, refused to recognize the league's preferred abbreviation and insisted on using the letters wpbl, even going so far as to change quotes from league personnel to insert the extra *P*.)

The new league needed a logo, and Byrne approached a local graphic artist named Rick Mock, who had created a logo for one of the slo-pitch franchises. Mock had heard of Byrne—which wasn't good. His own softball team had nearly joined Byrne's slo-pitch league, only to have the deal fall through when the owner heard about certain unpaid bills.

When Byrne approached him about creating a logo, Mock was glad to get the job but wasn't sure he would actually see his money. As for the idea of a women's league, "I guess I was like most people," he says, figuring "here's Bill again, trying something that nobody else has tried, and you know, it may work and it may not."

The artist sat down with a black Rapidograph pen and brush and went to work. The design should look feminine, he decided, so he sketched a woman with long hair with her arms raised, shooting a basketball. "I didn't want to get into other parts of the body and have to deal with not pleasing somebody who'd say, 'Well, you know, all the players aren't as petite as this player,' or 'The players don't have that type of body,'" Mock says. He worked the sketch into a *B*, giving the letter soft, rounded corners, and drew the other two letters to match.

In June 1977 Mock was paid $300 for the completed logo ("that ugly thing, I loved it," Byrne says), and the wbl had an image to go with its title. What the league needed now was a "name," a spokesperson who would have credibility with sponsors, the media, and players. Byrne picked up the phone and dialed a number in Logan, Utah, where the woman he wanted was working on her postgraduate degree at Utah State University. On the other end of the line, Karen Logan listened to what Byrne had to say, but she was wary. She had fallen for this before.

A few years earlier, women's athletics was just beginning to attract national attention. A paucity of meaningful athletics programs for women in high school and college had drawn relatively little attention until Congress enacted Title IX of the Education Amendments of 1972, designed to improve opportunities for females in education. The controversial law placed a spotlight on the status of women's and girls' sports, generating more than ten thousand comments during the regulation process and an unsuccessful lawsuit by the National Collegiate Athletic Association (ncaa) seeking to exempt athletics from its reach.

In 1973 a record 40 million viewers watched tennis player Billie Jean King defeat self-proclaimed male chauvinist Bobby Riggs in a famed "Battle of the Sexes." A year later, abc added women to its annual *Superstars* program, which pitted athletes against each other in events other than their normal sport. Among the contestants that year was a woman named Karen Logan.

Logan had earned her spot on the *Superstars* roster through her role as Most Valuable Player for three years on the All-American Redheads, a barnstorming women's basketball squad that combined Harlem Globetrotter–style antics with genuine basketball skill. An influential 1974 piece about the Redheads in *Sports Illustrated* opened with an eye-catching declaration: "If they were men, they would be famous. They would be rich. They would be on a first-name basis with Cosell, Schenkel, Whitaker and Gifford, perhaps even Cavett and Carson. They would have played before hundreds of thousands in the Garden, the Spectrum, the Forum, the Astrodome—tens of millions on television."

The SI writers joined seven Redheads (four of whom later played in the WBL) on the road and painted an appealing picture of the potential entertainment value of women's basketball:

> The Red Heads are slick ball handlers and their passes snap with precision. Many are thrown behind the back, perfectly. The women are wearing bright red lipstick and blue eyeshadow, as if they were going to the theater. But here they are, perspiring like mad and playing basketball like demons. They drive swiftly down the court. They shoot with deadly accuracy. They shout at each other, shrilly, crying out play patterns. Sometimes they shriek jokes at the men. Their precision dazzles the crowd and, even though they are playing against butchers and insurance men and car salesmen, the All American Red Heads are plainly a splendid basketball machine.

The star of the team, the article said, was Logan, "who is perhaps not very far below the unmatchable Babe Didrikson in natural abilities." Seeing her play, the authors wrote, "is like seeing a work of art. Her moves remind one of Pete Maravich." During her three years with the team, Logan scored 12,400 points, averaging 25 points per game.

After the article, Logan began receiving phone calls. One was an invitation to the *Superstars* competition. Another was from an attorney in Phoenix, Lee Bakunin, who had a fairly concrete proposal. With Logan's help, a traveling squad would serve as the prototype for other teams in a professional league to be called the Women's Basketball Association.

The timing seemed right to Logan, who disliked the level of control exerted by Redheads owner Orwell Moore. Another ex-Redhead was also interested, and the result was the Phoenix (later Indianapolis) Pink Panthers, which would generate interest in a pro league by playing men's teams, but without the comic aspects of the Redheads. The Pink Panthers hoped for a game against the Redheads, envisioning a Madison Square Garden appearance for what would have been the first professional women's basketball game.

"The league now consists of one team—admittedly an unusual format," the *San Francisco Chronicle* remarked, but landing investors wasn't easy. "If they expect to make money the first couple of years, we'll probably fold,"

Logan said. A number of people had expressed interest, but no one took the plunge. "It'd be the first women's pro league in history and everyone is waiting for someone else to do it so they can join in."

Time ran out, and backers never materialized. "We were just getting our heads above water when we decided it was too hard," Logan said. "It wasn't worth it any more." The Pink Panthers were out of business, and the first professional women's basketball league would have to wait.

Meanwhile, women's basketball continued to make inroads into the public eye. The first televised women's basketball game was on January 26, 1975, between Immaculata College, the dominant team in women's basketball at the time, and the University of Maryland. A month later, the "Mighty Macs" faced Queens College in the first women's basketball game ever played at Madison Square Garden. The game drew nearly twelve thousand spectators, many of whom left before the men's college game that followed—much to the surprise of Garden promoters, who paid the men's teams twice what the women received.

Later that year, Logan again drew attention to women's basketball by taking on former Los Angeles Lakers guard Jerry West in a nationally televised game of H-O-R-S-E, part of a *Battle of the Sexes* series inspired by the King-Riggs match two years earlier. The first two misses (West's *H* and *O*) were straight jump shots; then Logan, encouraged by the show's promoters, used a trick shot, spinning the ball on one finger, which she used to propel the ball into the hoop. West could not get the ball to spin, let alone finish the shot. Logan was still at *H* when West hit *E* on a missed outside jumper. "I can't believe it!" a teenage girl screamed.

In 1976 women's basketball was played for the first time at the Olympic Games in Montreal. No one gave the unheralded Americans much of a chance after finishing eighth in the World Championships the year before; indeed, expectations were so low that when the team actually qualified at the preliminary tournament in Ontario, the U.S. Olympic training grounds weren't ready for their arrival. "We had to kind of lay low for a couple of weeks until they could get the uniforms, bags, and all the paraphernalia that goes with it," Gail Marquis laughs.

The real contest in Montreal, everyone knew, was for the silver medal. The gold was assured to the venerable Russians, led by twenty-four-year-old Uljana Semjonova, one of the tallest women in the world at seven feet, with impressive skills to go along with her height. After being trounced by Japan and Russia, the United States upset Czechoslovakia to come away with the silver.

A few months later, Logan's phone rang again. This time a man named Jason Frankfort was on the line. Frankfort, a restaurateur and former stockbroker from New York City, was planning a twelve-team Women's Basketball Association to play a six-month, sixty-two-game schedule beginning in October 1977.

The WBA's commissioner would be Lois Geraci Ernst of Advertising to Women, Inc., creator of such memorable advertising campaigns as the Coty perfume's "If you want him to be more of a man, try being more of a woman" and the Clairol slogan, "You're not getting older, you're getting better." Ernst had a goal for the WBA: "I hope one day that little boys might say, 'When I grow up, I want to be a great basketball star—just like my mother.'"

In January 1977 Frankfort staged a press conference in New York City to announce the league's formation. While cocktail waitresses in spiked heels and satin shorts served drinks, Ernst opened the proceedings: "For centuries, you know what they've been saying about us women. 'Keep 'em barefoot, pregnant, and praying. But today we're changing that to 'keep 'em well shod, well paid, and playing.'" She then introduced Frankfort, the "chairman of the broads."

A company based in Columbus, Ohio—run by a man named Bill Byrne—announced that it would provide scouting reports to the league, and Byrne's National Scouting Association began contacting college coaches across the country. Reportedly, four franchises had been snatched up for $50,000, but in reality, Frankfort had no takers yet. "Everybody waited for somebody else to lend the credibility of his or her name or money to the WBA," *womenSports* later wrote. "Midway through this $100,000 waiting game, Frankfort's money ran out. So did his backers." Logan, meanwhile, wound up stuck with a $250 hotel bill.

Now, less than a year after that debacle, Logan found herself listening to Byrne's plans for yet another try at professional women's basketball. This time, she thought, maybe investors would actually materialize. "I just hope the people who are behind it have enough money to see it through for maybe four or five years," she said, "because by then there will definitely be a market for it and enough players with the skills to play professionally."

On October 11, 1977, the Women's Professional Basketball League, a nonprofit organization, was incorporated in Ohio by Byrne, Almstead, and a friend of Byrne's, Carew Smith, who had no involvement with the league. At a formal meeting that day, the three organizers issued bylaws, announced operating and playing rules, and created a board of governors to be filled by representatives from each team. The league would be headquartered at a building owned by Byrne in Columbus.

Two months later the WBL issued its first press release, announcing the solicitation of charter membership applications, and in January 1978 Byrne's group placed an advertisement in the *Wall Street Journal*:

WOMEN'S PROFESSIONAL BASKETBALL INVESTMENT
The Women's Professional Basketball League will begin play in 1978–79 and now has membership and territorial right investments available. Evidence from national research and market studies indicates the WBL has strong growth potential for its program which includes national marketing and television exposure.

Reporters, some more suspicious than others, took notice. "When we read that yet another effort is under way to start a new pro league, it's extremely difficult not to be skeptical and, unfortunately, even cynical about it," a Mississippi sports editor wrote. "Sports fans have been burned so often that they have become wary and distrustful of new ventures, of all the outrageous promises that accompany them, and of the financial backing they say is there but usually never is."

Doubters could point to any number of obstacles. To some, it was premature. The time for a women's pro league would be when the college game became a tough ticket, UCLA coach Billie Moore said. "Right now, you can walk right into any big contest in the country without worrying about being shut out at the gate. When that changes, the time for a pro league will be here."

Philadelphia writer Mary Flannery agreed, noting that the women's collegiate game was still in the "embryonic stage" in many parts of the country. Flannery speculated that perhaps a third of the nine thousand in attendance at the recent college finals in Los Angeles between UCLA and Maryland had been drawn by a genuine interest in women's basketball. "That number, from the second largest population in the country, does not auger well if you expect to attract fans for a 34-game schedule," she warned.

Others noted that now that women's basketball was an Olympic event, top players would likely forego a professional career to compete in the

1980 Olympics in Moscow. (Olympic eligibility required amateur status at the time.) The absence of such players would dilute a talent pool already disadvantaged by a scarcity of quality high school and college programs.

"Even those coaches most bullish on women's basketball think the idea of a pro league is premature," *womenSports* wrote a year before the WBL began. "Seven years ago, they point out, colleges were still playing six-woman basketball on a divided court. There were virtually no athletic scholarships until four years ago. Women's basketball didn't become an Olympic event until last year. And until very very recently coaches like Immaculata's Cathy Rush were producing championship teams on salaries of $1,500 and nonexistent budgets."

Many prospective pros had only begun playing organized ball a few years earlier. "Skeptics, among them several local sportswriters, say the quality of women's basketball simply hasn't come far enough for a pro league," reported the *Minneapolis Star*. "There have been improvements, they admit, but the women's game still bears too many blemishes: clumsy ball handling, no power plays under the basket, no towering shots from the outside, no awesome slam dunks, few fast breaks, no breathtaking moves."

Among the skeptics, however, were optimists. The WBL "might well deserve more than a passing glance by media and fans alike," the self-proclaimed cynic in Mississippi concluded. Women's basketball had advanced in quality, he wrote, and interest in the sport was growing. A sportswriter in Washington shared that optimism. "At some point in time, there will be women's basketball at the pay-for-play level, and it will be successful," he predicted. "Girls will shoot hoops in their backyard thinking of the day they'll be playing in the pros before packed gymnasiums around the country."

WBL bylaws named Byrne as president/commissioner (both terms were used), with broad responsibilities and powers. He was also granted a five-year employment contract executed by Almstead and himself at $50,000 per year, subject to increase (but not decrease) by the board of governors.

The founding documents also included certain financial incentives that, if the league succeeded, would prove lucrative for the three organizers. They were granted territorial rights to Florida, New York, Texas, and California, the four most populous states, and a percentage of gross revenues from licensing and nonlocal television broadcasts.

With financial details in place, Byrne's group now needed to distance themselves from Frankfort's aborted attempt a year earlier. "Jason Frankfurt did more to hurt women's basketball—you can print that—because what he would do, he would call a press conference and have everybody come in and nothing happened," Byrne says. Some writers couldn't seem to tell the difference between the two groups, and even some who did still had negative perceptions. Writing about the WBL, for example, one Chicago columnist began his remarks, "This is no gag."

League officials hoped for twelve teams, but the bylaws (and logistics) would allow them to start with eight. A June 1978 deadline was announced, which gave Byrne six months to find eight investors able and willing to part with a $50,000 entry fee and an estimated quarter of a million dollars in annual expenses.

One way to spark interest among investors was the tried-and-true method of hinting that another buyer was just around the corner. Thus, one early brochure identified thirty-five cities that were "under consideration for first-year memberships." Were they under consideration by the league? Yes. Were there applicants in those cities ready and able to buy in? Not always—in fact, rarely. Byrne worked hard to line up franchises, and virtually any nibble was enough to announce that a city was a "strong candidate" or "in discussion."

The league said it had received 144 applications for franchises and later claimed to have considered applications from "750 groups and/or individuals who expressed interest in becoming members of the League." Some of that hype was true. A group in Jackson, Mississippi, was indeed interested, especially if it could field a team of local players. "How many people would pay to see women's professional basketball in Jackson?" queried a local newspaper. Not enough, the group ultimately decided, and Mississippi passed.

In Washington DC the efforts of attorney Gary Minninsohn to line up investors looked so promising that the *Washington Post* pronounced "Women's Pro Basketball on the Way." Two months later, Minninsohn had faded from the scene, but the league announced that the nation's capital would still have a franchise, the Washington Wiz. Forty-four-year-old businessman Lloyd Fetherolf from Woodbridge, Virginia, "spent $50,000 and realized a dream," the *Post* said. By the end of July 1978, though, the *Post* reported that Fetherolf "has not signed a player, does not have a staff, a coach or an arena." He had, in fact, failed to pay the membership fee, saying he couldn't find a suitable arena in the DC area.

Other potential investors surfaced but did not sign on. Five businessmen in Tampa announced that they were "very interested." An x-rated movie theater owner in St. Louis put down a deposit but couldn't finalize arrangements. San Francisco investors were intrigued and had the money, but decided to wait a year.

By the league's first official meeting in June 1978, Byrne had secured commitments from six WBL franchises: Chicago, Iowa, Milwaukee, Minnesota, New Jersey, and Fetherolf from DC. The board gave him more time to find at least two more entries, and when Houston and New York signed on, the league now had the minimum number of teams that it needed. Other interested parties were still out there, Byrne reported, but existing owners decided to stick with eight. (When the DC franchise later fell through, league officials transferred it to Dayton.)

When the WBL tipped off its inaugural season on December 9, 1978, it had eight franchises—the Chicago Hustle, Dayton Rockettes, Houston Angels, Iowa Cornets, Milwaukee Does, Minnesota Fillies, New Jersey Gems, and the New York Stars. The game was afoot.

The Lights Go Up

President Jimmy Carter was two years into his term. A gallon of gas cost 63 cents, and a newly minted Susan B. Anthony dollar could buy six first-class stamps. Americans were reading Mommie Dearest, *listening to the disco tracks from* Saturday Night Fever, *and watching* Laverne and Shirley. *Pittsburgh Steelers quarterback Terry Bradshaw was the* NFL's *Most Valuable Player.*

In the visitors' locker room at the historic Mecca Arena in Milwaukee, a young man with curly brown hair stood before a dozen young women. In its day, the Mecca had seen NBA *and* NCAA *championships. Tonight, the arena would host the first professional women's basketball game.*

It was also a first for Chicago Hustle coach Doug Bruno. At twenty-seven, Bruno was younger than some of his players and had only been coaching for a couple of years. National news cameras and wire services were out there waiting, along with what everyone hoped would be a big crowd. Perhaps more than anything, Bruno's job now was to keep his players calm.

As the coach spoke, he was interrupted by an insistent British accent. "Well, please get to the part where you tell them how important it is." Bruno knew the voice; the woman was with the public broadcasting radio crew that had been following the team around for two days ("an Englishwoman who knew little about sports," according to the Chicago Tribune*). "Tell them how they have to win and go out there and fight," she directed.*

Bruno looked at her and then back at his players. An opportunity to ease the tension had just presented itself. "Remember, girls," he intoned, "the battle of Dunkirk was won on the playing fields of Eton. Now, go out there and win one for the Gipper!"

Across the arena, the home team's preparations were less dramatic. The Milwaukee Does (as in female deer) snapped Polaroid pictures of each other and then settled down to business while Coach Candace Klinzing began her pregame talk.

Klinzing, a Wisconsin native, had joined the Does "on a whim" some five weeks earlier when the team's first coach backed out due to an illness in her family. As coach at Russell Sage College in Troy, New York, Klinzing had won all but one game her first season and was undefeated the following year. From there, she moved to College of Lake County in Grayslake, Illinois, to develop its women's athletics program, coaching the school's volleyball, softball, and basketball teams to Skyway Conference titles over the next two years.

Klinzing explained her game plan to the Does players and how she wanted the offense run. She knew her squad was at a disadvantage. This would be Milwaukee's first competition against another WBL team, but Chicago had already played two exhibition games. To make matters worse, Klinzing's plan to scout the Hustle had been thwarted by a snowstorm that diverted her flight from Jackson, Mississippi, where the Hustle were playing, to Atlanta.

The Does were chosen to host the inaugural game, general manager Gene DeLisle said, "because we have a good arena, NBA and NCAA championships have played here, and Milwaukee is a good basketball town." The city claimed historical entitlement, touting in a half-page advertisement that it had hosted the first professional baseball game (1869), football game (1895), and basketball game (1896). "Plus, I think I asked for it first," DeLisle quipped. Actually, a little more thought went into it, says WBL founder and president Bill Byrne. The Does did have an excellent arena, and the location was right. "We're an upstart league and Chicago is right next door, so the travel is going to be nil," he figured. "You know it's going to be a rivalry."

Milwaukee staffers went all out in their preparations for the game, mailing hundreds of brochures to businesses, attorneys, and doctors, and sending players to bars and restaurants across the city. Managers figured out one potential market for the game early on: of the first one hundred phone calls received for tickets, all but two were from women.

To perform the national anthem, the team first approached pop singer

Helen Reddy (whose "I Am Woman" was a number one hit exactly seven years previously to the day) but were told that her asking price was $6,000. "When I heard that, I told her, 'See you later,'" reported public relations director Chuck Bekos.

They had better luck with opera singer Carol Neblett, a soprano of international repute who also happened to be married to Milwaukee Symphony conductor Kenneth Schermerhorn. "How did we get her?" Bekos asked rhetorically. "We *asked* her. She is doing it because she is enthusiastic about this being a first for Milwaukee and a first for women." Neblett had, incidentally, played basketball at the University of Southern California.

The night before the big game, Does management put the players up at a local hotel. In their rooms, players had butterflies in their stomachs. "We couldn't wait to just get down there and play," Barb Hostert recalls. "We knew that it had been hyped up for a couple of weeks, and now we wanted to play."

"This day, Dec. 9, 1978, may come to be remembered as one of the most important in the history of sports, comparable to the days when George Halas and friends founded pro football and Abner Doubleday thought of an extra use for a cow pasture," Ray Sons of the *Chicago Sun-Times* wrote. "The patter of sneakered feet in Milwaukee Arena will signal the birth of what may become the first women's professional league in a team sport to capture and hold national interest." December 9 was officially declared Milwaukee Does Day, and "I'll tell you, I almost cried when I read it," DeLisle said.

The anticipation in other corners, by contrast, was underwhelming. The December 9 issue of *The Sporting News*, for example, contained no mention of the game, other than an oblique reference in a column about women's basketball that opened with, "Are you uneasy with women's sports? I am." Ultimately, the writer conceded, "there must be a place for these female (basketball) teams because they are cropping up all over."

Game time drew near, and the starting lineups were set. Handling the point for Milwaukee would be a twenty-seven-year-old southpaw Brenda Dennis from Marshall University. Dennis had quit her job at a factory in Kentucky to drive to Milwaukee for tryouts, impressing management with her ball-handling skills and quickness on defense. "Brenda was quiet," Hostert recalls. "She was a very good athlete, a team player, somebody you could rely on."

At shooting guard was the team's youngest player, "Baby J," twenty-two-year-old Joanie Smith, a recent graduate from Arizona State with a degree in education. Smith was a deadly shot but had assumed that her basketball career was over when a broken collarbone benched her for most of her senior year. She was looking for a teaching job when friends told her that she had been drafted by the wbl. "She was a character," teammate Lynda Gehrke laughs. "She was the one that they usually picked to do the interviews. She had a great personality."

At forward for Milwaukee was Marguerite Keeley. Kansas's "Queen of the Center Court" began her career at Independence Community Junior College, earning All-American honors and setting a single-game record of 33 points and 33 rebounds, and finished at Wichita State University, where she averaged 20 points and 15 rebounds per game her senior year. "She was just nice," Hostert says. "She didn't swear, and she didn't really say much about people. She was big and tall—you couldn't push her around. She meant business when she was out there."

Also in the front court was five-foot-ten-inch Kathleen DeBoer from Michigan State, a finalist for that year's Wade Trophy as the best female college player. DeBoer was feeling lukewarm about graduate school when she learned that she had been drafted by the new professional basketball league. "She could snatch the ball out of the air like nobody," says Hostert. "Her rebounds—you would think somebody else was getting in there and she's up there taking it." DeBoer's enthusiasm inspired her teammates. "I can remember her being the one in the huddle, 'Come on, you guys, we can do this,'" Hostert says. "Pulling us together."

Rounding out the Does roster was the tallest player on the court, six-foot-two-inch center Lynda Gehrke from the University of Colorado, where she averaged 24 points and 12 boards per game. "She laughed a lot, and she was a hard worker out there on the court," Hostert says. Six months earlier, Gehrke had been moping about the end of her playing career when a friend approached her. "Did you see that they have a draft for a women's pro league and you got drafted?" Gehrke thought it was a lie. "That is a cruel joke," she replied. Now, she would be tipping off in the first professional women's basketball game.

For the Chicago Hustle, starting at guard was twenty-nine-year-old Karen Logan, the best known player on the team and in the league itself, the woman wbl organizers had called when they needed a spokesperson to lend credibility to the new league.

In the other guard slot was twenty-three-year-old Rita Easterling from

Mississippi College. Dubbed the "All American Girl" by Chicago press, Easterling did not drink or smoke, nor did her thick southern drawl utter swear words. Tonight, though, she was a little worried, having just come off some troubling exhibition games in Mississippi. "The biggest thing I remember about those is I got leg cramps real bad for the first time in my whole life, because it was so hot," she says. "I kept having to go in and out of the game because I kept getting cramps so bad."

At small forward for Chicago was Elizabeth "Liz" Galloway from the University of Nevada–Las Vegas, a superb rebounder even though she was only five-foot-six. "The Bandit" was also known as a defensive specialist with quick hands. She was a hard-nosed player who gave 100 percent of herself in practice, Coach Bruno said, the kind of player who "comes off the floor with her hair wringing wet and her pants good and dirty."

Filling the other forward position was Galloway's college teammate, five-foot-ten-inch Debra Waddy-Rossow, who had perfected a nearly un-stoppable turnaround jump shot in high school by practicing against a coach wielding a tennis racket. (When Waddy met future husband Winston Rossow in college, he tried an opening line on her that was not as effective with her as it might have been with others. "I'm a basketball player. I average 16 points a game," he said. "Oh?" Waddy replied. "Well, so am I. And I'm averaging 32.")

At five-foot-eleven, the tallest player on Chicago's squad was center Susan Digitale from Cal State, Sacramento. "Susie Dig," as Coach Bruno called her, was a native Californian, fun loving and outgoing. (In one of the earliest news photographs of the Hustle, Digitale—who said she used her hairdo to make herself look taller—was wearing a T-shirt at practice that said "Basketball players do it one on one.")

For Karen Logan, the first game would not be an ideal experience. For one thing, she found her responsibilities as assistant coach and league spokesperson distracting. More bothersome was a nagging injury that almost kept her from playing. During an open tryout in October, she had stepped on the foot of a walk-on and had broken a bone in her own foot. Now, several weeks later, the break was not fully healed, but Logan had little choice about whether to play. Both the WBL and the Hustle had capitalized on her name from the earliest sales pitches through opening day. She also wanted to play, and did so—"very painfully," she says.

When the Milwaukee Does and Chicago Hustle trotted onto the court, they were cheered by 7,824 people in the stands. It was everything that Does players had hoped for. "We practiced in the Arena a couple of times, heard our echoes and tried to imagine all those seats being filled," Smith said. "It was just excellent."

His players were "a little like Lewis and Clerk and Christopher Columbus," Bruno declared. "They're going out on a limb. They've given up good jobs, and they're taking a chance. They're not just talking about one game but the whole league." It was like a storybook tale, Dennis said; all she had ever wanted to do in life was play basketball. "It is hard for me to believe that I will be playing in the first pro women's game in America. It makes me feel like a pioneer."

For Gehrke, playing in the first game was a dream come true. "All of the spectators and fans—I never played in front of that many people before—and the big lights, it was just a different world completely." Gehrke felt that she was there for all women, to show that they had finally made it. "I was just holding my head up high thinking it was grand. 'Here we are, let us perform for you. Let us play this wonderful game and show you that we can play it, too.'"

Mixed with that sense of wonder were more practical considerations. "It's hard to have a sense of history when you're competing in a sporting event, because to be self-conscious when you are competing in a sporting event is, by definition, to fail at competing," DeBoer observes. "Tiger Woods, when he is winning the Masters, is not thinking, 'This is a historic moment.'" Easterling also brushed aside the historic implications. "I don't remember thinking about that," she says. "I just remember we were trying to get ready, and thinking about things we had to do to win."

Seven white players and three African American players lined up at midcourt, and the Does' public address announcer asked the crowd—"for once"—to give a hand to the officials, Mark Mano and John Katzler. "Surprisingly, there were few boos," noted *Referee* magazine (and, Mano was happy to note, they didn't get many catcalls during the game, either).

Mano was a car salesman from Racine, Wisconsin, who had to ask for time off to work the game. He had a "firm and direct" style honed by five years in the NBA, *Referee* wrote. By contrast, Katzler had a more amiable, gentle manner. "A warm, friendly, almost fatherly smile awaited each free thrower when official John Katzler administered the ball"—and even a wink when Logan disputed a call, *Referee* said.

At 1:44 p.m., Mano stepped to the center circle and tossed up the opening tip between Gehrke and Digitale. Chicago won the possession, and the first professional women's basketball game was on. Twenty-six seconds later, Milwaukee's Smith received a feed from Dennis and nailed a 15- or 20-foot left-side jumper (15 feet, according to the Milwaukee press; 20 feet, according to the Chicago press) and, the *Chicago Tribune* presumed, "a spot in the Smithsonian Institution in Washington, where the game ball is destined to wind up."

One second later, Smith was called for the WBL's first foul (Digitale would later become the first player to foul out of a professional women's basketball game), and Easterling's free throw put Chicago on the scoreboard. The second was a miss, but Waddy-Rossow grabbed the rebound and laid it in. 3–2 Chicago.

Crowd noise was a factor in the game, Gehrke says. "I'm a talker when I play. Being the big man in the middle, I would always be directing everybody, 'Look out, I've got your backside, you've got one out,' all that kind of stuff. No one could hear me because the crowd was so loud. It was upsetting to me because I'd never played in such a frenzy."

The first quarter saw heated action as Easterling picked apart Milwaukee's defense, making 5 assists, a steal, and a blocked shot. Waddy-Rossow dominated the scoring with 11 points, and Milwaukee's DeBoer was close behind with 8. After the first 12 minutes of play, Chicago led by 8 points, 34–26. Foreshadowing things to come, Milwaukee had missed 10 of 19 free throws, and Chicago only 2 of 14.

As the second quarter began, Gehrke rested on the bench while Gerry Booker subbed in at center for Milwaukee. Easterling and Digitale were still in for Chicago, along with Janie Fincher, Tesa Duckworth, and Toni Stachon. The offensive battle between the teams' highest scorers continued, with Waddy-Rossow racking up another 8 points and DeBoer another 10. Despite 6 more assists by Easterling in the quarter and continued problems at the free throw line (missing 5 of 10 attempts), Milwaukee had narrowed the gap to 3 points at the break, 54–51.

The first half was over, with only a few glitches. One involved television timeouts, a foreign concept to Klinzing (and most others in the women's game at the time). "That caused a couple of errors in my coaching in that first game," she recalls, "because they had said that there would be a TV timeout taken every so many minutes, and that if it was around the time that you would be wanting to take a timeout, you might as well wait for the TV timeout. Well, at one point in the game I wanted to call a timeout, but

I thought the TV timeout would be coming up, so I waited and that was a mistake."

Half-time entertainment was provided by Iowa Cornets ball-handling specialist Tanya Crevier. Crevier's tricks, which quickly made her a popular attraction throughout the league, included spinning a basketball on a soft drink can while a fan drank from it and feeding a volunteer chocolate pudding from a spoon with a basketball spinning on its handle.

While Crevier entertained the crowd, the teams hastily worked on their second-half strategies. Milwaukee knew it had to do something about Waddy-Rossow, who already had 19 points and 6 rebounds. "She was giving us fits," Klinzing says. After seeing the stats at halftime, the coach says, "I was like, 'whoa, we've got to stop her.'" Klinzing adjusted her defense in the post to cut into the forward's shots.

Chicago, meanwhile, focused on shutting down DeBoer. The Does had not had time to perfect screen plays to free her up, Klinzing says, so they turned to Booker for offense. Although Booker was Milwaukee's leading scorer (with 5 points) in the third period, the Does shot a dismal 26 percent from the field. Meanwhile, Easterling continued to accumulate assists—another seven—and Stachon hit three consecutive jump shots for the Hustle as the quarter wound down. At the end of three quarters, Chicago was up by 9 points.

The Hustle built their lead to 13 points less than a minute into the fourth quarter, but suddenly Milwaukee's Smith erupted, scoring on four straight possessions: a rebound and lay-up, a drive to the basket off a feed by Dennis, another drive, and a pair of free throws. In less than three minutes, Smith had single-handedly cut Chicago's lead to 6 points, and a driving lay-up by Dennis a minute later narrowed the margin to 4 points. Time out Chicago.

As play resumed, Milwaukee ratcheted up the pressure on Easterling, forcing her into 9 turnovers in the second half after only 2 in the first. The Does crashed the boards, out-rebounding the Hustle 17 to 9 in the quarter, and grabbed 6 steals. With 5:28 left in the game, Smith fed an open Booker, whose left baseline jumper tied the score at 81–81.

The crowd rewarded the Does' effort with a standing ovation. "Fans who were seeing the team for the first time and who probably never had heard of any of the players stood and screamed encouragement," the Associated Press reported. "The decibel level at times was comparable to that of an NBA playoff game."

The tie was broken thirty seconds later when Booker was whistled for goaltending a baseline shot by Waddy-Rossow (a rare call in women's basketball). The Does then went cold offensively. Nearly three and a half minutes lapsed with no field goal, and Booker missed 4 of 4 free throws. The Hustle held off the Does' rally, and two hours and two minutes after it had begun, the first professional women's basketball game was in the books: Chicago Hustle 92, Milwaukee Does 87.

On her way to becoming the WBL's first MVP, the Hustle's starting point guard scored 14 points, handed out 21 assists, and snagged 9 rebounds. "Guard Rita Easterling of Chicago would bring the ball up the court swiftly, then rifle a pass from midcourt to the baseline, giving a teammate an easy layup," the *Milwaukee Sentinel* praised. "Or she might continue toward the basket and zip the ball through the maze of the middle, setting up another shot." Waddy-Rossow was the game's high scorer with 30 points and 12 rebounds; Smith and DeBoer each had 22.

In the end, Milwaukee was doomed from the free throw line, making fewer than half (19) of their 39 attempts. "We were nervous," DeBoer theorized. "That's why we missed all those free throws. With a decent shooting percentage"—the Does shot only 33 percent from the field—"we would have pulled the game out."

Other than a few minor blemishes (the official play-by-play referring to a time-out by the "Milwaukee Bucks," for example), the first game was seen as a success. "The Does and Hustle put on a fairly good show, employing a fast paced, although sometimes erratic, style of basketball," the *Milwaukee Journal* declared. "There were no slam dunks or players going into orbit for rebounds, but there was plenty for fans to enjoy as the Women's Professional Basketball League (WBL) made its debut at the Arena Saturday," echoed the *Sentinel*.

After the game, Logan remained pragmatic about its significance. "Everybody says history was made here today," she said, "but it's not history unless we're all still here three or four years from now. Everything that happened today is all well and good, but if we're not here next year, what is it all worth?" One answer, some might suggest, could be found in the faces of dozens of excited young girls who surrounded players after the game.

2

Chance of a Lifetime

Tom Davis, assistant coach of the Dallas Diamonds, looked at his notes. Peggy Conover, Shaw College (Michigan). Scouting was a tedious but necessary process, and he picked up the phone. Conover's coach wasn't available, he was told (something about quitting in the middle of the season), but someone would get back to him. Three days later, someone did—a switchboard operator who had been to some of Shaw's games that season.

Davis started with his usual opening question about the player's position. "Does Peggy play inside or outside?"

"Do you mean the court?" she asked. "We play inside. Yes, we have an indoor court."

Okay . . . "Well, how does she run? What kind of speed does she have?"

"She can get up and down the floor." Silence for a moment. "I don't remember her not making it back up the floor."

"What is her jumping ability?"

"Well, for her weight, she jumps pretty well."

"What kind of quickness does she have?"

"What do you mean by that?"

Davis thanked the well-meaning volunteer. Peggy Conover was drafted by the Chicago Hustle.

Joy Holman sat nervously before the woman who had raised her. She had something to say, and she didn't think her grandmother was going to like it. Carrie Lee Jones had never been all that happy when her girl took up sports, anyway. That was a boys' thing. Mama hadn't discouraged her, but she'd made a point of not encouraging her, either.

Joy remembered the one high school game that Mama came to. *In normal basketball fashion, the tiny guard was getting bumped around by the bigger girls, and Joy could hear Mama screaming at them to leave her baby alone.* "Mama, they weren't doing anything to me," she explained patiently after the game. "I was doing it to them."

The family couldn't afford to send Joy to college, but a man who saw her play in high school helped with a scholarship to Benedict College. When Joy arrived there, an intern was coaching the women's team, but two years later the players demanded a real coach and, to their delight, actually got one.

After graduation, Joy heard about a new professional women's basketball league. She already had a job lined up in Charlotte at the nation's second-largest YMCA and had only three days to pack up and get there, but before she left, she and college teammate Gerry Booker filled out paperwork for this new league.

In Charlotte, Joy awaited word from the WBL while coworkers helped her train, going to the gym with her at lunch time, setting up cones and blowing whistles, and keeping her motivated. The more they talked, the more determined she became. "I am going to do this," she said.

When an invitation came for tryouts, Joy decided to go, but first she wanted Mama's blessing, which wouldn't be easy. Mama was old school: you got a good job and you worked. Joy would be giving up a good job to play a game. Her college coaches agreed to drive down for The Talk, and the four of them now sat in Mama's living room.

"Could I go to the tryouts for the women's professional basketball?" Joy asked, quickly rambling on. "I'm going to make more money. I'm going to be on TV and the radio, and I'm going to travel. I get to do what I really, really want to do." Holman glanced at her coaches so that they could "amen" before her grandmother had a chance to answer.

A moment passed, and then, "Whatever makes you happy." Joy was ecstatic, and to celebrate, she shot baskets late into the night with her boyfriend. When she got in, Mama was already asleep.

The next morning, Joy found Mama lying on the floor. The elderly woman had come home from shopping and collapsed. An ambulance arrived quickly, but the news was bad. It was a heart attack, and probably not her first. Nothing could be done. Together with her friend Gerry, Joy waited at the hospital, and a few hours later her grandmother passed away.

She had just lost her best friend and family. "You've got to go try out still,"
friends urged. No, Joy replied, "I don't want to do anything." She spent the
next few days soul searching. Was she supposed to feel sorry for herself? Was
she supposed to be strong and do what she needed to do?

She decided to go. "Don't call anybody and let them know what happened,"
she told her coaches. "I just want to get away." The day after Mama's funeral,
Joy boarded a plane to Minneapolis and then to Washington DC. The tryouts
were therapeutic, although she couldn't stop herself from crying at times.

Joy Holman was signed by the Dayton Rockettes. "It's God's blessing," she
thought. "I need this."

When the new Women's Professional Basketball League was forming,
spokeswoman Karen Logan was honest about one concern: Where would
the players come from? Women's basketball was hardly a developed sport
at the time. "There were a handful of players that I thought had fantastic
skills," she says, "but were there enough good players?"

Many players would have to come out of retirement. Former Queens
College star Debbie Mason and future WBL All-Star Janice Thomas had
jobs as department store security guards. Ann Platte was working at a Stop-
N-Go (where she had been held up three times). Mary Scharff was working
in the accounting department at an automobile manufacturing plant.

Even if women sometimes hadn't played for years, the league really had no
choice, WBL administrator Jane Rath said, because "obviously you don't have
144 super college seniors around the country." No, not in 1978. It was hard to
find that many great college players when so many lacked meaningful high
school experience. Several future WBL players such as Kathy Hawkins, Mara
Melbourne, and Paula Mayo had no high school programs at all; others
such as Heidi Mae Nestor, Deb Prevost, and Robin Tucker were able to play
only a year or two.

Platte remembers when her physical education teacher drove a group of
girls over to another high school for a game. She got to be a "rover" (allowed
to play on both ends of the court) and had a great time. "And then I never
played another game," she says. "That was it. We couldn't get any time in
the gym. We couldn't get it in the morning—the boys had intramurals.
We couldn't get it after school—they had sports. We tried to go up in the
balcony and practice, and they said we bothered them sometimes with balls
coming down. We couldn't get any facilities whatsoever, it was so male
oriented."

Gail Marquis got a few more games than that her senior year—five, to be exact. "That was our season: six games, three home and three away." Mo Eckroth's high school in Utah started a girls' basketball program her sophomore year, but it was pretty painful to watch, she says. There was no state tournament, and her team finished the season by playing three games in a row the same day. "It was awful. I can remember my parents left because they just couldn't watch it any more. I don't think they even made it though the second game."

When Eckroth got to the University of Utah, things were looking up. A few scholarships were available, and she got a new pair of shoes each season. At basketball powerhouse Queens College, the same pair of shoes was expected to last all four years, and there were no athletic scholarships. "You were always, I call it now still, second-class citizens when it came to athletics," Gail Marquis says. Each Queens player was assigned a hand-me-down yellow uniform (hers was too small), and if something happened to it, she would not get another.

That was still a step up from Platte's experience at Grand Valley Junior College, where players had to buy their own uniforms and iron on the numbers. Lynnette Sjoquist's team at Golden Valley Lutheran also bought their own uniforms at a local bookstore and were coached by a male sophomore. At North Carolina State, the women's team had no locker room; future WBL players Kaye and Faye Young had to change in a bathroom stall.

None of those obstacles mattered much to women who were drawn to the game, as many WBL players had been their entire lives. When Janie Fincher was five years old, her father tacked the rim of a bucket to the side of their house in Oklahoma; she spent hours tossing an old, flat volleyball at it. Janice Thomas had been playing since she was six years old, mostly in New York City schoolyards. Carolyn Bush-Roddy was inspired to try the sport in fifth grade after she saw a traveling team called the Nashville Redheads play. In Illinois, young Peggy Kennedy said she would always rather pick up a basketball than a doll.

Little Cheryl Engel spent hours in the gym with her father, a basketball coach. Accronetta "Neat" Cooper, six years old and sporting a knit cap with a bright tassel, started playing basketball with the older kids in South Carolina, and her father rewarded her with her own ball and a real goal. Donna Wilson was seven when she decided it would be more fun to play basketball than to be a cheerleader for the boys' team in Monroe, Georgia.

Glenda Holleyman was comfortable as a purely defensive player ("guard") in Tennessee's six-on-six system, and when her coach began grooming the tall girl for offense, she came home in tears. "Daddy, I don't want to shoot," she bawled. "I don't want to shoot." Eventually, the traumatized player learned not only to shoot but also to dribble, which was an advantage when the rules began to allow a rover to cross midcourt.

Of course, just because girls *wanted* to play didn't always mean that they got to play. Margaret English's house in South Carolina had a hoop with no net nailed to a wooden pole, but her brother Alex (a future NBA Hall of Famer) and his friends wouldn't let her join them. They were clear about that: "The girls played with dolls, the boys played with balls." Sue Peters's brother and his friends would let her into their games—but only if they didn't have enough boys for two teams. When they realized how good she was, though, she no longer had to wait for an odd number of boys.

On a tobacco farm near Olmstead, Kentucky, Brenda Chapman took aim at a basketball goal nailed to a tree near her family's barn. "I played basketball with the guys—they were all my buddies," she said in 1980. "I was a fanatic—basketball all year 'round. . . . Even when it was snowing outside, I'd be out there bouncing a ball." But when she was twelve, the boys left to play organized ball. There was no team for the young girl, and the future WBL scoring leader didn't play again until college.

Holly Warlick's family were very much into sports. She first played basketball in the third grade, and her father would help hone the future point guard's skills by setting up chairs in a gym for her to dribble around. Peggie Jackson's entire family was also athletic. "I had six brothers and three sisters. Both Mom and Dad played sports. We had two built-in teams," she said.

Maria Gross's father never missed a game when she and her sister played in high school. (Her mother saw one game, "and all she had to say was 'You and Margie are the prettiest girls on the team,'" Gross laughs. "That was the extent of my mother's interest.") Sandra Smallwood was recruited from her rural grade school by a nearby junior high. The buses didn't go that far, so Smallwood's parents drove her to school every day.

Not everyone began with that kind of parental support. Nancy Lieberman's mother punctured her basketballs with a screwdriver to keep her from playing that "boy's" sport. In the North Carolina countryside, Faye and Kaye Young's father wasn't thrilled about his junior high daughters playing basketball. "My mother was supportive, but my father—this has been a long time ago—my father thought that we shouldn't play, because we needed to come home and do chores and help out around the house," says Kaye. "My mom put her foot down and said 'Yes, if they want to play basketball, they can.' We were thankful for that."

Karen Aulenbacher's parents didn't object to her trying out for her high school team, as long as it wasn't too rough and she didn't do "masculine" things like lifting weights. Paula Mayo's father was a businessman and not very interested in sports, but her mother was at every game. "My mother, that's the one that supported us from the beginning to the end," she says. "She didn't miss."

When sixteen-year-old Queen Brumfield told a high school coach in Kentwood, Louisiana, that she wouldn't play basketball, the coach decided to try the girl's mother. "She didn't believe basketball was a proper thing for a young lady, but she listened to me," said Ann Smith, who mentioned the possibility that it could lead to a college scholarship. The elder woman agreed, with conditions: the coach would drive her daughter to and from games, and the team would pray before and after games. But even then, the first time Smith arrived to take Brumfield to a game, she learned the family was going to church instead.

Marie Kocurek had never played any sports in Corpus Christi and decided to try tennis one semester. After spotting the tall girl in the hall, though, the school's basketball coach asked if she wanted to join his team. Not really, Kocurek replied. "Well, you're going to whether you like it or not," he said, snatching her schedule and changing "tennis" to "basketball."

Anita Ortega's Puerto Rican father believed that "women should be housewives and mothers, not playing ball," she says, but he eventually came around. Ortega grew up in central Los Angeles and started playing basketball at the age of fourteen mostly for self-preservation; "it was either play basketball or get involved with illegal activities." (She later became a captain in the Los Angeles Police Department.)

Michelle McKenzie was about the same age when she began playing street ball with her brothers and neighborhood kids in the District of Columbia. "My parents were livid," she recalls. "They didn't want me playing basketball. Girls don't do that." When McKenzie was a junior in high school, the school's coach spied her shooting baskets in the gym one day and asked if she wanted to play. "I can't; my family won't pay for it," she said, but the coach was undeterred. She got the fee waived, and as McKenzie's career progressed, her parents warmed up to the idea.

If there wasn't a girls' team on which to play, some future WBL players were willing to improvise. Linnell Jones played on boys' teams in elementary school, but when she reached junior high some of her teammates gave her a hard time, and she quit mid-season. Sandy Rainey played one game with the junior high boys' team at her school in Wheeling, Illinois. Cardie Hicks once sneaked onto the San Pedro, California, high school team for her brother, who was ill. There were a few glitches (she didn't hear the coach yelling because he couldn't use her real name), but Hicks remembers that her 16 points that night included a dunk. The school was disciplined, she says, but the incident later inspired a movie.

When it came time to continue their careers in college, players like Jody Rajcula at Southern Connecticut State, Carol Blazejowski at Montclair State, or Darla Plice at Ashland College had one option: an academic scholarship or nothing at all. Title IX was gradually changing the landscape, however, and several WBL players became the first women to receive athletic scholarships at their schools, such as Kathy Andrykowski at Marquette, Kim Bueltel at Pepperdine, Harriet Novarr at Syracuse University, and Rhonda Kite at Oklahoma State University.

Margaret English landed a scholarship by happenstance. Her local tech squad was having a great season while her brother Alex's team at the University of South Carolina was struggling. A local paper picked up on the story and asked the siblings to play against each other for the camera. When the women's basketball coach at South Carolina State saw a photograph of Alex English and his six-foot-four-inch sister playing one on one, he quickly dialed the phone with an offer.

When Jessie Kenlaw arrived at Savannah State University, the school did not have a women's basketball program. She approached the school's president to ask for a team. OK, he replied—as long as she put it together, raised the money for uniforms, found someone to coach it, and scheduled the games. With the help of her college (and later Houston Angels) teammate Dollie Mosley, Kenlaw did it.

To reassure colleges that it would not interfere with their programs, one of the WBL's first announcements was that it would not sign any player who retained college eligibility. ("After college, bounce on over . . . ," its motto read.) Teams could draft juniors, but there were no "hardships"; women could not join the league early for any reason.

One third of the more than three hundred women who played in the WBL were drawn from a pool of twenty-six colleges. Indeed, nearly a quarter came from just thirteen schools: Montclair State (10 players); Wayland

Baptist College (8); Queens College(7); University of Maryland (6); North Carolina State (5); University of Tennessee (5); University of Nevada–Las Vegas (5); Cheyney State (4); Illinois State (4); Immaculata College (4); and University of California, Los Angeles (4).

Small colleges dominated women's basketball at the time, and with restrictive recruiting rules and few scholarships, most players weren't aggressively sought out, nor did they have much incentive to travel far from home. "Despite its marginalization by the sports world, women's basketball before the 1980s was as egalitarian a sport as you'll ever see," Ta-Nehisi Coates of *Washington City Paper* noted in 1998.

When she joined the wbl, Queens star Gail Marquis realized that some unknown colleges were putting out very talented players. Jackson State's Bertha Hardy, then playing for the New Orleans Pride, was an especially tough opponent, she says, "and I never heard of her. They played at places that I never heard of the schools, much less the players, and they were great players."

St. Louis Streak coach Larry Gillman was "talking to LeMoyne and Belmont [Colleges] because girls' basketball hadn't reached that stage yet," he recalls. "They were still in the boonies." (LeMoyne's coach recommended a couple of players named Tonyus Chavers and Debbie Washington, and Gillman agreed to give them a tryout. The coach couldn't line up a gym, so he and Streak owner Vince Gennaro took the women to a playground and challenged them to some two on two. He signed both of them.)

wbl coaches sometimes knew players from other teams. Iowa Cornets GM Rod Lein had coached Molly Bolin in college and knew what she could do. For the New York Stars, coach Al Cissorsky brought in Maria Gross and Mara Melbourne from his aau team, Al's Gals. Often, however, recruiting efforts depended heavily on college coaches. Chicago Hustle coach Doug Bruno had never seen his 1979 number one draft pick, Retha Swindell, play, but she got high marks from Texas coach Jody Conradt. In 1978 Queens' Debra Roelich was given a tryout after a recommendation by her coach.

Word of mouth was only one way of learning about unheralded players. Valdosta State guard Susan Taylor had been drafted by the Nebraska Wranglers, but she didn't want to go by herself, so a friend, Carol Chason, tagged along. When the Wranglers agreed to sign Chason, she knew it was because they wanted Taylor, the aiaw's fifth-leading scorer that year, but that didn't bother her. "That's the way life is sometimes," she says. "You make your own breaks, and you take what God gave you and you deal with it."

In Lake Charles, Louisiana, the boys' high school basketball coach came by Paula Mayo's house to see whether she wanted to try professional basketball. The coach knew a famous professional wrestler, Ernie Ladd, who lived in Houston and could make some calls to the team there, the coach said, if she didn't mind going to try out. ("Oh, no, I don't mind," she assured him.)

Linnell Jones was at tryouts for the 1980 Olympic team when University of Kansas coach Marian Washington asked about her dreams. "I told her that my dream since I was eight years old was to play women's professional basketball," Jones says, and a few days later, Washington called her at home in Kentucky. "Do you still want to play professional basketball? I've got someone that would be interested in looking at your skills, and he's going to call you," she said. Soon afterward, Jones got a call from St. Louis Streak coach Larry Gillman.

People like Washington were a valuable resource for WBL coaches, whose research abilities were limited by money and technology. Scouting the Olympic trials for the Houston Angels, "I was like Joe Detective or whatever," says Tom Davis. "[Assistant Coach] Greg Williams worked for Sony and so I had a little handheld tape recorder, and I would just sit there the whole time going, 'Number 80 dribbles well to her left and she's got a good jump shot, but she can't see the open person.'" Davis ended up with a pile of notes, but he had no clue who most of the women were until months later when the Olympic committee released the names of attendees.

Open tryouts were another way to find good players who might have fallen through the cracks. Patti Bucklew wrote the WBL after reading an article in a Pittsburgh newspaper, and she was invited to a free agent camp in Dayton with one day's notice. In Conroe, Texas, a junior high girl handed Karen Aulenbacher a newspaper clipping about tryouts for the Houston Angels. "Coach, why don't you try out for this?" she suggested.

Tryouts drew hopefuls from across the country and all walks of life. In Dallas, a security guard at the gym gave it a shot, along with an attorney who flew in from Denver. Others came from Arizona, Minnesota, and South Dakota. When the Diamonds held an open tryout in Tennessee, one prospect arrived at 5:30 a.m. on a bus from Macon, Georgia. That evening, coach Greg Williams dropped her off at a small store that served as the local depot. Two hours later, though, the storeowner called Williams. The bus had come early, and the woman was still sitting there with nowhere to go. Williams drove her to Knoxville, where she could catch a bus home.

Chicago's open tryout in 1980 drew more than fifty women, one of whom rode her motorcycle 1,400 miles from Virginia. Another had just lost her father the day before. Ten women appeared for open tryouts with the Dayton Rockettes in 1978. It wasn't until after the morning workout that organizers realized that three of them were high school or college players who would lose their eligibility if their participation were discovered.

Before coming to tryouts, many players had to decide whether they were willing to leave college without completing their degrees. (Because it was difficult for basketball players to carry full class loads, they often did not have enough credits for a degree at the end of four years.) Joanette Boutte had her degree but saw many of her colleagues facing a tough choice. Their scholarship would cover an additional semester after they were done playing ball, but not if they signed with the WBL.

Pearl Moore was in her last semester at Francis Marion College when she was drafted by the New York Stars. She agreed to miss a couple weeks of school to attend training camp and then to fly down to New Orleans for a game, but when she heard "Why don't you leave school, and we'll pay for you to go to summer school?" she said no. "And that was the best decision I ever made," she says. "I didn't want to leave, because I might not have gone back. So I finished my school." After graduation, she reported for duty. Katrina Anderson also decided to finish her degree at South Carolina before giving the WBL a try in 1979.

Margaret English needed another semester to graduate, but she wasn't worried about it. "I knew the college would be waiting for me to come back and finish my degree," she says, "which I did." Rhonda Penquite likewise figured "what's a year?" when she chose the Iowa Cornets over her student teaching requirements at Oral Roberts University. Queen Brumfield returned to Southeastern Louisiana University after her WBL career to finish her degree in social work. Nancy Lieberman received her degree from Old Dominion in 2000.

Players also had to decide whether they wanted to hold out for a shot at the 1980 Olympics. Several star players did, such as Wade Trophy winner Carol Blazejowski of Montclair State and Tennessee's Cindy Brogdon, who, *Newsweek* said, "may well have the purest outside shot in the game." The Amateur Basketball Association of the United States (ABAUSA) issued a stern warning to the 590 players trying out for the National Sports Festival in Colorado Springs that "if they even go to tryout camp with the intent to join the league, they lose their amateur status" and could be reinstated for friendly goodwill matches only.

League administrator Jane Rath speculated that some players might choose the WBL over the Olympics. "Those people who want to go to the Olympics will have to make that choice," she said, "but there are many people in men's basketball who skipped a shot at the Olympics to sign immediately with the NBA." Queens star Althea Gwyn declared that pro ball was just as important as the Olympics to her, and Milwaukee Does rookie Dori Zwieg agreed. "I feel it's even a greater honor to play in the first pro women's game than to be in the Olympics," Zwieg said. Others just assessed their Olympic chances as doubtful. The Olympic selection was too political, Penquite figured, "and the other thing I thought was, 'You know, if this pro basketball league does make it and I don't do it, I would forever regret it.'"

Offers from overseas were sometimes more tempting than an upstart league. Marquis had a comfortable life as an Olympian playing in Europe and wasn't going to give it up until the WBL had made it at least one year. Future WBL All-Star Heidi Nestor preferred to spend her first season in the Netherlands instead of Milwaukee. Mariah "Maggie" Burton Nelson was weighing an offer to play in France when she got a call from the New Jersey Gems. "So for about one nanosecond I thought, 'Where do I want to be, New Jersey or France?' And I had already been to New Jersey . . ."

Overall, far more women jumped at the chance to play in the WBL than declined. Why did they do it? "It wasn't the money," says Tesa Duckworth, who left a coaching job to try out in Chicago. "It was just the idea of getting to play." Maria Gross gave up a good position as a bond underwriter with an insurance company but has no regrets. "Oh, no—it was a once in a lifetime opportunity. I got to live in New York. I got to travel. It was fun."

In Pennsylvania, Patti Bucklew's father urged her to try out for the District of Columbia team. "I don't know about going so far away from home," Patti hedged. A few months later Roy Bucklew noticed that the DC team had been sold to Dayton—would she try out now? "Well, that's a little closer to home," she said, "I think I could try that." (After one season in the WBL, Bucklew didn't care that her contract was sold to California. "I was so into it by then that it didn't matter that I was moving three thousand miles away from my family.")

Kathy DeBoer's parents weren't quite as enthusiastic about their daughter joining the WBL. "I think my parents had a lot more hesitation than I did," she says. "They had been waiting for me much of my life to grow out of my obsession of wanting to play sports." Suzanne Alt's family was "all against it," she remembers; "they thought it wasn't a long-term career goal."

Even a short-term career goal was better than what some players had to look forward to. Krystal Kimrey's apartment in New Carrollton, Maryland, burned down a week before she was invited to try out for the New England Gulls. "I was completely wiped out," she recalls. "I had a couple pair of pants and stuff that was cleaned up by the laundry, but it was ugly. . . . I was working part-time for the YMCA running an after-school program for kids, making minimum wage—I didn't have a lot to lose."

Neither did Janie Fincher. Just a few years earlier, she'd had an epiphany while working at a Safeway grocery store in Oklahoma one stormy day when a customer bought a candy bar, a *TV Guide*, and a roll of toilet paper—then expected Fincher to carry the small package out for her. "It was tornado weather and it was just beating down out there with pea-size hail and everything, and she wanted me to carry it out for her," Fincher says. "After I did that I thought, 'You know what, I'm not doing this anymore. I have got to get a better life.'" The next day, she started making calls to see if there was somewhere she could play basketball.

Cheryl Clark had spent years with the All-American Redheads and figured her playing days were behind her. "I had just decided, 'I guess this is it, you know, the end of the road,'" she recalls, until another former Redhead, Karen Logan, called to say there was going to be a WBL team in Clark's home state of Wisconsin. "Gosh, I would like to do this," she thought, and the Milwaukee Does quickly signed her.

Vonnie Tomich was single, and no one was depending on her. "It's a whole different life when you're young and you don't care," she says. "It's like, 'Go ahead, I'll challenge the world.'" At that age, "shoot, you go for broke," says Nancy Wellen. "I am so glad I did it. Some people thought, 'You're crazy.' I had a couple of offers to teach, but I said, 'I can teach any time. I can come back to that.'" That's what Debra Waddy-Rossow told her husband when he encouraged her to skip the WBL for a teaching job. "Dang, Winston," she said, "I've got 40 years to teach. This is my one chance to be a pioneer."

"We all were willing to give up other things—family, jobs, security, whatever—to be here," Brenda Chapman said in 1978. "We're going to try to make it work." Vicky Chapman was a little nervous about giving up her position as a graduate assistant, but people had to take chances to get ahead in the world, she decided. Joanie French resigned a teaching job in Missouri to join the Dallas Diamonds. Randi Burdick resigned as assistant women's basketball coach at Rutgers without hesitation. "Someday I may be part of sports history," she thought.

Still, it was a big risk for many. In New Jersey, Wanda Szeremeta saw women quit good jobs, only to be cut after a week. "There were no guarantees of any sort, so a lot of my memories from that first year were watching the development of the league and watching how it affected all these different women," she says. Chris Critelli didn't count on the league to bring her financial security, which was important, she says, "because a lot of my teammates left their homes and families and they had kids. They were promised so much. If I got it, I got it, and if I didn't, it was just another way to play basketball. I truly played for the love of the game."

So did most other wBL players. "Not too many women were getting paid to play what they enjoyed except for golf and tennis," Kim Bueltel told herself. "Why not try and play in it at least for a year or two, and then go out and get a real job? I always wanted to just keep playing."

And that was the biggest allure of the wBL. "Forget all the failures of the league—these girls came in with a mission," says San Francisco Pioneers owner Marshall Geller. "They came into that league and it was like, 'This is our chance,' and they played that hard. They really played hard." The women of the wBL just wanted to keep playing a game that they loved. "Talent is a hard master," the *Washington Post* theorized about wBL players in 1979. "How many can resist following the path of their ability—even if that skill were pickpocketing?"

3

A Man's Game

I think women athletes will get a chance to show how well they can do in what has been called a man's game. • **Mike Connors**, co-owner, San Francisco Pioneers, November 1979

I told her to go to Paula and she goes to Coretta . . . Turn around, dammit! How many times do I have to tell you? . . . Move! Move! Jeez, what the hell are you looking at me for? . . . Goddamn, Augusta . . . Oooh, Wanda. • **New Orleans Pride coach Butch van Breda Kolff**, December 1979

HOUSTON, FALL 1978
Houston Angels coaches Don Knodel and Greg Williams watched their players run up the court. The Angels were now a couple of weeks into practice, and the coaches wanted to see what they could do against bigger, tougher opponents. Knodel rounded up the perfect volunteers, a group of truck drivers and other rugged workmen from his day job at a building supply company.

So far, things were looking good. The game was going back and forth, and the Angels were holding their own. Suddenly, a loose ball popped out, and two players charged after it: the Angels' Paula Mayo, a sturdy five-foot-ten-inch, 180-pound former track star who could run the 100-yard dash in 11 seconds, and one of Knodel's truck drivers. The two reached the ball at the same time and banged heads. As the coaches watched, the truck driver went down, and Mayo picked up the ball and went in for the lay-up.

Knodel turned to his assistant. "We've got a team!"

Marie Kocurek stood on the basketball court, talking to some other players after a tough loss by her Minnesota Fillies to division rival Iowa. Coach Terry Kunze approached. "Get your ass back into the locker room," he ordered.

Inside the locker room, Fillies players sat quietly as Kunze stormed in. "Gutless, f——ing bitches!" the coach shouted, kicking a large trash can. "Gutless, f——ing bitches!" He slammed his fist through a chalkboard.

Kathy DeBoer began to say something. "You shut your mouth or I'll shoot you back to Michigan," Kunze barked at her.

Furious at the coach's treatment of them, Kocurek rose to confront him. To her mortification, though, she began to cry instead, which made her even angrier. "Stupid women always cry; it just makes me mad," she thought.

Unable to speak, Kocurek sat back down. Kunze walked over and patted her head, but she threw his hand off. "I'm not your dog, don't pet me!" she snapped. As Kunze turned away, Kocurek had one last thing to say to him: "What you said today will never be forgotten."

And that, DeBoer says, is one of the biggest differences between coaching women and men. "Women personalize criticism so much more than men do. So if you're going to throw a fit after a loss, if you're going to come into the locker room and start throwing things around and just going crazy, there's going to be a price to pay." DeBoer admits she did some of it herself during her own thirteen-year coaching career, but warns, "Don't think for one second that women are going to walk out of the locker room and come back the next day and have forgotten about it."

A typical example, she says, was the time that Kunze thought she hadn't pursued a loose ball enthusiastically enough. "You chased that ball just like a damn woman!" he shouted. DeBoer yelled back at him ("I remember what I said, but I don't want it printed in a book"), and Kunze benched her. "I was hacked at him for three days," she says. "In fact, you can tell, it's 20 years later and I still haven't forgotten the comment. I am living proof we never forget."

Kunze often told DeBoer she would be a better basketball player if she didn't take everything so personally. "I wasn't able to deal with that as constructive criticism at the time, but now I realize it really was," she admits. "He was right. Everything was just a personal attack instead of, 'Oh, just let him be. Let him go crazy.'"

The assumption that female players were more sensitive than male players seemed to be a given in the WBL. "Coach," a reporter asked New Jersey Gems coach Don Kennedy after the team's first loss, "aren't you surprised that the girls aren't taking the loss any harder? I mean, being more emotional than men and all." And WBL players *were* more emotional at times. "There were a couple of games lost in the last minute and afterwards the girls would be crying," said Eric Nadel, broadcasting voice of the Dallas Diamonds. "I wasn't used to dealing with that." Tears were not uncommon on and off the court, whether due to a hard foul, or a trade, or a tough loss.

This natural compassion created certain obstacles, some coaches thought. During a Houston Angels game, Belinda Candler snagged a defensive rebound and dished it off to trigger a fast break, but as she started down court, she accidentally toppled her defender. Instead of rushing down court where she would be open for an easy basket, Candler ran over to help the other player up. Infuriated, coach Knodel called a time out. "Boy, did he chew Belinda out," teammate Patty Bubrig reported.

Steve Kirk likewise recalls an Iowa Cornets practice when action on the court came to a halt after a player was knocked to the ground. "I remember screaming, 'How can you stop playing? Just because somebody falls to the floor or gets knocked to the floor, nobody stop playing for even a second! In fact, step on them!'" And, eventually, he says, they hardened. The next time a player hit the deck, her teammates stepped on her.

Many women players lacked the natural intensity of men, Kunze concluded early in his first season with the Fillies. "They don't know what it takes yet." Kennedy had the same complaint in New Jersey. "You'll see the girls from both teams hugging each other," he said. "They'll have tea and toast together after a game. If they lose, it doesn't have that much effect on them. Right now I'm trying to develop more aggressiveness. Winning and losing's got to mean more."

Wanting to instill that kind of "game face" in his Cornets, Kirk required players to gather before each game for a team meal, but there was to be no talking or laughing; the women were to sit silently and think about the upcoming game. (One time, it was just an impossible task, Rhonda Penquite says. "It's like in church when you try to be quiet when you're a kid, and something just tickles you and you start giggling, and you can't stop. A bunch of us started giggling, and he just yelled at us and told us to get out on the bus.")

To help his team develop more of a killer instinct, Kirk ran a practice drill called "War," which had only one rule: Anything goes. Players could push, shove, hack, anything. "[Kirk] would push us down; he didn't care," says Charlotte Lewis. "He expected you to be able to make baskets when you were falling and when you were fouled. He expected you to be in that defensive position, to not to let them go even when you were getting hit."

WBL players weren't soft, says New Orleans coach Butch van Breda Kolff. One of the coach's most vivid memories from the league is when a player landed hard on the court, and he could tell she wanted to cry. "We've made a pact that we are going to try to get into men's basketball, and we're not going to do any of this crying stuff," he reminded her, and she gutted it out. The players wanted to prove a point, he says, that "as far as hitting the floor and getting banged up and so forth, there was no crying or anything like that. It was fun. I enjoyed it."

During the WBL's three-year existence, nearly all its coaches were men, often coaching women for the first time. Most female coaches made only brief appearances in the league. Dee Hopsfenspirger in Minnesota and Charlotte Adams in Milwaukee quit before the first season began. Milwaukee's Candace Klinzing was fired after a single game, Dayton's Linda Mann after two games, and Minnesota's Julia Yeater fourteen games into the season. (A year later, Yeater replaced Milwaukee's head coach when he quit midseason.) Only one female head coach, New Jersey's Kathy Mosolino, made it through an entire season.

The short life span of women coaches in the WBL generated occasional jibes. After an exhibition contest between the Fillies and a local media team coached by hockey publicist Mary Ann Young, for example, the *Minneapolis Star* quipped that Young had retired after the game—"making her the only female coach in the WPBL this year not to have been fired."

Why were there so few female coaches in the WBL? Different explanations were offered. Women were starting to draw decent pay and newfound security in college coaching, *Sports Illustrated* surmised, not to mention improved budgets attributable to Title IX. They weren't likely to make a speculative leap to the WBL. "Top female college coaches were reluctant to give up secure, and in some cases very well-paid positions, to join the new venture," as *Ms.* said.

Women also might not like the atmosphere, Mosolino theorized, at least by the third season when most WBL coaches had come from men's programs. "I think they're afraid to take the chance," she said after a New Jersey Gems game against the St. Louis Streak. "How many women do you know who want to subject themselves to this? [Streak coach Larry] Gillman was not only screaming at his players, he was screaming at my players, too."

The most common reason given for the predominance of male coaches in the WBL, though, was a scarcity of competent female candidates. "There are only a number of qualified women, oh goodness, you can get hung for saying something like this," Gems owner Tom Brennan said in 1978. "But women coaches are still developing. They're just coming into their own on the college scene." As Stanford University coach Pam Strathairn said in 1981, "the best coaches come up through the ranks, but doors had been closed to women in sports for many, many reasons, so there weren't many who had that kind of experience."

Before the passage of Title IX in 1972, women's basketball teams, if they existed at all, were often directed by physical education teachers or volunteers, WBL founder Bill Byrne pointed out. Apart from their willingness, these coaches, most of whom had been schooled in the old six-player, half-court game, lacked the qualifications usually found in coaches of men's teams.

Many WBL players had been taught by people who "know less than nil," New York Stars coach Dean Meminger said, and it was his job to "deprogram" them. In Houston, Don Knodel also felt he had to spend too much time teaching his Angels basics. "Small details, things the gals weren't shown in college or high school have been slowly but surely worked into each player's repertoire," the *Houston Chronicle* reported. Knodel wasn't criticizing the level of coaching the players received in college, the coach emphasized; "they just didn't get as good of coaching as most boys do."

Because of that history, male coaches were needed to advance the women's program, van Breda Kolff argued. "I know a lot of women libbers are going to hate me for this, but women coaches have done a poor job of training women basketball players," he said. "The girls leave college knowing very little about things like blocking out, rebounding, setting picks and shooting over screens. It's not a question of whether these things are feminine or anti-feminine. They are part of basketball and the women players who want to win want to learn them."

The ideal for many WBL owners was a coach with NBA connections. Picking a coach was like drafting a player, Stars owner Ed Reisdorf said. "Sure you want the best you can get, but you want somebody people have heard of." (Reisdorf landed Meminger by asking the NBA Players

Association's Larry Fleisher if he knew any former players who might be interested in coaching a women's team.)

To the amazement of many—including his wife—former Boston Celtic "enforcer" Jim Loscutoff agreed to coach the WBL's New England Gulls. Other scores from the NBA were former head coaches Larry Costello, whose Milwaukee Bucks had won it all in 1971, and van Breda Kolff, whose Los Angeles Lakers went to the NBA finals in 1968 and 1969. "Both coaches have done their share of towel throwing, chair kicking, sideline screaming and swearing," wrote the *Republic Scene*.

Before taking the helm at Milwaukee's WBL franchise, Costello first had to be convinced that women were coachable. Giving Chicago Hustle coach Doug Bruno a call, Costello said he had some questions—about three and a half hours' worth. He biggest concern soon became clear, as Bruno recalls the questioning: " 'Okay, where do you stay? . . . But can they run plays? . . . How do you get there? . . . Okay, you have to fly. But can they run plays? . . . Where do you practice? . . . Can they run plays? . . .' It just never stopped," Bruno says. " 'Can they run plays? Can they run plays?' "

Getting such high-profile male coaches into the WBL was not made easier by observers who depicted the move as humiliating. A *New York Daily News* feature on Meminger casually opened with, "It was a job many men with his credentials would hardly have considered. Here was Dean Meminger, college All-American, key reserve on an NBA championship Knicks team, an athlete respected for intellectual and physical talent, a man presumed to have a future wearing a three-piece suit on some NBA bench sometime, asked to coach a *women's* basketball team."

Coaches like Costello and van Breda Kolff plying their trade in the women's league was beneath them, wrote the *Republic Scene*: "It's like Muhammed Ali hiring on as a sparring partner, LeRoy Neiman making a living as a house painter, or Ansel Adams working the window at a Fotomat hut."

Costello had initially dismissed the Does' offer outright, he admitted, but he did not consider it beneath him. "These girls are really good athletes, and they're responsive," he said. "Some people might think it's a comedown for me, from the NBA to here, but that's not it at all. I've got no ego hangups, in the first place. In the second place, what I'm doing is a living and it's basketball."

Was it embarrassing to be coaching women, the *New York Post* asked Meminger. No, he replied, he was coaching athletes who just happen to be women. He was a "liberationist," Meminger said, and the WBL was part of a larger social struggle: "I think one of the last barriers males want females to enter is professional sports. That's the last barrier of male macho, the sacred sanctuary of maleness. . . . Being black, I've always had these feelings. The women's movement is nothing but a microcosm of the black movement, one and the same."

As part of that movement, some players expected WBL coaches to adapt their traditional male terminology. "I try to stay away from 'girls,' and instead use 'persons,'" Kirk said in 1979. "But I've had some trouble. Sometimes it comes out 'guys,' sometimes 'men,' and once I even yelled, 'OK, you jocks, get in there!' I got an elbow in the ribs from Bruce [Mason] who said, 'Coach, they don't wear 'em.'"

Kunze especially had to watch himself; he was coaching two players (DeBoer and Kocurek) ready to pounce if he slipped into gender-exclusive language, says DeBoer, who was traded to Minnesota midseason. When she arrived, the coach had already been warned: "If you say 'man-to-man,' she's going to correct you and say, 'There aren't any men here; just say player-to-player.' We couldn't do the 'three-man' weave; it was the 'three-player' weave. 'Don't call us girls, we are all in our twenties, we're women now.' I was totally into that."

In Houston, local media praised Angels players who took a different approach. "We don't think anything about it when Coach Knodel says something about man-to-man defense," a *Houston Chronicle* writer quoted Patty Bubrig. "That's what we called it at school, too. It would be silly to call it anything else." That statement, the writer declared, "kills the notion the Angels are a band of women's libbers hung up on terminology."

New Jersey's Kennedy said he did not plan any changes from his years of coaching boys. "I'm going to treat them like basketball players," he said. "My son told me, 'Dad, you won't be able to yell at them like you used to.' Well, I'm going home to gargle and get ready."

Meminger also saw no need to treat women players any differently than men. Comparing himself to a professor in the classroom, the Stars coach said he had twelve students. "When I'm teaching, I'm teaching a mathematical science. I don't ask if they are male or female—does a professor ask if his students are men or women in a college classroom?—just 'Do you have the ability to learn the science of basketball?'"

But coaches like Meminger brought with them an approach that many players found disturbing. When the San Francisco Pioneers signed him as their head coach in 1980, "everybody said that we were crazy," owner Marshall Geller recalls. "In a way we were, because Dean had no patience with these girls, none. He would go crazy." At one Pioneers game, two sportswriters watched Meminger yelling at a player. "He's an ass," one concluded. The other agreed. "He's got that girl so crazy she doesn't know whether she's coming or going," he said. "He'd never get away with that in the NBA."

Meminger and Gail Marquis "banged heads" most of the season in New York, but she still ranks him as one of her best coaches. Nonetheless, Meminger's language, particularly referring to players by "some part of your body, your anatomy, you know," irritated her. "I don't get motivated by the cussing and swearing or the hollering," she says.

Other players, though, weren't bothered by the coach's style. "I loved Dean," says Sharon Farrah. "He taught me a lot. He had a fiery temper and a lot of passion for the game, and he really did get into it." That he did. "He would say, 'You mother-f— —ing p— —ies, get out there and play some basketball!'" recalls Molly Kazmer (then Bolin), who signed with the Pioneers because she wanted to learn from Meminger. "He would be screaming this at us with moms and their kids right behind. We thought it was hilarious. We were never offended by it, but that is how he talked to us."

It certainly was, says teammate Margaret English. "What the— —are you doing? Get your— —down the floor!" Although English was from a religious background, the salty language didn't offend her, mostly because it wasn't directed at her. (She was sidelined with an ankle injury.) "Now, if I was out there, I think I would have said something to him and let him know that I think he should approach us differently," she says. "Being an adult, I think he should have a little more respect for us as players. Some of the girls would just cry. He was so tough."

Most WBL coaches weren't inclined to soften their language during games. "To this day, I still remember we were having a practice game like at a Catholic grade school or some place in a small town in Iowa," Cornets player Mo Eckroth says, when coach Steve Kirk called a time-out. "He made the most, you know, 'We've got them right by the—,' and he actually said it. There's all these little girls and they're like, 'Okaaay.'"

In Houston, Knodel and assistant coach Williams decided they weren't comfortable with the coaching style they were trying to use, and one Saturday morning the two discussed their approach. The problem, they decided, was that they were treating the Angels like ladies instead of like basketball players. "We quit softpedaling our coaching," Knodel reported. "Greg and I started yelling at them just like we would a man" (including, on occasion, "strictly X-rated" commentary).

Yes, Knodel yelled at them, Glenda Holleyman says, but she liked his approach. "He said, 'This is what we are going to do,' and we worked hard enough to learn it until we could get the job done. You know, all coaches scream and holler, but he didn't put you down and cuss you and things like that. He was definitely a gentleman and respected us, too, as women."

That distinction is why women can accept some coaches shouting at them but not others, St. Louis Streak player Ann Platte believes. "If you tell a player when they are doing good and let them know that you believe in them, it's a lot easier to take the negative criticism. Treat them with respect as players and as women, then it's easier to take yelling."

But being yelled at was a new experience for many WBL players, who had never been coached by men, or by coaches who raised their voices. Minnesota's Kocurek, for example, was one of eight Wayland Baptist College alumna who played in the WBL. The Flying Queens had been mentored by Dean Weese, a famously low-key coach who did not swear or push his players or allow them to curse on the court. "Under extreme pressure and unbearable provocation he may be heard to utter softly, 'Damn,' without an exclamation point," said the *Dallas Times-Herald*.

The only female coach in the 1980–81 season, Kathy "Moss" Mosolino, was also more of a nurturer, according to Gems player Jill Jeffrey. "She expected people to act like professionals and do the things that they were supposed to do," Jeffrey says. "We would sit down and strategize a lot about how to combat the Nancy Lieberman press with Dallas, or just figure things out that way. It was a very different experience for me than college because she was not a disciplinarian type dictator. It was more of, 'Hey, guys, we are professionals and we're in this together, we've got to figure out how to beat this team.'"

Contrasting with such laid-back approaches was an aggressiveness by other coaches that was jarring at times. One confrontation between a WBL player and coach in practice became especially notorious in the league. "I was *stunned* at what took place," a fan who witnessed it complained to the team's owner. Events began when the player missed a lay-up and muttered something to herself. "What did you say?" the coach asked.

"I said, 'shoot.'"

"No you didn't," he replied, "you said 'shit.' Do you want to talk shit? Let's talk. Go over there and stand in that corner and think about what you said."

A couple of fans were watching, the player noticed, and members of a men's team were trickling in. The coach repeated his instruction, and the player walked over the bleachers and sat down. "I said stand in the corner." Suddenly, she realized what he was doing. Some fans who sat in that part of the gym occasionally brought with them a small dog, who had defecated in the corner. Look at it, the coach ordered.

The player turned around and saw her entire team standing behind him. "You talk about humiliated?" she says. "Hell, yeah, I was humiliated. I looked him in the eye and I didn't bat an eye. I think he wanted to see me cry." The coach ordered her to squat next to the mess. "Not only do I want you to look at it, I want you to smell it. That's what shit is." Turning around, he strode back to the court. "Let's go practice."

Teammates weren't sure what to make of it. "Well, that is a situation where you could take things one way or another. He could have been doing it in a joking kind of way, or he could have been serious," one says. "I don't know. With stuff like that, I just tried to block it out and not get involved in it. That was a problem that they had that they needed to work out."

How a player reacted to a coach depended in part on her temperament, says New Orleans Pride player Kathy Andrykowski. "It can be all new to you or you could be very used to it, but if you don't let it affect you and your play and your attitude, then it's fine. It goes in one ear and out the other." Her theory was put to the test under van Breda Kolff, who, *Sports Illustrated* once noted, "never uses a dainty word when a more colorful one will suffice."

Van Breda Kolff's language was "flowery," Pride player Paula Dean confirmed. "After he's told us something to do two or three times and we continue to do it wrong, then naturally he's gonna yell. And I mean *he yells*—and screams and cusses and carries on." That was initially a shock to players like Sandra Smallwood and Andrykowski, whose previous coaches would never dare utter a swear word, but the key, Andrykowski says, was recognizing that van Breda Kolff was an excellent coach. "You listen to what he says, you drown out the bad things and the loud voices, and you take note of the constructive part."

Pride players knew that his comments weren't personal, van Breda Kolff said. "They know my bark is worse than my bite. I yell at 'em and I'm mad at 'em, but the next day everything's fine again—as long as they do what I tell them." Van Breda Kolff may have joked about coaching females—"the women smell so much nicer" in time-outs, he said—but he supported them and their ambitions, Pride guard Sybil Blalock says, so his manner of expression was not important. "It's what you are trying to tell me, because I'm trying to win."

That kind of coachability was refreshing for many wbl coaches who had previously worked with less receptive men. "Guys have a tendency to think they know it all, but women players are willing to learn," New England Gulls Coach Jim Loscutoff said in 1980. Players were moody and unpredictable, "especially that time of the month," he says, but "they listened to everything you did or tried to tell them to do. They were just happy-go-lucky."

Loscutoff's successor in New England, Dana Skinner, also felt that women had a healthier attitude toward the game. For men, it often became too important a piece of their lives, he believes. "I found the women I worked with to be much more agreeable, much more cooperative. They just wanted to be part of a successful franchise, and they were willing to pay an enormous price to get there."

Knodel also liked that aspect of his job. "They look at you and they listen and they go out and do what you tell them to do," he said. "They question very little, but then they don't have the big ego to feed like most men's teams. They're team oriented, too. They cheer for each other, not like the members of a men's team do, but in a real sense. They really want each other to do well."

The players also wanted the league to do well, which meant educating the public about the "new" women's game. When the wbl formed, *Houston Chronicle* writer John Wilson admitted in 1979, he had never seen women play full court, and he doubted that women's basketball could be a viable sport. After watching four Angels games, though, he was a convert. "It is a bona fide athletic contest played with vigor and considerable skill," he wrote. "And it makes an exciting spectator event."

Steve Kirk had likewise been a self-proclaimed "chauvinist" toward women's basketball before agreeing to coach the Iowa Cornets. "I guess there's a little chauvinism in every man when it comes to women's basketball and I was no different," he admitted. "People who have never seen women play have an idea that all women play a 3–2 zone, walk the ball up the floor and that it's a slow, boring game. But it's not so. . . . These women can run, they can shoot and they can get physical."

Just how "physical" a WBL game should get was fodder for much debate. In one California Dreams game, sportswriter Ed Cole wrote, the only question was "whether the crowd of 601 were watching basketball or rugby." Cole was especially concerned about feisty Dreams guard Muffet McGraw, whose "frail frame seemed ill-suited to the wild play."

Early WBL spokeswoman Karen Logan argued that, for the WBL to succeed, it needed to capitalize on players' skill, grace, intelligence, and strategy. The league's selling point was "beauty of motion," she said, and it was essential that the WBL curb the physical play she already saw developing. "Most of the coaches teach power basketball," she said. "They teach women to brutalize each other. If you want to see that, you should go to women's wrestling or roller derby."

Minnesota Fillies owner Gordon Nevers didn't want to see the WBL turned into the men's game, either and after one tough game in Houston he insisted that the rules be reevaluated. To the dismay of league officials, the "Angels" routinely overwhelmed opponents with swarming, in-your-face defense, becoming known as the Houston "Muggers" (and rightly so, Angels forward Paula Mayo says). They featured halos on their uniforms and wings on their warm-up jackets, columnist Joe Soucheray noted—"the kind of wings made familiar by a motorcycle gang."

Referees were letting players push and shove because they assumed it was inherent to the game, Nevers told his fellow owners, but there was no precedent for professional women's basketball, so owners—not officials—should define just what "pro ball" meant in their league. "The WBL is not the NBA," he argued, "and we should begin developing the League with the foresight to keep the women's game marketable."

The owners unanimously adopted a motion that "The League continue with the WBL rules as written with continued emphasis being placed upon the interpretation of those rules by the officials and the players which will not cause the style of the WBL games to become like that of the National Basketball Association (NBA) or men's collegiate basketball." (They were sending mixed messages, officiating supervisor Steve Zebos later said. "Early game criticisms ranged from too many whistles to allowing too much contact. Obviously these complaints are at both ends of the spectrum, and there's no way we can satisfy all factions.")

De-emphasizing the physical aspects of the game in favor of its more "feminine" traits was one way that officials hoped to avoid comparisons with the National Basketball Association. "We're not the NBA, but we don't want to be," Iowa general manager Kate McEnroe said in 1979. "We're the wbl, selling our unique game and finesse." The two leagues were entirely different, Brenda Chapman noted. "Look at me and a guard in the nba. They're 6–5, maybe 6–7. I mean, do they expect us to come close to that?"

Yes, apparently; many observers insisted on holding the wbl up to the nba in assessing its worth. That is an inherent problem with women's sports, said Chip Campbell, a former lpga publicist then working with the pga, in 1984. "The women who played in the old women's pro basketball league (wbl) play great basketball and would make the rest of us look like paraplegics, but they're compared to the nba. They just don't grow big enough or jump high enough."

Women might lack the strength to dunk or crash the boards dramatically, but they were generally better shooters than men, said Tex Winter, then the men's coach at Cal State, Long Beach. (When they were willing to shoot, that is. "The trouble with women is that you gotta prod 'em to shoot," San Francisco Pioneers coach Frank LaPorte complained. "No kidding.")

The women's game also emphasized more teamwork. "In the men's National Basketball Association, much of the game is feeding the ball to a tall center who stuffs it into the basket," the *Chicago Tribune* noted. "That center is the star. But in the wbl, the quintet of players works as a team, getting the ball close to the net. Men rebound balls off the board. The women aren't tall enough to do much of that. So theirs is more of a team game, working patiently with one another to get the ball where one of them—and not always the same woman—is in the best position to shoot."

A New Orleans Pride game was like a "time warp," *New Orleans Times-Picayune* sports writer Peter Finney said during the third season, with the women playing basketball like the men did from the 1940s to the 1960s. "No slam dunks. More pattern play than one-on-one. More screens. More passing."

There was nothing wrong with a throwback, Finney added. "It's like going into an antique store and discovering how things used to be before 5–10 guards began to stuff, before 6–10 centers began moving like 6–4 forwards, before the men got so good, sheer talent nudged technique off the stage." That "old fashioned" style was appealing to students of the game like van Breda Kolff. "I liked the way [the Pride] played," he says. "Moving the ball, moving yourself, trying to get good shots, playing together, playing as a team."

wbl players also approached the game with a tremendous enthusiasm.

The difference between the NBA and the WBL, *Chicago Sun-Times* sports editor Ray Sons wrote, was "more than the obvious difference that has had poets raving for centuries." Rather, he said, quoting Costello, "These kids give you 2,000 percent. They come to work with smiles. And they're so damn attentive."

If comparisons to the men's game were made, WBL officials hoped they would emphasize this passion. They didn't, and when quality of play was at issue, the outcome was usually unfavorable. "The women's game lacked the exciting individualism of the National Basketball Association, the *Minneapolis Star* concluded after one WBL season. "There are no backboard-shattering slam dunks. No dunks for that matter. And there are no breath-taking behind-the-back passes."

The *San Francisco Chronicle*, which was generally supportive of the Pioneers, was also blunt at times. "To the fan used to watching the NBA, the WBL is very different," a column read in 1981. "For one, it's played below the basket, no great loss because the beauty of basketball is in precision passing and teamwork, not merely in being able to touch the top of the backboard. But what is so lacking is a grasp of the fundamentals, crisp passes, well-executed plays. There have been times this year when it appeared that a WBL team couldn't beat a pickup squad of under-sized high school guys."

Women, of course, had been playing full-court basketball for less than a decade, and programs for them were an afterthought in many schools. Those factors, along with physical differences, produced some weaknesses in the women's game. "By the time a boy is in the ninth grade, he knows how to break a press, he's already developed a court awareness," Meminger said. "Many of the girls never picked up a basketball until they were in high school, so they're that much further behind when they get here."

The fact that most fans could achieve the feats of female but not male professionals was seen as either good or bad for the WBL, depending on one's perspective. *San Francisco Chronicle* writer Bruce Jenkins considered it an obvious drawback, but his colleague Glenn Dickey felt that it was easier for the typical fan to relate to the women's game. "A lot of men will find, as they have with tennis and golf, that it is easier to identify with the women's game than the men's," he wrote. "You don't drive a golf ball like Jack Nicklaus, nor hit a serve like Roscoe Tanner—and you don't shoot a jump shot like George Gervin, either."

One clear plus for the WBL was that its players were more accessible off the court than their NBA counterparts. "The women are less jaded," one fan wrote to the *Chicago Tribune*. "They still smile at you and have time to talk to you. . . . Women still play for the joy of playing, and it shows." It would be at least ten years before women "catch up with the men in egoball," San Francisco fan Lee Glickstein predicted.

Of all the differences between the WBL and the NBA, two were inherently unique to the women's league. The first was a consequence of male-dominated coaching and management, which inevitably led to accusations of "fraternization," whether true or not. Chicago coach Bruno often heard smirking remarks about his job. ("You're going to New York with ten women? I'd love to go to New York with ten women.") Dallas Diamonds broadcaster Eric Nadel was "traveling all over the country with 12 healthy women basketball players," a columnist noted. "Of such things are smutty novels and X-rated movies inspired."

Even Iowa Cornets gentleman owner George Nissen was the target of some teasing. A news photograph in the Iowa Women's Archives of him signing the first contract in the league, that of attractive Molly Bolin, who is seated beside him in the state governor's office, has been doctored so that Nissen actually appears to be writing "MEET ME IN THE LOCKER ROOM LATER."

At one time or another, claims of relationships surfaced in nearly half the WBL franchises. Sometimes the accusations seemed little more than retaliation. In San Francisco, for example, favoritism by Coach LaPorte toward number one draft pick Pat Mayo did not sit well with some teammates. "Then they started a rumor—you get this in pro sports like any other thing, it doesn't matter if it's men or women—that she was having an affair with Frank LaPorte," owner Marshall Geller recalls. "Well, if you knew Frank LaPorte, Frank came out of coaching an all-Catholic school up here. Frank, in my opinion, was Mr. Straight Arrow."

On other occasions, there was merit to the suggestion. During one road trip, a coach invited a WBL player to his hotel room. There, he handed her a note expressing romantic feelings for her and asked if he could kiss her cheek. Another coach frequently bothered women in whom he had a romantic interest, a player alleges, and especially one teammate in particular. "I think he knew that she couldn't stand him, and he just started dogging her until she quit." Other teammates left for the same reason, the player says. "You talk about sexual harassment, it was huge on that team. Huge."

Molly Bolin ran into similar problems with a Pioneers investor. "Today it's called sexual harassment; back then he had a 'crush,' " she says. "I would go, 'Why are you calling my house? I'm not interested.' I kept telling him over and over, and the guy would just not give up." One day, she arranged to meet him for a talk. "Look, you've got to leave me alone," she said bluntly. "I don't want anything to do with you, and that's it." He got the message.

In Milwaukee, a wedge grew among Does teammates over a relationship between a player and general manager Gene DeLisle. Yes, something was going on, the player says, but it wasn't by choice: "He kind of had me locked and barreled; he had threatened me into being around him more than the others." She knew what her teammates thought but couldn't escape the situation, she says, which worsened until she called the police when he showed up in her hometown. "He just wouldn't leave me alone. So, yeah, that isn't a happy aspect of it."

A happier relationship developed in New Orleans, when Pride forward Sandra Smallwood began dating general manager Steve Brown near the end of the 1979–80 season. They didn't worry that it would create conflicts with the coach, because no one would believe that Brown could pressure van Breda Kolff. "If you knew Butch," Smallwood laughs, "he wouldn't take orders from anybody." She and Brown are still together.

Another experience unique to the WBL was strictly biological. One afternoon at training camp, a coach's high draft pick told him she was going to quit. "Oh, that's nice," the frustrated coach replied. "What's the problem?" After some hedging, she finally told him: she was pregnant. Oh. "I didn't have to worry about this with boys," the coach said unnecessarily. "I just got an education that day," he says now, that "coaching girls is different than coaching guys."

At the end of the 1978–79 season, the Houston Angels were in a fierce title run against the Iowa Cornets when Houston coaches noticed that Glenda Holleyman's game seemed off. Before the final game, Holleyman told Coach Knodel what she thought the problem might be, and a red flag went up. Pregnant? If Holleyman wanted to play, owner Hugh Sweeney declared, she would have to sign a release:

> I, Glenda Holleyman, in the event of injury to me or my unborn child as a result of participation in a Houston Angels basketball game or workout hereby release the Houston Angels, Women's Basketball Productions, Ltd., and Women's Basketball Productions, Inc. of any

and all responsibilities to me in any form. I requested to participate and play and assume full responsibilities to me in any form. I requested the opportunity to participate and play and assume full responsibilities of action, myself. In accordance with this agreement, I hereby accept by affixing my signature.

Holleyman signed the waiver and went through warm-ups as usual but never came off the bench. "I got to play in every game but the very last game," she says with regret.

4

In the Locker Room

We are not attempting to provide members of the media a peep show. • **Chicago Hustle general manager Chuck Shriver**, December 6, 1978.

Women. Locker rooms. It was an intriguing combination for men covering the new Women's Professional Basketball League.

Women in *men*'s locker rooms was already a hot topic. Only two months before the WBL tipped off, a federal judge in New York declared it illegal for Major League Baseball to exclude *Sports Illustrated* reporter Melissa Ludtke from the locker room at Yankee Stadium based solely on her sex. With the furor from *Ludtke* still in full swing in late 1978, many male sportswriters saw the new women's league as the perfect opportunity for some turnabout, or at least a juicy storyline.

The topic of locker room access in the WBL first arose in the summer of 1978 when an Iowa columnist, critiquing the morality rules imposed on Iowa Cornets players (no drinking, smoking, swearing, or drugs), concluded his light-hearted feature with, "The next thing you know, the Cornets' management won't allow reporters to interview the women in the locker room."

Sure enough, three days after *Ludtke*, an Iowa headline proclaimed: "Women's locker room off limits to male reporters." The Cornets' locker room was not an appropriate place for men, general manager Rod Lein announced. To avoid legal problems, all reporters would be banned from the dressing quarters. The *Ludtke* ruling was an invasion of the athletes' privacy, Lein felt; "there is a difference between a girl and a boy."

The representative of a men's rights organization responded by demanding that he be allowed into the Cornets' locker room. "I would like to interview some of their players," Don Lamb wrote. "In view of the recent court decision in New York that allows women reporters access to men's locker rooms, I feel I should be allowed to have locker room interviews. If denied, I will seek legal help to enforce my right to equal opportunity." (He did not follow through on the threat.)

Lein's decision to exclude all reporters drew some criticism. "That reminds me of a time some jerk back in grade school hit a nun with a snowball and the entire grade school didn't see another recess," wrote Denny Holton, a columnist for the *Cherokee Daily Times*. Holton disagreed with *Ludtke* ("men and women should stay in their own locker rooms"), he said, but "if you can't keep female reporters out of men's locker rooms, you aren't going to keep male reporters out of female locker rooms. It's as simple as that. It's called the equal rights movement or 'what's good for the goose, is good for the gander.'"

Sensing a potential dispute—*read*: publicity—league officials quickly issued a press release titled "Who's Who in the WBL Locker Room?" "The historic first game of the WBL will not be without controversy," they declared. The release mentioned Lein's views and added that Chicago Hustle president John Geraty agreed with them. ("Men with men and women with women," he was quoted.) WBL president Bill Byrne's position was somewhat vague: "The League will cooperate with the courts to permit equal opportunities for all reporters but will never compromise the individual privacy of the players," he said.

The Minnesota Fillies, meanwhile, announced that male reporters would be allowed in their locker room. "Minnesota is the first team in the league to announce an open locker room policy," owner Gordon Nevers said. "The women think it's a good idea."

Three days before the inaugural WBL game on December 9, 1978, Chicago announced that its locker room would in fact be open after games. "We are not attempting to provide members of the media a peep show," general manager Chuck Shriver said. "In the first place, women's locker rooms are constructed differently than men's and those players who want to shower and dress can do so in complete privacy. In the second place, we think the whole 'controversy' over whether or not to allow men reporters in a women's locker room is a tempest in a tea pot."

Some male sportswriters wanted to see (so to speak) for themselves. In

New York, Al Mari was assigned to cover a Stars home game against the New Jersey Gems for a "family newspaper." Mari knew that women could now enter baseball locker rooms, he said, and that they sometimes interviewed male players in various stages of undress. "So, with no tongue in cheek, I approached representatives of both the Stars and the Gems before Thursday night's game," he wrote. "The question was obvious: Could I enter the locker room after the game?"

No problem, Mari said he was told by both teams, and when the close contest (a 100–99 Stars victory) was over, he was ready. "An intense effort by Kathryn Solano of the Gems had been lost in the shuffle, and as I walked toward the locker room, I noticed Solano sobbing on the bench," he wrote. Mari didn't want to impose on her and approached Janice Thomas of the Stars instead. "Excuse me," he said. "Would you mind if I come into the locker room to interview you?" Sure, she replied, he could come in after the players dressed. "How about as you shower, and after you come out?" he asked.

"Don't be ridiculous," Thomas said with a smile. "We're talking now, aren't we? You didn't come here to see us with no clothes on, did you?" No, he assured her. "I'm all for reporters coming in to the dressing room," she said, "but me, well, I don't know. It's kind of a personal thing. Female reporters, that's a little different."

Mari said he had no better luck with New York's Kaye Young. "I think it might bother some of the other girls," she said. "It wouldn't bother me." Really? Mari queried. A man walking around naked women? "Well, it might be awkward," Young amended. "It might take some time getting used to. We could use publicity and more reporters covering our games. As I said, it's probably some of the other girls that would mind."

Mari approached wBL administrator Jane Rath with his findings. "I guess that the girls aren't ready for that, right now," she joked. "Are you sure you didn't come here just to get into the locker room and see naked girls?" No, he had seen thousands of naked girls, Mari told her ("in magazines"). But it was clear that he wouldn't be seeing any in the Stars locker room that night. "You win some, you lose some," he concluded.

After the Minnesota Fillies' home opener, male reporters waited outside the locker room for the required five minutes, then went in. "The relatively historic moment passed without controversy," the *Golden Valley Post* reported. No conflict arose after the San Franciso Pioneers' home opener, either. "When it was over, the question remained as to how the women professionals would handle their post-game interviews," the *San Francisco Chronicle* noted. "Would men—or women, for that matter—be allowed into the locker room?"

The answer was yes, but as it turned out, there wasn't room for interviews anyway. (Cramped locker rooms were a common WBL feature. In the visitors' locker room at Minneapolis Auditorium, Chicago player Janie Fincher said, "we sat so close together we had to be careful two people didn't put on the same sock.")

The post-game scene in the WBL gave it a certain charm, the *Chronicle*'s Bruce Jenkins wrote. "Male reporters, wondering what it would be like to invade a women's locker room, have found the WBL's policy remarkably open. In every league city they are welcome to come right in and, in most cases, stay as long as necessary for interviews." The league had managed to combine privacy with accessibility, he concluded.

WBL players often dressed somewhere other than the locker room. Most visiting teams showered at their hotels, preferring it to facilities that were generally designed for men (less privacy), or were questionable for other reasons. In Houston, for example, Chicago players found a mouse in the visitors' locker room. "In some locker rooms the floors hadn't been swept for weeks, paint was peeling off the walls and bugs were crawling all over the shower-room floors," Iowa Cornets guard Tanya Crevier said in 1979. "In our first year we can't expect the greatest, but it would be nice to take a shower without worrying about athlete's foot."

Some franchises avoided locker room issues by designating an interview area elsewhere. Iowa provided an intermediate room, and in San Francisco, interviews were conducted in socializing areas, mostly for practical reasons. "There's hardly enough room for us in there, let alone anybody else," Pat Mayo said. "We'd be glad to let you in, but it would be a joke." Jenkins thought it a better arrangement anyway. "How would you feel hanging around while someone sitting next to you is waiting to undress?"

Locker room access was also a non-issue in New Orleans. "The women are aware that publicity helps them," Pride official Ken McCloskey said. "It's completely relaxed; everybody's happy with it. Coach (Butch) van Breda Kolff is generally available and we have a lot of room. It's nothing unusual; nobody's walking around nude or anything like that."

Dallas had a "huge dressing room," a staffer said, "but most of the male writers down here would just as soon not go in. It's like going into somebody's closet, if you want to do that, fine." (Accidents did happen, as when a male reporter there walked in on St. Louis Streak player Adrian Mitchell bare from the waist up.)

New Jersey had no locker room restrictions. "Oh, we would have welcomed anyone to cover our team," Wanda Szeremeta jokes. "I don't think we would have kicked *anyone* out of there." Neither would Houston. Several Angels players were already used to dealing with male reporters from their college days, coach Don Knodel pointed out. "But I know our girls are young ladies and will not display a striptease act in front of any of the reporters, male or female."

One Houston sportswriter said he was looking forward to the experience, though. "The women's pro league is going to provide the first true test as to the equality of the sexes," wrote John Wilson of the *Houston Chronicle*. "Not in the game, but in the dressing room." Female reporters had won their court victories allowing them into men's locker rooms, he said, and now there was a women's place for men to go into.

Women who went into men's dressing rooms said it was an emotionally neutral experience, "that it is no different than any other work task, such as filing papers or checking groceries, that they are able to switch off any possibility of a genetically programmed response," Wilson said, but he made no such pretense. "Taking my cue from President Carter who chose to be truthful in his famous interview with *Playboy* (admitting that he had 'lusted' in his heart), I am going to confess that I am looking forward to visiting the Angels dressing room," Wilson wrote.

Alas, he was to be disappointed. Wilson was admitted to both locker rooms after the Angels' home opener but reported, "The only thing is that nobody dressed in the dressing room, or should I say undressed." Both teams arrived and left wearing their uniforms, and the only clothing removed was when Chicago player Karen Logan took off her shoe to apply ice to her foot. As Hustle point guard Rita Easterling was being interviewed, teammate Janie Fincher stuck her head in the doorway. "Is that man still here?" she asked. "I have to go to the bathroom."

5

Playing by the Rules

There was one guy out in Iowa who tossed me because he thought I gave him the finger. If I give you the finger, you are going to know that I gave you the finger, and you are going to get some words with it, too. • **Gail Marquis**, New York Stars

How many steps do I get? • **Tonyus Chavers**, Minnesota Fillies, complaining about a traveling call

This is no disco. • **Referee Bob Christian**, February 4, 1981

We're getting outhomered at home! • **Donna Geils**, Chicago Hustle, January 2, 1981

BOSTON, 1981
New England Gulls coach Dana Skinner, feeling frustrated, approached one of the referees. "This is ridiculous!" he exclaimed.

"I'm calling a fair game," the official insisted.

"I'm not looking for a fair game!" Skinner replied. "Every time I go on the road I get hammered, for heaven's sake. I can't afford to have you call a fair game at home!"

As the first league of its kind, the WBL was free to set its own rules of play. The league faced a slight dilemma: it did not want to be compared with the NBA (although it was), but it also did not necessarily want to be compared with the college game. Early on, owners envisioned a hybrid set of rules, combining some aspects of each, but eventually adopted "professional" (NBA) rules instead, with a few minor variations. Now all they needed was to round up officials to monitor the games—which was not always as easy as it sounded.

THE OFFICIALS

Charged with enforcing the WBL's rules of play were one hundred or so men under the direction of Steve Rainer, a thirty-eight-year-old referee from Columbus, Ohio, where the league was headquartered. Appointed the WBL's first supervisor of officials in September 1978, Rainer was first assigned to compile a roster of qualified officials, and by December he had accomplished the task, putting together a mix of high school and college referees—all men.

The irony did not escape the WBL Board of Governors, who wondered why none of the officials in the Women's Professional Basketball League were women. It wasn't for lack of trying, Rainer insisted; only one qualified female had applied, and she wasn't located near a franchise. He assured the owners that he would keep looking for women, and by the end of the season he had recruited Phyllis Devaney to work games in New Jersey.

Initially it took some officials a while to get used to WBL procedures. "It's a tough game to officiate, I know," Hustle coach Doug Bruno said, "and those guys work hard. But all I ask is that they sit down and read the rules before the game. My girls have to pass tests on the rules, so if they have to know them then the refs should, too."

Often they did. During a game against Minnesota, Bruno told Tesa Duckworth to go in for Janie Fincher during an injury time out. Under the rules, Fincher wouldn't be allowed to return, Duckworth pointed out. "I know, but don't worry," Bruno replied. "Those guys don't know the rules." Actually, they did—Bruno was caught when he tried to sneak Fincher back in.

One of the season's more bizarre officiating gaffes occurred near the end of that game. As reported by the *Chicago Tribune*, Fincher was standing on the sideline when a nearby referee threw the ball at her—but she wasn't looking at him. The ball hit Fincher squarely in the face and knocked her, unconscious, into the Minnesota Fillies trainer. ("What happened?" she asked later. "Well," teammate Karen Logan replied, "you sat on that trainer's lap for an hour, and he had his way with you.")

Only two weeks into the season, the WBL received its first formal protest of an official's decision. The league discouraged protests—even threatening one cost $500—but for $1,500 it would review a ruling. On this occasion, Milwaukee argued that it should have been awarded free throws when the

Iowa Cornets committed their second foul in the last two minutes of the half.

The Cornets were furious (general manager Rod Lein tried unsuccessfully to get a court hearing before the next game), but Byrne ruled for the Does. The December 29, 1978, game was resumed on January 28, 1979, at Iowa, with Milwaukee's Kathy DeBoer at the free throw line and the Does leading 66–54. Milwaukee won, 101–96.

A later challenge was a bit more unusual. In March 1979 the injury-plagued Minnesota Fillies arrived in Chicago with only eight players. Five of the Fillies fouled out, but because WBL rules required at least five women on the floor, two of the disqualified players kept playing. Each subsequent foul by them cost a technical free throw—or so the officials thought. The rule actually imposed a technical when the players *remained* on the court, even before they committed another foul. The Hustle protested, and Minnesota's 141–139 victory was reversed. Half an hour before the next Fillies game in Chicago, the two teams resumed play with 5:29 on the clock and Minnesota leading 116–111. The Hustle won, 129–124.

Overall, officiating in the WBL's first season was fun, says referee John Katzler. "The players were pleasant, and they didn't pay a whole lot of attention to the officials, unless you really blew a call." Even then, criticism by the women players, compared to that by men, was relatively mild. Vocal abuse was rare—"women, you know, they give you that hurt look"—and coaches largely behaved themselves. (That began to change the next year, when several franchises hired NBA veterans as coaches. "They brought with them their good habits," Katzler quips, including four-letter vocabularies and short tempers.)

Fans were a different story. WBL official Dan Korvas had two fantasies, the (*Arlington Heights* IL) *Daily Herald* reported. "One is to toss his whistle toward a heckler in the stands and shout, 'OK, if you think you can do better, then you try it.'" The other was "to get together with a bunch of other refs and go in where one of those guys works and boo him while he's trying to do his job."

Chicago crowds were especially abusive, Korvas said. "They're crude. They're cruel. It aggravates you to a point." A local sportswriter wondered aloud if Hustle fans went to the games to cheer the players or to boo the referees. In Dallas an enraged New Orleans Pride fan threw three plastic cups at referee Bob Dietz. "As the cups sailed over Pride coach Butch van Breda Kolff's head, he ducked, smiled and watched the police escort the inebriated young man out of the Convention Center," the *Dallas Morning News* recounted.

Heading into its second season, the wbl took an impressive step to improve perceptions of its officiating, signing John Nucatola, a long-time nba and ncaa referee enshrined in the Basketball Hall of Fame a year earlier, as its supervisor of officials. Although Nucatola's officiating experience was limited to men, he was supportive of the wbl and its players. "I'm more than impressed with this women's league," he said early in his tenure. "The girls shoot well, pass and dribble with coordination and have more of a team concept than some men's clubs I've watched. . . . They dive after the loose ball and give 110 percent effort every time out."

Nucatola brought with him a dozen nba officials whose jobs were eliminated earlier in the year when the men's league reduced game crews from three to two. The new supervisor also helped recruit two female referees and created a ranking system. A nicely bound wbl rules booklet was distributed, and game pay was bumped from $50 to $75, plus expenses.

Some observers were not impressed. "wbl officiating can border on the ludicrous," the *New Orleans Times-Picayune* opined. "The wbl uses nba rejects, and they do all the hilarious things bad officials are supposed to do: they'll make simultaneous conflicting calls; they'll inadvertently distract a player who's shooting a foul shot; they'll run into the players. They'll be the only two people in the arena to miss blatant fouls. They can be so inept that opposing coaches every once in a while glance surreptitiously at each other and grin."

The media, of course, added to the perception by happily pointing out mistakes. Two officials in one Pioneers game were "neither adept nor consistent," the *San Francisco Chronicle* casually remarked. The *Dallas Times-Herald* had fun with one sequence of events during game two of the 1981 Dallas–New Jersey playoff series. Dallas's Rosalind Jennings was called for a breakaway foul on New Jersey's Carol Blazejowski, but the culprit was actually Retha Swindell. The officials then realized their mistake, the paper said—and assessed the foul on Kim Bueltel.

A mix-up between the numbers 10 and 11 cost the Dayton Rockettes a game, the *Dayton Daily News* alleged. With 5:24 left in regulation play, the Houston Angels' number 10, post player Paula Mayo, was whistled for her sixth foul and headed for the bench. The scorebook, however, showed only three fouls, and Mayo returned to a chorus of boos from the mathematically astute Dayton crowd. Later, it was discovered that half of Mayo's fouls had been charged to her teammate, number 11, Karen Aulenbacher, who was surprised to foul out with only three fouls. Houston went on to win in overtime, aided by two key free throws by Mayo.

During halftime at a New Orleans Pride home game, general manager Steve Brown was in the midst of an interview about officiating when New Jersey Gems coach Howie Landa wandered by. A *Times-Picayune* reporter described what happened next:

> What began amicably enough as banter about the quality of WBL officiating quickly turned into a white knuckle argument that saw the two accusing each other of complaining about bad officiating only when his team was on the losing end of the score.
>
> With a volunteer group of cheerleaders in the background screaming "We are the Pride of New Orleans!" Brown and Landa seized one another by the lapels and dragged each other outside, where they could be heard uttering such schoolyard roosterings as "Get your hands off me," "Don't put your hands on me again," and "You yell in my face one more time and we're gonna got at it for real."
>
> Finally the security police arrived and busted up all the fun.

Even mild-mannered WBL coaches occasionally lost their cool. After a home game in San Francisco, normally soft-spoken Pioneers coach Frank LaPorte rushed out onto the court to confront official Ed Deritter. The two exchanged words (shouts, actually) until fellow referee Paul Wilson grabbed his colleague from behind and dragged him away.

The WBL's most serious officiating dispute occurred during a televised game in Chicago on March 7, 1980, a heated contest between the Hustle and the St. Louis Streak that was heading for overtime. Heightening the tension was the fact that some of the Streak players had been traded by the Hustle and were now facing their former team. Technical difficulties had also been sufficiently frustrating to prompt a note in the official play-by-play in the third quarter that, "due to scoreboard errors, score is not totally accurate." With a minute and a half left in the game, the play-by-play simply read "Helter Skelter."

Over the past few months, Hustle coach Bruno had become convinced that opponents were intentionally roughing up his tiny point guard, Rita Easterling. She had been hurt several times that season, including serious knee and shoulder injuries, and she seemed to get undercut a lot, Easterling says. "I think he felt that some of the players were just out to hurt me."

Only one day before the Streak game, WBL president Bill Byrne had warned Hustle owners about Bruno's temper, specifically two "chair-throwing incidents" he had heard about. The first was in Houston. "I guess he was watching Bobby Knight too much," Easterling laughs. As Greg Williams, an assistant in Houston at the time, recalls, "He just couldn't take it any more, with the old homer officiating. He made Bobby Knight's toss look like minor league."

Byrne claimed that Bruno tossed a folding chair "30 feet across the floor at an official, barely missing two players." That's ridiculous, the coach says. "No chair was ever thrown across the floor in Bob Knight style, all right? Did I kick a chair over at my own bench? Yeah. But not thrown, that's not true. For me to come off like I'm Bob Knight—I never abused my players, and I hardly swear at all," he says, then admits, "but at the same time, I was a nut."

The other incident mentioned in Byrne's telegram had occurred three weeks earlier in New York. Following an early technical foul for coming out onto the court, Bruno did it again in the fourth quarter. ("I just couldn't sit there and take it any more," he said.) Hit with another technical, Bruno headed to the locker room and, along the way, picked up a metal folding chair and slammed it to the ground. Unfortunately for the coach, Nucatola was seated nearby and wrote a firsthand report to Byrne recommending discipline.

Now, with the Hustle rallying against the Streak, the inevitable happened: Easterling was knocked to the ground. It was clearly intentional, she says, but she thought there was no whistle. Bruno thought the same thing, that referee Mark Mano was calling only a time out. "Is that all you can say—20 second injury time out?" he yelled repeatedly. (Mano had, in fact, called a foul.) The coach was finally hit with a technical, his second of the game. Bruno had always gotten along well with this referee, he felt, but Mano didn't realize this time that he was truly angry. "We got mad at each other, but now I'm much more serious and he thinks I'm just playing."

Fincher watched from the court as events unfolded. "Doug had his fist up in the air bouncing around like a boxer," she recalls. "The next thing I know he is out there in the middle of the floor and has (Mano) in a head hold." Bruno had run out onto the court and tackled Mano, swinging at him and trying to bang the official's head on the court, the *Tribune* reported. "It finally took three security men to pull Bruno off the referee and drag him from the hall."

Hustle president John Geraty also had to be restrained, and fans rushed to attack the officials. "The fight between Bruno and Mano triggered at least three other fights as about 70 persons, including fans, stormed the court," *Chicago Sun-Times* reporter Lacy Banks wrote. "Fans on the court and in the stands threatened and cursed Mano, his colleague Stan Harris and Chicago area head official Tony Tortorello."

Mano ordered some fans ejected, and the police were summoned to restore order. After a 25-minute delay, the game continued, with the Hustle winning 128–123 in overtime. "I truly believe the refs, if not consciously, subconsciously gave Chicago the game because they were afraid of a riot," says the Streak's Ann Platte. "The Chicago fans were fanatics." After the game, police officers formed a line to protect the Streak as they ran to the locker room, and escorted Mano out of town.

At WBL headquarters, Byrne was still at work when the phone rang with news about the fracas, and Vice President Dave Almstead called the television station to get the tape. "I went over it and over it and tried to figure out if it was premeditated or instigated or what have you," Byrne says, and he summoned Bruno and Geraty to New York. "Tapes don't lie. I didn't have to tell them anything, there it was."

Byrne liked the young coach, but he had no choice. He fined Bruno $1,000 and suspended him for the remaining two games of the season. "This is the type of action the league can not afford and will not tolerate," his telegram read. Bruno said there was no defense for what he did, and that he had expected even stiffer punishment. "I know I will never do it again as a coach," he declared.

Mano was still angry. "I was really entertaining some thoughts of taking him to court to let him know that this was not acceptable, because this hadn't happened before and a precedent was being set here," he recalls. He demanded a public apology and got it. Bruno issued a statement ("I deeply regret my actions of March 7th, and I feel I owe a public apology to the Women of the WBL, the referee profession, specifically Stan Harris and Mark Mano, and to the Chicago Hustle fans and Basketball fans throughout the country"), which he repeated at the next home game. In honor of their suspended coach, Chicago players yelled "Doug!" as they came out of each huddle.

Finally, national media turned an eye toward the WBL, but the league did not want that kind of publicity. Requests came in for copies of the game film, but league officials refused to release it. "All the news shows wanted it," says Lynn Arturi, a New York Stars player who worked in WBL headquarters. "Everybody would want to see it. A coach and a referee? You've never seen that in the pros, wrestling on the floor."

Bruno does not recall any punches but acknowledges that the scuffle turned into a wrestling match. "It was embarrassing; it was stupid," he says. "It has no place in sport." Mano accepted the coach's apology and says Bruno's image wasn't really tarnished by the incident because officials knew it was not typical of him. "[Bruno] wasn't that type of a person," Mano says. "He just lost it one night."

It all came down to emotion, Hustle player Jody Rajcula says. "He loved us. You had a guy like Doug Bruno that was taking a chance in coaching these women. He knew what a lot of them had given up, and he would fight tooth and nail to protect his players."

The following year, the WBL began its third and final season with disturbing news on the officiating front: Nucatola had resigned as supervisor and was "blowing the whistle" on the league. The league owed money to at least fifty referees, Nucatola said, but he had been kicked out of a league meeting at which he raised the issue. "I just couldn't take it any longer," he said. "This was the worst experience I ever had in my 34 years as a pro basketball referee."

He was replaced with fifty-year-old Steve Zebos, a three-year WBL official who had played with the NBA's Philadelphia Warriors in the 1950s and was now a history teacher and referee in the Chicago area. No significant rule changes were voted in, but officials were told to cut back on the number of fouls called, "meaning the play is tougher, and now includes sweat, grunts, groans and elbows," *Minneapolis Star* columnist Doug Grow wrote. "In the past, it seemed that the referees were trying hard to make women's pro basketball a *ladylike* affair."

Meanwhile, the league drew more bad press by firing Mano. At an exhibition game in Chicago, the referee approached interim commissioner Sherwin Fischer, who was also part owner of the local franchise, about expenses due for two games the prior season. Fischer said to call him, but Mano wasn't satisfied, and at half-time he slipped Fischer a note that read: "It seems senseless to keep calling about the $60. The games were on Feb 29th and March 7th (The Doug Bruno Fight). You claim the Hustle sent the checks in. Bill Byrne claims you never sent the checks. For me to keep calling only deducts from the $60. I'm frankly tired of the run around. I really don't feel like leaving the game without the $60. I feel you can get me the money tonight. Appreciate your attention to this matter please."

Irritated with Mano's approach, Fischer recommended that he be fired. Mano, in turn, began gathering information about unpaid wages, and in January 1981 he sent Fischer a list of names, dates, and amounts allegedly owed to eighteen wbl officials, with a warning: "We will refrain from using the press any more until the end of January. After that it's no holds barred. Judging from the current officiating problems in Chicago alone, reporters must be foaming at the mouth for more ammunition."

Zebos was unimpressed. "Forget this guy," he advised Fischer, claiming that Mano had recently asked for his wbl job back. "He can do nothing—he's just talk." (Zebos later hired a lawyer himself to recover unpaid compensation.)

Meanwhile, the influential *Referee* magazine (published by Mano's brother Barry) turned up the pressure with a December 1980 cover story that flayed Fischer, Zebos, and Byrne, setting out one tale of mistreated official after another. One unnamed referee, for example, said that Byrne had dismissed his inquiry out of hand, suggesting cavalierly, "You've probably drunk up more than that at our parties anyway."

The controversy did not prevent the wbl from recruiting a full complement of officials for its 1980–81 season. As usual, they had to re-orient themselves to wbl rules early on. St. Louis owner Vince Gennaro shot an angry letter to headquarters, complete with diagram, after officials required players to follow a "new rule" on lining up for free throws that wasn't actually a wbl rule. (They apparently were thinking of the ncaa.) "How can we spend $300,000 to $600,000 per year and hire officials who don't know the rules!" Gennaro exclaimed.

Unlike their milder counterparts from the first season, players were more actively joining the fray. Two of the top five recipients of technical fouls that season were women, and both from New Jersey. (The other fouls went to three male coaches.) Only two games into the season, Gems coach Kathy Mosolino's first visit to the New Orleans Superdome was cut short by two emphatic T's. ("I was a young coach, remember?" she laughs.) In the grumbling department, Mosolino held her own against male colleagues; at different times, the lively coach knocked over a chair, threw papers onto the floor, and matched hot-tempered St. Louis coach Larry Gillman "shriek for shriek."

Equally vocal was Gems rookie Carol Blazejowski, the league's leading scorer and technical foul recipient. "I haven't been impressed with it [the officiating]," she told the press, "and that's putting things mildly." Blazejowski often didn't put things mildly, says Katzler—"she was one of the more vociferous ones in those days." In the first two months of the 1980–81 season, the Blaze racked up five technicals in four different WBL arenas. "Officiating is officiating, but when you are a targeted player, sometimes it gets old," she says now. "So you have to do it [complain] every once in a while. You make friendships after the game."

Although complaints about officiating are inherent in competitive sports, the WBL had an unusual feature, reminiscent of early NBA days, that invited more than the usual skepticism. To save expenses, referees did not travel to away games during the regular season. Instead, home teams provided—and paid—the officiating crew, which led to frequent accusations that calls favored whichever team was signing the paycheck.

"In this game as well as many others the referees tend to favor the home team," *Sportswoman's T.E.A.M. Basketball Digest* publisher P. G. Wethall wrote in 1980. "For example, in the second quarter [Chicago Hustle center] Inge Nissen committed two separate hacking fouls within 30 seconds of each other, with the referee looking right at her. Most players will do it if they know the referee is blocked out yet both these were obviously seen by the referee and one of them was heard throughout DePaul's Alumni Hall."

As evidence of such "homering," coaches and sportswriters cited occasional eye-opening disparities in free-throw shooting. After one home game against the California Dreams, for example, local press acknowledged that a "friendly whistle" had sent the Chicago Hustle to the foul line 50 times to the Dreams' 25. Chicago, on the other hand, insisted that the Iowa Cornets were getting to the line 17 more times at home than the Hustle.

In February 1981 Dallas Diamonds president Dave Almstead compiled figures over a one-week period that he said showed "poor (if not partial) officiating in New Orleans." One example, he said, was a game in which New Orleans was awarded 36 more free throws in a game that Minnesota lost by only 7 points. On another occasion, New Orleans shot 40 free throws to 18 for St. Louis, with a final score differential of 8 points.

The league brought in neutral referees for its first playoffs, and Byrne announced plans to do away with local officiating crews during the regular season, but the more costly change was not implemented, and complaints continued to surface. New Orleans referees identified Pride possessions by calling "our ball," one fan complained, and St. Louis officials often congratulated Streak players who made baskets. The league began charting each franchise's average number of fouls, home versus visiting team, the results of which seemed to support some of the objections. Most notably, visitors in New Orleans were whistled for nearly 8 more fouls per game than the hometown Pride.

Late in the third season, the Pride decided that officiating in a road game against San Francisco required drastic measures. With just under five minutes remaining, four of his nine players fouled out, two more injured, and his team trailing 124–106, coach Ray Scott refused to send his players back on the court. The official explanation was that New Orleans could not continue because it had only three players, but, Scott said, "It was our choice to leave because the officiating was so atrocious."

That's how Sybil Blalock remembers it. "We were putting ourselves in a position where we could get hurt," she says. "That's the only time in my entire career I have been in that situation—and I hate to criticize officiating—but it was really bad. At some point you have to honestly consider your safety."

In hindsight, the "home court advantage" might not have been as bad as everyone thought, says three-year New Jersey Gems player Wanda Szeremeta. "I complained at home. I complained on the road. I complained everywhere I went. So, homering, no. Because I would get teed up in New Jersey as much as I did in Minnesota or Chicago." (Or Houston, where she received a technical for "calling an official an obscene name.")

Coaches are the wrong ones to ask about officiating, Greg Williams admitted. "We see things one way—our way." Pride general manager Steve Brown agrees. It's a terrible job, he says. "I think I've refereed one high school game and swore I would never do it again. We went to Chicago and used to think it was impossible to win a game up there because of the refereeing. Was that true? In our minds we believed it, but who knows? You know, it's part of the game."

THE RULES

FULL-COURT FIVE ON FIVE. WBL games were played with five players on each team, using the full length of the court. Although all colleges played five on five at the time, the format was not a foregone conclusion in some parts of the country. Until 1971, girls and women in the United States played a half-court game, with six players per side, and when the

WBL opened play, half a dozen states still favored six-on-six competition at the high school level. Ultimately, litigation and public pressure led all but Iowa and Oklahoma to switch to the five-player game during the WBL's first year.

LENGTH OF THE GAME. The WBL originally intended to play four 10-minute quarters (a hybrid between the NBA's 12-minute quarters and college's 20-minute halves), but at the urging of Milwaukee Does general manager Gene DeLisle, the WBL Board of Governors voted in the NBA rule instead.

Some commentators questioned a 48-minute game for women. After the WBL's inaugural game, *Women's Basketball Newsletter* opined that the 12-minute quarters "caused an exciting game to be at times boring." *Basketball Weekly* writer Clifford Smith added his voice. "Forty minutes is the college length, and seems just right," he said. "Word is, 48 minutes is a little too long." After the second season, Minnesota Fillies owner Gordon Nevers recommended switching to four 11-minute quarters, which would allow most games to finish within two hours, enhancing fan appeal and helping to sell television time. The original rule remained in place, however.

SHOT CLOCK. As in the NBA, WBL teams were required to take a shot within 24 seconds. Originally, the WBL rule book borrowed a 30-second limit from the women's college game (college men did not yet have a shot clock), but DeLisle successfully urged adoption of the NBA rule. The shot clock, owners believed, would generate higher scores. WBL fans were promised 80- or 100-point games on a regular basis—and got them. (In 139 of 167 WBL games in 1979–80, for example, at least one of the two teams reached the 100-point mark.)

ILLEGAL DEFENSE. The WBL adopted the same definition of an illegal defense as in the NBA. Players were not allowed to defend specific areas of the court ("zone" defense); rather, each player was required to guard another player.

WBL coach George Nicodemus took advantage of this rule early with his infamous "clear out" play. Four players would rush to the sidelines, drawing their defenders with them, and a guard would then go one on one up the middle. Greg Williams, Houston's assistant coach at the time, remembers the play well from preseason scouting. "I went back to Coach (Don) Knodel and said, 'This is ridiculous. If they're going to allow this, we might as well play a two-on-two league.'" The rules committee later declared that defenders did not have to stay with players too far from the basket, "so that ended that fiasco."

Teams managed to work around the rule anyway, says Angels player Glenda Holleyman. "Of course, we're supposed to play man-to-man. And of course, you find ways to make your zone not look like a man-to-man." As did most NBA teams, WBL coaches often bent the rule. In one game, for example, Chicago needed to stop the onslaught of a Dallas Diamonds power player. "A cleverly disguised zone defense (it's illegal, you know) finally slowed down the marvelous 37-point 20-rebound performance by 6–3 Alfredda Abernathy," the *Tribune* reported. "Zone? What zone?" Hustle coach Bruno smiled. "That's a help-out man-to-man. Same thing Bobby Knight uses. He never calls it 'zone.'"

THREE-POINT SHOT. The WBL's second season (1979–80) saw one major rule change: adoption of a three-point shot. The trey originated in the American Basketball League, a 1960s pro league developed by Harlem Globetrotters founder Abe Saperstein, and was popularized by the American Basketball Association, a rival to the NBA from 1967 through 1976. In the late 1970s the NBA, facing dwindling television ratings (more than a 25 percent drop between 1978 and 1979), began eying the spicier elements of its former competitor's game and voted to experiment with a three-point shot.

Basketball purists were appalled and wanted nothing to do with the ABA's glitziness. "They don't want to see multicolored basketballs, sequined sneakers, trampoline takeoff pits for slam dunkers, or three-point baskets," the *Los Angeles Times* reported in 1980. Red Auerbach, general manager of the NBA's Boston Celtics, was among the critics. "I say leave our game alone," he said. "Putting in the 3-point play reminds me of a team that trades four, five and six players every year. Everybody starts panicking. TV panicked over the bad ratings."

Such resistance to the three-pointer in the NBA led some WBL owners to question whether the women's league should follow suit. Why had the NBA adopted the rule? San Francisco owner Marshall Geller wanted to know. Perhaps to counter the effects of man-to-man defense, Nucatola speculated, and to de-emphasize the power game inside, but Geller was not persuaded. The NBA had lost a lot of money in recent years, he noted, and the WBL might do the same if it copied the men's rules with a "me, too" attitude. Would the WBL even be considering a three-point shot if the NBA hadn't adopted it? After all, the board had rejected the shot just one year earlier.

Other owners saw a potential for added excitement. "We are in the entertainment business," New York Stars co-owner Steve McCarthy argued, and the decision should hinge on two questions: How can I get hurt? and How can I make money? To Minnesota's Nevers, the prospect of changing the outcome of a game in its late moments was especially appealing. The board adopted the new rule by a 10–4 vote.

NBA teams largely ignored the new shot ("Anyone who has actually seen a three-point basket, please contact the Audubon Society, rare bird division," *Saturday Review*'s Jonathan Evan Maslow wrote in 1980), and the WBL followed suit—especially as the distance was the same as in the NBA, 23 feet 9 inches from the center of the basket and 22 feet in the corners, well beyond the range of most WBL players.

The Houston Angels did not attempt a single three-pointer in the 1979–80 season. The Milwaukee Does launched only 8, making none. Out of 10 attempts, the Minnesota Fillies netted 2, one of which was a buzzer-beating 55-footer. Only one Iowa Cornets player made a trey. By far, the most ambitious team was the Chicago Hustle, which attempted 33 three-pointers, but sank only 2. Other than Muffet McGraw's 2 for 3, the California Dreams were 0 for 9.

With these statistics in mind, the WBL's rules committee considered moving the line in to 22 feet at the top and 21 feet on the sides, which would increase accuracy and create more excitement, Nevers said. It would also "be in line with the fact that all of our measurements are for our game," he wrote in 1980, but the question was buried under other pressing business.

Interest in the long-distance shot picked up in 1980–81, but accuracy did not. Apart from 1 for 2 by St. Louis's Rowanna Pope, New Jersey Gems guard Tara Heiss led all players with 4 out of 12, or 33 percent. Second was Dallas Diamonds star Nancy Lieberman, who went 2 for 10.

AT THE SCORER'S TABLE. In Houston, one of Tom Davis's duties as director of operations (a fancy title he gave himself) was to run the 24-second shot clock. "You got any experience?" a referee asked in his first game. "Oh, yeah, yeah," Davis assured him, adding under his breath, "About two minutes' worth." (At least there *was* a shot clock in that game; after being kicked out of their regular facility for nonpayment, the Houston Angels had to play once at a high school that didn't have one.)

Scorekeepers weren't always experienced, either, and no one really knew the final score of a 1979 game between the St. Louis Streak and California

Dreams, the *St. Louis Post-Dispatch* reported. "Apparently, the official scorer did not know what he was doing. Nor did the official timer. Baskets were either recorded late or not recorded at all. At one point, Dreams owner Larry Kozlicki threatened to protest the game because of the scorer's ineptitude." The Dreams won (apparently), but for an hour afterward, Streak personnel sat in the stands while scorekeepers tried to sort out what had happened.

No particular format was required for official WBL play-by-play, and scorers were somewhat free to improvise. Chicago's were often colorful:

Farrah fast break layup . . . Marquis cripshot . . . Sanborn 16 foot set-shot rightside . . . Travnik left handed hook shot . . . McGraw driving layup . . . Hileman 10 foot leanin jumper . . . Caldwell 17 foot desperation jumper . . . Rajcula one-footed over the shoulder prayer shot . . . K. Young spinning lay up . . . D. Burdick 6 foot floating jumper off glass . . . Stachon 10 foot turnaround no-look jumpshot

Milwaukee also provided nice detail:

McWhorter turn around jumper from Prevost . . . Morales drives the lane off Greene feed . . . Nestor rebound and layin . . . Gamble baseline jump from White . . . Griffith lean-in jumper off Chapman pass

Other franchises were less descriptive, even monosyllabic:

[Minnesota] Swindell (drive) . . . Wilson (court long pass) . . . DeLorme (left key) . . . Sjoquist (fast break) . . . Duckworth (turnaround) . . . Koopman (open underneath) [St. Louis] Loyd bsk good fl by Galloway . . . Platte 5 ft glide [Iowa] Thomas corner . . . Lewis lane [New Jersey] Tatterson hook . . . Martin tip . . . Meyers under basket . . . Comerie one hander . . . Browning steal and layup . . . Geils oj break [New Orleans] Hardy 14 jump . . . Wayment layup from Peters . . . Brogdon 18 jump from Farrah . . . [New York] F. Young elbow foul on rebound Caldwell shoot XX . . . Moore layup from Craig . . . Bender side jump from Thomas . . . Melbourne jumper from lane . . . Fletcher 10 foot left side bank shot [California] Scharff, 12' jumper . . . Basket Cook [Dallas] (Bruton under (Shoemaker) . . . Barnes 18' outside . . . Steal: Browning . . . Lieberman folo.

San Francisco's play-by-play seemed the most picturesque. Readers might see, for example:

> McKinney from sweet 16 . . . Haugejorde 5' bank left . . . Williams pullup 10-footer . . . Kennedy runnin' jumper 12 ft . . . Hansen muscles inside . . . Mitchell running hook from 8 feet . . . Ortega finger tip lay in . . . Hicks head and shoulders, dribble drive, lay in . . . McKinney around-about- hook . . . Fincher nuttin' but net 6 ft . . . Digitale in traffic & 1

In an early game in New Jersey, a hapless scorekeeper scratched through several entries before finally conceding, "Stats are screwed up." Another confused Iowa players Tonyus Chavers (a six-foot-two-inch African American) and Tanya Crevier (a five-foot-three-inch white reserve player), adding after the game, "Replace the name Chavers where the Crevier is due to an error" (which explained why "Crevier" was substituting for six-foot-one-inch Doris Draving and six-foot-two-inch Charlotte Lewis).

TECHNICAL FOULS. The fine for a technical foul in the NBA, where the average salary at the time exceeded $100,000, was $75.00. The fine for a technical foul in the WBL, where the average salary was closer to $10,000, was—$75.00. "The only thing wrong with this league are common sense and dollars and sense," New Orleans coach Butch van Breda Kolff said. "That technical cost me $75, just like the NBA. Only I'm not making $300,000 any more." After his second T in as many games, Philadelphia Fox coach Dave Wohl predicted dourly, "If this keeps up, I'll owe the team money, instead of them having to pay me."

Nearly half of the WBL's coaches were suspended at one time or another for unpaid technicals. Owners showed little interest in reducing the fine, though. Keeping coaches in line was important for the fans, Zebos believed. The WBL "is a 'big League' and not a 'bush league' operation," he wrote; bench misconduct must not go unchallenged. "Do not allow (coaches) to become the center of attraction with constant griping and gestures from the bench," he directed his referees. "The fans are there to see the players perform—not to watch a coach harass or intimidate the officials. Keep them in line!"

Working Hard for the Money

You quickly get the idea these women like the game. It sure isn't the luxury. • **Mark Everson**, *New York Post*, December 15, 1978

For the players, the jump to the pros is like joining Basketball Anonymous. At least in college there were fans. Cheerleaders. Reporters. Maybe even a band. What do the Diamonds get? . . . Row on row of comfortable, empty seats. Average annual salaries of $10,000 (about one-tenth that of NBA stars). Co-op living, part-time jobs. Chauvinistic media treatment. And on bad days, torn ligaments in pursuit of glory. • ***Texas Observer***, April 11, 1980

CEDAR FALLS, IOWA, JANUARY 15, 1979
The Iowa Cornets were up before dawn, filing into their Corn Dog bus to get from last night's home game in Cedar Falls to this afternoon's home game in Des Moines, 129 miles away. The trip would take a little over two hours, plenty of time to freshen up and wash their uniforms for the game.

Throughout the Midwest, the winter of 1978–79 had been one of the most severe in memory. Banks in Chicago were offering emergency loans, Milwaukee was buried under constant snow and record lows, and Iowa was seeing some of its worst storms of the century. Shortly after leaving Cedar Falls, the Cornets found themselves heading into a white nightmare.

Hours later, while the Minnesota Fillies warmed up at Veterans Memorial Auditorium, the home team's bus crawled behind a snowplow that was clearing a path through drifts sometimes as high as the bus windows. "We're going to forfeit our own home game," Rhonda Penquite thought.

Nearly six hours after leaving Cedar Falls, the weary bus driver pulled into the parking lot at Veterans. They were ten minutes past tip-off, and the Cornets quickly hauled their luggage into the gym. There was no time to do laundry; they would just have to wear their uniforms from last night. But as they pulled them out, the women realized that the uniforms were completely stiff—frozen in sweat.

The players stood them in a corner, hoping they would thaw out enough to wear. One hour after the game was supposed to begin, the Cornets donned their dirty, frozen uniforms and went out to play for the few hundred fans who had braved the storm. "We warmed up faster than our uniforms did," Connie Kunzmann quipped.

Watched by a sympathetic reporter from the *Washington Post*, the Iowa Cornets pounded on a gym door in Elizabeth, New Jersey, in early 1979, hoping to be let in out of the cold to practice. (They eventually got in, but not to practice—a local girls' game had preempted the pro team's practice time.) "Is this how it feels in the NBA?" assistant coach Bruce Mason asked.

Not exactly, the *Post* replied. "In the National Basketball Association, players don't sleep three and four to a room to save pennies as the Cornets did here. Nor do they dress at the motel, then arrive at the game with 14 players and coaches (and all their belongings, including one guitar) crammed into two rented station wagons."

Nor did NBA players practice at 6 a.m. and 7 p.m. so that players could hold a second job. Minnesota Fillies players worked part-time as sales clerks, in the warehouse of a local florist, selling insurance, substitute teaching, or whatever other job would let them be gone for days at a time.

New Jersey Gems player Denise Burdick commuted from Pennsylvania every day after work. "Practice was over at 9 or 10 p.m., and she would drive all the way back two or three hours to get back to her road construction job," trainer Ron Linfonte recalls. "This girl, she would drag herself into the gym." Her teammate Kathy Solano worked as a lifeguard and swimming instructor all day, then went to Long Island for practices. "I drove an hour and a half in and an hour and a half home every night. That is how badly I wanted to play," she says.

When Gail Marquis arrived at tryouts for the New York Stars in 1979, Coach Dean Meminger had a message for the players: "This is not the NBA. This is not at all the NBA. Don't even think of it like that." The National Basketball Association had been through its turbulent years, but it was now more than thirty years old and major league in every sense. For Marquis, it was a necessary lecture. She had been playing professionally in France, where she had been treated very well. "I had this crazy idea that the WBL was like the NBA," she says, but she was quickly disabused of that notion.

WBL players worked under conditions that would seem primitive to many college or YWCA teams, *Physician and Sportsmedicine* wrote early in the first season. "But the women players don't mind at all. Adaptability is their strong suit. They practice anywhere, make use of whatever equipment comes with the particular gym, and do their conditioning in neighborhood parks and playgrounds near where they work or live."

The magazine might have been a little generous in its assessment of other women's programs at the time. Granted, some schools were progressive. "In college we had weight rooms, a training table and super facilities, but this is the WBL's first season," said Cornets player Nancy Rutter from the University of Missouri. "We can't expect everything to happen overnight." (Indeed, Missouri's program had only evolved after Rutter's freshman year, when there were no scholarships, no locker room, and the women's team did not play out of state.)

Faye Lawrence likewise compared her Philadelphia Fox unfavorably to Temple University. "Temple gave us the red carpet compared to this," she said. "It's tough. We're going to Houston on the same day as the game. At Temple, we would go a day ahead. I guess I was spoiled in college." Most women's programs, though, were not as advanced as *Sportsmedicine* seemed to think. When Eastern Kentucky University's Cindy Lundberg arrived at the Milwaukee Does, she was delighted to learn that her uniform shirt would have her name embroidered on the back; she'd never had that in college.

"You have to remember women athletes are used to second-class status," Minnesota player Kathy DeBoer said in 1980. "Like most of us who just came out of college, we weren't used to making—or needing—much anyway. We're agreeable to doubling up in rooms on the road, sharing expenses and learning to live cheaply. Demands made on us are not unreasonable." It was no big deal, Dallas players said, to take turns gathering up dirty uniforms after practice to wash them; they were used to it.

Not so with eight WBL players from Wayland Baptist College, a small school with a prominent women's basketball program. "Hutcherson's Flying Queens" even had a private plane for road games. Those same players were now expected to ride buses for hours on end. "Many of us came from college programs that were very well known and established," says former Flying Queen Valerie Goodwin. "And then you go into the pros, and basically it's an infant mentality. It's starting from scratch teaching people about the women's game."

It was an abrupt transition for former Wayland Baptist coach Dean Weese, head coach of the 1979–80 Dallas Diamonds. WBL president Bill Byrne remembers getting a call from the new coach. " 'Now, we play New York one night, and then New Jersey. How do we get to New Jersey?' " asked Weese. Byrne was exasperated. That Wayland bunch were just spoiled little brats. "I told him right to his face, 'Do you know what? For Christ's sake! You had a college team where the guy flew you around on planes and did this and that. You're in a pro league now.' " Byrne arranged ground transportation to the Diamonds' next game.

How WBL teams got to their games depended largely on two factors: geography and money. Teams on the East Coast could often take a train, and Midwest teams could drive to several venues. Players in those franchises spent a lot of time in buses and vans. "It's rough," Minnesota All-Star Marie Kocurek said. "We play in Chicago. We play a run-and-gun game up there and we only had eight players to work with that night. . . . Then we drive over to Bettendorf, get in at four in the morning and have to play that night. Now that's rough. That's rough on men. That's rough on women. That's rough on gorillas."

Traveling by ground was made more difficult in the first two WBL seasons by unusually severe weather conditions. In early 1979, the Chicago Hustle could not get to Milwaukee for a game against the Does. It would normally have been a six-hour drive from Cedar Falls, Iowa, where they played the night before, but the *Chicago Tribune* reported that "Saturday night, even snow plows were ordered off Iowa highways—snow and high winds were shutting off all travel."

Heading to Des Moines, a Minnesota Fillies bus inched cautiously past ditched trucks, and when they arrived, "the whole city, the *capital* city, was shut down. The streets were barely navigable, even on foot," wrote a *Twin City Reader* reporter traveling with the team. The snowstorm was "so severe that visibility was about 1 percent, and that was only through the *side* windows," she recounted. (Cheryl Engel remembers that bus ride well. The team had traveled half the night to get to a game the night before, then found itself on the harrowing trip to Iowa. The players complained at the time, she says, but in hindsight it wasn't so bad. "It's so funny to look back on it because it seems like when you're young, it's all exciting.")

In Mississippi, a visiting women's basketball squad from LeMoyne-Owen College gawked at a curious sight: a bus, newly painted with the image of a woman shooting a hook shot against an outline of the state of Iowa. Tonyus Chavers was in awe. "They must be professional if they have their own bus," she thought.

And what a bus it was. The Corn Dog was a $30,000 green and gold 1964 Greyhound with eight-track stereo, restrooms, beds, and dining area. "It was carpeted on floor, walls, ceiling," Penquite remembers. "It had speakers all the way back and it was probably one of the first buses that had television and VCRS in it. They had the seats to where they would turn around and then (make) a table there, so we could have a couple of tables where we could play cards or something."

When the Corn Dog pulled into town, people flocked around it, wanting to meet the players, general manager Rod Lein recalled years later. So did the police at times, says Molly Kazmer (then Bolin). "We saw you," a highway patrol officer would say. "Let us escort you in from here." (When the bus was pulled over for a less happy reason, an autograph or free poster usually took care of the problem).

Other teams were at the mercy of less glamorous transport. When a bus carrying the Dallas Diamonds to their hotel after a game broke down, the driver of a car behind them shuttled the players to a nearby hotel. On its way to an exhibition game, Chicago's Hustle Bus limped into a gas station, where arrangements were hastily made for the women to carpool. ("Hey! Take my girlfriend!" the mechanic offered.)

The Hustle were soon back on the road but then got lost, driving around in circles before finally arriving at the arena. (Getting lost was not uncommon in the WBL. On one Dallas road trip to New Orleans, a bus from the airport to the players' hotel got lost, as did the next one from the hotel to Tulane Gymnasium. The same thing happened in New Jersey, and the Diamonds were an hour late to a game against the Gems.)

WBL coaches often served double duty as drivers. Hustle coach Doug Bruno was behind the wheel of one of the team's two vans one night when he became drowsy. "Just let me pull over for ten minutes," he said and settled in for a nap on the side of the road. "After ten minutes, we woke him up and he went on, like he was refreshed and ready to go again," Rita Easterling recalls.

The San Francisco Pioneers flew to all of their games, so it was a rude awakening for Anita Ortega when she was traded to Minnesota in 1981. "I came here and found out we had to travel eight hours by car to Nebraska for a game, then travel eight hours by car back home right after the game," she complained. "I think that's ridiculous; I don't think that's a sign of a professional team."

For geographic reasons, the St. Louis Streak had to fly to all of their away games, which was easier on the players but harder on the wallet. To save money, Streak planners got creative. Eastern Airlines had a hub in Atlanta, and fares were cheaper if one was willing to route trips through there. "We saw a lot of the Atlanta airport," coach Larry Gillman laughs. "Like when we would fly from St. Louis to New York—through Atlanta. When we would fly St. Louis to Los Angeles—through Atlanta. How about this one? St. Louis to Minnesota and Chicago—through Atlanta." The New York Stars once flew back to New York from a game in Chicago and then out to San Francisco, a "rather strange itinerary" to save money, the *San Francisco Chronicle* speculated.

Another cost-saving measure was to fly standby. In the midst of a fourteen-game winning streak, the Stars were scheduled to play a road game against the California Dreams. "We didn't leave New York probably until about 12:30 in the afternoon to play a game at 7 o'clock that evening," Gail Marquis recalls. "We didn't arrive until 4 o'clock off the plane. This is a professional team, sitting in the airport on standby. How are you going to get 16 people on standby?"

Schedules were not always put together with convenience (or tiredness) in mind. In 1980–81, New Jersey played four nights in a row in four different cities. "We would sometimes have to be on the airplane in our uniform, running here and there," says guard Jill Jeffrey. "We would just kind of paste it together with chewing gum and smoke and mirrors."

The travel itself was often tedious. "Waiting in hotel rooms," Fillies player Cindy Lundberg says is her most vivid memory of her professional days. "Waiting for the game to start. Waiting for the plane to take off. Waiting—always waiting." Donna Murphy's life was "basically practice, traveling, and games. Practice, travel, and games the entire time," she says. "I didn't really get to enjoy the city of St. Louis."

During long trips, players napped or read or played cards or talked with teammates. A Chicago Hustle plane trip, as described by a *Tribune* reporter, went something like this: Tesa Duckworth did needlework. Mary Jo Peppler analyzed her teammates' handwriting. Debra Waddy-Rossow slept (and, when awakened by Liz Galloway to provide a sample for Peppler, wrote, "My name is Debra. I wish Liz wouldn't bother me with stuff like writing. Thanks.") Sue Digitale amused her teammates by reading from an advice column about the effect of alcohol on men's sex drives.

On a typical Fillies bus ride, Janet Timperman and Sue Wahl-Bye played Mastermind with coach Terry Kunze. Marie Kocurek stared out the window. Kathy DeBoer read Bill Russell's *Second Wind*. Donna Wilson, Katrina Owens, and Pat Montgomery chatted. Scooter DeLorme played backgammon with owner Gordon Nevers. On the trip back, the hungry players were refused service by a truck stop manager who said the place was too crowded. "God is testing us, Gordon," Nevers' partner Dick Higgins said.

One "luxury" that players could always find on the road was the mandatory halftime treat: two dozen oranges in the locker room. Whether they would also find a trainer (a staffer charged with preventing or ameliorating injuries) was less certain. The Nebraska Wranglers took care of their own injuries unless they were serious enough to warrant a doctor's visit and also did their own pregame taping. "The assistant coach was trying to tape my ankles and I said, 'That's all right, I'll do it myself,' because he was so pitiful," Janet Flora laughs.

The New Jersey Gems lucked onto a young trainer who also worked with the Cleveland Indians and had sophisticated equipment such as an ultrasound machine. Ron Linfonte wasn't always paid on time, but it didn't matter. "It was such a great experience that I didn't care," he says. "I would have done it for nothing." (The Gems' first trainer, Ethel Holevas, had originally come to try out for the team, and was provided a blue gym bag with a box of bandages, scissors, gauze pads, two cans of germicide, a tube of floor burn ointment, and some spray disinfectant. What she really coveted was an ice cooler.)

Trainers were usually among the first to be sacrificed in lean times. During the Stars' title run in 1980, management announced that the team's trainer, Rick Capistran, would not be joining them for the championship game, but he did anyway. "He made the drive from New York to Iowa himself with a couple of other fans," Marquis marvels. "We all got together and gave him all kinds of kisses and hugs when he arrived. He taped all of our ankles, our thighs, attended to all of us, and we had to take up a collection to make sure that he ate."

Trainers for the Chicago Hustle and the NBA's Chicago Bulls later cooperated in a study that compared injuries in both leagues. One noteworthy conclusion, reported in the *American Journal of Sports Medicine*, was that the women were nearly five times more likely to experience a sprain, most often an ankle, and were twice as likely to suffer a strain or contusion. The greater incidence of sprains suggested a need for better conditioning, the report concluded.

Without question, conditioning was far different in the WBL than a generation later. The most common method was jogging, often because players had no other options. New Jersey, for instance, practiced at a gym with no weight room. "I always ran because there was no place to do anything else," Gems player Jo-Ellen Bistromowitz said. (She also got in an extra workout by running up the stairs to her apartment—on the twenty-second floor.)

Better conditioning might have cut down on injuries as the study suggested, but its authors were also laboring under the misapprehension that working conditions were "essentially the same" in the NBA and WBL. Unlike the men, WBL players were still riding all day and sometimes all night, playing in unforgiving facilities with slippery floors, dead spots, and missing tiles, wearing the same pair of shoes they wore in college, and practicing and playing in extreme temperatures.

The Met Center in Minneapolis was kept at 55 degrees even during games. "How cold is it?" *Minnesota Star* columnist Bob Fowler asked. "Well, Marguerite Keeley didn't start for the Fillies, but started a trend. She opened the game on the bench by wearing gloves. Soon teammates were shivering in sweat shirts, with the hoods over their heads, while wrapping jackets and towels around their legs." Carol Blazejowski remembers freezing in an ice skating rink where her New Jersey Gems played (the court was laid directly over the ice), as fans huddled in their coats. "In today's day and age, they wouldn't even consider playing under those conditions," she says. "But you know, who cared? If you hurry and run enough, you get warm."

At the other end of the spectrum, the St. Louis Streak's training camp was held in 110-degree heat with no air conditioning. Players' noses were bleeding, and some nearly passed out. Renee Rutland waded into an outdoor fountain to cool off. Linnell Jones was overheated, but she was afraid she might feel bloated or get cramps if she took a drink. "I remember that heat, but I remember such a determination to make that team that when he would say 'break,' I would just go sit down and pour water over my head."

Although managers usually scrimped when they could, they were generous at times with accommodations. After one of their usual nine-hour, four-leg trips to Dallas, the Streak stayed in the exclusive Loews Anatole Hotel, which boasted nine restaurants, a swimming pool, and racquetball courts. Staying on the *Queen Mary* during road trips to California is also a fond memory of many players. Even the less plush accommodations weren't bad, says Chicago's Sue Digitale. "I mean, they weren't eerie, you know?"

When the purse strings tightened, the nice hotels had to go, and the Iowa Cornets sometimes crammed as many as six players into one room. Money could also be saved getting to the games. "We hitchhiked a few rides from the hotels to the coliseum for games," Nebraska Wranglers player Genia Beasley recalls. "You surely don't think we rented vans? I remember riding in the back of an electrical truck that's open in the back from our hotel in New Orleans to the Superdome." When the San Francisco Pioneers had back-to-back games in New Orleans, it was cheaper to put them up at a hotel between games than to fly them home, so the players got to spend a few days in New Orleans during Mardi Gras.

The chance to travel was a significant benefit of the WBL. "Professional athletes have a unique opportunity to see more of the world and the nation than almost anyone in any other walk of life," the Chicago Hustle's player handbook noted, and it was true. "Some of the girls just chose to stay in the hotel room," Nebraska player Janet Flora says. "Not me! I had to get out and see what was around." Her team had a curfew, but there was time to visit Fisherman's Wharf and ride the trolley in San Francisco, and to go down to Bourbon Street in New Orleans. Many players had never been to WBL cities before, let alone with time to spend sightseeing, shopping, and socializing.

"The first time we went to New Orleans, we had these fat jackets with 'Iowa Cornets' on them and we walked as a group down the street, so people would turn around and look," Molly Kazmer recalls. "Even when we went to New York City, we were so naive. We were open-mouthed. Looking in, there would be girlie shows going on or something and we would say, 'Oh my God.' We wouldn't go in, but we looked when the door was open. We were just sticking out like sore thumbs." Wearing matching jackets on their time off was one way of making a team more visible, and most players didn't mind. If the WBL was to survive, they figured, it was their responsibility to do whatever they could to promote the league, whether standing on street corners in uniform (which didn't attract as much attention in San Francisco as it would have in her home town in Michigan, Pioneers player Kim Hansen noted), or endless promotions at schools and in the community.

During her three years with the Gems, Wanda Szeremeta made many such appearances. "I did all this for free, because I felt obligated to promote the league," she says. "I was born in the pioneer era for women's sports. I didn't put my hand out and say, 'Look, it's going to cost you if you want me to come speak to you.' Who knows—maybe I was a lousy businesswoman."

A few Iowa players became a little too enthusiastic during one promotional assignment at a local grocery store. "We were supposed to be kind of hanging out in this grocery store and handing out 2-for-1 coupons to our games," Kazmer says, but a snowstorm kept people at home, and there weren't many targets. Spying an elderly shopper, the players rushed toward her. "We were chasing an old lady down the aisle trying to give her a coupon," she laughs. "She was scared to death of us, wondering what we were trying to do to her. That was one of our running jokes for the next couple of years—'Remember how we used to chase people down in grocery stores during a snowstorm to make them come to our games?'"

Although WBL players needed to reach out to potential fans, they also needed to be cautious. The Hustle handbook warned of "pests" who would seek autographs, pictures, and personal favors, but the guidelines also reminded the women that "it is the interest of the fans and their attendance at our games that ultimately helps pay the bills, including salaries."

No problem—most players were happy to interact with fans. "I thought that was a neat experience," says Patti Bucklew, who was surprised the first time someone asked for her autograph. Being approached for an autograph was a thrill, Lynda Gehrke agrees. "It was like, 'Somebody really wants my autograph? Little old me?' I was so proud." (That helped make up for the "fan" in Milwaukee who boomed out at every game, "Hey, Gehrke, your name rhymes with turkey!")

In different cities, fans set up booster clubs, helped players move, did their taxes, wrote letters to the editor, and worked hard to promote their teams. Some became part of franchise lore, such as Chicago's Chrome Dome (Bill Holcumb) and the Hustle Mustle Club.

On rare occasions, WBL players were surprised by a fan's actions. A male fan in Chicago repeatedly managed to get Janie Fincher's phone number to ask her out to eat vegetables (having read somewhere that she liked them). "He would go to any length to get my unpublished number, and I must have changed it seven or eight times," she says.

One Thanksgiving morning, a rare day off for Fincher was spoiled by a knock on the door at 6 a.m. It was the police, they announced; someone had been caught messing with her car. Outside, Fincher recognized the would-be thief as the boyfriend of a young teammate. "What are you doing? Why in the hell are you trying to steal my car?" she demanded. "How did you find out where I live?"

He had followed her home from practice, he admitted. He was in love with her. "I just wanted a piece of something you owned, something special to you," he said. He was looking for Thanksgiving cards or other personal items. Fincher was disgusted. "So tell me, maybe I'll take the hint or something, but don't go steal my car," she chided. The young man started to cry. She felt sorry for him and told the officers to let him go.

In Dayton, Rockettes players were "totally oblivious to the whole thing of being a professional athlete" until someone followed them home after a game one night. The fan turned out to be nice, Michelle McKenzie says, but the incident made her realize how vulnerable players could be. Minnesota Fillies players were so naive that they provided their home addresses for one early news article.

"If professional sports has a lunatic fringe, isn't the WBL close to it?" the *Washington Post* asked. "Surely, this is the ragged edge of liberation for women." WBL players "are proud not to be treated like women these days. They are pioneers, founding sisters, who have proudly signed a long-term contract with hard times." Not lunatic, perhaps, but passionate. "I know the feeling of insecurity about the league, but I love the game so much I'm going to take my chances and go day by day," Dallas's Debbie Stewart said. "Most of the girls on the team feel the same way—I'd even mow grass this summer to hang around."

That passion was exemplified by the players on one troubled franchise. "Once, not so long ago, women played basketball for nothing, for love of the game," the *Post* wrote in December 1979. "The Washington Metros are still playing for nothing. They have not yet been paid this season." Several players hadn't been able to afford a visit with their families over the holidays, and some who did had returned to find their clothes locked in a store room because their rent hadn't been paid.

Leaving on a road trip, the Metros traveling squad gathered their food and gave it to the players staying behind. Care packages from home were also shared with teammates, like the collard greens that Dianne Caudle's mother sent, along with $10 to buy some meat. When newly acquired player Janie

Fincher arrived from Chicago with food in hand, she immediately made an impression on her four roommates. "All of those canned goods I had and the bologna and bread I went and bought at the store, those girls thought it was a delicacy," she recalls. "We chowed down like they hadn't been eating for six months."

The Metros practiced on an outdoor tennis court—in the middle of December—because they couldn't afford a facility, and had to borrow ankle tape from opposing teams. Some players couldn't afford gas to drive to practices, and only five sessions were held at which the whole team was present. "Coach, I need money for gas," one player told Nat Frazier, who pulled out a dollar bill.

Paydays came and went, but instead of a check, the Metros were each given $100 so that they would have "dollars in their pockets," WBL vice-president Dave Almstead said, while the league tried to straighten things out. "You can't beat life at the top," the *Chicago Tribune* wrote sarcastically.

But when New York Knicks player Toby Knight watched the Metros take on the visiting New Jersey Gems, he couldn't believe what he was hearing. They hadn't been paid? "You'd never be able to tell it by the way they're playing," he said. That's right, the *Washington Star* reported. "They know times are tough but it was tough on the men, too, once, they say. Besides, they are pros and pros don't quit."

The desire to keep playing a game they loved allowed the teams to take advantage of players, Donna Geils suggested when her Gems played Washington. "They tell you you're the pioneers. That's the carrot they hold in front of your head," she said. Metros player Carmen Fletcher felt some of that frustration. "Maybe men feel like whenever they get women together in a group or a team, they feel like a pimp and can do with them as they please," she said.

Byrne resented the implication. "I get mad when men or women say we're exploiting women," he snapped. "Their salaries aren't too bad for 4 months work." (Of course, that assumed the women actually received the salaries. But even when the money wasn't paid, it wasn't really exploitation, Susan Summons says. "If they gave me a tight uniform and my shorts were up to my butt, that would make me feel exploited as a woman," but money problems were "just a shortcoming of the operations of the program.")

Bouncing paychecks wasn't unique to the Metros; at one time or another, more than half of the WBL players experienced no pay or slow pay. "My husband would wait outside practice on pay day with the car running so we'd be the first ones at the bank," the California Dreams' Muffet McGraw recalled in 1998. "Sometimes, just the first couple of checks would clear."

Teammate Michelle McKenzie was also nervous. She was about to lose her car, but at least she and her roommate, Patti Bucklew, had enough to eat — sort of. "I remember just eating spaghetti," McKenzie says. "I got so sick of it. Because we knew we needed carbohydrates, we would eat spaghetti, and the luxury item was having sauce with it. Spaghetti with sauce — we were living high for that day."

In Philadelphia, several Fox players had their phones disconnected, and they couldn't afford flights home for Christmas. The Fox's Christmas party was "less than joyous," the *Philadelphia Inquirer* noted. "Hell, yes, I'm worried," guard Faye Lawrence said. "I've got a car payment due. I can't even go out New Year's Eve. I'm busted. I've got four dollars to my name."

Three Minnesota teammates shared a one-bedroom apartment. Nancy Dunkle had the bedroom, Kim Hansen slept on the living room floor, and Anita Ortega slept on the dining room floor in a sleeping bag. They all shared Hansen's car and ate rice. And more rice. "We eat rice with vegetables, with meat, and with, er, everything. We eat rice with rice," Ortega said.

Chris Critelli squeezed into a small Chicago apartment with three others. "It was a little pantry, honestly the size of a walk-in closet sort of thing, and they put a bed in there and put my bag in there and that is where I stayed," she recalls. "It was pretty bizarre." When the New Jersey Gems fell behind in salaries, players economized. "I was living in this old hotel with cockroaches," Karen Logan says. "It didn't even have a kitchenette. We had to go past the drug-rehab floor where people were passed out in the hall."

New Jersey captain Wanda Szeremeta liked her owners but had no patience for financial shenanigans. When her paycheck was returned for insufficient funds, she announced in the locker room, "Look, my check bounced. I don't know if any of you guys have tried to cash your checks, but I'm not going to suit up for tonight's game." The other women continued dressing. "You know, this could happen to you," she added, but it didn't faze them. Szeremeta suited up and then walked over to a team owner staffing the ticket booth. As each person bought a ticket, Szeremeta held out her hand for the cash. When she reached $300, she rolled up the money, stuffed it in her sock, and went to warm up.

Houston Angels coaches felt guilty asking players to practice when they weren't being paid, and finally Coach Don Knodel made a somber announcement at the team's Christmas party: "We have a game in San

Francisco tomorrow. Greg [Williams, the assistant coach] and I will be out at the airport at 7 a.m., and if five of you show up, we will go. If you don't, we will understand, we'll just forfeit the game."

The next morning, the Angels coaches watched as eight women arrived, the remnants of last season's championship team. For others, the hardships weren't worth it. "Nancy Kuhl, our number one draft pick, she said, 'The heck with that,' and she just left and went home to Pennsylvania," Williams recalls. "We never saw her again."

Before the 1981 WBL championship game in Omaha, Nebraska Wranglers players met in the locker room. Except for some rent money, they hadn't been paid for a couple of months; should they call it quits? Marie Kocurek spoke up. "I don't think the league is going to make it beyond this year," she said. "I want to play one more game before I retire." They owed it to future generations to finish the season, Charlotte Lewis believed. "We wanted to see another professional league come out of it, even if that one failed. I think that if we had quit, then there would be no hope for us now because nobody would have faith."

Players wanted a chance at the title, to experience the pride of winning a championship, Holly Warlick recalls. Even worse, arch rival Nancy Lieberman and her Dallas Diamonds would claim it if the Wranglers walked. "Forget that," Genia Beasley concluded. "Not an option." What it really came down to, says Carol Chason, was that they just couldn't give up. "The people you had on that team loved basketball, and I guess to some extent we had a vision of what could be one day. If I had to go back and do it again, I would, because I think you've got to suffer through those hard times to get to the good times."

7

Makeup Game

Oh, that she were Ludmilla, the Russian shot-putter, bilgewater blah and built like a baked potato. No one would question her legitimacy then, for she would look like a professional athlete. Trouble is, even in her worst moments, 27-year-old Janie Fincher looks more like a professional cheerleader than a professional basketball player. Witness the honey-blonde hair, the eyes of jade, the supple body that's enough to make a grown man howl in the moonlight. She could be Miss January if she chose, but what she really wants is for people to accept her as a jump-shooting, rebound-snatching, shovel-passing pip of a guard who just happens to be beautiful.
• **Michael Davis**, *Parade*, January 18, 1981

Can men learn to appreciate a girl for her beautiful jump shot? Will women want to watch the girl next door press full-court? • **Kathy Martone**, (New Jersey) *Daily News*, July 1978

Molly Bolin stood at the counter, cashing her WBL paycheck. "You're a basketball player?" the teller asked. "You don't look like a basketball player." Bolin had heard it before. So had the Chicago Hustle's Janie Fincher, and their response, invariably, was the same: "What is a basketball player supposed to look like?"

In the 1970s, that was an important question for WBL officials. The general public's impression of women's basketball—both the game itself and those who played it—was relatively uninformed. Players no longer stood around in skirts waving their arms around, but what kind of woman would want to race up and down a full-length court, or crash the boards, or play college basketball with no chance of a scholarship? It just wasn't done, at least not by "normal" people.

"Whenever you pioneer something, it is a difficult thing to do," says Iowa Cornets player Rhonda Penquite. "Especially to pioneer something so new, and so against societal grain at that time when women weren't really athletes, and if you were, there was a stigma that went with it." That kind of disapproval was, literally, a foreign concept for Chicago Hustle player Inge Nissen. When the Great Dane arrived at Old Dominion University after years of playing in Denmark and France, she discovered a widespread attitude that athletics "wasn't a feminine thing for a woman to do. And, frankly I was shocked. I had never been exposed to that before."

It was the American mindset that Karen Logan took into account when putting together the Chicago Hustle team, she says. She hoped it wouldn't always be that way (and it no longer is, she feels), but WBL players had to project a certain image if the league was to succeed. "We will not hire one girl on our team who looks masculine," she told the *Logan* (UT) *Herald Journal*. "The only way society will accept our team or league, in general, is for us to show that it's a normal thing to do. It must be family entertainment."

Having heard a sportswriter look for "a good-looking player, so we could use a picture in the paper," Logan also concluded that appearance might affect how the media covered the league, and it seemed to at times. "I'll tell you how to make money with this franchise," one sportswriter said at a New Orleans Pride game. "You round up Dallas Cowboy cheerleader rejects and put 'em on the court. You'd pack the place every game and it wouldn't matter if you lost 180–0."

Whether they were trying to dispel prejudiced notions of their readers or actually shared such notions themselves, "there were a number of newspaper articles I read where the sportswriters would almost be speaking with surprise: 'There are nice looking women out there!' " Logan says. Thus, for example, an early *Houston Post* article praised the Houston Angels, "who, by the way, are not so unattractive, so indelicate, so huge and hairy as one might imagine."

Another writer, complimenting Carol Blazejowski, wrote, "The young lady they call 'Blaze' does not fit the expected mold of a basketball phenomenon. She is not outsized with gargantuan arms and legs and hands like ham hocks. At 5 feet, 10 inches and 145 pounds, she is an attractive miss who could pass for the girl next door."

The stereotype of women athletes as "Ludmillas" was, ironically, reinforced every time helpful writers exclaimed that WBL players seemed 'normal.' "A lot of women can look pretty," *Mademoiselle* wrote. "But how many can be beautiful and still score fifty points a game?" Off the court, dress and demeanor of Minnesota Fillies players was that of "robust, athletic, but not unfeminine or unusual young women," the *Minneapolis Star* noted.

The Houston Angels "want to be called 'ladies'" but would perform like athletes on the court, the *Houston Chronicle* reported. "No worrying about broken fingernails, no calling time out to find a misplaced false eyelash and no stopping to check smeared lipstick." The *Chicago Tribune* illustrated a lengthy feature about the Hustle's battle against sexism with a large photograph of Tesa Duckworth curling her hair in the locker room, the caption of which assured readers, "Though they play the game with the same zest as their male counterparts, Chicago Hustle players are distinctly feminine off the court."

Such coverage had "worked miracles" for the image of women athletes, *Women in Business* wrote in 1980. "No longer are they thought of as unfeminine misfits." Indeed, some were now thought of as sex objects. WBL officials hoped that an article focusing on a "curvy 5–9 beauty" like the California Dreams' Jane Ellen Cook would appeal to male fans, some of whom might go to a game "just because they want to watch the players jiggle," the *Tribune* noted.

Some fans were indeed interested in the "bods." One male season ticket holder's collection of Hustle photographs, sold online in 2002, reflected an unusually high number of close-ups of the posteriors of Chicago players Donna Geils and Inge Nissen. "Yeah," Hustle guard Rita Easterling says, she occasionally was given those kinds of photos. "People would come up and hand you pictures, and that's what it was. A lot of them was just your breasts or your butt or whatever. . . . Maybe he was trying to tell me what he was looking at."

Did it offend superstar Molly Bolin if fans came to see "the cute blonde in shorts instead of the professional basketball player?" asked the *San Francisco Chronicle*. "I don't really see how that could bother anybody," she answered. "It's flattering. But it doesn't offend me because I'm confident about my playing. If all I could do was sit on the bench and look pretty, I'd be offended. Call it looks, or good play, or whatever. The bottom line is putting people in the stands."

With that goal in mind, many WBL players were willing to go along with league efforts to enhance their appeal. "I did just about everything to help make that league work, including getting hairdos," says three time All-Star Althea Gwyn. "But you reach a certain point (where you think), 'Well, I can only look so feminine or such and still be me.' . . . I'm not going to walk around in a bikini tryin' to play no basketball. We sweat. I'll just say, 'Put me in realistic parts.' It was tiring, trying to live up to an image that you're not."

Gwyn told New York Stars officials, "You've got Faye and Kaye for that," and the Young twins were indeed a wbl marketer's dream: good looking and skilled. "If I had anything to do with a team that had a pair of attractive and personable blonde twins on it as the Stars did with Faye and Kaye Young, I'd have sent all sorts of pictures of them to the press," wrote Larry Cole of the *New York Daily News*. "Granted some of these pictures might have appealed to male chauvinistic pigs as well as real sports fans, but male chauvinistic pigs buy tickets, too."

The "Dannon Yogurt twins" landed the first national ad campaign featuring female professional basketball players, but most people assumed they were just actresses pretending to play, Faye Young said. "I'm not sure what people expect real basketball players will look like."

Stars management treated the twins as players rather than marketing tools, Faye Young says, but they were still expected to put marketing above basketball at times. "I do recall that we went in once to the owners of the New York team and said, 'We do not want to miss practice. If you're going to schedule other kinds of engagements for us, please schedule them around practice.' We felt very strongly about that."

On the court, members of the New Orleans Pride were "basketball players first and women second," the *New Orleans Times-Picayune* said. "But they *do* have their hair done before home games." Yes, they did, says Sybil Blalock, and most of them also put on makeup. It wasn't a requirement (not everyone did it), but rather a suggestion by the team's owners to help gain public acceptance.

Before their first road game, Pride coach Butch van Breda Kolff walked onto the court expecting to see his players shooting. "Where are they?" he asked. In the locker room? "What the hell do they have to go there for? They've got their uniforms." (wbl players often changed into their uniforms before coming to the arena.) The coach headed for the locker room, and there they were, he says, "sitting in front of mirrors putting on mascara and putting on lipstick. So I sat there pretending I was there to fix my hair and all that."

Blalock had no reservations—"none whatsoever"—about making up before games. "There is the love of the game and that's why you play, but it is a business. Within reason, if you want to be successful, it's like any other business. If they ask you to wear a business suit to your job, how many people question that and refuse to do it?" Teammate Sandra Smallwood shared the same view. "You can't be so naive as to not think that doesn't matter, no matter what gender you are," she says. "It wasn't really brought up, but I felt everyone did their best to enhance their qualities, because it was important."

Minnesota Fillies owner Gordon Nevers was not going to get that kind of cooperation from two of his stars. Marie Kocurek and Kathy DeBoer maintained that appearance was irrelevant, that the sport could sustain itself. "You're entertainment," Nevers repeatedly told them, but Kocurek wouldn't accept that. "No, we are athletes, we play basketball," she insisted. He could never get through to her, Nevers says. "I never felt that I could get where she would hear what I said and believe it."

Neither would DeBoer. "I was angry about it, but I understood the incongruity in it because it was all around us," she says. "I had been a girl jock, if you will, for my whole life, so the tug-of-war between being cute and pretty and tough and strong and physical and aggressive was something that we lived everyday." Would DeBoer adapt to the struggle by putting on a little makeup for the fans? "Oh, no, I was totally counter-culture," she says. "Are you kidding me? No, I just went the opposite direction. I protested, all that kind of stuff. That was in my feminist ranting days."

Nevers noticed. "Kathy and Marie are very nice-looking women, but it was almost that they didn't want to look like women, they wanted to look like a 'basketball player,' " he recalls. "They thought they were puristic basketball players, and they weren't showcasing women playing basketball as much as they were showcasing basketball at the time. We really didn't realize that we were out there on a mission. It was a *show*."

Years later, Kocurek concluded that she had been idealistic. "In hindsight, he is correct," she says. "We are entertainment. I just thought if you play the best you can, that if you do well, you win, that is why folks want to come and see you play. That wasn't the only reason why folks came."

Were WBL players athletes who happened to be women, or women who happened to be athletes? Could the women's game sell itself, or would it take something spicier? The answers were not always clear. "Women's team sports was something that was completely outside the box," DeBoer says. "It was such a new concept that they didn't know from a marketing concept what they were trying to do. Were they selling basketball or were they selling women? Was this some kind of a skin show, or were you actually trying to market a sport?"

On one hand, owners wanted attractive players to showcase. On the other hand, they wanted to win. "They were torn between wanting to put great looking ladies out there and also win games," Logan says. "They were torn between an appearance they wanted and a win-loss record. So everything went 'looks vs. skills vs. appearance vs. public image vs. crowd appeal vs. talent.'"

One option was to "fill the twelfth spot" (choose nonstarting players) with a pretty face. "We have to have a real good-looking girl, even if she can't play," a WBL owner told Logan. Thus, for example, one general manager surreptitiously photographed women at the 1979 Olympic trials for the team's owner, who was looking for "marketable" players.

St. Louis coach Larry Gillman remembers using that criterion on one player. "Her hair was blonde down below her rear and she was a little sparkplug hustler type," he says. "I kept her, I think, as the twelfth player. I mean, she could go in and run your offense and stuff, but she wasn't going to win a championship, you know?" He didn't care about a player's race, Gillman says, "What I cared about was appearance. I wanted people that were going to try to represent the whole thing in a nice way; meaning that you wanted to see a little femininity." In Dallas, coaches Greg Williams and Tom Davis made light of the whole concept. Scouting some prospects, Williams pointed at a player who wasn't showing much, skill-wise, but was quite attractive. "What about her?" he asked. Davis was surprised. "You can't possibly mean that girl with the blonde hair?" Yes, Williams said, he did. "Sure, let's go up and see if we can sign her hair."

The role of appearance in assessing women athletes has evolved, Logan contends. "I think that right now in the WNBA, nobody spends a lot of time trying to figure out, 'Well, she looks normal,' or, 'Boy, is she ugly,' or, 'She's got to be a lesbian,'" she says. "We're at the point now where the people that are in sports are just a cross-section of everyone, and we accept that. It wasn't like that back then. So Janie Fincher immediately was a find because she is great looking and a good ball player."

The Chicago Hustle player in question was an attractive blonde forward who quickly became well enough known in Chicago to be identified in headlines by just her first name. "Janie Fincher was a very, very attractive girl and a very good player," Minnesota owner Nevers says. "When she was on the court, everybody was watching the game."

There wasn't a general manager in the WBL who wouldn't kill to have her on his roster, Michael Davis wrote in *Parade*. "To be blunt, Fincher puts fannies in the bleachers, and that's what the financially whipped WBL needs—fans who'll shell out six bucks to watch a game that has been a bastion of male supremacy since its inventor, Dr. James Naismith, nailed a peach basket to a wall long ago."

Hustle coach Doug Bruno would like to think that Fincher's popularity was due to her basketball skills and not her appearance, "but I think it was a combination," he admits. Fans and media alike seemed mesmerized by the blonde's curves. "Breathe deeply, Janie, breathe deeply," a male fan yelled one night when Fincher was at the free throw line.

This particular player "would be worth the price of admission if she did nothing more than take pre-game stretching exercises," *Chicago Sun-Times* sports editor Ray Sons raved. While professing to help Fincher "shed her image as the Chicago Hustle's sex symbol," *Tribune* writer Bill Jauss then described her as someone who "makes the world around her a little less dull," with her "blonde hair, her delicate features, her model's figure, and her extra-short shorts."

When it came to photo shoots, the papers inevitably wanted Fincher. "You can go anywhere in society now and they are going to take the blonde, you know, 24 by whatever the measurements are for a number 10 body," says teammate Jody Rajcula. (The press loved the fact that Fincher's number was 10, also the name of a highly publicized movie starring Bo Derek. Some teammates even thought Fincher picked the number for that reason.)

Nevers acknowledges that WBL owners discussed the benefits of attractive players but denies that such considerations drove any of his decisions. "In league meetings, people would talk about the Mollys of the world, and the Janie Finchers of the world, and Annie Meyers of the world," he says. "There were some very nice-looking women in the league. That certainly never influenced my judgment of what we did."

It did with other franchises, he believes. "I think some of us, as owners, might have confused goodness with beauty, if you will. Instead of enlarging on how good a person was, some were worried about how pretty their people were." Such considerations were given too much weight for Dallas

Diamonds owner Jud Phillips's taste. "There was so much emphasis on attractiveness," he says. "'This girl is attractive, let's try to promote her.' To me it was, 'Let's promote who can play basketball.'"

One example of an overall package in the WBL, Donna Orender (then Geils) says, was Bolin, who had looks and "unbelievable" talent. "She could hit from anywhere. She really was amazing." There was no denying Bolin's skill, and the media's preoccupation with the All-Star, All-Pro, all-time WBL scoring leader seemed natural. But was an article touting "Basketball's Sexiest Shooter," complete with Bolin posed provocatively in a bathing suit, too focused on something other than her playing skills? That piece, which ran in the *San Francisco Chronicle*, illustrated the competing considerations of players and owners trying to promote this new animal.

By the time the *Chronicle* article appeared, Bolin was used to accusations that she was selling out her gender. She had, after all, been the focus of the most controversial (and successful) promotion in the WBL's history. Heading into her second season with the Iowa Cornets, Bolin needed more money. She had a child to support, especially during the winter when construction work was scarce for her husband, and the pay raise she had been offered by general manager Kate McEnroe wasn't enough.

McEnroe had just renegotiated player contracts (downward, for some) and was concerned that giving Bolin too much of a boost might create dissension. The franchise also needed to devote more resources to promotion and marketing. As she thought about it, McEnroe realized that the solution to both their problems was, literally, standing right in front of her. What if the Cornets bankrolled posters of their star, with the profits to go to Bolin? Celebrities like Loni Anderson and Farrah Fawcett had made posters a hot item in recent years.

The black-and-white Bolin posters quickly sold out. The first showed Bolin in her road (dark) uniform, with a Cornets jacket draped over one shoulder and a basketball resting against her thigh. The other was a classic "Farrah Fawcett" knockoff: Bolin in a one-piece swimsuit, reclining, with tennis shoes perched atop a nearby basketball.

The inevitable controversy followed. Bolin was a "pinup" girl. The swimsuit poster "seems to suggest the Iowa farm girl of the traveling salesman's dreams rather than Molly Bolin, the married woman with a four-year-old son." The Cornets star knew that some would consider it exploitative, but said the team didn't have a professional-quality action photo. Besides, she argued, "It's all about putting people in seats, isn't it?"

After seeing the success of Bolin's posters, Chicago management approached Fincher about doing a poster of her own. When newcomer Chris Critelli first met with Hustle staff, the poster caught her eye. Well, she thought, now she knew why her New England Gulls coach Dana Skinner said every WBL team had a "T&A." When the Canadian player had asked what that meant, Skinner's explanation ("tits and ass") had surprised her. She didn't think it had been a factor on the Gulls team, but looking at Fincher's poster, she assumed it was in Chicago.

One reason to focus on pretty players and "femininity," some thought, was to counter the stereotype that female basketball players must be lesbians, even though there often was no correlation. Participating in women's team sports in the 1970s was still so novel that many people speculated about the "femininity" of those who did it. "That's their problem," Rita Easterling declared. "Who says being competitive and playing an aggressive game has to be reserved for men?"

Nonetheless, Fincher was often asked if there were a lot of lesbians in the WBL. "My first response is to say, 'It's none of your business,'" she said. "My second is to remember that this has happened to all women who have been pioneers in cross-gender professions. You just have to learn to put up with stupid questions." If people had to ask such questions, it was because of their own insecurities, she said. Yes, homosexuality existed in the WBL — just as it did in the NBA and the NFL.

Some players were concerned not only about fan perceptions of their sexual orientation but also about their own bosses' views. At a ribbon-cutting party in 1979, one drunk team official approached a player. "Are you a fag?" he slurred at the bewildered woman. "Screw you, fag." He then wandered off to confront another player. Sort-of-out lesbian Mariah Burton Nelson says her confidence was shaken when San Francisco Pioneers coach Frank LaPorte mentioned that their uniforms were designed by "a bunch of faggots."

Although she was "kind of scared," Nelson decided to take part in a gay pride parade. Suddenly, she made eye contact with a local television reporter with whom she had sparred earlier in the summer (in response to questions such as "Do the men in your life approve of you playing basketball?"). *Uh oh*, she thought. She considered calling to beg him not to say anything, but decided it would be against her principles. The next day, a teammate said that word had gotten back about Nelson being in the parade, and that afternoon LaPorte waived her. "He said, 'You're not tall enough,'" but the six-foot-two-inch Nelson was skeptical. "I said, 'Frank, I'm the tallest person on this team.' And he said, 'Well, then, you're not quick enough.'"

A league consultant fed the belief that the WBL should worry about sexual orientation, reporting that a potential sponsor was balking because the league image was seen as "dykish." (To counter that, he said, he would show it pictures of attractive players.) If a corporation refused to sponsor the WBL out of concern for the image of women basketball players, "I would have to say they probably came from people who never met the young ladies, or never went to a game," says Charlie McCabe, former marketing director for Manufacturers Hanover, a major sponsor of the WBL and women's basketball. "I knew these people. I knew they were attractive, both mentally and physically. They were good people."

No one went to greater lengths to ensure that his team conveyed a positive image than California Dreams owner Larry Kozlicki, who enrolled his players in a program at the John Robert Powers charm school. "That was a riot," Dreams player Patti Bucklew says. "Here you have a bunch of jocks who don't know the first thing about modeling going in there. They taught us how to walk down the little runway and turn around, and how to get in and out of a car with a dress on. They showed us prettier ways to cut our hair. It was quite interesting."

The staff were friendly, and some even attended Dreams games, Bucklew recalls. (At the end of the course, the agency gave players T-shirts that read, "We'd rather dream in California than hustle in Chicago.") "It was a challenge for the people who worked at John Robert, and it was a challenge for us to put up with it," she says, "but that was just one of those things where you don't question it, you just go do it."

Kozlicki said he was surprised that so many players objected. "You have to spend a lot of time playing basketball to make it to the pros," he was quoted in *Mademoiselle*, "and that means you've never had a chance to sit around learning makeup techniques. I thought the girls would be grateful for the chance."

Responding to grumbling from his players, Dreams coach Mel Sims brought the matter to a head during a practice, as reported in the *Orange County Register*. "How many of you think the classes are a waste of time?" he asked. A few hands went up. "How many of you think it is a *complete* waste of time?" A few more hands. Well, stick with it, the coach said. "You may not see the benefits now, but it may help you later."

To Sims, the biggest benefit would be learning to handle the media. "It's not that we don't think they're ladies," he said, "although I guess they do teach them things like eating and dressing. But I'm more concerned that when they are interviewed by the press—and they will be interviewed—they are able to reflect a positive thought. Women athletes are not used to being in the limelight."

That is largely what he had in mind, Kozlicki says: media or image training, much like Olympic athletes receive. Some Dreams players were indeed flustered at the prospect of public speaking. After a good game with her former team in Dayton, Michelle McKenzie had been called out of the locker room for an interview. What made this day different? Why did you have such a great game? McKenzie had no idea what to say. Finally, the exasperated sportswriter tried again. "Well, what did you eat for breakfast, for God's sake?" That was an easy one. "Well, I had a bowl of Rice Krispies." The next day, the article announced that McKenzie had "snap, crackle, and pop" in her game.

Gail Marquis sensed similar unease among her teammates. "Often some of the African Americans players didn't want to be out in the limelight, didn't want to be in the forefront," she says. "Like J.T. (Janice Thomas) might be someone you would want to talk to, but she didn't want to, she just wanted to play ball." (No kidding, says Stars owner Ed Reisdorf; Thomas would come up with any excuse to avoid appearances, one time even claiming she didn't have money for the subway.)

Even UCLA star Ann Meyers, who later made her living as a television analyst, froze when first thrust into the spotlight. "Basketball has helped me grow a lot," she said at the end of her college career. "I used to shake my head to answer questions, I was so afraid of speaking. I used to turn down invitations to speak at dinners. Now I have come out of my shell; I have confidence in myself."

McKenzie learned a lot at charm school, she says, but then laughs. "It was so sexist. Of course, now we think back on it and laugh. We think, 'Did men have to go through that?' No, I bet not." If management wanted Dreams players to present themselves in a certain way, it was her duty to attend, she figured. "They did go to extremes to modify the John Robert Powers program, like they had us walk in front of the camera, and speak in front of the camera, and basically go over things like how you would sit. It was interesting, but it became kind of a comedy routine because we found it kind of funny after a while."

Nonetheless, McKenzie learned some skills (such as how to set a proper table) that carried over to her adult life, and she probably would have gone willingly if the course had been optional. To Vonnie Tomich, the "grooming" program was not an issue. "It was very minor, and I only remember doing it maybe only once or twice," she says. "It wasn't like walking around with a book on your head or anything like that. It was probably way overblown as far as making that a big deal."

In a blistering feature on the experiment, "How to Be Charming While Dribbling," *Ms.* ran a sarcastic cartoon in which women played with books balanced on their heads and exclaimed, "Oh! Please help yourself to the ball!" The general view of Dreams players was that it was a promotional vehicle, the article reported. It was possible; Chicago Hustle players were "made over" at a fashion show (costing Ethel "Poco" White her Pocahontas-style braids), and Dallas Diamonds teammates were sent to a makeover session at the Texas state fair, which Valerie Goodwin found "a little off the wall."

Twenty years later, both the charm school and the Bolin poster drew harsh criticism from Indiana University doctoral student Sheila Shroeder, who saw the poster as an example of "apologizing" for female athletes by overemphasizing their femininity and heterosexuality. "Apologetic behavior has haunted women's sports because of the constant tension between womanhood and athleticism," she wrote. "It became the dominant discursive defense for professional female athletes, and it remains intact today as a tattered hand-me-down from the WBL." The poster was "more closely aligned with 'porn' than corn," University of Iowa doctoral candidate Shelley Marie Lucas declared in 2001.

But today's standards cannot be applied to the 1970s, Logan says. The WBL either had to adjust to public perceptions or die. "We're in a new sport, and we have to play by the rules that will sell that sport," she said in 1978. Kazmer agrees that the general public did not have a positive view of female athletes at the time. "This is before the Jane Fonda aerobic movement, for God's sake. Women weren't even supposed to sweat."

Coupled with television ads in which Bolin invited viewers to "let the Cornets warm up your winter," the question was inevitable, though: "Are the Iowa Cornets, a successful group of professional women, really sexist pigs?" sportswriter Chuck Offenburger wondered. The players' actions did the talking, McEnroe replied. "Most of them could be making more money teaching than they make playing ball, but they've been willing to make all kinds of sacrifices to get professional sports for women off the ground."

Offenburger's conclusion? "Aw, to heck with sociology. Gimme a Molly Dolly poster."

Teammates had mixed feelings. "I've never been into using sex for advertising and publicity," Penquite says, but she acknowledges, "it was good for the Cornets. It got us a lot of attention. At the time, I think we rolled our eyes," but she adds that she doesn't like to see women used that way. Nancy Wellen does not recall taking offense. "She was certainly attractive, and she was one of our best players. I thought Molly was a good role model, and I just didn't think it was any kind of exploitation. I thought it was smart marketing." And if the campaign happened to generate a little controversy, McEnroe says, she wasn't going to complain about the extra publicity.

Cornets ads were geared toward a male audience, McEnroe acknowledges, which was probably a sound strategy, considering the league's inability to attract female fans. Initially, women had been seen as a target audience. Sponsors would be especially interested in reaching out to the women's market, WBL vice president Dave Almstead predicted in 1978. "There's a tremendous amount of money involved in advertising products for a woman's identity," he said. "They want to latch onto this for the advertising possibilities."

It soon became apparent, though, that women were not supporting the WBL in large numbers. "It would have been natural to expect a heavily female crowd as the San Francisco Pioneers of the Women's Professional Basketball League played their home opener last week," Glenn Dickey of the *San Francisco Chronicle* mused in 1979. Instead, the crowd seemed typical for a sports event; there might have been a few more women in the audience, but not many.

Pioneers owner Marshall Geller said he had tried to reach out. "You tell me how to get the women there," he stated. "We talked to every women's group in the area." Nevers had no better luck in Minnesota. "I get a lot of lip service from the women's groups," he complained, "but they just talk. They say, 'We're behind you 100 percent.' But they never buy tickets."

The toughest challenge facing the WBL, *Saturday Review's* Jonathan Evan Maslow wrote in 1980, was to convert women into sports fans. "Will the millions of women who participate in sports pay to watch them? Will feminists support their sisters? Will the game ever really appeal to readers of *The Female Eunuch*?" Yes, one Minnesota writer predicted; now that women had a chance to participate in pro basketball, feminists would not let the league die. Not so, author Ted Vincent countered in his 1981 book *Mudville's Revenge*:

> Among the feminists of the 1970s there were those who saw little place for women's professional sports, which seemed like a female copy of the macho win-at-all-cost sports system of the jocks and media hucksters. These feminists felt it a virtue of women that they were generally reluctant to become the spectator fanatics who purchased a sports team's season tickets. It was argued that rather than copy the men, a preferable approach to sports for women would be the creation of informal mass participation on a grand scale.

"There is truth to that statement," says Nelson, a self-described "angry young feminist" at the time. "There *has* been a lack of understanding between feminists and athletes." Nelson, author of *The Stronger Women Get, the More Men Love Football* and other works on gender and athletics, says she did not feel that way. "Personally, I've always seen sports as the *embodiment* of feminism: an opportunity for women to develop strength, cultivate teamwork and leadership skills, bond with our sisters, and define for ourselves how women should behave. What could be more feminist than that?"

In 1979, Houston sportswriter John Wilson chastised feminists absent from Angels games: "Where were all the women libbers in the sports world during the Angels season?" he wrote. "Where were all of the women who complain about the lack of coverage in the media of women's sports? Where were all of the libbers who protest women don't get a fair break in athletics?"

A year later, a Minneapolis columnist issued a scathing rebuke to women not supporting the Minnesota Fillies:

> For some time now, we men have been submitted to diatribes about the inequality of women in this world. They get paid less, you say, and promoted less often in jobs, you say, and ignored in sports.
>
> There are screams for equal money for girls' athletics in the schools. OK, so they get equal money and become proficient and are drafted by the Minnesota Fillies.
>
> And you women won't support them. . . .
>
> OK, women, get out to the Met Center and change that image.

You don't have the excuse any more that you don't read the sports pages because they are male-oriented.

This column isn't on the sports pages.

Women had not been socialized to attend sporting events, but that was slowly changing, California Dreams coach Sims said. With "the women's liberation thing . . . , it has become fashionable for the parents to watch daughter play her basketball game. It used to be they would go to son's game and the girl went to hers by herself." That has changed significantly from the WBL era, Carol Blazejowski says. "There used to be dad and his little boy, and now dad cares about his little girl, hoping that some day she can play on the great court of Madison Square Garden, and making a commitment to her career."

A primarily male audience for the WBL had been predicted by some from the start. "The ad companies have figured out a long time ago that mostly men watch women's gymnastics and figure skating, for example," prospective WBL investor Arnold Coopersmith said in 1978. "If anybody doubts that, just let them pay close attention to the commercials on those shows the next time. What do they try to sell you? Shaving cream, beer and cars, that's what." Sure, women liked to watch sports, he said, but it was still men who bought most of the tickets.

If that were the case, it didn't bode well for a professional women's basketball league. "The traditional purchasers of tickets for athletic events—men —still seem to prefer women in skirts, not sneakers," a Minneapolis sportswriter said as the Fillies' second season approached. Other than a few individual sports, "the hardrock sports customer's attitude is chauvinistic," concurred a *Dallas Times-Herald* writer. "The perspiring female form has limited appeal."

Women had made significant strides in prize money and exposure for individual sports. Billie Jean King was a familiar name even to those who were not tennis enthusiasts, and newcomer Nancy Lopez was already well on her way to a twenty-year career on the golf course. But acceptance of individual events wasn't enough, King said. "Until team sports are accepted the same way they are for men, we haven't arrived." WBL players, she said, were "really the pioneers now for women in team sports."

The idea of women's team sports was just counterintuitive for some. "Whether it is cultural reasons or genetically programmed, we react more favorably to seeing women participate in sports that are esthetically pleasing," Wilson wrote. "That is, in sports in which there is a certain gracefulness."

If some men were put off by the physical competition, what would draw them to WBL games? Appealing uniforms, perhaps. The Chicago Hustle's uniforms were designed to "flatter" the female body, but were an acquired taste for some players. "Believe it or not, the only time that I felt there was exploitation might have been when I was with Chicago," Jody Rajcula says. "The darn uniforms were so damn *short*. They were cut, I thought, to show more skin and not for the reason that we had athletic bodies. They wanted to put more males in the stands." ("I guess the more they could see, the more they liked it," teammate Rita Easterling says.)

New Orleans Pride players did not appreciate a similar suggestion to abbreviate their uniforms. "Mrs. (Claudette) Simpson said she wanted our shorts shorter and tighter," Sandra Smallwood reported, "but I like 'em the way they are. I think they're too short now, and I'm always pulling 'em down." (That was still an improvement on the original plan, according to pride manager Steve Brown. "The first year she wanted to put them in skirts on the basketball court or some such thing," he says. "It was too far out for me to comprehend.")

The style for uniform pants at the time was short for men and women, but "there was a sexual component to it" in the WBL, San Francisco player Anita Ortega felt. Sue Hlavacek laughs when she looks at her old Philadelphia Fox gear. "Talk about sexist," she says. The bottoms were brief running shorts, and the uppers were basically tank tops, "thin little silky, sleazy things." At the time, though, she didn't think twice about wearing them.

New York Stars management "wanted the shorts to be very *short* shorts," Faye Young recalls. "We just sort of put up with it, because we didn't think it was a big deal." Nelson didn't complain in New Jersey, either. "I was coming from France where they wore like bikini bottoms for shorts," she says. "Maybe that's why I thought they were sort of regular American uniforms."

Milwaukee Does warm-ups were tight bell bottoms, and Lynda Gehrke remembers asking, "How are you supposed to move around in these things?" Still, they were far better than the "sleazy, bikini type uniform" someone had originally suggested to Does management. Another rejected proposal that Dallas owner Jud Phillips recalls was a man who wanted to put the Diamonds in high-heeled sneakers and short skirts. "That is the most ridiculous thing I have ever heard in my life," Phillips replied. "This is basketball, this isn't Miss America or whatever."

Less obvious ways to convey a softer image for professional women's basketball included the naming of some teams. "Somehow I can't take seriously an organization that gives its teams such distasteful nicknames as Fillies, Hustle and Does," a Minnesota sportswriter opined. "I think those designations are an affront to the female athletes who play in the WBL." (Nevers disagrees when it comes to his Fillies. The logo, five horses running in sync, conveyed a sense of power, he felt. "I loved that logo," agrees player Cheryl Engel.)

The "Hustle" generated a few wisecracks. "Is a singular member of the team a hustler?" Wilson asked. It was a "name that would fit better in an intramural league of bawdy houses," wrote *New Jersey Monthly* columnist Steven Levy, who also wondered what individual players were called (Hustler? Hustle woman? Hussie?).

The "Angels," the "Dreams," and the "Gems" reflected a passivity or appeal unique to females; if not sexist, such names were at least "syrupy," a *Texas Observer* writer thought, or "foofoo," as Milwaukee player Cheryl Clark puts it. (Some WBL players joked about starting a team in Hawaii and calling it the "Honolulu Leis,'" Nelson said.)

Most Does players did not object to their nickname—a play on Milwaukee's NBA team, the Bucks ("Does, Bucks, it made sense," says Barb Hostert)—but the *logo* was another matter: a big-eyed, long-lashed, curvy female deer with a bushy tail dribbling a basketball. "We weren't that thrilled about it," Cindy Lundberg says diplomatically. "It was horrible!" Hostert exclaims. "We all hated it."

The logo "conveniently resembles a playboy bunny," Lewis and Clark University student Heather Meyer wrote disdainfully twenty years later. "With her classic hourglass figure, tight and orderly hairstyle, kissable lips, sweet and innocent eyes, small feet, big breasts, and tight shorts does she look ready to play ball?" It was pretty sexist, Lynda Gehrke concedes, but she thought it was kind of cute, anyway. "I thought, 'Whatever it takes to get basketball for women out here.' I didn't care. 'At least they're trying.'"

8

Ball Games

Women are being forced to play with the same size basketball as the professional male player who is substantially taller, heavier and stronger. In short, Debbie Brock (4'11") is expected to function in the same manner with equal success with the same equipment as Kareem Abdul Jabbar (7'2"). No wonder women's basketball falls short in comparison with the men's game. • **Karen Logan**, modified basketball proposal, 1977

That was a slap in the face. Women don't need consolations to make us play better. • **Marie Kocurek**, Minnesota Fillies

All women's and girls' games in the world today use a basketball that is 28½ to 29 inches in circumference and weighs between 20 and 22 ounces, often referred to as a "women's basketball." Until the modified ball was adopted for use in the wbl, the official women's basketball had always been the same dimensions as the men's basketball.

The first basketball designed for the sport (rather than borrowed from soccer, as Dr. James Naismith had done) was specified to be 30 to 32 inches in circumference and 18 to 20 ounces. Over time the weight increased to 22 ounces as the leather used in manufacturing the balls changed.

In 1934 the Joint Rules Committee reduced the circumference to the 29½ to 30¼ inches presently used by men, hoping that the smaller ball would improve ball handling and generate higher scores. "The chief advantage would be in more accurate passing and more expert dribbling and shooting," noted Thomas A. Knudson in his 1972 study of men's amateur basketball rules.

For the next forty years, men and women played with this standard ball. In 1975, former Los Angeles Lakers star Jerry West faced former All-American Redhead Karen Logan in a game of H-O-R-S-E in a televised "battle of the sexes." Both shooters were skilled (each made 24 shots in a row before West finally missed), but as the competition wore on, Logan realized that she was lucky West was staying within her shooting range. "It was quite obvious that if he had gone five to eight feet out further to shoot, I would have been in trouble because of the size and the weight of the ball," she recalls.

Logan won the contest but began thinking about how other sports had adapted to women. If a basketball were smaller but had the same wide seams for grip, women's shooting ranges would increase, she figured. She contacted the governing body over women's collegiate athletics, which agreed to let her make a presentation.

She couldn't get a prototype to take with her, but Logan put together a written proposal "to upgrade the overall quality of women's basketball" by adopting a basketball one inch smaller and proportionately lighter in weight. Her analysis began: "Almost all sports, with the exception of basket-ball, vary the size, weight and nature of the equipment to compensate for the physical size and anatomical differences of women. These compensations are designed to insure equal mobility for women within the same rule structure of each sport. Thus, by not handicapping female athletes with oversized, misfit equipment, the quality of the product is preserved."

The basic motions of shooting, passing, and dribbling with a regulation basketball were all more difficult for women because they had smaller hands and less upper body strength, Logan wrote. "How much would a female bowler's form suffer if she had to bowl with a 20 lb. ball?" Tennis rackets came in different weights and grip sizes, volleyball nets were lower for women, golf tees were shorter, shots (for the shot put) and javelins were lighter and smaller, hurdles were lower, and softball pitching distances were shorter, she noted.

Logan identified nine specific advantages she believed would result from adoption of the modified ball:

1. Improve overall quality and mobility of the game by eliminating the physical handicap imposed by using equipment originally designed for men.
2. Make basic skills easier to teach. Many skills are limited by size and strength.
3. Increase shooting range and make the transfer from the dribble to the shot easier and quicker.
4. Improve all ball handling skills which will cut down on turnovers.
5. Will allow a faster, controlled game (if desired).
6. Will no longer handicap a smaller girl's ability to perform basic skills.
7. Will improve the game from a spectator point of view.
8. Will make available a leather model for junior high and high school competition.
9. The only other smaller ball available at this time is a junior rubber ball not suitable for competition.

As she addressed the committee, Logan quickly concluded that her efforts would not bear fruit. She was one item on a long agenda, and although some members seemed mildly interested, others were adamantly opposed. One major objection was a lack of statistical data showing that the smaller ball would improve the game. It was just common sense, Logan countered. "We don't ask 7-year-olds to play with a big ball; you give them a junior ball and lower the basket. Why would we ask women to play with the same equipment as these guys that are 6'8"–7'?"

The committee did not accept Logan's proposal ("they shut me down pretty quickly," she commented), but a year later she found a more receptive audience in Bill Byrne, who happily embraced the idea for his newly formed WBL. "Karen came to me and said, 'You know something? The women need the smaller ball,'" Byrne recalls. "I said, 'I agree with you.'"

To columnist Joan Ryan, the adjustment only made sense. "Women have been slow to discover that altering the dimensions of the game is not a sign of inherent weakness," she wrote. "Quite the contrary, it is the first evidence of their economic intelligence. If women athletes are compared unfavorably to their male counterparts by the ticket-buying public, it is obvious that turnstiles will soon rust shut."

Once the decision was made to use a smaller ball in the WBL, the question arose: Reveal the difference to the public? "If you put this size ball in a woman's hand, it's going to look proportionately the same as the man's ball in a man's hand," Logan remembers the discussion. "So, do we tell anybody, because they'll think we're rigging the game?" She preferred to disclose the fact that they were creating something unique for women, but "that's up to you guys," she said.

It was an easy call for Byrne, who saw an opportunity for publicity, not to mention licensing fees if he could convince a manufacturer to come on board. Byrne went to work. He taped that year's AIAW championship game and determined how many turnovers were due to ball handling. He also calculated the number of women's and girls basketball programs in the United States that might later adopt the modified ball if it proved successful in the WBL. "Once it became a reality (at all levels of play), it was another market, millions of dollars worth of balls," Byrne recalls pointing out.

Wilson Sporting Goods took the plunge, agreeing to manufacture and market the smaller ball, which WBL organizers hoped would produce $50,000 yearly in royalties. At the first owners' meeting in June 1978, vice president Dave Almstead took the podium to announce the innovation. "The ball has been designed to accommodate the anatomical difference between men and women," he said—to which a voice from the back of the room shouted, "Viva la difference!"

Although credit for the idea was widely given to her in early news articles, Logan wondered if anything more formal should be done. "Should we, like, patent this or something?" she asked Byrne and Chicago Hustle president John Geraty. As she recalls it, Byrne said a patent might be possible if there was a unique feature to the ball's design, and she asked if she should get a lawyer. "Oh, no. We'll take care of you, don't worry about that," Logan says she was told.

Meanwhile, she was curious about the league's financial arrangements with Wilson. "WBL" was emblazoned on the balls, and nobody other than the league's official licensee was manufacturing them. "I am guessing that there was stuff going on in the league and their agreement with the league that excluded me," Logan concluded. She didn't get any money but, "what I did get, what I thought was really interesting, was a non-stop supply of tennis shoes from Wilson."

In St. Louis, Donna Murphy remembers shooting around with her teammates when someone came to collect their basketballs. "They threw these little bitty balls out to use," she says. "I thought it was a junior ball, and we all kind of laughed and were fiddling with it," but the players grew to like it. "We very easily got attached to it, because you could palm the ball and put it out there and pull it back like you were Dr. J." (By then, the basketballs were uniform. Some of the first ones were a little warped, New Jersey Gems player Mary Jean Hayek noticed early in the WBL's first season.)

Outside the league, reaction to the new ball was mixed. One pocket of resistance, Byrne says, were school officials unhappy at having to purchase separate balls for their women's programs if the modified ball caught on. "The athletic directors came after my throat," he says. "They would say to me—I can't use the words—but they would say, 'Bill, you're out of your mind. Do you realize what this would cost?'" Yes, Byrne said, he did: "You guys would have to stop passing down used balls to the women; they're going to have a ball of their own."

Other criticism came from WBL players, such as All-Star Marie Kocurek. "That was a slap in the face," she felt. "Women don't need consolations to make us play better. It was an insult when they gave us a smaller ball saying women need something smaller so they can handle it. That pissed me off."

Carol Almond liked the new ball, but some colleagues didn't. "They may not have been used to it, but they also might have seen it as 'women are lesser,'" she says, "sort of a slam on women's basketball." Sybil Blalock was one of them. "At the time, I think I saw it as something that they sort of picked on to say that women just can't handle the bigger ball, that's why we have to change, so it's not really basketball," she says.

For other players, the new ball was welcome. "I absolutely loved it," Kathy Solano says. "I'm a point guard, and at 5'6" I've got good-sized hands. I felt I could do a lot more with it." Holly Warlick was another fan. Players could shoot from farther out with better accuracy, she noticed, and control the ball better while dribbling.

Even more intriguing to WBL officials than improved ball handling was the possibility that a smaller ball might bring the dunk to the women's game. "I think it's going to happen," public relations director Tim Koelble said in June 1978. "Most people don't think a girl can stuff the ball unless she's 6-foot-10. Now, the girls will be able to do more with the ball."

The desirability of the dunk was generally assumed; 516 out of 701 high school and college women's basketball coaches and officials surveyed in early 1978 favored allowing it. The WBL also hoped to counter critics like the *Chicago Tribune*'s David Israel, who refused to attend a WBL game "until they sign someone who can dunk and break a backboard." The women's game was hindered somewhat by the players' inability to dunk, the *Albuquerque Journal* wrote in 1981, "a sure crowd pleaser in the men's game."

With that in mind, WBL officials were excited when the San Francisco Pioneers signed a guard named Cardie Hicks in 1979. "Besides their first-round pick the Pioneers came to yesterday's draft armed with a free agent who may be a first in the WBL, a player who can dunk the ball," the *New York Times* reported. Even though she was only five foot eight inches, Hicks had been photographed performing a two-handed jam while playing in the Netherlands. She had a phenomenal vertical leap and "can dunk the ball and toss in jump shots with equal dexterity," the *San Francisco Chronicle* raved.

Hicks dunked often in practice and warm-ups, colleagues confirm, and also during pregame warm-ups of the 1981 WBL All-Star Game, where Albuquerque High School boys' basketball coach Abe Estrada was in the stands with writer Claire Hellstern. "Look at her going up there for a slam dunk," he exclaimed. "That is just as good as a man's game."

Hicks also tried to dunk during the All-Star Game itself, only to have the ball bounce off the rim. "She twice came within a sliver of dunking a basket and sent chills and thrills throughout the crowd in the middle of the fourth quarter," Hellstern wrote. Without question, Hicks could dunk, Pioneers owner Marshall Geller confirms. "I saw her dunk ten times in practice, but she was never able to do it in the games."

As fate would have it, on December 4, 1979, Hicks found herself all alone at the head of a fast break and was preparing to go up for a dunk when something snapped—literally. She felt her legs weaken, and laid the ball in, then headed to the bench. "My legs were just kind of shattered and my body just shook," she said after the game. Bumps could be felt on both legs, and the news was not good. The Pioneers star had a stress fracture—three, in fact, two in her right leg and one in the left. The "dunk specialist" was out for most of the season.

Nineteen years later, hopes for dunking in the pro game were again raised when the WNBA signed seven-foot-two-inch Margo Dydek from Poland, who could dunk easily and often did so in practice and warm-ups. Once again, though, fans were to be disappointed; Dydek refused to dunk, considering it not only risky (opponents might undercut her) but also "not polite." The first known dunk in a professional women's basketball game came on July 30, 2002, when Lisa Leslie of the Los Angeles Sparks dribbled from half court on a fast break and unexpectedly jammed the ball through with her right hand.

AFTER THE WBL

One month into the WBL's 1979–80 season, Karen Logan was out of the league, and recognition of her contribution to designing the new ball seemed to be fading. Worried that she was "getting screwed," Logan consulted a lawyer in New York to see if she had any rights with respect to the ball. She had maybe a 50–50 chance, he said; he could seek a temporary court order preventing league play with the ball until the issue was decided. Logan told him to go for it.

"We're talking a multi-million dollar thing here," the lawyer said. Not necessarily, Logan replied; the ball hadn't been adopted yet at other levels. "Well, this is going to be big," he repeated. "I need a $10,000 retainer to start this action." That was all the money Logan had in the world, which would leave her not only unemployed but also broke. She couldn't do it. "I just went away—end of ball," she says.

When the WBL ended in 1981, the ball remained in limbo, as the idea of a "women's" basketball remained controversial at the amateur levels. "I can't believe the high schools and colleges are still resisting that change," former Chicago Hustle coach Doug Bruno wrote that year. They were, though. Survey results in 1978 from the National Association for Girls and Women in Sport (NAGWS) sent a clear message. The vote on question number 16—"Should a smaller size ball be adopted?"—was 630 no to 61 yes.

In 1982 the first published study using the WBL ball did not lend support to its adoption. Researchers in Canada found "no differences shooting from 12 feet out, in passing errors, ball handling errors, passes attempted and rebounds," which surprised them. One possible explanation, they said, was that "sending" and "receiving" activities offset each other. "It is easier to send a small ball and easier to receive a large ball," the presenters noted, and except for shooting (a pure sending task), many basketball techniques such as dribbling and passing involve both sending and receiving skills.

In October 1982 a Women's Basketball Coaches Association (WBCA) survey revealed that many members felt the smaller ball might improve the game, but most remained undecided. Nonetheless, WBCA members voted at their annual convention in March 1983 to endorse the change, which nudged the joint college rules committee into exploring the issue further.

At that time, very little research had been done on women's basketball equipment. In 1962, a physical education teacher in Illinois conducted the first known study of the effects of a smaller basketball on girls. Jean Cione wasn't opposed to women using men's equipment (as an All-American Girls Professional Baseball League player in the 1940s, she had used a regular baseball), but she felt that the standard basketball was too large and heavy for girls to develop proper motor skills.

"I was always a bit disturbed about the fact that women, girls, didn't develop more skills in basketball," she says. "I felt that if there was a smaller ball, one that they could handle with their hands and their arm and shoulder strength, that they would be able to develop patterns and be able to execute much like boys and men do."

Cione set up an eight-week study with 97 high school girls and a fifteen-week study with ninety-three college players. Having a ball specially made was impractical, so she ran three tests with a junior basketball to measure shooting, passing, and catching skills. No real difference was found among the college participants, and at the high school level, only ball handling varied significantly. However, the small-ball group still did better on all three tests than the control group, even though they began at lower levels on two of them.

Apart from those results, Cione thought motivation might improve for some girls to whom "the regulation basketball represents an insurmountable obstacle to successful performance in basketball." She also noticed full finger and elbow extension and wrist snap with the smaller ball, and that movement seemed to be concentrated in those areas rather than the shoulder. Overall, players with the smaller balls "used their whole bodies in a more efficient manner," she concluded. Cione was a believer and bought junior basketballs for her own students.

Two decades later, the effects of a smaller ball were again under examination. This time, thanks to the WBL, researchers had an intermediate ball to use in their studies. One series, funded by the NCAA and Wilson Sporting Goods, was a five-stage study by Dr. William S. Husak of Cal State, Long Beach.

Stage 1 involved 363 high school girls and college women, both athletes and non-athletes, whose skills were tested with "large" regulation basketballs and "small" WBL basketballs. Husak reported improvement in skills of all groups with the small ball except high school athletes who, he speculated, were not as advanced in developing improved skills as college athletes.

Stage 2 surveyed 335 high school participants in college camps in five western states. Before the camps, most players were opposed to a smaller ball, Husak noted, but after exposure, "the attitude had almost reversed." The players felt that the larger ball would help rebounding and defense, but the smaller ball would be an advantage in other areas, such as shooting range and consistency, passing distance and accuracy, dribbling, dunking, speed of the game, and offense.

Stage 3 had 170 college and high school students (selected from tryouts for two summer developmental leagues) play games with the regular ball and with smaller balls from Wilson. Among the results were fewer blocked shots and steal attempts with the smaller ball, longer shots, and greater accuracy. Although the review did not disclose any other significant differences, a majority of players, coaches, and officials remarked on improved "crispness of play," reflected in longer outlet passes, sharper passes, and better ball handling.

Stage 4 was a statewide opportunity presented when South Dakota adopted the smaller ball for its 1983–84 school year, after which Husak measured the response. "In general, the players' attitudes toward the small ball were overwhelmingly positive—over 90 percent of the women preferred the smaller ball and liked the idea of playing with the ball," he said, and a similar percentage of coaches and officials also approved.

In stage 5, all 1983–84 Empire State Conference games used "the women's basketball developed by Wilson Sporting Goods for the (now defunct) professional Women's Basketball League," while inter-conference games used the regular-sized ball. The smaller ball resulted in significantly more rebounds, fewer turnovers, and fewer steals, Husak reported. There was no difference in free-throw shooting percentage, and the larger ball was better for short-range shots. The smaller ball was popular with players; by the end of the season, one athletic director reported, "when we put two racks of balls out (for practice), our kids all went for the smaller ball."

Overall, Husak concluded, "the skill performance of women basketball players was enhanced by a smaller basketball," and it was preferred by the vast majority of participants. "As a result of these changes, it can be expected that the game of basketball will be faster and more exciting for players and spectators and that players will be able to master basketball skills to a greater degree using a ball more in proportion to hand size." (Husak noted, however, that the smaller ball was bouncier off the backboard, one result of which was more missed lay-ups.)

In a study conducted in 1983 by Bette Harris of Longwood College and Jackie Dailey of Bowling Green State University and funded by Wilson and NAGWS, 754 camp participants were divided into two groups, one using the regular basketball and one using the smaller ball. From skill test results the authors concluded that "the smaller basketball made a significant difference in performance even for players who did not practice with it."

The U.S. Girls' and Women's Basketball Rules Committee had these studies before it when it met in Reston, Virginia, on April 18, 1984. It also had the results of the most recent surveys of college coaches and officials, which were far from conclusive. Even the WBCA, which had voted yes on the smaller ball a year earlier, was divided, with only 57 percent of its members favoring it. "I don't think you have many fence riders on this issue," said Betty Jaynes, the WBCA's executive director. "You either want it or you don't."

Those who wanted it were looking to make the women's game more appealing, says Jill Hutchison, president of the rules committee at the time. "I think there was a feeling that if we had a smaller ball, then perhaps we could get to a dunk, and because that was such a big part of the men's game, maybe that would help the spectator interest in the women's game."

There was "a ton of controversy" on the issue, though. "On the other side of the argument was that we were taking away the purity of the game," Hutchison says: "Are you going to stay with the real game or lower your standards for women?" Eventually many opponents who weren't interested in the dunk yielded to the suggestion that ball-handling skills and shooting accuracy would improve. "That ultimately became the biggest thing that sold people on it," she recalls.

One thing that apparently did not impress the committee was that the WBL had used the smaller ball. "At the time, the college coaches didn't have a lot of respect for the pro league," Hutchison says. "They didn't feel like that was the role model they wanted to follow. They felt like the college game was probably the premier game at the time." There was also some skepticism as to the WBL's motive for adopting the smaller ball. "I think they thought the pro league did it to be flashy and things like that, rather than for really advancing the game."

On April 18, 1984, the rules committee announced that it had voted 12–4 to adopt the smaller ball beginning in the 1984–85 season. Reactions were mixed, to say the least. "I think it is a historic day for women's basketball," said Nora Lynn Finch, assistant athletic director at North Carolina State. "I think basketball died," said Frances Garmon of Texas Christian University.

"What are we going to call it, baby ball?" (Some did indeed adopt the unflattering nickname—Hutchison's own account of the change was titled "The Baby Ball"—or variations like "mini-ball" or "the incredible shrinking ball.")

Principal objections to the smaller ball included the following factors:

COST. Most schools normally replaced two or three basketballs a year, and adoption of the smaller ball would require schools to buy an entire set of basketballs at one time. "Women's and girls' programs in the late '70s and early '80s weren't blessed with lucrative budgets," Hutchison notes, and replacing all of a program's balls at once "seemed like a daunting task."

WINDFALL FOR SPORTING-GOODS MANUFACTURERS. Twelve basketballs multiplied by more than a thousand college programs equaled a whole lot of basketballs to sell. "I still maintain it was all a plot by the ball manufacturers," UNLV's Sheila Strike-Bolla said in 1986. (It also meant endorsement revenue for some groups. Within two weeks of the announcement, for example, Baden was already putting out WBCA-endorsed balls.)

EFFECT ON INTERNATIONAL PLAY. Critics worried ("big time," Hutchison says) about whether using the smaller ball would handicap U.S. teams in international competitions, especially the Olympics, which used the larger ball. Husak's study, however, reported that college players saw little adverse effect in switching from the smaller to larger ball.

TIMING. Many felt that the smaller ball should be implemented in the high schools first. Others complained that school budgets were already set, and basketballs had already been purchased for the upcoming season.

CREDIBILITY OF THE WOMEN'S GAME. "I think when you make a physical change, changing the ball or lowering the basket you make a statement that 'We can't play this game,'" Louisiana Tech's Leon Barmore said. Olympic gold medalist Anne Donovan was also concerned. "I think that when we make an achievement now—if a girl dunks—it's going to be because it's a smaller ball," she said. "It's not because we're doing anything better; it's just because they've made it easier for us."

The deed was done, though, and Hutchison urged detractors to give it a chance. "The use of the smaller basketball has become a reality," she wrote in 1984. "To those of you who support its adoption, we hope it is all you hoped it would be. For those of you who are opposed to the smaller basketball, your voices have been heard. Perhaps your most viable option is to utilize the basketball for one season, critically evaluate the strengths and weaknesses, and prepare your arguments for next spring."

No real movement was made to convince a new NCAA rules committee to reverse the decision, and coaches prepared for the change. St. Joseph's coach Jim Foster cruised local sporting goods stores until he found one with an old WBL ball. "I'm surprised what it shows, to tell you the truth," he said. "It seems the ball is easier to pass and to catch."

But how did the rules committee know what dimensions were best suited to the female hand? It didn't, former WBL player Brenda Pitts argued, and the modified basketball wasn't the right size. "In comparing the average hand size of female basketball players with that of male basketball players and the surface area of each basketball that the hand size covers, the female still is at a disadvantage even with the new smaller ball," she wrote in *The NCAA News*.

The Rules Committee should have determined the optimal size, Pitts maintained, rather than simply adopt the WBL ball. "Who decided the ball should be one inch smaller in circumference and two ounces lighter?" she asked. "A sporting-goods company developed this ball after a request from a fairly well-known female player in 1978. She thought that women should have a smaller and lighter basketball. However, no research was conducted to determine the proper fitting for the female hand." Pitts had studied the use of the new ball by a high school team and had concluded that additional experimentation was needed.

One season later, the women's ball was still a hot topic. A sampling of quotes in the 1986 NCAA press guide ranged from "love it" to "hate it":

Those who speak in terms of losing the integrity of the game by making the ball smaller must be blessed with larger hands than the average woman. The smaller ball has allowed our players to pick up the tempo, make more accurate passes, feel more comfortable taking their shots and improve their ballhandling during play. It has added a great deal of excitement to the game. Bill Craig, Framingham State.

I don't think it has changed the game significantly one way or the other. I feel it hinders the girls' opportunity to play in recreational settings which are coed. I still disapprove of the concept. Chris Weller, Maryland.

I disapproved at first, but now have had a change of heart. The players love it, and what they feel is good about the game makes their playing so much better. Our field-goal percentage and free-throw percentage have all risen. Pat Fisher, Lafayette.

After one year, I see the ball causing many changes in our game, and not producing the effects that were stated for reason of change. The ball has given another job to the guards, who now have to check out and rebound, since it is so light. It has lessened the effectiveness of the big peoples' game, and has not helped shooting percentages or cut back on team turnovers. . . . Rene Portland, Penn State.

I was always in favor of the smaller ball and still am. I think it is only reasonable that the equipment used in sport fit the physical needs of the participants. Cindy Scott, Southern Illinois.

I didn't see any reduction in turnovers, or any improved shooting percentages. In fact, I found that good shooters were missing very easy shots—the put-backs and short jumpers. . . . Besides the statistical background, I am opposed to the ball because I don't think women's basketball needs to qualify any aspect of the game. We've made great strides, but now if caliber of play improves, some people will say it's because of the smaller ball, rather than more talented athletes. Jody Conradt, Texas.

Over time, the new ball became more widely accepted. On March 26, 1985, the National Federation of State High School Associations, representing forty-six states, voted to phase in the women's ball over the next four years. ("When it happened, boy, everyone thought I would become a millionaire," Byrne says, "but I got nothing. You can't patent a wheel or a ball.")

Some players continue to express mixed feelings about the modified ball. Its smaller size and lighter weight create more room for error, more missed lay-ups, lowered shooting percentages, and an argument that women do not play "real" basketball, they assert. Those concerns aside, in 1997 the Women's National Basketball Association (WNBA) chose the smaller ball because it had then been in use at the college level for more than a decade. In October 2004 the modified ball was adopted for use in all international women's competition, including the Olympics.

Color Commentary

The Kentucky State University women's basketball team settled into a restaurant for lunch. Linnell Jones, the team's only black player, decided she'd have some tacos. When the food was delivered, though, she cringed. "Excuse me, there are some bugs on my lettuce," she pointed out.

"Oh, I'm sorry," the waitress said. She took the tacos and returned with some others.

Jones looked at them. Oh, man. "Excuse me, there are more bugs on my lettuce," she said. The waitress returned with another plate, but once again there were bugs. "You should wash the lettuce, you know," Jones suggested.

"I'm so sorry. Do you want something else?"

Forget it, Jones decided. This restaurant is just dirty. "No, that's fine," she said. "I don't want anything. Just give me my money back."

Jones sat with her teammates, laughing and having fun while the others ate, but twenty-five years later a thought came to mind. She had been the only black person in an all-white restaurant in a virtually all-white town. Her teammates' food was fine. "Maybe they just didn't want me in there."

Linnell "Nurse J" Jones was one of 48 African American players on the 1979–80 WBL opening roster (out of about 160 total players). Except for a couple of Hispanic women, the rest of the players, all but one of the principal investors, and two of the head coaches in the league's three-year history were white.

Was racism a problem in the WBL? Some players thought so, according to an article by sportswriter Lacy Banks in the April 1980 issue of *Ebony*.

"This is a White girls' league, and it's run by White men," Banks quoted an unnamed player. "They (owners) feel that because pro women's basketball is a new product, they can't afford to have it dominated by the Black girls, and that's why they're trying to play up the White stars like Ann Meyers (whose $145,000 contract is tops in the league), Rita Easterling (last year's Most Valuable Player), Molly Bolin and (No. 1 college prospect) Nancy Lieberman."

There is no question, says Ann Platte, a white player, that the WBL tried to glorify some of its white players. Her St. Louis Streak teammate Adrian Mitchell was "an incredible ball player," she says, but received relatively little recognition. "I'm sorry, [Ann Meyers] was a good ball player, but there were a lot of ball players better than her—black ball players. They tried to build Meyers up. We had one game when she got four fouls and they called a time out, and there was no doubt in my mind the refs and the owner agreed they couldn't let her come out, because she was the big white hope, and the crowd had come to see her."

New York Stars forward Althea Gwyn, whose All-Pro credentials followed a highly publicized career at New York's Queens College, wondered if color was a factor when Meyers signed with the WBL at four or more times anyone else's salary. "She had national name recognition. I had New York name recognition. It was like, 'What's the difference?' Why was she marketable and we weren't?" At the time Gwyn sensed that the league felt it needed a certain image, "a nice, middle-class white woman to push this league," and she was willing to accept it. "I wanted a place to play and if that's what it took, as long as the league would survive, then I'm happy with that part of it," she says. "As we know, it was also going on in the men's game."

In the late 1970s, racial disparities were being debated in all the professional sports leagues. "Let me say this to you about race, color, creed, any of that bullshit," says WBL founder Bill Byrne. "If it was [an issue], I never found it, and if I had found it, I would have ended it."

Byrne's first roommate was a black football player named Jim Hayes, who later played for the Houston Oilers in the 1960s. "Jimmy and I would travel, he couldn't stay in the same hotel, or I couldn't stay where he stayed, but we did," Byrne says. "Talk about breaking the ice. In women's basketball, the black and white thing is just so easy for me, because in sports you don't look at that."

Byrne did perceive that some potential WBL sponsors were sensitive to race, however, and WBL owners were keeping an eye on the National Basketball Association, then suffering a dip in popularity that some blamed on a predominance of black players. Initially, the WBL's roster was approximately 40 percent black, compared to 70 percent in the NBA. "I think that there were an awful lot of white girls in the game," Dallas Diamonds owner Jud Phillips says, but that was consistent with women's basketball in the 1970s, particularly the fact that women's college programs had a higher percentage of white players than men's.

The WBL's figures were also affected by the occasional selection of white players to maintain certain ratios between the races. (The WBL "would rather have 10 white players lose than 5 blacks and 5 whites win basketball games," rival league investor Tony Mercurio accused in 1980.) During one draft, a team bypassed a highly regarded guard because she was black, and took a white player instead; then it lucked out when the other guard was still available later. In the same draft, a team owner directed the coach to select an "attractive white player" rather than another black player he was considering.

"Afterwards, we swore we wouldn't get into that stuff again during a draft," said a staff member. "We know who the best athletes are and we want them, no matter what color they are." (The staffer says he was told to be careful in discussing race in case the conversation was overheard. "When you're calling up about players, you had to refer to them as ones and twos, rather than, 'Is so-and-so black or white?'")

Viewing certain white players as window dressing was not always fair to them, says one black player. Her franchise promoted a certain white player heavily but did not give her as much playing time as she deserved, the teammate felt. "I think they were trying to let some people know that there was some white girls on the team," she says. "They would start her, and we always said that she played the first seven minutes and then she would sit the bench for the rest of the game. I thought that was so mean."

Before arriving at the Iowa Cornets, Tonyus Chavers heard about a meeting attended by Coach Steve Kirk earlier that year. "Without cutting any words, the message was basically, 'We want this league to be a league that is going to showcase white players, so we don't want a lot of black players on the team,'" she says. "He took insult at that because he was feeling like, 'I just want to get quality players on the floor, why should it matter how many black players I have, how many white players I have.'"

There was "a little bit of an undertone" in the league that "it's going to be hard for us to sell blacks," Kirk says, but he was never directed to consider racial factors by either his Cornets or Nebraska Wranglers owners. "I never got any pressure at all on whites and blacks, and I never made any choices that way either. That would have taken the fun out of it for me." Although Cornets manager Rod Lein believed that a certain presence of white players was necessary for marketing, Iowa's relatively small number of minorities was simply because very few blacks tried out for the team, he says.

Midway through the wbl's third season, the number of black players had risen to half (44 out of 87). All wbl teams had 5 or more black players except the Chicago Hustle, with 4 out of 12, the Dallas Diamonds, with 4 out of 10, and the New Orleans Pride, which had only 2. The Pride's racial mix was the subject of some speculation in the *New Orleans Times-Picayune*. The team began the season with only 4 black players out of 12, it noted, and both the first two players shipped out to cut costs were black (Beverly Crusoe and Betty Booker).

The trades seemed racially motivated, the paper hinted, but Pride player Sybil Blalock doesn't think so. "I would have to adamantly deny that," she says. "If it's true, I was very naive. I never in any form or fashion felt that." Couldn't happen, says first-season manager Steve Brown, a "crazed liberal back in those days" from New York. "Wouldn't have happened"—not if coach Butch van Breda Kolff had anything to do with it. "Butch looks at everybody the same. He likes you better if you drink beer with him, but other than that he's okay."

Van Breda Kolff had approved one of the trades (Booker), the coach said, but wanted to keep Crusoe, a member of the 1978–79 small college champion, the University of Dayton Flyers. Crusoe reminded him of Magic Johnson, van Breda Kolff said during training camp, "the kind of player who when made by God was meant to play basketball." Her trade had been arranged by Pride owner Claudette Simpson. The Simpsons never raised concerns to him about racial composition, van Breda Kolff says, but Mrs. Simpson did point out one reality to the *Times-Picayune*: "If I had fielded an all-black team out there, no one would have come out."

That same season, two veteran Chicago Hustle players (Liz Galloway and Debra Waddy-Rossow) wondered aloud if they were waived in order to keep the team's ratio of black players to four, but coach Bill Gleason denied it. "There is no color line on the Hustle as far as I'm concerned," he said. "My decision to trade players was never based on race. I've coached black and white players for years." She didn't like the cuts, Hustle guard Rita Easterling says, but she did not perceive any racial motivation for them.

Still, the issue percolated after players heard what appeared to be racially disparaging remarks that team officials had inadvertently recorded on a scouting tape.

Another franchise in 1980–81 traded two black players, including a veteran, for a pair of future draft picks, but it had nothing to do with race, a staffer said. One player was a promising guard, but she had fomented racial tension by publicly predicting that two teammates would make the final cut only because they were white, upsetting one of the players (who, ironically, *had* been drafted partly because she was white). The coaches decided that the threat to team harmony outweighed the guard's potential. The other trade was due to a poor efficiency rating at training camp. "It wasn't that she was black, but that she was not doing what we needed of her," the staffer says.

San Francisco co-owner Marshall Geller felt no racial pressures. "None whatsoever," he says. "In fact, remember Willie Brown [the first African American mayor of San Francisco] was one of our owners, so it was never an issue. We never talked about it. It was whoever could play the game." In Minnesota, owner Gordon Nevers says, racial considerations were not an issue with his team, and his Fillies had a solid black-white mix. "Never once was any decision ever made on our team based on color or anything else, not even close. We tried to get talent."

Management in Dayton definitely did not impose a black-white ratio; in fact, only two players on the Rockettes roster were white. "If anything was going to happen as far as racial issues, the team wouldn't have been pre-dominantly black," says Rockettes player Michelle McKenzie. ("We would have been the ones with the racial tension," jokes white teammate Vonnie Tomich.) The black players did predict that if a newcomer was brought in, "she won't look like us," player Joy Holman says.

No racial considerations went into New York Stars' draft, owner Ed Reisdorf says—nor could they, as he didn't know what players looked like when he drafted them. "There were no videos, and I certainly wasn't calling teams to find out about the people," he says. "We didn't know until somebody showed up." Reisdorf says he wanted a racially balanced roster anyway, to appeal to a broader spectrum of fans. (The Stars would have lost a major sponsor if the team hadn't been racially balanced, says Charlie McCabe, marketing director for Manufacturers Hanover. The New York–based bank, the biggest sponsor of college and professional women's basketball in the late 1970s, would not sponsor a program unless it was racially diverse.)

Other than greater promotion of white players, there was no bias against her black teammates in St. Louis, Platte felt, because coach Larry Gillman was not prejudiced. "If Larry had one redeeming quality as a coach, he didn't care if you were white or black," she says. "He treated you all the same (which wasn't very good, incidentally), but he did not discriminate at all."

Houston Angels management saw African American players as a potential marketing advantage. "There should be a large proportion of minority players, and this should help draw an audience from the minority community," owner Hugh Sweeney wrote in a 1979 investment memorandum. When Tom Davis, self-styled "director of operations" for the Angels, was asked how many blacks were on the team, he couldn't remember. "Oh, you're just saying that," the questioner accused, but Davis said it was true; he had never bothered to count.

The Angels did indeed have a high percentage of black players, which, after the team claimed the first WBL title, prompted Lacy Banks to write: "Despite the fact that the predominantly Black Houston Angels won the league's first championship last year, the general opinion among Black players is that the WPBL, in its economic infancy, is trying extra hard to keep White players in the majority and in the forefront in order to better appeal to the majority White market."

Inequality in promotional opportunities between white and black players is mentioned often by WBL personnel. "If a cry of racism did come up, it would probably be in the marketing of teams," says Gail Marquis, and Cardie Hicks agrees. "Everyone heard about Ann Meyers, everyone heard about Nancy [Lieberman]. They didn't hear about Althea Gwyn, they didn't hear about these other athletes," she says.

Some of the disparity was because many black players were from less-publicized college programs, Charlotte Lewis believes. "We can't really fault them if they were just ignoring black players [although] a lot of people see it that way, because they fail to look at the fact that a lot of the white players within the right schools got the publicity coming through the championships, where a lot of the black players came from smaller schools," she says. "They weren't in the limelight. They needed the big name players to promote the league."

But prior exposure could only partly explain the relative lack of promotions featuring black players. Among the players most heavily featured by the WBL were Molly Bolin in Iowa, Janie Fincher in Chicago, and Faye and Kaye Young in New York. None of these women were particularly well known before joining the league, but they did all have something in common: they were white and blonde.

"I sometimes thought blue-eyed blondes were getting more than their share of attention," says Kirk, and he wasn't the only one. The perception that blondes were heavily favored in the WBL is widespread. "Maybe my contract could have been bigger, maybe I could have been a bigger part of the marketing, and I think that was probably because I wasn't blonde," says Anita Ortega, one of the few Hispanic players in the WBL.

"Every team had a blonde," laughs Rosie Walker, the 1980–81 MVP. Although officials recognized the value of a dominating black player like Althea Gwyn, her teammate Donna Orender (then Geils) says, "I think the league tended to go with blondes. I can't tell you a dark-headed girl that was marketed. . . . We had the twins, Kaye and Faye, who were good players, and they got a tremendous amount of attention. They were just really attractive women. Then there was Janie Fincher who played in Chicago, and everybody thought she was the cutest, most gorgeous thing ever. She got tons of attention. I think there was just a natural resentment because, you know, they certainly weren't the *best* players. They were *good* players."

One of the best players was Rosie Walker, who dominated the WBL in 1980 much like Shaquille O'Neal dominated the NBA early in the twenty-first century. Apart from local coverage, Walker performed her feats in relative anonymity, but she accepted it. "Being black, that was part of it, but—you've got to print this—the league was just getting started," she says. "People do what they know to do. It's what they are told to do. They did what would keep the peace in the league. I really don't blame them."

Did the promotional success of her blonde teammates disturb Gwyn, a three-time WBL All-Star? "I'm not going to sit here lying and say no," she says. "Everybody wanted to be where they were. They had a product to sell, and that is what they were looking for then, two twins—two white twins—and they were not bad looking women. So even though you were envious, you knew why." If it helped the league, Gwyn says, it was all right with her. (Besides, she adds, nobody could be mad at the sweet Young sisters from the South. "You felt like you needed to protect them up in New York.")

At times, a focus on white players seemed counterintuitive. For an appearance in Chicago's Cabrini-Green housing project, the Hustle assigned

Sue Digitale, Rita Easterling, and Fincher, all white players. The women thought it would be fun to play on an outdoor basketball court, but police quickly arrived. "Ladies, you need to leave, this is not a safe area," they said. The women could see kids hopping out of windows with basketballs. It's okay, they said, picking volunteers for some three on three. "The cops kept trying to get us to go away," Fincher recalls. "Finally, more cops showed up and told us to leave." Two people had been shot on that court the day before, the officers informed them.

More troubling to some of their teammates was why Hustle management had sent three white players to an inner-city project. "It was several weeks later that Liz [Galloway] or Debbie [Waddy-Rossow] said something about it," Fincher recalls. "'Oh yeah, they really like us so much, that's why they sent white folks down to kids who look up to us.'" Fincher realized that she was right. "You know, that was kind of a stupid thing. Why wouldn't they send positive black role models down there to those kids?"

Within the WBL teams the players—black, white, and Hispanic—overwhelmingly report no racial conflict. "That's not something that I experienced at all," Kathy Solano says of the New Jersey Gems. Players of both races got along pretty well, Nebraska Wranglers player Genia Beasley says. "Everyone had been playing with every kind of race [in college], so we didn't have all the racial tension," adds New Orleans forward Sandra Smallwood. Occasionally, minor spats arose, Iowa Cornets player Mo Eckroth recalls, such as music played on the bus ("it was always black"), but she never sensed a real problem.

The most serious race-related incident reported involved a conflict among women on the same team. Players were summoned to a hotel room in Chicago, recalls a player who says she was present, and as the white players sat on a bed next to the window, some black players flipped out switchblade knives. "They said, 'We're tired of being treated like we're less than anybody else,' and they slammed the door and locked it," the player says. "Of course, those of us from the Midwest were a little bug eyed, and somebody else started crying."

She was surprised to hear her teammates' perception, the player remembers. "Sometimes you don't even know that other people are picking that up. We finally convinced them that we didn't feel that way. But that was the first time I'd ever seen a switchblade in my life." The situation was defused by a street-smart white player who assured the other women that they did not consider themselves superior. "She talked our way out of it," the player says. "You can tell her thanks." The air was cleared, and it was agreed that no one would talk about the incident.

White players could not always comprehend what their African American teammates were going through, Kathy DeBoer acknowledges. "I certainly learned some things from Donna Wilson and Trish Roberts [two black teammates]." One lesson came when the women were looking for a place to stay in Minneapolis. "When we were trying to get an apartment lease, if I would call and ask if they had any apartments available they would say, 'Yeah, you can come out, one or two bedroom?' If one of the black kids or one of the southern kids would call, they would say they didn't have anything available."

The realization was unsettling for DeBoer. She remembers Wilson, who was from Georgia, talking about racial bias in the northern United States. "I, as a Yankee, was always kind of defending that it was better for blacks in the North," DeBoer says, but Wilson enlightened her. "She said to me one day—and I will never forget it—'You know, maybe it's where I grew up, but I don't agree with you. In the South, if you're black, nobody beats around the bush as to why you're being treated the way you are. In the North, they pretend that it doesn't matter, but it does.'"

That subtle racism was hard for Wilson to deal with, DeBoer realized. "'I would rather know where I stand,'" DeBoer remembers Wilson telling her. "'When I walk into a place, there are places that I can sit and there are places that I had better not sit. In a restaurant up North, I come in and I sit down at a table, and if I'm not at the right table nobody comes and serves me.' It was something that I had never thought of. It was a perspective to me that was eye opening."

10

Changing the Lineups

These women thought a no-cut contract meant that you got fired if you ever need stitches. . . . They thought whether you won or lost and how hard you played was as important as how much you got paid. They thought traveling coach had something to do with Greyhound, rather than coming up short in first class and having to sit in the back section of the airplane. . . . Listening to them talk about how much fun they were having was enough to make any red-blooded American sports fan question his values. There was most definitely something wrong with them. They weren't complaining about the food, they weren't whining about the hotel accommodations. The WBL could be taken no more seriously than a speed-skating team from Key West. Until now. • **David Israel**, *Chicago Tribune*, November 30, 1979

MILWAUKEE, JANUARY 1980

Coach Doug Bruno had been thinking. His Chicago Hustle did not have a lot of size, and this season it was catching up to them. There was a Milwaukee Does player he had his eye on. . . . Bruno went looking for Hustle president John Geraty. "Let's go get Charlene McWhorter," he said. "They won't trade her. Why don't we just go get her?"

"What do you mean?" Geraty exclaimed. "The bylaws say you can't go get her. You can't just go steal a player."

"John, she's not being paid. If she's not being paid, we can go and do whatever we want." The coach had made up his mind. "I'm going to do it. I'm going to get her."

Bruno was nuts, Geraty declared. No, just desperate. The men drove to

Milwaukee and bought McWhorter dinner ("and don't you know I was grateful for that meal," she says). Why don't you come to Chicago, Bruno suggested, since you're not getting paid? Think about it for a few days.

McWhorter was unsure what to do, and she decided to ask her agent, a young lawyer in Massachusetts named Scott Lang whom she had never met. Sleep in and skip the Does' road trip the next morning, he advised. "That's ludicrous," she thought; she had never missed a game in her life. The idea plagued her all night, but when her teammates left, McWhorter wasn't with them. The next day, Bruno backed his van up to her door.

"There isn't a dadgum thing Milwaukee can do about it," Bruno figured. The move was later reported as a trade.

One of the most jarring awakenings for many WBL players was the reality that a team's lineup could change at any time, often with no notice. Only three weeks into the inaugural season, Milwaukee players Terri Conlin and Cindy Lundberg knew something was up when they were summoned to the front office. "Once they called us and said we want to see you in our office, that's the shock—'Uh-oh, something is going on,'" Lundberg recalls. And it was: they had just been traded to Minnesota. "We turned to each other and said, 'Well, that's life in the big city.' We packed up our cars and went."

"You definitely feel like cattle when you're being traded," says Suzanne Alt. "I got called one afternoon at 2 o'clock, and I was on a plane the next morning and played the following evening in New York. Basically, offense was explained to me on a piece of paper." Tonyus Chavers had just returned home from dinner one night when she got a call from St. Louis coach Larry Gillman. Be on a flight to Iowa at 7 a.m., he told her.

Gillman was always looking for that perfect combination. "I nicknamed him Trader Vic because he would call me every day with a trade proposal," laughs Greg Williams, who coached with the Houston Angels and Dallas Diamonds. "I mean every day. It was hilarious. Some of his trade proposals were just unbelievable." Then again, one never knew what might interest the person on the other end of the line. A WBL coach once pitched a trade candidate this way: "She's 6'1", a good attitude, white, good mobility, owns a car, can shoot outside, and is a good rebounder."

Bringing new players into the mix didn't always make a team better, Fillies owner Gordon Nevers admits. "I think a lot of times you think you are plugging holes, and all you are doing is creating a bigger sore than you had before." Changing players sometimes destroyed whatever chemistry a team might have. A case in point is the 1980–81 San Francisco Pioneers, who had made it to the playoffs as an expansion team the year before. Less than a month into the new season, the team was self-destructing. "Something happened to us," says Pat Mayo, and it clearly had:

Center Nancy Dunkle was openly criticizing coach Frank LaPorte, who, in turn, gave his players a public lecture.

Players were complaining of favoritism by the coach toward Mayo.

LaPorte worked out a trade to send new arrival Doris Draving to the Chicago Hustle, but Pioneers president Marshall Geller overruled him, forcing the league to cancel it on a technicality. (It was negotiated on a weekend, which wbl operating rules didn't allow, and it hadn't been confirmed in writing.) Draving, meanwhile, totaled her car in an accident, and wasn't focused on her game.

Cindy Haugejorde, a talented rookie, wanted the ball a lot ("and if she didn't get it—whew!" laughs teammate Margaret English). Pioneers guard Anita Ortega finally became so annoyed that, during one practice, she "stopped, walked over to Haugejorde, and handed her the ball."

"The question is," wrote the *San Francisco Chronicle*, "are these player problems, or coaching problems? Do you trade the players, or get a coach who can shut them up and make the most of their considerable abilities?" The growing dissension in the Pioneers locker room culminated in Pat Mayo smacking another player. The two women were arguing, English says, and Mayo walked over, put her mouth guard in ("I guess she expected the other player to punch her back in the mouth"), and popped her teammate in the face. "She broke her nose," English recalls. There was "an incident in the locker because someone was mouthing off," Mayo admits, but she doesn't like to talk about it.

The Pioneers players later apologized to each other, Cardie Hicks reported, but the damage was already done. Mayo, voted team mvp by Pioneers fans, suddenly announced her retirement at the age of twenty-three. She had been sidelined with severe bronchitis for weeks, and she suspected she was about to be traded "somewhere cold" by the new coach, Dean Meminger. "I just turned my uniform in and said that I didn't want to be a part of this any more," she says.

Meminger had indeed been busy on the phone. First, he sent Dunkle to

Minnesota. (When she didn't make the trip right away, the Fillies owner called to ask when she planned to report. "When God tells me to," she replied.) Heidi Nestor was then shipped to New Orleans, and rumor was that Ortega was next.

Although she led the Pioneers in scoring and minutes played the season before, Ortega wasn't surprised to be on the chopping block. Meminger was trying to bring an East Coast style to the West Coast, she felt. She, too, ended up in Minnesota. "I got off the plane in St. Paul, and it was something like 56 degrees below zero with the wind chill factor," she recalls. "And I thought, 'What the hell am I doing here?'" Only four Pioneers players were now left from the beginning of the season. "It just wasn't my kind of team," Meminger said.

Sometimes players had input in the decision. Tesa Duckworth knew that Chicago was going to recruit taller players, and she asked to be traded to New Orleans, which was closer to home. San Francisco traded star rebounder Kim Hansen to Minnesota because she wanted to play nearer her home in Michigan. Donna Simms kept New Jersey from trading her to "the boonies" by offering to take a pay cut instead. In New York, Donna Geils talked a small claims court judge into declaring her a free agent after some missed paychecks, and then she negotiated a move to New Jersey, after refusing a trade to St. Louis.

During the 1979–80 season, Iowa Cornets coach Steve Kirk approached Nancy Wellen before a game against the Fillies. How would she feel if he traded her to Minnesota? Well, she might get more playing time now that she had recovered from a knee injury, Wellen decided; it was all right with her. Good, Kirk replied—report to the visitor's locker room. Wellen was handed a Fillies uniform, and forty-five minutes later, she was playing against her old team. "It was a little wild," she laughs.

In college, basketball teams stayed fairly constant, but at the professional level, "Players aren't performing well, they're out of here. Coaches aren't winning, they're out of here. That's a whole new ball game," Michelle McKenzie says. In 1978–79, twenty-two women suited up with the Fillies for at least one game, and by the end of the season, only two original members remained. "I think he was always looking for that one or two or five super-duper, fantastic, charismatic players," player Cheryl Engel says of Nevers. "He just didn't quite understand how to build a team rather than just acquire a team overnight."

That kind of turnover was not unique to the Fillies. Only two members of the first-year New Jersey Gems returned for a second season, and the 1980–81 New Orleans Pride had only three women from the prior year's playoff team. In 1980 St. Louis Streak coach Larry Gillman began the season with an entirely new roster. "Gillman is a regular Dutch scrubber," the *St. Louis Post-Dispatch* wrote. "That is, when he cleans house, he cleans house." The women fresh out of college were just a lot better, Gillman said. "These rookies are all from a group that played college ball for four years on a scholarship. I'd say it's a pretty good trend throughout the league."

Unquestionably, the skills of 1980 graduates were far better than classes just a few years earlier. "There is some super talent on this team," Iowa's Alt said before the first season, "but players coming out of colleges will be better than we are. That's because kids are getting exposed to basketball at a much younger age and the coaching is continually getting better."

To keep pace, veteran Donna Geils routinely spent hours alone in the gym working on her game. (Geils was one of only twenty-one women to play substantially all three years in the WBL; the others were Molly Bolin, Gerry Booker, Belinda Candler, Vicky Chapman, Tanya Crevier, Scooter DeLorme, Sue Digitale, Doris Draving, Rita Easterling, Janie Fincher, Anita Green, Vivian Greene, Althea Gwyn, Marie Kocurek, Connie Kunzmann, Paula Mayo, Wanda Szeremeta, Janice Thomas, Joan Uhl, and Donna Wilson).

WBL players often felt they were competing at all times, not just against other teams, or against each other for playing time, but against the unknown prospect who might walk in off the street. "It almost seemed like every time the team got together you're still trying out, because they're constantly bringing in other people for you to go against," recalls Martha Hastings. Mo Eckroth was so stressed during her year with the Cornets that she couldn't keep food down and lived on nothing but Mountain Dew. Although injured players weren't supposed to be cut, fear of being sent home and a desire to play outweighed pain at times. When Eckroth broke a thigh bone — taking a charge from teammate Molly Bolin in practice, she says — she kept quiet for a few weeks until she couldn't keep from limping. (Getting between Bolin and the basket was at one's own risk, Houston Angels Karen Aulenbacher says; she suffered a broken pubic bone from a Bolin drive.)

"I saw Rita Easterling play an entire season on a knee that would have had most $200,000 male pros under a sunlamp," Chicago coach Bruno wrote in 1980. Mary Ellen Carney impressed Hustle staff when she broke a bone in her right hand at tryouts and tried to keep playing.

When Paula Mayo suffered a knee injury, the team's physician advised her to sit out a game. No way, she said—just tape it. She scored nearly 30 points in the first half. After Nancy Lieberman injured her foot in January 1981, she got treatments at her hotel and a hospital on the road. Should she have kept playing? "You can't keep her out," coach Greg Williams said.

In Dayton, Vonnie Tomich played on two sprained ankles. "I can't get up in the morning and walk now," she says, "but you know, making that All-Pro was everything I wanted in the world that first year, and I would have gone if they would have put a cast on my foot." When Iowa's Wellen hurt her knee around Christmas, she stewed: stay out and possibly lose her job, or play. "I tried to come back too quickly, thinking I could get over it, and I hurt it again in a game in January," she recalls. "When you play pro basketball, you feel a lot of pressure to continue to play. You don't want to be out because there is always someone right there getting the opportunity to play."

Not only might current players lose their jobs or their teammates at any time, but often they were required to provide a place to stay for the women who might be replacing them. The apartment shared by St. Louis Streak teammates Donna Murphy and Rosie Thompson played host to several such guests. "I'd come home and there's somebody on the couch, and Rosie would say, 'By the way, Coach called and he wanted such and such to stay here,'" Murphy recalls. She usually didn't mind meeting the newcomers, but it did bother her that the team didn't reimburse any of the extra utility or grocery expense.

The situation was awkward all the way around, says teammate Ann Platte. "Can you imagine that you're going to a strange city and trying out for a team, and all of a sudden you're dropped off on somebody's doorstep? They didn't have any money. We weren't making much money. We had to feed them and put them up. We felt like a Motel 6." Sometimes things got worse: one woman stole from Platte's roommate and then tried to pass a bad check. "I was like, 'No way,'" Platte recalls. "I didn't trust her any further than I could throw her. We really had to put up with a lot."

Watching teammates move in and out of the Milwaukee Does was painful, Lynda Gehrke says. "One day you were there, and then they would say, 'Hey, we traded you. You're gone.'" Carol Almond's worst memory of the WBL was not knowing who would still be there the next day. "It just seemed like everybody was leaving. That was what was so different coming from college (where) your team is your team. In the pros for that year we had a different team every day."

November 24, 1979: Ann Meyers (New Jersey Gems) enjoys
a good play during her first WBL game. Teammate Wanda
Szeremeta is smiling in the background. *WBL Archive.*

The New Jersey Gems celebrate their first win of the 1979–80 season. From left to right: Pam Browning, Jennifer Savio, Martha Hastings, Donna Geils, and Ann Meyers. *WBL Archive.*

All-time WBL scoring leader "Machine Gun" Molly Bolin (Iowa Cornets). *Photo courtesy of Tony Fiore.*

Mary Jo Peppler and Karen Logan (Chicago Hustle) harass a Houston Angels guard in a December 22, 1978, game. *WBL Archive.*

Hattie Browning (Dallas Diamonds) goes in for a lay-up in the fourth game of the Championship series against the Nebraska Wranglers, April 18, 1981. The Wranglers, from left to right: Susan Taylor, Holly Warlick, Carol Chason, Rosie Walker, and Charlotte Lewis. *WBL Archive.*

Nancy Lieberman (Dallas Diamonds) dribbles into the
paint, surrounded by New Orleans Pride defenders Kathy
Andrykowski, Cindy Brogdon, and Sybil Blalock. *WBL Archive*.

Althea Gwyn (New York Stars) tries to keep the ball from Sue Digitale and Janie Fincher (Chicago Hustle) during a first-season game in 1979. *WBL Archive.*

"Chicago's Sweetheart" Janie Fincher (Chicago Hustle). *WBL Archive.*

Joanie Smith (Milwaukee Does) takes it up against Rita Easterling, Debra Waddy-Rossow, and Janie Fincher (Chicago Hustle). *WBL Archive.*

Dean the Dream: the New York Stars announce the hiring of
Dean Meminger as coach for the 1979–80 season. *WBL Archive.*

The Iowa Cornets enjoy a Christmas bonus from team owner George Nissen. Back row: Annie Nissen, Connie Kunzmann, owner George Nissen, Rhonda Penquite, Doris Draving, Denise Sharps, Tanya Crevier. Middle row: Debra K. Thomas, Kathy Hawkins, Suzanne Alt, Molly Bolin, Mary Schrad (seated on chair). Front row: Joan Uhl and Robin Tucker. *Photo courtesy of Doris Draving.*

The Dannon Twins: Kaye and Faye Young (New York Stars) in the first national advertising campaign to feature women professional basketball players. © 2006 The Dannon Company, Inc. All rights reserved. Reprinted with permission.

Sherwin Fischer: from co-owner of the Chicago Hustle to WBL commissioner. *WBL Archive.*

Liz "the Whiz" Silcott (St. Louis Streak), Adrian Mitchell (Chicago Hustle), and Anita Ortega (San Francisco Pioneers) relax before the 1979–80 WBL All-Star Game. *Photo courtesy of Anita Ortega.*

Michelle McKenzie (Dayton Rockettes) reaches for a rebound in a first-season game. In the background is the Minnesota Fillies no. 42, Marie Kocurek. *Photo courtesy of Michelle McKenzie.*

The Minnesota Fillies a few weeks before they went on strike in 1981. Front row: Scooter DeLorme, Anita Ortega, and Angela Cotman. Middle row: Nessie Harris, Nancy Dunkle, and Donna Wilson. Back row: Kim Hansen and Coretta Daniels. *Photo courtesy of Anita Ortega.*

Washington Metros players Lisa Schlesinger (with the ball), Carmen Fletcher, and Willodean Harris at preseason practice in 1979. *Photo courtesy of John W. Albino.*

In the huddle: Coach Doug Bruno (Chicago Hustle). *WBL Archive.*

Chris Critelli of the New England Gulls takes a shot while Tina Slinker prepares to rebound in a December 18, 1980, game. *WBL Archive.*

Pearl Moore (St. Louis Streak), the all-time leading scorer in women's collegiate basketball with 4,061 points. *WBL Archive.*

George Nissen (owner, Iowa Cornets) signs a contract with Wilson Sporting Goods to produce the first "women's" basketball. Left to right: WBL president Bill Byrne, Nissen, Wilson representative Dave Runnells, WBL vice president Dave Almstead, and Fred "Curly" Morrison. *WBL Archive.*

Connie Kunzmann (Iowa Cornets) goes up for a lay-up against Vicky Chapman (Houston Angels). *WBL Archive.*

San Francisco Pioneers forward Cardie Hicks mugs for the camera with teammate Pam Martin during the 1979–80 season. *Photo courtesy of Anita Ortega.*

Battle for the board: Patti Bucklew (Dayton Rockettes) and Nancy Rutter (Iowa Cornets) in a first-season game in 1979. *Photo courtesy of Michelle McKenzie.*

The 1978–79 Houston Angels, the first professional
women's basketball champions. *WBL Archive.*

Players usually tried to make new teammates comfortable after a trade, because they had lost colleagues themselves. Wellen was at home with roommate Nancy Rutter when they got the call that Rutter had been traded to Dallas. "Nancy was literally on a plane that afternoon, and her parents came up to get her things the next day," Wellen says. "I think after you have experienced that, you realize that it is not really the player's choice in all cases, so the other players were pretty good about helping someone integrate in."

There was still some awkwardness when arriving at a new team, says Adrian Mitchell. "They felt like family, and you're coming in trying to take somebody's spot and they don't want to give it up." Mitchell knew from experience, having been a pawn in the wbl's most controversial trade.

Early in the 1979–80 season, Chicago Hustle player Janie Fincher's minutes were declining. She was quite popular in Chicago (and, not coincidentally, quite attractive), and angry phone calls to Coach Doug Bruno's home followed a game in which she played only eight minutes. The Hustle then left on a road trip, expecting to be joined on their return by a new player who had just finished her practice teaching requirements. Someone would have to be taken off the roster to make room.

On November 26, 1979, Fincher arrived at practice, and Bruno steered her to a back room to give her the bad news: she had just been traded to the Washington Metros. Fincher was stunned. "Why?" she asked, starting to cry. "Was it something I've done?" No, it wasn't, Bruno says now; it was his best judgment as a coach. Bruno thought replacing Fincher in the lineup with rookie Adrian Mitchell would help the Hustle adjust to changes on other teams. "It was just dollars and cents. How do you get more people out there? How do you make it work better? It was a right decision, but a bad decision."

Fan reaction to the trade was swift, and fierce:

"Say it ain't so, Chicago Hustle. How could you possibly have traded Janie Fincher?"

"You've taken the smile and the sunshine out of the Chicago sporting scene. Just as Mary Pickford was 'America's Sweetheart' over a half century ago, so Janie Fincher was 'Chicago's Sweetheart.'"

"It's been two weeks and I am still in shock about Janie Fincher. How can the Hustle be so stupid as to let her go?"

"The public reaction was very strong, because people loved Janie, as well they should," Bruno says. "She had a great game." Fans donned black number 10 armbands (Fincher's number) and wielded "BRING BACK JANIE!" signs. The Hustle front office was deluged with phone calls, and Bruno quickly regretted his decision. "Getting rid of Janie was probably one of the most unpopular moves in recent Chicago sports," he said less than a month later. "Things were getting pretty grim around here."

It was a learning experience for Bruno. "It's not just all about who's batting cleanup and who's still on first, as Abbott and Costello would say. There's a dynamic that includes the fan," he says. "There's a dynamic that includes trying to grow women's sport. There's the concept of 'Don't fix what's not broke.' But I was young, and I was just being sincere when I made the move." Bruno says he also learned a lesson about not pushing rookies too quickly. "The pressure on Adrian was more then she should have had to deal with."

Sportswriter David Israel said he still wouldn't attend a Hustle game (because he "doubted that women had the ability to play basketball competently, competitively, or entertainingly"), but he would at least take the team more seriously now. What bothered him about women's basketball was the naïveté, he wrote. "Here were a bunch of folks playing for fun, not greed. Here were idealists who loved the game, not the attention. Here were athletes who thought of the team first and themselves second. The whole business had to be suspect. It wasn't basketball as I had been raised to know it." But then the Hustle traded Fincher. "For cash. It was heartless. Cruel. Mean. Ruthless. Cold-blooded. It was wonderful. It was just like the NBA."

It wasn't wonderful for Fincher, who was given bad credit cards by the Metros for her drive to Washington. "I had to sneak out of the freakin' hotel in the middle of the night and drive away because I found out the credit card was no good," she grouses. In the middle of a snowstorm in Ohio, Fincher's truck began acting up, and she decided to find a place to stay the night. But as she stepped out, she accidentally locked herself out with the engine still running, and had to wait hours until a police officer arrived to unlock it. "I shed some tears, and I got angry. Then I got hurt, and then I'd get angry, and then I'd get hurt," she recalls of that time in her life.

Chicago press tracked Fincher's plight with the Metros, whose players hadn't been paid since the season began. "We thought the Washington franchise was sound," Hustle president John Geraty insisted in mid-December. "Then, after we learned the players weren't being paid, Doug said 'that's not fair; we owe it to Janie to get her back.'" Fincher was skeptical when a fan called to say that the team was trying to bring her back, but the story was confirmed by a Chicago sportswriter. "You've got to be kidding," she exclaimed in her Oklahoma drawl.

"Janie's back!" a *Tribune* headline blared on December 20. The Metros had folded, and the league had agreed to void the trade. Or maybe not. "The Janie Fincher saga took more twists and turns Friday than the wildest soap opera," the paper mused two days later. Instead of sending Fincher back to Chicago, the league had placed her into a dispersal draft with other Metros players. Chicago had the fourth pick, and after the first three went by, Fincher expected to hear her name. The Hustle, though, had traded the slot to Iowa, who selected a post player. St. Louis coach Larry Gillman grabbed Fincher with the fifth pick. "Well," Fincher figured, "I guess I'm not going back to Chicago."

"Will Janie escape St. Louis and return to Chicago?" the *Tribune* asked. "Stay tuned." Hustle managers were infuriated. Fincher was supposed to return automatically to Chicago, they argued. Now they would have to pay ransom for her—and Gillman wanted Adrian Mitchell. Darn right he blackmailed the Hustle, Gillman says. "Chicago wanted her back and we weren't going to give them the rights unless they gave me Mitchell, because I thought Mitchell was an All-Star." (She was.)

Chicago gave in, and Fincher was on her way back. (Hustle owners weren't done paying, though; before Fincher would re-sign, she extracted $1,000 from them for expenses.) "Maybe all this wouldn't have happened if I were really unattractive," she acknowledged, referring to the fans' clamor, "but I don't think the fans brought me back so they could stare at me sitting on the bench. I have to play exciting ball, too."

Apart from trades, injuries, and waivers, lineups also changed at times because players simply decided to call it quits. Maria Gross decided to end her pro career after one season when she was traded from New York to the California Dreams. "You had to pay your own expenses, and if you made the team, you were reimbursed," she recalls. "Well, you were having to go compete with everybody on the West Coast, so I didn't even go."

Players had any number of reasons for retiring. Jan Ternyik took a head coaching position at the University of San Francisco. Christy Earnhardt hadn't liked the feeling of having her team's owner throw in the towel midseason. It bothered Valerie Goodwin that Dallas coach Dean Weese (her college coach) had been fired, and she accepted an offer from Stephen F. Austin State University.

Kathy Solano was disappointed that her team hadn't made all of its contract payments. "I felt if the management was not going to make a solid commitment to us as players and to this team and this league, then I didn't know that I wanted to sacrifice again for the following year," she decided. Krystal Kimrey, who never received a paycheck with the New England Gulls, wanted more stability in her life than "not knowing when you are going to get paid, where your next meal is coming from, if you're going to get stranded in California."

In St. Louis, Darla Plice was already discouraged by her team's poor finish the season before, and then she was offered a teaching job. "I think I got my taste of it and knew what it was like, and knew that I was ready to move on," she says. Tesa Duckworth had played two years, but she knew the group coming out of college in 1980 would be the strongest yet, and she could see the handwriting on the wall.

Ann Platte didn't intend to retire, but fate conspired against her. After being swept up in Gillman's mass waiver in St. Louis, she was invited to try out for the Iowa Cornets. Before she left, however, she lent her car to someone, who lent it to someone else, who then caused an accident. Platte didn't have any money, she was facing insurance problems over the accident, and her car wasn't drivable. She had no way to get to Iowa, and her professional career came to an end.

For others, doubts about the WBL's future took their toll. In December 1979 Washington Metros guard Jodi Gault was traded to the California Dreams. She packed her bags, flew out West—then turned around and flew back after sitting down with Dreams consultant Cathy Rush to explain, "I just don't think things are really stable. It's just not for me." Kaye Young drove to St. Louis after a trade by New Jersey, but it didn't feel right to her any more. "I remember watching one of their games, and I remember getting back in my car and driving back home," she says. Young just didn't believe the league was going to make it.

Another car heading out of St. Louis belonged to Donna Murphy. She'd had enough, she decided—of the WBL, of her coach, and of basketball. She was going back to school. The good Lord had a plan, Murphy says, and it was Betty Booker, who was sleeping on her couch while trying out for the team. When Booker made the roster, she could take over Murphy's half of the rent.

Murphy told her roommate that she was leaving and then packed her car, tearing the vinyl in her haste to get on the road. A snowstorm moved in, but Murphy didn't care. With the car's single windshield wiper flapping the whole way, she drove home to Kentucky. "That was about the happiest moment of my life," she says.

11

Standards of Conduct

Molly Bolin rushed around the hotel room. She and her Iowa Cornets team-mates had overslept, and the rest of the team and coach Dan Moulton were downstairs, impatiently waiting in taxis that would take them to the airport.

Clothes flew as the women hurriedly packed. Grabbing some miniature wine bottles the trio had smuggled off an airplane, Bolin shoved them under her coat and headed downstairs. Team rules were pretty clear: no cursing, no smoking, no alcohol. Still, the women had figured a little indulgence wouldn't hurt. Bolin stuffed the bottles into the trunk of the cab, tucking them into a travel bag so they wouldn't break.

Arriving home, the confused coach drew some wine bottles from his bag and held them up. The team's travel carriers all looked alike, and Bolin had accidentally shoved the contraband into Moulton's bag. No one claimed them, but the coach would have seen three distinctly red faces if he had cared to.

The WBL's Iowa franchise was corny, and proud of it. To symbolize its home state, owner George Nissen dubbed his team the Iowa Cornets, named its bus the Corn Dog, chose yellow and green uniforms, and had an ear of corn as its mascot. "We were an Iowa team," he says of his vision of wholesome "cornography." "What do you get from Iowa? Corn. We are not the Cornets, musical. We are the Cornets, Iowa. I just thought it was good."

The nickname wasn't well received in some corners. "Local embarrassment about Iowa's corny heritage had put the 'Iowa Corn Song' in mothballs at the University of Iowa, and many in the state blanched when Nissen not only chose 'Cornets' but made sure everyone got the point by choosing corn's primary colors for the team," the *Des Moines Register* reported. "Cornets" conflicted with the industrialized image that the Iowa Development Commission was trying to convey, the agency protested.

Even the team's own announcer seemed embarrassed, Nissen remembers. "He would yell out, 'New York!' [Then] he would kind of be apologetic when he would say, 'They are from Iowa . . . you know . . . the Cornets.' " Nissen ignored the critics, though. "Can't we be secure enough about our heritage to advertise it now, rather than ashamedly hiding it?" he asked.

Whether others groaned or not, it was clear early on that Iowa intended to hold itself up as a model franchise, at least when it came to public morality. Months before the opening tip-off, Cornets coach George Nicodemus announced that his players would be governed by certain standards of conduct. "They will be ladies, first of all. I don't use foul language in front of girls, and I don't expect them to." Other vices were also off limits. "If a girl smokes, drinks or is on drugs we don't want her," he said, and that included a glass of wine with dinner.

No other WBL franchise had such restrictions. Indeed, a *Dayton Daily News* writer was pleased to see Dayton Rockettes players unwind after a game with some Hudepohl 14-K (a Cincinnati beer). "When one sees them quenching thirsts with beer, you *know* they are professionals," he wrote. The *Chicago Tribune* likewise congratulated player Chris Critelli for successfully hustling unsuspecting men in free throw shooting contests at a local sports bar, with an ice-cold beer at stake. (She especially enjoyed challengers who didn't like losing to a woman, the paper reported, because they would inevitably demand another game—another free beer for Critelli.)

Given the openness of such conduct elsewhere in the WBL, Nicodemus's restrictions were fodder for some humor. "There's something bothering me about the Iowa Cornets," the *Register*'s Ron Maly wrote. "I mean, what kind of professional team is it that won't allow its players to smoke, drink, or use drugs? . . . What a letdown. Here I was, all set to go out and cover a bunch of hard-living, whiskey-swigging, pot-smoking women who are 'up' for every game."

With tongue in cheek, Maly predicted a dire effect on sponsorships. "There will, of course, be no Lite beer commercials," he wrote. "The way team officials are thinking, they don't even want the Cornets watching beer commercials, much less appearing in them and making money off them."

(A better candidate for a beer commercial would have been New Orleans Pride coach Butch van Breda Kolff, who always enjoyed a brew or two after games, and who often popped a can in the locker room. "I do the public relations for Miller High Life," the coach joked, and at a New Year's Eve party hosted by the Chicago Hustle, van Breda Kolff "obtained about 90 cans of his favorite brew," writer Claire Hellstern said. "Either he had a distribution truck outside or Santa Claus.")

Molly Bolin (now Kazmer) understood what Nicodemus hoped to achieve with his standards. "As pioneers, we were trying to establish what a professional was, and what you did to be a professional," she says. "Being in Iowa where it is so conservative, it's real important, obviously, to have a good image: 'We don't smoke. We don't drink. We don't do anything wrong. We are perfect and we play basketball, and you've got to be just like us.'"

For players like Tanya Crevier, who "didn't do any of those things anyway," there was no issue, but the rules didn't sit well with others. "Most of the girls on the team are 21, 22, 23 years old, and they're going, 'Hey, who is going to tell me what I can and cannot do when I am of legal age?'" Kazmer recalls. It was one thing to be cautious when representing the team, and another to dictate conduct during free time. "A lot of the girls were objecting to having our people tell us what to do. . . . We thought we were doing something rebellious by having a simple wine on the plane."

When Nicodemus later tried to carry his rules over to the Milwaukee Does, he was not supported by management. Indeed, Does general manager Gene DeLisle often went out with players and bought them drinks. "He wined us and dined us," an unidentified player said in a 1979 *Milwaukee Sentinel* article. "Even after George set up a no-drinking rule. He'd say when we were out, 'Hey, it's all right, I'll talk to George about this in the morning.'" The Does players had a standing joke, an unnamed starter reported. "When we check into a hotel, we all say, 'Where are we going to check into?' And someone answers kiddingly, 'a bar.' Or we'll meet up with someone in the hall and say, 'Hey what room are you in? B-A-R.'"

Bar hopping was, in fact, part of Milwaukee's marketing strategy. In one early promotion, management sent Does coach Candace Klinzing and her players on a limousine tour of local bars. "They would park the limousine, bring the girls into this bar, introduce them as the Milwaukee Does, the guys would all buy them drinks, and they would sit around and talk with different people in the bar," Klinzing remembers. "Then they would go on to the next bar and do the same thing." There was nothing wrong with the idea, PR director Chuck Bekos told the coach. "This is how we are going to get the word out that these are the girls."

The next day, players couldn't even make it up and down the court. "So I sat them down, and I said, 'I don't care if they want to take you out and entertain you with the bars or buy you a drink," Klinzing says. "You want to be courteous, sip it, but don't drink it. Here you are at practice and you can't do a gol-darn thing.'" The team did spend a lot of time in bars, Cindy Lundberg says, but mostly by choice. "I never thought I had to be there," she says. "We were pretty agreeable back then. I just went with everybody else." Partying was accepted in the Does organization, Barb Hostert says. "You could smoke dope. You could drink, any of that stuff. No wonder we were the worst team."

Illegal drug use was prohibited by the standard WBL contract, but not everyone complied. One player who joined a new team midseason remembers walking into an apartment that she was to share. "There are four women on the couch, and there's cocaine all over the table. I couldn't believe this. I walk in here and they go, 'Do you want some?' I knew what it was, I wasn't that naive, but I'm going, 'No, it's okay.'" Another player was irritated to see a teammate snort cocaine on a flight. "You just don't respect people like that, especially me, because I don't drink or smoke or nothin'," she says.

WBL coach Dean Meminger was well known for his use of recreational drugs, even during halftime of games. "He liked to get high, so there would be times on the road I would be exhausted after a game, and he would pull me out of my room and stand there and go into all of his philosophies until about two in the morning," one player recalls. "He's higher than a kite, and I'm half asleep going, 'Just let me go.'" Meminger (who later went public about his drug use) often came "stoned" to practices and once even forgot to bring any basketballs.

During one close game, a frustrated Meminger called a time-out to yell at his players. "You could hear him in the arena," a staffer recalls. "'You dumb this, ba-ba-ba.' He sent them back out on the court, the game starts, and all of a sudden I look over on the bench and Dean's not there." Instead, an assistant coach appeared to be in charge. "Where the hell is Dean?" the staffer wondered and went looking for him. "He's had enough," someone said. "He went out to score some coke."

For some WBL players, encountering occasional drug use was awkward. "You're not mama's little girl anymore," recalls Joanette Boutte. "You're out there playing professional ball with professional women. They had habits that you're not used to, but you know, it's the real world. So I had to grow up and accept certain things." Some teammates might not consider it "cool" that she didn't drink or smoke, Boutte figured, but that was her belief system.

Tanya Crevier, a South Dakota farm girl who played in Iowa's relatively safe environs for her first two seasons in the wbl, had no reservations about leaving for the big city when she was signed by the San Francisco Pioneers. "I knew where my morals were, and I had a Christian foundation," she says. "I knew the Lord was going to protect me wherever I go." Players didn't seek to impose their values on each other, says the Pioneers' Margaret English, who was also from a religious background. "I had a job to do. I did my job and I minded my own business. Everybody kind of went their separate ways."

Linnell Jones's fondest memories of the wbl were reflective moments along a riverbank in St. Louis when she was with the Streak. "I had just recently recommitted my life to Christ," she recalls, "and I used to go off to this river over there and just listen to my gospel music and kind of meditate and focus." Jones and two of her teammates joined a local church and enjoyed discussing their faith.

Occasionally even the most devout young women found themselves tested. Streak coach Larry Gillman remembers a game in which Pearl Moore "used language that I wouldn't have used" to a referee. On the flight home, he noticed Moore and Rowanna Pope reading the Bible together. "Pearl, are those the same passages you used with the referee?" he called out. (Finding language that Gillman wouldn't have used in 1980 takes some imagination. When Jane Ellen Cook, another player with deep religious convictions, asked the coach if he would refrain from swearing during practice, it was an easy answer—"Hell, no.")

12

The Money Men

It was a bunch of guys trying to survive. A lot of guys had no money and were trying to pretend that they did have money. Some guys were honest, and some guys weren't. • **Judson Phillips**, owner, 1979–80 Dallas Diamonds

I bought this team for $100,000, and I'd say that in a few years, it could be worth four or five million. • **Larry Kozlicki**, owner, Nebraska Wranglers, March 1981

EN ROUTE FROM HOUSTON TO DALLAS, 1979
The small plane's engine sputtered. The radio was already dead. Passenger Michael Staver could feel the wind from the storm whipping the plane around and knew that the man in the pilot's seat, his friend, was worried. The wings were starting to ice up, the pilot reported; they might not last much longer.

He was going to die, Staver knew, and it suddenly dawned on him: What had he really accomplished in his thirty-three years? Yes, he owned a successful real estate company, but that was just business. What lasting monument would he leave? The plane limped into Dallas, and though Staver survived, the feeling that he should do something meaningful in his life didn't fade.

On January 18, 1980, a television newscaster announced that the local wbl franchise was folding, and Staver perked up. Something meaningful . . . This was it. His sister had played basketball in high school, and owning a professional sports team had been a lifelong dream of his. Staver put in a call to the Women's Professional Basketball League—the Dallas Diamonds would be his gift to the City of Dallas.

Kate McEnroe watched as her Iowa Cornets battled the New York Stars for the WBL championship. A few months ago, she would have been down there in the thick of things, making sure everything off the court went as planned, but now she was just one of three thousand other fans.

A year earlier, the league's twenty-four-year-old public relations director had accepted owner George Nissen's offer to become the only female general manager of a professional sports team. She had just one year of experience, but a year in the WBL was like five years anywhere else, she figured. It had literally been her life — she slept, ate, and drank women's basketball.

The Cornets were popular, they had a shot at the title, and she was working with the league's most beloved owner. What could go wrong? But a WBL team's fortunes rose and fell with those of its owner, and McEnroe learned the hard way that events across the world could bring dreams to an end.

The three hundred women who played in the Women's Professional Basketball League would never have had the chance without the men who bankrolled the venture. None of those men were driven by a passion for women's basketball (many had never even seen a game before), but they believed that the sport had potential, that it would grow in popularity — and, of course, that it would produce a nice return on their investment.

It wasn't a coincidence that nearly half the WBL's owners were initially drawn to the league by an advertisement in the "business opportunities" section of the *Wall Street Journal*. They were entrepreneurs, hoping to get in on the ground floor of something that might become the next National Basketball Association or the next National Football League, ignoring the cynicism all around them.

They came from all walks of the business world. Joseph C. Reither (New England Gulls) was a teacher-turned-liquor-store-owner. Louis Deitelbaum (Dayton Rockettes) was an insurance agent. Larry Kozlicki (California Dreams, Nebraska Wranglers) was a tax attorney. Bob Peters (Milwaukee Does) was an inventor and owner of a tool manufacturing company. Robert Milo (New Jersey Gems) ran an advertising agency.

"One has to wonder what in the world would possess someone with a little extra cash to buy a women's basketball team," the *Republic Scene* mused in 1980. "It's not what you'd call your low-risk investment. It's more of an extravagance, really, like something out of a Neiman-Marcus catalog: for the man who has everything, *including* a chocolate Monopoly set, how about a full- court, perfume-scented team that will shoot 44 percent from the floor, 73 percent from the line and 100 percent of your money."

"The odds against an owner's finances holding up until good fortunes arrive are so high that, by comparison, pork belly futures are a gilt-edged investment," wrote *Sports Illustrated*'s Sarah Pileggi. Maybe that was the point, some suggested; maybe WBL owners were just looking for a tax shelter.

"There were some attorneys who sold some people on a [tax] loss carryover," Cornets owner Nissen says. "They didn't care anything about what was the sport or the game or anything, it was some kind of financial doing." A *Tank McNamara* cartoon in 1978 depicts a cigar-puffing blowhard investing in a new women's professional basketball league. "Oh, I think I got 50–60 thousand my tax man wants me to get rid of," he declares. "Are the teams (har har) charged for a time out (har har) if one of the girls snags her panty hose going for a loose ball (har har)?"

Such motives would explain why several owners were tax lawyers, skeptics figured, but one of those lawyers, New York Stars owner Ed Reisdorf, denies it. "People who say that don't really understand the value of having a deduction," he says. "I mean you can give money to charity and get a deduction; you don't really have to create a business to do it. There was no tax advantage to this deal, believe me."

"I don't know if anybody did it to save money or to hide money, or take tax credits for their losses, because everybody lost," Minnesota Fillies owner Gordon Nevers says. "Obviously we started out with the idea that we were going to make it." Where did they get that idea? The expected surge in women's athletics sparked by Title IX, for one. "I've known that women's sports are coming on strong," Nevers said in 1978, "but when I saw the numbers about what's happened in the last four or five years, I just feel that this is going to go very big."

Rosy marketing projections were also enticing. The league's first preliminary marketing plan, for example, estimated annual revenue from $88,000 to $350,000 per WBL team, based on seventeen home games and "conservative" ticket sales of three thousand. The most persuasive factor of all, though, was WBL founder Bill Byrne, who knew what it took to sell franchises. "Byrne was very clever with a very low franchise fee," Reisdorf says. "You think you're going to get into professional sports for $50,000. Of course, that was almost an irrelevant amount, and the real costs came when you start flying 13 or 15 people around the country, back and forth and back and forth. It adds up pretty quickly."

Byrne was a heck of a salesman, Dallas Diamonds owner Jud Phillips says. "This is the kind of thing that would not have got going unless you had somebody like Bill Byrne to spearhead it." Phillips became interested after his wife read about the WBL in *People*. "She's not a real sports fan and I wouldn't call her a real feminist, but I wouldn't call myself a real feminist either," he says. "It looked like a good opportunity. The franchise was $100,000, and at that time the baseball teams were selling for $15–20 million or whatever, so I figured at some point I could turn $100,000 to $200,000."

With his brother Jim (they owned several McDonald's restaurants together) and their attorney, Ira Tobolowsky, Phillips bought a franchise in Dallas. "He didn't buy a basketball team, but a toy he'd long saved for," columnist Skip Bayless wrote. Hundreds of thousands of dollars later, Phillips put his toy away, returning his franchise to the league. "I have three grown kids today that weren't born then and I haven't really gone through it with them," he says. "Someday I will go through and show them the $300,000 scrapbook that I have."

After Phillips reached his financial limit, the Diamonds were taken over by Staver. "I know it's crazy, damn crazy," Staver said in 1980. "Some think I've gone off the deep end, and maybe I have. I don't know if *I* can pull this off, because I don't know if *anyone* can." The Diamonds would be his social contribution to a city in which he began with nothing but a small loan seven years earlier. "He seems sincere, if not a bit misguided," Bayless concluded, and the *Dallas Times Herald* echoed the cynicism. "Of all the precious metal commodities in which Staver might have invested—gold, silver, Diamonds—he picked the only one with very little future."

So did Hugh Sweeney, a tennis promoter and former pro who initially wanted a World Team Tennis franchise until he saw the team's budget. "When they revived him, Sweeney caught the next plane back to Houston," the *Houston Post* quipped. "A few weeks later, a salesman called offering a gift for the man who has everything: a women's basketball team." Sweeney believed that women's sports were on their way up, and put down the $50,000.

"Whatever you do, give Hugh Sweeney a shot in the arm," says Byrne. "We were kind of blasé and dull. When Hugh Sweeney showed up at the draft, he added so much color, so much fun to the league." Sweeney was indeed a character. In the 1950s, he was the world's tallest professional tennis player (six-foot-six), and the only one still wearing long trousers on the court (he considered them more dignified). Although he had played at Wimbledon and traveled the world, he was not a rich man.

By contrast, the owners that investment banker Marshall Geller lined up for his San Francisco Pioneers were both well heeled and well connected. "What got us very enamored of this whole thing was the fact that Title IX had just started being talked about in the colleges, and was starting to be implemented," Geller says. "We were beginning to see that women and our daughters were getting involved in sports like soccer and tennis and golf. And I am an optimist. I have a saying, 'I've never met a rich pessimist.'"

Co-owners in the Pioneers included actors Alan Alda (*M*A*S*H*) and Mike Connors (*Mannix*), assemblyman (and later San Francisco Mayor) Willie Brown, former San Francisco 49er Gene Washington, attorney Phil Ryan, socialite Ann Getty, and former Oakland Warriors coach Clifford Raye. Although he hoped for a return on his investment, Geller admits to other advantages of buying a women's basketball team. "San Francisco is somewhat of a liberal city, and there was a great desire by a lot of people there to see women progress," he says. "I did very well business-wise because of the notoriety of being the founder of the Pioneers."

On the other coast was the New York territory of Reisdorf and his partner, Steve McCarthy, another tax lawyer. "I pretty much bought it as a birthday gift for my wife," Reisdorf says. (Terry Reisdorf was interested in sports and eventually ended up managing the team.) "When we got into it, it was going to be a passive investment for both of us, but it definitely did not end up that way. It's the kind of thing that just sucks up all of your energy. It was such an exciting adventure."

Even when the decision to invest is driven by money, there is something different about professional athletics, Reisdorf believes. "You get passionately involved with sports. You lose your perspective when your passions take over like that."

Houston Angels assistant coach Greg Williams got a taste of that when he attended an owners' meeting in 1979. "They were all so competitive," he remembers. "They all wanted to win the championship so bad, and that came out in those meetings. They were just brutal. In fact, two guys got in an argument and one of them asked the other one to step outside in the alley to settle it." Byrne remembers a time when New York's McCarthy became angry with Minnesota's Nevers. "He's a New York street guy—he got up and said, 'Hey, stop the meeting. Come on Nevers—outside!'" Byrne told them both to sit down.

Another heated moment came in 1980, when a frustrated Ed Reisdorf declared that anyone could have 98 percent of his New York franchise for $250,000. Geller called his bluff—"Sold!"—and the dialogue went downhill from there. (Geller knew he was getting Reisdorf's goat. "He was just playing a game there; he wasn't selling it.")

Reisdorf didn't appreciate Geller's flippancy. "Geller made a comment that really brought up my ire," he recalls. "We were sitting at opposite ends of this long table—I remember it vividly. I walked around and he was sitting in his chair and I pointed my finger at him to say, 'You know, you can't say things like that.' He started to jump out of his chair, and I hit him and knocked him out, so it was a very short episode." A recess was called, the minutes reflect, to allow "tempers to cool."

Geller shrugs off the incident. "It happens in league meetings," he figures. "I can tell you, if you have the league minutes, they probably don't reflect even half of the battles that went on there." The two men have no lingering ill will, Reisdorf notes. "I've seen Marshall since then, by the way, and it is just a big joke between us."

Women's sports were going to take off, Reisdorf was convinced. If an owner could buy a team for $50,000 and hold on for a while, one day it might be worth millions. Those hopes seemed to come true in December 1979, when national news reported that the Houston Angels had been sold for $1 million.

The new owner was a man named Richard Klingler, who introduced himself at an Angels practice. Sitting with his players in the bleachers, uneasiness washed over Greg Williams. "He started talking, and he talked about *this* loud [a murmur]. We were straining our ears to hear him. He just didn't come across as someone who had just bought a team for a million dollars. We were like, 'What's going on here?'"

Checks started bouncing, and Klingler's payment deadlines came and went. It was then revealed that the sale was a "devilish hoax," as sportswriter Lacy Banks put it—the buyer was a laborer with no real assets. "He was like a machinist in a machine shop, and didn't any more have a million dollars than you and me," Williams says.

Klingler just wanted the attention generated by such a major announcement, speculates Tom Davis, director of operations for the Angels. "You gotta give him credit; he didn't take a gun and shoot anybody for publicity." (A few months later, Chicago Hustle owners rejected a million-dollar offer that was not a hoax, according to co-owner Sherwin Fischer. "I knew the guy; it was legitimate," he says, but he and co-owner Larry Cooper thought they could do better in the long run. Fischer shakes his head. "We turned down a million bucks.")

"You know what?" Fillies owner Nevers said in 1979. "I wouldn't take a million if you offered it to me right now. I wouldn't entrust it [the Fillies franchise] to anyone else." Nevers was an eternal optimist, in spite of losing more than half a million dollars his first two seasons, and was the only sole owner to last all three years in the wbl. Why did he stick with it? "Stubborn," he says. "In my lifetime, I have never been a quitter. I've left things, but I have never left things on a sour note."

Nevers had a lifelong interest in sports and pitched for a Triple A baseball team until a leg injury ended his career. After that, he worked at the Werness Brothers Funeral Chapels, eventually becoming executive vice president and part owner until the business was sold in 1976. Meanwhile, he consulted with an occupational specialist who suggested that he should be in professional sports management. When Nevers saw an ad for a new women's basketball league, he figured it was meant to be. (His former occupation did generate a few puns. The owner hoped he wasn't "digging a hole for himself," one sportswriter quipped. Another said he could imagine the headlines: "Fillies Die in Last Quarter" . . . "The Stiffs Can't Make Free Throws" . . . "Fillies Face Grave Situation.")

Another optimist was the owner of the St. Louis Streak. Vince Gennaro's curiosity was piqued when ten tall women boarded an airport shuttle he was riding to a hotel near his apartment in Chicago. They were the Houston Angels, he learned from Glenda Holleyman, who talked him into attending their game the next night. A lot of young girls were at the game, he noticed, and they seemed to revere the basketball players.

It reminded Gennaro of the excitement he felt as a five-year-old boy attending his first New York Yankees game, which stayed with him over the years as he followed his favorite players. Gennaro realized that the whole notion of role models in a team sport did not exist for women as it had for him. He made some calls, quit his job at a consulting firm, and he and his wife "put down some roots and tried to build an organization and put women's basketball on the map."

Although Gennaro was from Chicago, that rich territory had been snapped up early by John Geraty, a friend of Byrne. The first investment meeting for the franchise was attended by half a dozen men, including Sherwin Fischer, owner of a personnel service, and Larry Cooper, a local bankruptcy lawyer. "It was a very strange meeting," Fischer recalls. "Here you're going to be involved in professional basketball, and nobody really knew what they were doing." Over time, Fischer and Cooper became the only owners, and in February 1981 they tried something novel: offering 37 percent of the Hustle's stock in a public sale at $10 a share, with a $100 minimum purchase.

The response was good, Fischer says, especially considering the circular's warnings (the stock posed a "high degree of risk, and should only be purchased by people who can afford to lose their entire investment") and an advisory from a local stock analyst ("If you want to spend $100 to have a nice piece of paper to hang on your bathroom wall, ok, but you wouldn't find an investment banker in the city who would endorse this offering for anything other than its emotional value").

The sale generated over a hundred thousand dollars, he says—not including one prankster's check for $7,500,000,000—and the league decided to try it with other franchises. "We were just about to start that when Minnesota came tumbling down on us," Fischer says, referring to a walkout by Fillies players. (See chapter 18.) When the wbl later folded, the Hustle had to return investors' money.

In New Orleans, former New Yorker Steve Brown wanted to keep professional basketball in the city after the nba's Jazz moved to Utah. When he read about the wbl in *Sports Illustrated*, in an article that began with a favorable quote from Julius Irving, Brown's basketball idol, a light went on. "The very next day I started trying to put this team together," he said.

A year later, Brown was reclining beside a pool in the Bahamas when he realized that the man next to him was none other than "Dr. J" himself. Brown spoke up, telling Irving about the results of his words in si. The quote wasn't entirely accurate, Irving said, but that didn't matter to Brown. It had inspired his dream, and this was his chance to say thanks. "It sort of was a sweet moment as a fan of the game," he recalls.

To bring a wbl team to New Orleans, the stockbroker approached one of his clients, Dr. John W. "Billy" Simpson from Covington, Mississippi, who owned several buildings and cofounded a local hospital. Simpson initially dismissed the idea, but his wife had other ideas. "I take a mother's viewpoint when I see what inspiration the team can be to young girls with potential in the athletic field," Claudette Simpson said. (The Simpsons had one son and six daughters.) She urged her husband to reconsider, and Dr. Simpson took the plunge, the two of them becoming involved in every aspect of team management.

The most endearing of all WBL owners was Iowa's George Nissen, inventor of the modern-day trampoline. As a child, Nissen had noticed that circus trapeze artists ended their routines by dropping onto a net, sometimes bouncing back up. At age sixteen he put his curiosity to work, and in 1934 he completed the first trampoline. After winning national gymnastic titles in college, Nissen and two schoolmates became "the Leonardo brothers," traveling around to carnivals and schools demonstrating the new jumping device.

Forty years later, Nissen's trampolines were fixtures throughout the world, and he was ready to try something new. His company had recently merged with another, yielding stock that could be converted to cash. "Of course, anyone that has worked all his life without cash doesn't know what to do with it," he jokes.

The idea of a local women's basketball team intrigued Nissen. "I always had it in the back of my mind why didn't girls have more sports coming up. I could see that in the future," he says. "I remember when the men's football started in Chicago [the Bears], it was like $5,000 or something like that." He also figured that halftime shows could showcase his trampolines. Over the next two years the Cornets owner became immensely popular among players and fellow WBL owners alike.

In 1979, though, Nissen's fortunes would take a drastic turn. He was in Iran at the time, following up on a handsome deal he had struck after meeting the shah of Iran at the Asian Games the year before. "I put in all of the gymnastic equipment for them and sold it to the Iranian people," he recalls, a terrific opportunity—except that the shah and his backers were about to be violently deposed. ("The revolution was in process, which I didn't anticipate," he says. "I guess I should have, but I was well treated there all the time.")

The people Nissen was working with were put to death. "It was an emotional shock to listen and see their executions on television," he said, and months later it was still hard for him to talk about. While billionaire Ross Perot was launching a dramatic rescue of employees kidnapped by the new regime, the Iowa Cornets owner was also fleeing the country. "He got his men out and I got out too, just because I was too dumb to really be scared," Nissen says.

Nissen was safe, but he was stuck with a multimillion dollar project that had just collapsed. The company he had begun setting up in Iran had already received orders from Saudi Arabia, which Nissen had used to obtain bank funding. "The contracts were coming in, but they took my word for it and all of that," he says. "When [the Ayatollah] Khomeini came in and all this stuff came crashing down, I got hooked for the loan. I paid it all."

Schools were also cutting back on trampoline purchases, and Nissen's investment in a women's basketball movie (*Dribble*) had set him back hundreds of thousands of dollars. Cutbacks had to be made. Cornets staff took pay cuts, and up to half a dozen players crammed into hotel rooms on road trips. Nissen began looking for investors, and on January 25, 1980, he sold 60 percent of his Cornets stock to a man named Dick Vance, a former disc jockey who now leased a local cable television channel. Another 20 percent went to the team's first general manager, Rod Lein.

Cornets coach Steve Kirk watched Vance announce his ambitions at a press conference. "He kind of went through all of this talk; all of these women were going to make more money," he says. The players seemed enthused, but Kirk had his doubts. "They were just eating it up, but I had been around enough I could read him, streetwise." Something didn't seem right. "As a businessman he was just blowing smoke up the rear end of these girls. 'This guy is such a bullshitter,'" Kirk thought. "'He doesn't really believe in us.'"

With Vance's arrival came the departure of general manager Katie McEnroe for "personal reasons"—namely, her disgust at his vision of the team. "They wanted to rename the Iowa Cornets as Dick's Dolls," she says. "It wasn't the franchise that I had built up." The Cornets accused the Dallas Diamonds of "tampering" with McEnroe and threatened a $1 million lawsuit, which infuriated Diamonds owner Michael Staver. (He had spoken with candidates for a general manager position recently, Staver admitted, but both McEnroe and he denied any impropriety, and McEnroe stayed in Iowa.)

The new Cornets owner, meanwhile, was taking heat for a show on his cable channel that had allegedly defrauded three hundred viewers who bought vacation packages through it. "We were kind of the butt of a few jokes there in Iowa," Molly Bolin later recalled. "People would be interviewed on the news saying, 'Well, I bought this vacation and I didn't get it. He owns the Cornets, so I guess I own one of the Cornets, but I don't know which one.' We were going, 'Oh man, this is so embarrassing.'"

"I didn't know him to investigate," Nissen says now. "At the time, my family and everybody said, 'Enough. Get out if you can.' " Vance's ideas were good, it seemed; "I thought that he got the point, but the guy was a crook." He had been "suckered," Nissen realized when Vance's check bounced, and the buyer faded from the scene. "He skipped the state," Kirk says. "He was a piece of work, this guy."

For McEnroe, it was too late, and she watched the championship game from her seat in the bleachers. "It was one of those moments I will always remember," she says wistfully. "I couldn't be there at the very end."

13

Wrong League

I am 5-foot-9 and weigh 175 pounds and haven't shaved my legs in 38 years. I have a better chance of dancing with the Radio City Music Hall Rockettes than Ann Meyers has of playing basketball in the NBA. • **Dave Kindred**, *Washington Post*, September 13, 1979

Officials of the women's league claimed that she was slighting her sisters—effectively telling them that the WBL wasn't good enough for her. Sportswriters railed that she was only after money and publicity—how did a woman dare pretend that she could play ball with the big boys? • *Mademoiselle*, March 1981

Ann was smart. She had an opportunity with the Pacers. Who wouldn't have taken it? • **Wanda Szeremeta**, New Jersey Gems

On July 17, 1978, the Houston Angels used the number one pick in the inaugural WBL draft to select a five-foot-nine-inch senior from UCLA named Ann Meyers, who had just led the Bruins to the 1978 AIAW national championship. Meyers was a natural athlete (she played seven sports in high school) and had the added advantage of honing her basketball skills as a youngster against her father, who had played at Marquette, and her brother, Dave Meyers, a future NBA guard. She was, as legendary UCLA men's coach John Wooden said, "the one who really got women's basketball going. She was a complete player and a great ballhandler." Getting Meyers onto a WBL roster would clearly be a boost to the young league.

She declined. Finishing her degree was Meyers's first priority, she said, and she was two quarters short. She also wanted to maintain her amateur status for Olympic competition. For Meyers, representing her country had been a dream ever since reading a biography about Olympian Mildred "Babe" Didrikson in the fourth grade. Meyers had been a member of the silver-medalist Olympic basketball team in 1976, and now she wanted to play under coach Sue Gunter in 1980, when the United States had a chance at gold.

And so a year later, WBL officials were stunned to hear that Meyers had signed a contract with the Indiana Pacers of the National Basketball Association ("the only signee in NBA history to show up in a skirt for the occasion," the *Miami Herald* quipped).

Meyers had received a phone call "out of the blue" from Sam Nassi, the new owner of the financially troubled Pacers. Until Nassi's intervention in May 1979, the fate of the Pacers had been uncertain from season to season, the franchise preserved only by a telethon in 1977, and propped up by a group of local businesses in 1978. Nassi was from Los Angeles, where Meyers's UCLA team had just won the national championship. "How would you like to try out for the Indiana Pacers?" he asked.

Meyers recognized that it was a "total publicity situation on his part," but Nassi's call came at just the right time. Conflicts had arisen with USA Basketball, and Meyers had grown uncomfortable with that relationship. Surrounded by younger teammates, most still in college, Meyers perceived that her age had become an issue. "I just felt they thought I was too old at 24," she recalls. She was ready to move on.

If signing Meyers was a promotional gimmick ("like Bill Veeck signing a midget when he owned a baseball team," Seattle Supersonics owner Sam Schulman said disgustedly), it worked—the Pacers training camp opened under the watchful eye of every major publication in the country. "*Wrong League*," read the headline in *Time*. It was a publicity stunt, many said, "Disneyball" (as in fantasy), according to Dave Kindred of the *Washington Post*. The Pacers were claiming "this wasn't a big joke, a stunt, hype, or a gimmick," a Minneapolis writer said. "If you believe that, you'll believe anything."

WBL officials were furious. It was the "initial step in a large-scale ploy by the National Basketball Association to undermine the WBL," New York Stars owner Ed Reisdorf fumed. New Orleans Pride manager Steve Brown fired off a telegram to the Pacers refuting the "propaganda" that Meyers was the best woman basketball player in the land, betting $5,000 that she could not win a one-on-one shootout against a player from the WBL. "Ann Meyers would be an average player in our league," he said. "Maybe she'd start with some teams, maybe not."

Discounting Meyers' abilities was rather farfetched, but a sportswriter in Minneapolis added to the verbiage. "As good a basketball player as Meyers is, she couldn't have carried [Denise] Long's Underalls," he declared. "Long was the best female basketball player this country has ever produced."

The reference was not coincidental. A decade earlier, Long had been the first female drafted by an NBA team, after making national headlines as a high school player in Iowa, scoring what was then a record 6,250 points in four years, including 111 points in a single game. (In Iowa's six-on-six basketball, three players on each squad were assigned exclusively to offense, and it was not unheard of for "forwards" to average 60 or more points per game.) The 1968 state championship battle between Long's Union-Whitten and archrival Everly was covered enthusiastically by national media.

In Long's senior year she was summoned to the superintendent's office for a phone call. Congratulations, the caller said—she had been drafted by the NBA's San Francisco Warriors in the thirteenth round. Long figured it was a prank, but suddenly she was invited to appear with Johnny Carson on the *Tonight Show*, and sportswriters were on the phone from across the country. "Immediately, friends and fans of Franklin Mieuli, the Warriors' owner, snickered over what they called a 'great publicity coup,'" Jim Enright's book *Only in Iowa* reported, but Mieuli protested. "Denise Long is the best girl player I've ever seen, and I'm confident she can compete against boys," he said.

Long headed for training camp in California, where she worked out with the Warriors and was photographed shooting over six-foot-eleven-inch Nate Thurmond. Her NBA adventure was to be short-lived, though. Commissioner Walter Kennedy quickly voided the draft pick, citing the league's prohibition (at the time) against signing high school students. Mieuli arranged a $5,000 college scholarship for Long and organized an amateur "all girl basketball league" to play before Warriors home games.

After a year at the University of San Francisco, Long returned to Iowa. In 1978, she tried out for the WBL's Iowa Cornets, but she had been out of basketball for several years. "What's hard is trying to stay up with these college players," she said. "The last time I was in decent shape was 1968." (She later did have a chance to play in a Cornets game, thanks to general manager Rod Lein.)

In May 1975, after the NBA's New Orleans (later Utah) Jazz drafted a

Russian player whose chances of playing in the United States were virtually nonexistent, general manager Bill Bertka's teenage daughter approached him. "You did something different this year, so next year why don't you draft a woman on your team?" she challenged him. "Why not," Bertka replied. "You never know. . . ."

Two years later, the Jazz did just that. In the seventh round of the 1977 NBA draft, it selected Olympian Lusia "Lucy" Harris, who had redefined the role of a post player in the women's game. "Ever since talented 6–3 Lusia Harris of Delta State University planted herself under the basket and shoveled in 47 points at a Madison Square Garden shootout between DSU and Queens in 1976, people wondered if there could ever be another player like Harris who could dominate the game," said D. D. Eisenberg of the *Philadelphia Evening Bulletin*.

Harris was picked in the draft immediately after Alvin Scott of Oral Roberts University, who played eight seasons with the Phoenix Suns, and two slots before 1976 Olympic decathlete Bruce Jenner. She had no interest in following up on her selection by the Jazz, however, and declined to try out for the team. ("It was later revealed that Harris was pregnant, prompting jests that the Jazz had actually drafted the rights to her firstborn," wrote team historian Dave Blackwell.) Two years later, Harris would have another chance at professional basketball when she finished out the 1979–80 WBL season with the Houston Angels.

After overcoming the initial shock at Nassi's call ("What? Who is this?"), Meyers had no reservations about giving the NBA a try—even if some within the Pacers club did (Coach Bob Leonard personally flew to California to talk her out of coming)—and in September 1979, she joined other hopefuls at training camp. "Ann Meyers is a very good basketball player fundamentally," an Indianapolis sportswriter concluded. "She passed the ball well, she didn't back off even though the players gave her few courtesies. And, she wasn't the worst player in the tryout. . . . Still, it was obvious right away she didn't have the physical ability—quickness, the size to shoot over big players, strength—to play men's basketball. But, really, there were moments when she didn't look lost out there, and you had to admire her spunk."

Meyers was cut on the third day but maintained that she had been a legitimate prospect. "I thought I got robbed," she says. "I thought I could sit the bench as well as anybody else, and look better in a uniform." At a 1979 press conference in Minnesota, Meyers said, "I felt I was doing as well as the others. I played the best basketball of my life during those three days. I had the same disappointments as anyone else who gets cut by an NBA team."

Seated nearby, WBL All-Star Marie Kocurek rolled her eyes, and a reporter asked if she had something to say. "No, I don't," Kocurek replied. "I didn't say a word." At the time. "That's a lot of crap," she said afterward. "She knows she could never play in the NBA. Saying things like that doesn't help us [in women's basketball] because everyone knows it's not true. We have to sell our own game."

Meyers's tryout was a recurring debate in women's basketball. "No woman can play in the NBA," said Nancy Lieberman, then a senior at Old Dominion. "Ann Meyers, Nancy Lieberman, or anyone else has to work hard to show what we can do in our own sport." (A year later, though, amid rumors that she might be a late-round NBA draft pick, Lieberman said she would give it a try if drafted. The difference, she said, "is that Ann honestly felt she could make it. I wouldn't feel that way. I'd do it because of the challenge.")

Meyers was betraying her gender, Minnesota Fillies owner Gordon Nevers felt. "She's a great basketball player in her own right, but why hasn't she promoted women's basketball?" he complained. "She seems more concerned with Ann Meyers than a place for women pros to play. I hated to see a person with her ability sham herself like that."

And it was a sham, many were convinced. "That was nothing more than a publicity stunt for her and them," Chicago Hustle player Janie Fincher declares. "You will never convince me in a million years that that chick thought she was going to be able to stay in that league." (Another theory, articulated by California Dreams general manager Bob Joseph, was that Meyers went through the Pacers stint to increase her leverage with the WBL.)

Meyers's size alone generated much of the skepticism. "We didn't like that at all," says WBL player Tonyus Chavers, but her objection wasn't to Meyers trying out; rather, it was to the NBA picking someone so small. "We felt like we could have sent some big girls in there to bang with those guys for real. How is she going to try out? She isn't even tall enough."

Nancy Dunkle, an Olympic colleague who signed with the WBL the same week as Meyers's tryout, was a little worried. "I just can't help but think that something might happen to her," she said. "I'm really concerned because I know how sensitive she is. I hope she doesn't get hurt." Dave Kindred concurred, speculating in his *Post* column that, in the NBA, Meyers "would set a pick only after notifying her next of kin."

UCLA teammate Anita Ortega knew that Meyers didn't have a realistic chance of remaining with the Pacers ("no NBA team was going to have a woman on it," she was sure), but the opportunity helped women's basketball by showing what women could do, she felt. "Annie Meyers has got guts," 1976 Olympic teammate Charlotte Lewis says. "She has got guts, and she went and stood up for what she believed. I would have thought less of her if she didn't." Many WBL players would have done the same thing, no question about it, says Gems teammate Wanda Szeremeta.

Either way, Meyers wasn't going to be troubled by reactions to her tryout. "I couldn't afford to listen to what the other players were saying," she said. "I can't see any player turning down an opportunity like that." It might have been a promotional scheme, she acknowledged in 2001, "but to me, it was an opportunity of a lifetime most men don't get. I didn't want to say 'what if' years later."

After the tryout, Meyers decided that she missed playing. If she signed with the WBL, however, she would lose her $50,000 Pacers contract. That made negotiations a little difficult. The average WBL salary was, after all, about one-fifth of what she was asking. Houston was not interested in a $50,000 price tag, and the team sold the right to approach its draft pick to the New York Stars, thought to be a good match for such a high-profile player.

In the end, New York could not meet the price. "We don't want to bid against the NBA and we don't want to start a bidding war within the WBL," Reisdorf said. "We were very willing to pay her what a star in the WBL would make, and we pointed out the fringe benefits she would derive from playing in New York, but we were unable to reach a settlement on her base salary."

Next up was New Jersey. Gems owner Robert Milo wasn't put off by the figures he was hearing and paid Houston $20,000 for the right to talk to Meyers. "She is someone a lot of people will want to see because she had the guts to do what she did," he said. "She will bring excitement to the league and help other teams fill seats. She will also be the superstar, which our league needs."

After a five-hour negotiation with Meyers's agent, Milo announced that terms had been reached. "I did it!" he enthused. Bringing Meyers to the WBL was, he said, "our contribution to the future generation of women's sports in America." The Gems then scheduled a press conference at Giants

Stadium to announce its prize. "Everything went smoothly, except—Ann Meyers failed to show up," the *New Jersey Herald* reported. "In its own small way it would have been like Jimmy Carter failing to show up for the inauguration, Charles Lindbergh being a no-show for his ticker tape parade or Mickey Mantle skipping Mickey Mantle Day."

That wasn't her fault, Meyers says; she warned Gems management days earlier that she had a prior commitment to speak on the West Coast and that she couldn't make it. "I hadn't even signed anything, and they were calling a press conference," she says. "I'm not there, so how does that make me look? Right off the bat, I'm not feeling too good about this." As it turned out, bad weather rolled in, and outgoing flights that evening were grounded anyway.

"Meanwhile, Gems' president Robert Milo was left holding an unsigned contract at what he had hoped would be an event comparable to the Jets' signing of Joe Namath and the Cosmos' signing of Pele," the *Herald* wrote. Milo tried to ease the awkwardness, joking, "When I picked my staff for the Gems I left out one person, a weather forecaster," but the paper hinted at intrigue, noting a comment from Meyers that she still wanted her lawyer to look over the contract.

Ironically, Meyers's newsworthiness was demonstrated by the fact that missing the press conference in itself drew press from Los Angeles to Philadelphia. (In her absence, reporters turned to team captain Szeremeta. "They asked Wanda if she was better than Ann Meyers," recalls teammate Martha Hastings. "Wanda looked at them and said, 'Better what? Better looking?' It was hilarious.")

A few days later, Meyers signed on the dotted line and then had to contend with her new colleagues' perceptions. "Ann Meyers isn't God," All-Star Althea Gwyn complained. "I don't think she's in the top 3–4 in the league and she's getting all this money without proving herself."

Although WBL players were prohibited from discussing their salaries, it was widely publicized that Meyers was making at least $50,000 ($140,000 over three years). Many players thought it was ridiculous, Sharon Farrah says. "They just wanted to play and make enough money to make ends meet. They weren't trying to get rich."

Szeremeta wondered what the reaction to Meyers would be among her teammates, but she said that it was positive and that the players respected Meyers. Hastings also saw no hostility. "Ann is a really nice person, so people didn't hold it against her," she says. "I didn't have any problem with it. If other players did, I wasn't aware of it."

The impression lingered, however, that Meyers had insulted her peers by accepting an offer from the Pacers after turning down the wbl. "It may have been good PR for her, but it undercut the wbl's attempts at serious sport," wrote Jere Longman of the *Dallas Times Herald*. The women's league "was made to look second-rate" by her Pacers stint, Ted Vincent accused in his 1981 book *Mudville's Revenge*.

Meyers insists that was not her intent. "I felt [the wbl] was a new league, they didn't have the stability, I didn't really know who the owners were and some of the coaches," she says. "Not to say that I wasn't excited to be a part of the league, but the nba came calling on me. How do you turn it down? When somebody offers you that kind of money in the '70s, fifty thousand dollars, even today it's a huge amount of money. And I thought, 'Where else am I going to make that kind of money?' The wbl, what were they paying? Six to fifteen [thousand dollars], if they were lucky?"

Meyers was a popular topic at the Chicago Hustle's preseason training camp, the *Chicago Tribune* reported, where players saw her as anything from an opportunist to a traitor. "My first opinion was that she did it for the money," Sue Digitale said. "My second opinion is that I wouldn't do it for the money—for any amount—and that she sold our league short. We don't need her." League mvp Rita Easterling was also disappointed. "I feel she was not thinking of us," she said. "We took the chances last year when the wbl was new."

To the Hustle's Janie Fincher, "[Meyers] signing was kind of an insult to us, like our money wasn't good enough. It was embarrassing because we are supposed to represent the best in women's basketball." Adrian Mitchell, though, wasn't bothered. "I would have done the same thing and so would most of the other players in the league," she said. I don't think I could make an nba team, but for $50,000 I'd sure try."

In New York, Gwyn predicted that Meyers might be the target of more than the average number of elbow jabs: "after all, she put down women, and that's what we are." Looking back now, Gwyn says, "I guess that was jealousy talking. I felt that she had knocked the league, but as I look at it, I also knew it was all about the money and all about publicity. She probably made more just for trying out with them than I made in the whole year." Did Gwyn give Meyers any of those elbow jabs? "I don't remember," she says coyly. "I think she might have tried to drive in there, and I think that she might have been met with some opposition, but I can't swear by it." (Gwyn emphasizes that she would never have intentionally hurt Meyers.)

Szeremeta doesn't recall seeing anyone "go after" her teammate; Meyers did end up on the floor a lot, but it was part of the game. "When you have someone who has been labeled the best player in the league, people are always going to be after your head," she says. That's true, agrees Karen Aulenbacher, and she was one of those people. "My aim was to knock Annie Meyers clean off the floor," the former Houston Angels guard says. And she did—three times in a row in one game—but it wasn't because of the Pacers tryout, she says; Meyers was just so good that she needed to be distracted.

Indeed, Meyers was expected to do Big Things in the WBL. "Meyers is the woman that the Women's Professional Basketball League hopes will do for it what Joe Namath did for the American Football League," wrote Mel Greenberg of the *Philadelphia Inquirer*. It would take time before Meyers established herself as the league's "savior," the *Herald* noted, but she had been in town only minutes before she was already signing autographs.

Although the media touted Meyers as the "franchise player," she did not feel that team management treated her that way. Like many players, upon her arrival she requested a uniform number with personal significance to her (number 15, her college number). Sorry, that uniform had been stolen. Couldn't another one be made? she asked. No money, she was told. Well, how about number 6, her Olympic number? Sorry, that number was already assigned to another player. "I don't want to get my ego too out there or step on anybody's toes, but I'm thinking, 'You're bringing in a player that's supposed to be your franchise player. Doggone it, you can't even give me my number?'" Meyers says. "And as trivial as that sounds, a number is very important to the identification of a player. So things didn't start off real great."

To the public, Meyers tried to downplay expectations. She was just a rookie, after all, she said. "I know a lot of people expect me to do great things, but I don't know what I can do. I'm no superstar, just another player." But number 14 had generated too much ink, and her salary was too big, to sell that line. Critics wanted her to prove she was worth all the fuss.

"For someone who was supposed to be The Franchise, Ann Meyers had an inauspicious beginning with the New Jersey Gems," a *Chicago Tribune* column sniffed after Meyers missed a lay-up and two free throws early in her first game. She did end up with 16 points and 10 rebounds in 24 minutes, the writer conceded, which "augured well for the future."

Some observers weren't looking at the right factors, a *St. Louis Post-Dispatch* writer argued. "To rate her on the basis of scoring—which some people apparently have done—is an intolerable injustice," Cal Fussman wrote. "She is the game's most complete player. Dribbler, defender, shooter, stealer, rebounder, rallier, picker, passer—Meyers is a Renaissance Lady of Basketball."

Most opponents in 1979–80 employed a simple strategy against the Gems: mob Meyers. After a tight game in Minnesota, a local columnist observed, "the Fillies entered the contest seemingly intent on roughing up Meyers, and they were able to do so—knocking the 5–9, 135-pound Meyers to the floor repeatedly." Meyers said she was having trouble adjusting to being fouled on nearly every shot. "People ask me about my 35 per cent shooting, and that's the reason. But I have to get used to it."

A month into the season, the *Tribune* was a convert, declaring that Meyers "showed a Chicago crowd Saturday why she's worth every dollar of her $140,000 salary package with the New Jersey Gems." So was the *New Orleans Times-Picayune*, which said Meyers's 34 points, 13 boards, and 3 assists proved "why she is the WBL's top drawing card." The Chicago Hustle's organist pounded out "Jesus Christ, Superstar" when Meyers entered the court, and the crowd gave her a standing ovation.

One evening as Gems trainer Ron Linfonte was taping Meyers for a practice, he glanced up into the stands. "Gee, that guy looks familiar," he said. "That's Don Drysdale," Meyers replied with a smile. Linfonte was impressed; Drysdale was a future Hall of Famer from his pitching days with the Brooklyn Dodgers. "What's he doing here at our practice?" he asked.

Meyers looked slightly embarrassed. ABC was filming a piece on her, she said; Drysdale would be interviewing her over dinner, so the trainer needn't worry about giving her a ride after practice. "I guess they hit it off," Linfonte says. Evidently—Drysdale was "Meyers' biggest fan," the *Star-Ledger* said, attending many of the Gems' games, and the two later married.

Meyers gradually emerged as, if not a savior of the league, at least a beacon. "If the Women's Basketball League (WBL) is to survive its embryonic years, it is going to have to have more players like Ann Meyers," the *Christian Science Monitor* wrote. That kind of media interest itself was a welcome change. "Everywhere we went they had a press conference, but of course, they only wanted to talk to Ann," laughs Hastings.

When the 1979–80 season ended, Meyers had averaged a remarkable 22.2 points (fifth in the league), 10 rebounds (sixth), 6 assists (third), and 5 steals (first) per game, but that was the last the WBL was to see of her. When the 1980–81 season rolled around, the star was nowhere to be found. "No one, it seems, is quite sure where Ann Meyers is," the *Post-Dispatch* reported. "When asked of her whereabouts, a spokesman for the New Jersey Gems . . . said, 'That's a good question. We'd like to know where she is, too.'"

Meyers had been in absentia for nearly a month, and rumors were flying. She wanted to renegotiate her contract because of the money being paid to new rookies, *Sportswoman's T.E.A.M. Basketball Digest* assumed. Or perhaps she wanted to play closer to home. "It is ironic that the WBL, while still in its infancy, has come far enough that Meyers is considering breaching her contract so she can go home to California to play for San Francisco," the *Boston Globe*'s Lesley Visser wrote.

On November 7, 1980, Gems general manager Ed Kozma sent Meyers a telegram: "Because of your failure to honor the terms of your contract, we put you on notice to return your company car immediately and further wish to inform you of a $200 a day fine for missing training camp commencing 11/6/80." Meyers wouldn't be there, she said, because she hadn't received all the money under her contract from the prior season. Her final check from the Gems for $10,000 had bounced.

"It was the principle of the thing," she says. Her relationship with Gems management had been rocky at times, in part because of unreasonable expectations, Meyers says. "They would ask you to do appearances, but they didn't want to pay you for it. They wanted you to show up at a dinner reception with some of the sponsors or fans afterward—well, were we obligated to do that? Are you trying to make this a college thing, or is this a pro thing? We were treated like girls, not women, not a profession."

Meyers felt it was important to take a stand. Still, she missed basketball. "I was constantly on the phone with my brother, saying, 'Should I go back?'" The Gems' new coach and teammate Carol Blazejowski had asked her to reconsider. "I wanted to play with Blaze," Meyers says, "but I couldn't, because of the organization. It left a bad taste in my mouth."

In January 1981, Meyers traveled to Omaha to work out with the Nebraska Wranglers. (It was "kinda cool" to practice with such a legend, Wranglers rookie Janet Flora remembers. "I thought she was going to be bigger than me, but she wasn't.") The Gems objected, pointing out that Meyers's contract dispute was still in arbitration. If Meyers signed with Nebraska, attorney Lyndell Carlin Jr. warned, the Gems would sue. "They blackballed me," she says. "And the rest is history."

An arbitrator finally closed the door on the Meyers holdout, ruling that New Jersey still held all rights to her. "I look back today, and I think, did they care?" Meyers says. She wondered if the arbitrator really took a professional woman basketball player's claim as seriously as he would have a man's claim. "I'm sitting there in the arbitration, and I was just stunned, because it was my understanding that bouncing a $10,000 check was a federal offense. And that just didn't seem to matter." (However, "neither the Gems nor the WBL itself are totally blameless in this matter," the arbitrator added.) The ruling was issued in May 1981, too late to matter to the WBL, which closed its doors not long afterward. Meyers ended up losing money by giving up her Pacers contract but says she is not bitter. "It was new, and everybody was trying to learn," she says. "A lot of mistakes were made, but a lot of good things came out of those mistakes. No question in my mind, the WBL was the forefront of what the WNBA is today."

Another WBL player later ventured into "the wrong league." In the summer of 1980, Old Dominion star Nancy Lieberman joined a summer league with NBA players in preparation for the WBL, and a year later she was invited to play in the Los Angeles Lakers summer pro basketball league. ("Beating the Supreme Court to the punch, the Lakers put a woman on their bench Sunday night," the *Los Angeles Times* quipped. Sandra Day O'Connor had been nominated to the nation's highest court two weeks earlier.)

Coaching the summer team was assistant Pat Riley, who did not seem thrilled with the idea. "[Lakers owner Jerry] Buss suggested he wanted to give her a look, a tryout," he said. "I believe in the chain of command." So did the Lakers trainer—to a point. Handing Lieberman a bag, he sent her into the locker room with her male teammates and then watched as the young woman drew out her workout gear—including a jock strap. Lieberman wasn't fazed, though. "Yo, trainer!" she called. "This jock's too small. If you want me to play I'm going to need something much bigger!"

Lieberman held no illusions about competing in the NBA at her lean five feet ten inches. "I fall into the category of midget in this league," she acknowledged; indeed, she was one of only two players under six feet in the entire sixteen-team league. "Pound for pound, inch for inch, Nancy Lieberman is the greatest woman basketball player ever," wrote columnist Skip Bayless. "But no matter how big her heart, the redhead will always stand 5–10 and weigh about 150 and be white and never, ever play in the NBA."

When Lieberman stepped onto the court in a qualifying game against the Atlanta Hawks, half the crowd cheered, and half booed—"another victory perhaps for the Moral Majority," suggested Jim Poyner of the *Dallas Morning News*. She ended up with two missed shots (she was fouled on the second, Riley insisted) two assists, and a foul. In 1986 Lieberman became the first woman to play in a men's professional basketball league, the United States Basketball League.

14

Out-of-Bounds

He is the worst that ever lived. • **Martha Hastings**

Let me tell you, the man had "666" written across his skull. • **Ann Platte**

That guy was crazy. I mean, I didn't dislike him. He was just crazy. • **Vonnie Tomich**

Oh, boy. • **Pearl Moore**

DORVAL AIRPORT, MONTREAL, 1986
Gwen Lord had just seen someone off at the airport when she recognized the familiar face of a former student. "Liz!" Lord walked over to have a word with the other woman but quickly realized that something was wrong. The woman's appearance was disheveled, and she wasn't making much sense. She was staying at the airport, Liz said, because she was waiting to tell the prime minister "what had been done to her."

Lord was saddened. This woman, later picked up as a vagrant, was Elizabeth Silcott, one of the greatest—and most controversial—basketball players in Canadian history. Six years earlier, she had also been one of the greatest—and most controversial—players in the Women's Professional Basketball League.

Few players in the WBL generated as much excitement, or as much furor, as Elizabeth Silcott of the St. Louis Streak. "Liz the Whiz" was an anomaly in the league: one of the few black players to become a major draw, a short, older player who was unstoppable by anyone—except, perhaps, herself.

Silcott was originally from Montreal, the only daughter among four

children born to a West Indian railroad worker and a Canadian government employee. Silcott's family was one of two black families in a white
neighborhood, and she was subjected to verbal abuse at times, but she
became close friends with a white girl who lived just six doors down the
street.

"Silcott the girl was fun and adventurous," Linda Rajotte recalls. "She
was the one to walk on fence rails instead of the sidewalk. She was the
one who took me down the back alley behind a bakery to ask for free
bagels." (They usually scored one bagel each, hot from the oven.) In high
school Silcott's playground-honed skills led her basketball team to the city
championship. "We were the only two players on the school basketball team
never to be substituted during any game—ever—during the five years we
played," Rajotte says.

After high school Silcott became a remarkably successful, but increasingly
troubled, basketball nomad, as chronicled in the 2001 documentary *Slipping
through the Hoops* by Elitha Peterson Productions. Before her college career
began, though, Silcott was jarred by the brutal murder of her older brother,
who was found in a ditch, strangled with piano wire.

In 1972 a coach helped Silcott get a scholarship to the University of British
Columbia. In spite of her height (she was only five-feet-six), Silcott could
break any defense, and she twice led UBC to the Canadian championship.
The strange behavior that plagued her career was already beginning to
emerge, though. As a member of the Canadian National Team, Silcott
constantly vexed coach Jack Donahue. She played well, but she was undis-
ciplined and refused to work hard in practice. Teammates resented her, and
she was eventually waived. She had a poor attitude, the coach concluded.

Looking for a place to land, Silcott ended up shooting baskets one day in
the gymnasium at Montreal's Loyola College. "You'd better come have a look
at this," someone advised coach Pat Boland, and she did—quickly adding
Silcott to her team, which immediately went from "pretty bad" to winning
the Quebec championship. Meanwhile, the Canadian National Team got a
new coach as it prepared for the upcoming Olympics, and Silcott was given
another chance. Led by their Most Valuable Player, the Canadians suddenly
became a force in international basketball, defeating every opponent at least
once in the 1975–76 season.

"But even when she was at her best during this time, there was a side to
Liz that made her a difficult, if not impossible, teammate," Sylvia Sweeney
said. To those she played with, Silcott seemed "eccentric," "childlike," and

emotionally and socially immature. She refused to warm up or practice seriously, and she laughed at teammates from the stands as they ran suicide drills. Canadian sportswriter Bob McDevitt noticed her erratic behavior and shouting matches with the coach. "There's something terribly wrong here," he concluded.

Just days before the 1976 Olympics in Montreal opened, coach Brian Heaney kicked Silcott off the team. The timing seemed "particularly cruel" to Silcott, Boland thought. It "tore her heart right out," her brother Bobby Silcott said. And instead of having a chance to medal as expected, Canada lost every game. "I'm sure why we failed at the Olympics and did so poorly was because we spent two years depending on a great player like Liz, then you take her out of the lineup at the eleventh hour," Canadian player Chris Critelli said.

A year later, the National Team had yet another new coach, Don McRae, and even after hearing the stories, he allowed Silcott back on the team. "No matter what the warning signs were, no coach could resist Liz," Sweeney said. While the team was on tour in Poland, Silcott's teammates insisted they couldn't go on with her, and McRae told Silcott he was sending her home. Her teammates ultimately relented, and Silcott made it through the rest of the season. She then enrolled in the University of Waterloo to get her master's degree in recreation, again single-handedly turning a mediocre basketball program into a powerhouse, and her 28.7 points per game earned her All-Canadian honors.

In 1979 Silcott ventured to the United States to try her luck with the Women's Professional Basketball League. Although at twenty-eight she was one of the wbl's oldest players, she was "an outstanding physical specimen who plays with the quickness, speed and stamina of the league's youngest players," sportswriter Lacy Banks praised. She signed with the St. Louis Streak, and the fireworks soon began. The league's most volatile player was about to meet the league's most volatile coach.

On the bench for St. Louis was thirty-year-old Larry Gillman, a former men's basketball coach at East Carolina University whose intensity disturbed many Streak players. "You'd practice, and in the end he would just tell everybody, 'You are all just a piece of shit,' and walk out of the room," says Martha Hastings. "He would do that all the time. He was a nut." Draft pick Glenda Springfield Scott reported to training camp but left early. "I think she was really scared of me," Gillman says.

She wasn't the only one. To this day, the coach's name evokes strong emotions. "Excuse my language, but he was a bastard, and I don't say that about too many people," says Ann Platte. Carol Almond is more diplomatic. "I know I was young and maybe not as tolerant as I am now—well, a little more immature too," she acknowledges, "but yeah, he was kind of crazy, I thought. And he wasn't any fun to play for. He motivated by fear and aggression."

During one road game in Minnesota, the Streak were joined by owner Vince Gennaro for the halftime locker room talk. While discussing second-half adjustments, Gillman noticed that player Jeannie Loyd did not seem to be paying attention. "Jeannie!" he yelled. "What did I just say?" Loyd teared up, Gillman says, because she didn't know the answer. "Jeannie, you know what?" he asked. "Poor Vince over there is paying you a salary to pay attention and to listen, not to sit there like a dope!"

Streak guard Pearl Moore remembers a time she was guarding a player on the wing at practice when she saw a guard dribbling into the lane. "I'm thinking, 'Which is the closest to the basket, the girl going down the lane or the girl standing out there?'" She hurried over to the ballhandler, who then dished a pass to the now wide-open wing player for an easy jump shot. Gillman "went off," Moore says, and she walked out. She returned the next day, and neither said a word about the incident.

Did Gillman have a temper? "With the players?" he asks. "I never had a temper with ownership or anybody outside. Your temper with the players was not really a temper, it was discipline." When he wanted to get his point across, he did; he had no intention of coddling players. "I think they had a hard time adjusting to me."

Darla Plice didn't have a problem with Gillman, but she wondered if coaching in the wBL was really his true desire. "I believe he knew the game, I just think he had some frustrations, maybe, coaching women," she says. "I think he had visions of bigger things, and this was just kind of a filler for him." Whether players disliked Gillman depended on their own reaction to him, Plice thinks. "If you let him get to you, then you had problems, but if you just kind of blew it off and took it with a grain of salt, then you didn't have a problem with him."

St. Louis media often questioned the coach's interaction with his players. "I didn't really care," Gillman says. "The press made me out to be a tough guy. My job was just to try to win games." If the players were offended, "well, they were getting paid. What is it, recreation?"

The Streak coach was not the kind of man who would put up with much attitude, even from a star player. "Larry Gillman had a very strong personality, and a lot of conviction about how to do things," says Gennaro. "I think Liz, who was an extraordinary talent, was frankly a little difficult to harness. She had a lot of independence in her own way. So you had two strong-willed, very independent people banging heads with one another."

The two didn't even make it to the first game. When the 1979–80 season began, Silcott was nine hundred miles away, having gone back to Canada. "The problem was, Elizabeth didn't like to practice," Gillman said. ("That's an understatement," says teammate Tonyus Chavers.) No, Silcott countered, she left because Gillman had "insulted" her a lot in practice.

The Streak opened with four straight losses, but then, suddenly, Silcott was back. The timing wasn't coincidental, Gillman theorized. "Most super players find training sessions drudgery," he said. "When she wasn't consistent in practice the trouble started. Once the season starts, there is hardly any practice. Now, the games are fun for Elizabeth."

Very fun. "If Elizabeth Silcott earned her livelihood in a high-profile sport, she could name her price for endorsements," the *St. Louis Post-Dispatch* raved. "Until such time as the Women's Pro Basketball League comes of age, this amazing young lady's skills will remain hidden under the proverbial bushel." The night before, fewer than three hundred people had seen Silcott pour 46 points into a double-overtime thriller against the San Francisco Pioneers.

Gillman proceeded to structure his team around Silcott, and the Streak's fortunes rose or fell with its star ("so goes the team as Liz goes," Almond says), but most of her teammates did not seem to mind. Other talented players had egos and wanted their piece of the action, Plice says, but she never saw any real resentment of Silcott's dominance.

"Liz the Whiz was a magician," Chavers declares. Play 1 was to get the ball to Silcott, she says, "and Play 2 was get it to her again." That's about right, according to Gillman. "I used to set up a 1–4 offense. Most people set up a 1–4 four across and one at the top, right? When I put the 1–4, I put them all down on the baseline, two people in the corner and two at the low posts. I would give Silcott the ball at the top, and just let her go," he says. "She would either score or get fouled every time. No matter what they did, they couldn't guard her."

Other teams were well aware of what was coming if teammates passed to Silcott. The guard was a "black hole" (balls went in and didn't come back out), says New Orleans Pride forward Sandra Smallwood. Once Silcott had the ball, "it was pretty much going to be a one on one—she was going to the hoop." But knowing what Silcott was going to do and stopping her were two different things. "Spread out the offense, give Silcott the ball and the results are academic," the *Post-Dispatch* said: "Two points."

Attendance at Streak games picked up as word spread about the Whiz. Early in the season, she set a new WBL scoring record in a remarkable performance described by the *Post-Dispatch*:

> It was after Liz Silcott had scored 50 points on shots from every-where but the towers of Union Station and from every imaginable position—including the tuck, twist and double-pike positions—that The Whiz put on a show worthy of Broadway.
>
> With 34 seconds remaining in Wednesday night's Women's Basket-ball League game at Kiel Auditorium and the St. Louis Streak leading the Minnesota Fillies by three points, Silcott took an inbounds pass at halfcourt and began to dribble out the clock. Manipulating the ball with the glib precision of a Marques Haynes, the former Harlem Globetrotter, Silcott slipped between and maneuvered around the Fillies. Four hounds furiously chased Silcott for 20 seconds before the magic ended when The Whiz passed to Streak forward Venita Griffey, who was standing alone under the basket. The two points insured the Streak's 93–90 victory.

"Silcott is so brilliant, she's almost boring," the *St. Louis Globe-Democrat* enthused. With that brilliance came attitude, though. She was "cocky" and "arrogant," some teammates felt, but Silcott said she was just standing up her for herself. "Coaches treat you too often as a non-entity and women, especially blacks, are supposed to be ignorant, gullible and take all that foul language and crap," she said. "I don't appreciate that. People had better respect me properly or I won't perform for them. It's just that simple."

The Streak were now 10-2 since their 0-4 start, but the same conflicts that led to Silcott's preseason disappearance still lurked beneath the surface. ("It seems like there was a dispute daily," Almond says.) Word spread that the rookie was rather "head-strong," or a "head case." "I remember what a phenomenal athlete she was," says Tom Davis, director of operations for the Houston Angels that year, "but I also knew what kind of fruitcake she was as well."

Silcott wasn't that much of a problem at first, Gillman says, but after a while she became a little tough to handle. The coach says he was thankful to keep her together for two or three months. "I'll tell you, I enjoyed winning. She made me look good, but boy, oh boy, would she drive you crazy." Evidently—just five weeks into the season, Streak managers admitted they had talked to several clubs about trading Silcott (although they were having second thoughts after two 40-point performances).

Matters finally came to a head in mid-January 1980, when Silcott publicly demanded a trade. She and Gillman could not get along, she said. As an example, she mentioned a recent close loss. Gillman "came over and said, 'You shot eight of 15 from the foul line. You lost the game for us,'" Silcott accused. "Here I was mentally drained from the game. I had scored 34 points and had 10 assists and tried my best and then he said I lost the game. I don't think it was called for. I was hurt." Gillman had also told the press that Silcott was fundamentally unsound and immature (both of which were largely true).

Another sore point was her salary, which was lower than the reported league average of $10,000. Gillman, however, said there wasn't much interest in Silcott at other teams, which Houston assistant coach Greg Williams confirms. "Liz was crazy," he says. "I don't know if Liz could stand anybody. Liz had her own agenda. She burned her uniform once. I don't know the whole story, but there were stories about her." Gillman was often calling to pitch trades, usually involving Silcott, and Houston's coaches joked about what it would be like to have her on a team. "We would go, 'Will you please run a suicide today, just one? The rest of the team has run ten.' She just had a reputation of being unmanageable."

Perhaps not unmanageable, Gillman says, just difficult. "She never missed a practice," he emphasizes. "If she didn't come, she would have been out on her butt a lot sooner." Everyone—teammates, owners, and coach—made concessions because of Silcott's talent, Gillman said. For example, he didn't yell at her as much as he would someone else. "The coach is a disciplinarian who has said on more than one occasion, 'I rule this team.' The player is a free spirit who has a casual attitude toward defense (although she turned five steals into 10 points Thursday night)," the *Post-Dispatch* summarized. "No understanding has been reached between the two conflicting philosophies."

St. Louis owner Vince Gennaro acknowledged the dilemma. "Without her we're a team without 34 points, eight assists and five steals a game," he said. "I don't know what will happen. I don't want to play without her. And I don't want to play against her." The fans didn't want to play without Silcott, either. At the next home game, "Trade Gillman" and "Liz is the franchise" posters were wielded by some of the record 3,430 fans who watched a battle between division leaders (won by the New York Stars in spite of 38 points from Silcott).

Interest in the Streak was growing, not only among fans, but also in the media, as reflected in superior game stories and action shots, and in other, more subtle, ways. Box scores, which had been limited to halftime and final scores and player point tallies, began to include other tidbits. Scanning the box score from a close game against the California Dreams, for example, readers could now learn that Adrian Mitchell not only had 24 points but also had 10 rebounds, 5 assists, and 2 steals.

The discontent between Gillman and Silcott seemed to simmer down for a while, but in early February 1980 came a headline shocker: "Streak's Silcott Is on Suspension." The player had contacted another team to suggest a trade, Gennaro said. "The problems are with money and her ability to get along with the coach. It's a combination of both. I just don't know if we can solve them permanently."

Again, Silcott's take differed. It was a publicity stunt, she declared. Yes, she had talked to the general manager of the California Dreams, but only about a friend who had joined the team. They did not discuss a trade, she insisted, although the situation in St. Louis had not improved. "I really don't know what to do," she said. "I can't deal with these people any more. Did you hear Larry scream at me during the last game? It's getting worse every game. Perhaps it would be better for me if I were traded."

She got her wish. The San Francisco Pioneers had lost some players and were looking for a spark. "By that time it was getting to be, 'OK, the heck with what's going on with the rest of the league, let's just try to keep some semblance of a team out on the court,'" says Pioneers president Marshall Geller. "Let's have some excitement to it. Let's score some points and maybe win some games." (Silcott was leading the league in scoring at the time with 33.1 points per game, along with 5.8 assists.)

Geller had heard the rumors about Silcott, but he figured some of it was Streak management's fault. "She told us that they treated her awful, and we said to her, 'Look, we're nice people, we're honorable people, we'll pay you when we owe you money. We just expect you to play, and we expect you to be part of a team and so forth.'"

On February 11, 1980, Silcott was packed off to San Francisco for a fifth-round pick in the 1980–81 draft and guard Lisa Brewer—who then refused to report to St. Louis. "Thirty-three points per game for nothing," the *Post-Dispatch* lamented. The Streak's owner, though, said that Brewer was secondary in the trade, which was prompted by Silcott's demand for more than $100,000, including certain incentive clauses. Her salary had already been bumped from $6,000 to $10,000.

It was the money, not the attitude, that forced the trade, Gillman says. "The moping in practice, we looked the other way. I've had guys that were bigger problems than that." Gillman knew how good Silcott was, but he didn't think she was irreplaceable. (She was—the Streak lost their next twenty games.) "I thought we could change things around and still win because she was a pain in the ass. But if I look back on it right now, I would have just said, 'Hey, either you'll play for the $6,000 and shut your mouth or go home,' and I wouldn't have traded her."

Silcott "kept it together fairly well" with the Pioneers for a while, Geller says, but conflict again surfaced. "It just ended up being a disaster." The Pioneers, second in their division at the time with a 16-12 record, suffered two successive losses. "Losing at home twice is a surprise any time, but especially because the Pioneers were expected to be much improved after the addition of high-scoring Liz 'the Whiz' Silcott," wrote the *San Francisco Examiner*. Silcott seemed to have "considerable trouble" working in with the team, it noted.

It would take time to fit Silcott into the system, Pioneers coach Frank LaPorte said optimistically. "Our other players don't know what she's going to do, where she's going to go, when she's going to give up the ball. So instead of moving and creating passing lanes they were standing around." Her new teammates were especially unhappy with Silcott's "ball hogging," the *Dallas Morning News* reported; in 28 minutes per game, she was taking nearly 15 shots.

"Silcott never really worked out," Geller says. "She was a tough act, a very unhappy lady." There was always something, always a problem, he recalls, and he finally decided, "I've got to stay away from her or I'm going to throw her off [the team]." Her new teammates hated playing with her, and the Pioneers lost yet again. Finally, LaPorte placed her on the inactive list with two games left in the season.

"For Silcott to be effective, the team must be built around her, which means she must be with the team from the start," concluded *Chronicle* columnist Glenn Dickey. The coach also had to be hard-line, Gillman believes. "Frank couldn't win with her because Frank was just—God bless him—a wonderful, softer guy than I was."

After the 1979–80 season ended, the Pioneers traded the rights to Silcott to the Dallas Diamonds for "future draft considerations." When the details didn't work out between those teams, the Pioneers traded her again, this time to an expected Florida franchise for a third-round draft pick. When the Tampa Bay Sun dissolved, Silcott declared herself a free agent.

A WBL franchise had just been awarded in New England, and Silcott flew there for tryouts. Already on the Gulls roster was Chris Critelli, who had played with Silcott on the Canadian National Team. Silcott was a troublemaker, Critelli knew, and she didn't want to be on the same team again. She approached Gulls coach Jim Loscutoff, a nine-year veteran of the NBA's Boston Celtics. "Listen, I played with Liz on my national team," she told him. "It's disruptive, and I can't do it any more."

Critelli was surprised at Loscutoff's response. "Chris, I have seen hundreds of Liz Silcotts in the NBA, and she is not making this team," he said. But Silcott was very good, one of the best players in Canada; Critelli didn't want to be responsible for the franchise losing that kind of talent. "No, just send me to another team," she offered. Forget it, Loscutoff said. "She's not making the team." Critelli was impressed. In Canada, her coaches had all believed—or wanted to believe, because of Silcott's sheer talent—that they could "fix" her.

Silcott's next stop was a brief stint in New Mexico with the newly formed Ladies Professional Basketball Association. That league folded after only a few games, though, and her brilliant career was over. "If you had to sum up this league, and you had to talk about one player," Gillman says, "it would have to be Silcott, because she was like the league. It didn't last, and she didn't last."

Silcott returned to Waterloo, Ontario, where she was essentially aimless, reappearing unexpectedly at the doorstep of former coaches. She was picked up for vagrancy at a Montreal airport in 1986, and another former teammate saw her begging on a street corner. That same year, Silcott called Sweeney and asked for $35. The conversation was strange, Sweeney thought, and she convinced Silcott to meet with her.

Silcott was diagnosed with a longstanding mental illness and was admitted to a psychiatric hospital. "She certainly acted like it," says Geller. So why didn't anyone realize it earlier? "If she were young and playing today, would her illness have been diagnosed and treated earlier?" UBC athletics historian Fred Hume asked in 2002. Without question, the level of sophistication, particularly in women's sports, was much lower at the time, and even obvious physical ailments escaped attention at times.

Midway through the 1980–81 season, for example, New Jersey Gems player Jill Jeffrey became ill with increasingly severe abdominal pain during a road trip. "Everybody on the team had their own philosophy as to what it was," she recalls. "You know, 'Do more sit ups. Take a hot bath.' They were jumping on my stomach." Finally, she was diagnosed with appendicitis.

In Chicago, Hustle guard Janie Fincher found herself unable to make a simple lay-up. "I would approach the goal and get real close to it, and then all of a sudden it would become a big blur. I would lay it up there, and it wouldn't even be close." One day at practice, the frustrated player stood in front of the basket, staring up at it and wondering, "Why can't I shoot a lay-up?" Because she needed glasses, she later learned.

While still in college, one future WBL player began acting bizarrely. "We would be in practice, and we'd be running a scrimmage, and all of a sudden [she] would start walking around in circles," recalls a teammate who also played in the WBL. An extended hospital stay revealed nothing. "They removed all of her hair and she wore a bandanna, but they never found out what it was." Surprisingly, it did not interfere with her basketball career. "[She] was just so good and wanted to play," her teammate marvels.

With athletes, behavior that would normally raise concerns is often shrugged off as mere eccentricity, Sweeney believes. When those around her reached their limit with Liz Silcott—and they all did—they attributed it to arrogance or immaturity, not a deeper problem. "No one noticed she was in trouble," Sweeney said in 2001. "All they said was, 'Liz *is* trouble.' Were we all so focused on winning, so focused on using her talent, that we just couldn't see her for who she was?"

Twenty-five years after her spectacular WBL season, Silcott lived in a group home in Hamilton, Ontario, on government disability. Her condition required medication, with multiple side effects, and her memories were mostly gone. Once in a while, Vince Gennaro thinks back on that night in 1979 when Liz the Whiz Silcott scored 50 points in a single game. "For a very brief moment, the Streak was absolutely the focal point of St. Louis sports," he remembers. "And that was exciting."

15

Benched

Pursuant to the direction of the Board of Governors of the Women's Professional Basketball League, at their meeting held September 8, 1980, you are hereby terminated for cause from all positions held in the Women's Professional Basketball League and WBL Properties effective immediately. • **Robert J. Milo to William J. Byrne**, September 18, 1980

WBL founder Bill Byrne has especially fond memories of his creation's first season. "We started with eight, and finished with eight," he says proudly. League officials put everything they had into the cause that year. "It wasn't a job, it was a way of life for all of us," says public relations director Kate McEnroe. "People lived, ate, and breathed it, working seven days a week, 365 days a year. I think we took off Christmas Day, and that was about it."

When it was over, the hard work had paid off. None of the owners made any money, but all of the teams made it through the season. (It did require a little scrambling when the Dayton Rockettes began to list, and the league infused nearly $100,000 to get the franchise through the season. Although Dayton was a sore point, it didn't generate much fallout, McEnroe says. "I think we skated because it was so young.")

The management scuffles that eventually ended with Byrne's ouster began in earnest during the WBL's second season. "It was so nice that first year," Byrne says. "Forget about the second year. . . . The power moves started and the money became different, and the third year it was another matter."

As the 1979–80 season started, the WBL had seven new teams (including one transplanted from Dayton), and newcomers were inquisitive. What about franchises that weren't paying their players? asked Steve Brown, general manager of the New Orleans Pride, at a contentious WBL Board of Governors meeting on October 5, 1979. A team that owed money to any player should be barred from the draft, he urged, and the player should be able to declare herself a free agent. The league could make up the unpaid salary and fine the member. Brown's motion was seconded by Marshall Geller, manager of the new San Francisco Pioneers, but was tabled.

Two other owners questioned the league's advertising and promotion efforts, but Byrne ruled them "out of order" when they requested a copy of the budget. Did promotions director Nancy Sarnoff even have a budget? Chicago Hustle co-owner Larry Cooper interrupted. Not exactly, she said, but she was reimbursed for expenses. Perhaps the league could hire a professional merchandiser, suggested Eric Kraus, a principal with the new Philadelphia Fox franchise. It was too close to the season, the board decided, and the motion was withdrawn.

Meanwhile, a few original members complained about a requirement that they buy their merchandise from WBL licensees. The Minnesota Fillies had made their own arrangements for shoes, owner Gordon Nevers said, and he also wanted to license Fillies caps himself. The Hustle would likewise buy from whomever they chose, Cooper declared. No, vice president Dave Almstead warned, the rights to logos, club names, and so on were held by WBL Properties, which would "take whatever steps necessary" to enforce its contract.

Cooper and co-owner Sherwin Fischer were now Chicago's representatives at WBL Board of Governors meetings—they had been forced to leave a meeting in May 1979—replacing former Hustle president John Geraty. ("As we progressed, there was no money except from Cooper and myself to put into the team," Fischer says, and they felt that Geraty was too close to the players.)

Now the two men were dogging WBL management. "Cooper and Fischer fought me hand and foot," Byrne says. "They fought me daily, but that was great for me. I didn't give a shit. They would come to meetings, and I would look at them and bring the meeting to order, and they would hide behind each other."

The Chicago group were the most focused of all the owners, says Geller. "They wanted control of the league. They wanted to throw Bill Byrne out and they wanted Sherwin in." Geller was annoyed at the pair's suggestion that the league needed Chicago as the "flagship" of the WBL. "I kept saying, 'Are you guys crazy? The league doesn't revolve around Chicago to begin with. The league is going to make it in L.A. and New York, and Chicago is going to be important, but why should we let you become the commissioner?' There was a battle. You have no idea of the battles."

But Byrne's relocation of WBL headquarters to expensive New York City offices had irritated otherwise supportive owners like Geller. "What in the world does this league need offices on Park Avenue when they don't have a TV contract?" Geller recalls thinking. "If you have a TV contract, I don't care what you do. If you don't have a TV contract, then put your offices on Second Avenue or Third Avenue."

A month into the 1979–80 season, Byrne came under fire again when the Philadelphia Fox and Washington Metros franchises collapsed. "The league has been financially mismanaged from the top by Bill Byrne and Dave Almstead from the very beginning," Fox coach Dave Wohl said. Byrne had signed player contracts knowing the team had no owners, he accused.

Byrne denied it. "Contrary to what folk think, those teams really had owners," he insisted. "I still have in my possession signed checks and approved membership papers. But they turned out to be bad checks and I was left holding the bag."

That was not entirely true. On September 28, 1979, Eric Kraus was granted a Philadelphia team, but the agreement also required the league to arrange $250,000 in funding before the season started. Kraus was only required to put up $20,000 in cash; the rest of the $100,000 franchise fee wasn't due until the investment money materialized, which never happened.

Almstead told the press that the league had funneled about $100,000 into the Philadelphia operation while searching for new owners, but Byrne says it was his money, not the league's, that kept the two franchises afloat. "I gave them credit cards, that's how stupid I was, instead of folding."

Byrne didn't give a damn about the people in the league, Wohl said, "he just wants the reputation of being at the top, like Pete Rozelle, Larry O'Brien and Bowie Kuhn." The Fox had received no help from Byrne and his "sidekick" (Almstead), he asserted. "We call them Bonzo and Howdy Doody. We'll call up and say, 'We have a phone bill for $1,800 that's three months overdue. The phone company says they're taking out our phones,' and they'll go, 'Well, stall them.'"

Byrne still seethes about Wohl's accusations. "Dave Wohl was so detrimental and lied," the league founder says—and that's all he will say. Fox players were "victims," a *Philadelphia Inquirer* article declared, and the WBL a "schlock pro league." Almstead fired off a bitter reply. The piece resembled a gossip column with "the distinct taint of crucifixion rather than journalistic license, even in its broadest sense," he wrote. Because salaries were spread over twelve months, players had actually received more money than they were due at that point, he claimed. Wohl disagreed. "I'm just generally bleeped at the way these kids have been treated," he said. "If I had the money, I'd sit down and write out their paychecks myself."

One month later, Byrne took another hit when Dallas owner Jud Phillips called a press conference to announce that he was closing the franchise. He had taken in less money than he spent on advertising alone, Phillips says now. "We couldn't find any investors. I probably lost my voice talking to people trying to sell them partnerships. Sophisticated businessmen weren't going to do it. It was a pie in the sky deal."

An hour after Phillips said the team would officially close its doors, the other owners held an emergency conference call. They were wary of operating the franchise themselves, but to lose another team would be devastating. A new owner stepped in, but the incident generated more bad publicity.

"There's talk of impeaching Byrne during all-star break," the *New York Post*'s Peter Vecsey claimed. Not exactly—at their next meeting the owners gave Byrne a unanimous vote of confidence "for his actions in his official capacity with the League in relation to his efforts in founding, developing and operating the WBL." (Perhaps not coincidentally, they were also reminded of Byrne's employment contract at that meeting.)

Cooper came away from the meeting feeling good about the WBL's future, he said. "Sure, we've had some problems. Every new business does. But we talked about those problems and decided that we still have 12 solid franchises operating—thanks to Commissioner Byrne. Nobody could have put this together better than he did." New York Stars owner Steve McCarthy added his own endorsement. "We feel he's doing a marvelous job and have asked him to stay on through next year."

The respite did not last long, and by the end of the season, owners were unhappy with Byrne and Almstead again, this time for a deal the two cut with a group that took over the Houston Angels. After losing $275,000 in his first year, Angels owner Hugh Sweeney had found a backer willing to provide funds, but there was a catch. The franchise would be pledged as collateral, and the league had to cosign for the loan.

In September 1979 Byrne signed an agreement obligating the league to pay Gerard Haynes $100,000 to redeem the franchise if Sweeney didn't repay the loan. The agreement was later renegotiated to encourage Haynes to advance more funds, with the league on the hook if Sweeney did not cover the notes by June 15, 1980. The deadline arrived, and Haynes' attorney, Earl D. Elliott, promptly made demand. The league could either pay up now, he offered, or dip into its merchandising rights and future membership fees until Haynes got his $250,000 back.

The June 15, 1980, board of governors meeting in New York City was a pivotal moment in the WBL's history. Atop the agenda was a cash flow problem that Byrne hoped to resolve with an emergency assessment against each team. Before the meeting, though, several owners met privately to discuss the future of league management (specifically, Byrne's role), ending in a move to turn league operations over to an executive committee consisting of St. Louis Streak owner Vince Gennaro, Chicago Hustle owner Larry Cooper, and New Jersey Gems owner Robert Milo.

Byrne saw the change for what it was—a coup. A staffer had warned him before the meeting that half the owners were plotting against him, but Byrne had at least five or six votes if he fought it, he calculated. "I went a little crazy in New York," he says. "I remember that day at Rockefeller Plaza where we called a recess to a meeting. [New York Stars owners] Steve McCarthy and Ed Reisdorf were sitting where they ice skate in the summertime. We were sitting under a nice canopy having lunch, and I said, 'Steve, I am going to resign today.'"

McCarthy urged him not to, Byrne says, and suggested an alternative. "Here's what we'll do. We'll keep the league office here. We'll move the New York Stars in there. You become the general manager and run the New York Stars. I'll back you for any other money to do it."

"No, they've had enough of me and I've had enough of them, and it's time for me to go," Byrne says he told McCarthy. He figured "that Chicago group" was going to force a move of league headquarters. "Steve, if they move this league office to Chicago, it will kill it. It will kill it," he said.

The men returned to the meeting. There, Byrne says, he looked around the table. "I knew where the votes lay, always knew." By his count, he would have the tiebreaker if he tried to force the issue. Instead, he accepted the changes, which he now says was a mistake. "Hindsight, I would have never run. I would have held on for the league. . . . If I had gone back into that meeting more forcefully . . ."

The owners were ready to toss Byrne out because "he was just absolutely impossible," says Geller. "Bill had a very bad habit. He used to tell you that he sold three new franchises and tomorrow the money is coming in," which would have helped struggling teams. "But the money never came. So it finally got to a point where everybody wanted to throw him out."

Minnesota owner Gordon Nevers felt it was time for a change. "After two years of promises, two years of grandiose conversation about what was going to happen, I think that a lot of us were a little disenchanted with what we were being told was going to happen and actually what did take place," he says. Gennaro believed that a greater level of leadership was needed to move the league forward and to build what owners envisioned. "Well, Bill, I think you have brought this as far as you can bring it," he told Byrne. "You might be right," Byrne replied.

It was a tough afternoon for Byrne. "When I walked out, all I took was my briefcase," he says; he asked his secretary to send on whatever material the new managers wanted him to have. "I never did get it," he says. "I don't know what happened to it, probably one of them got it, or they shipped it to Chicago."

Not so, Fischer said; when league records arrived in Chicago, they didn't include financial documents, especially for merchandising revenue. "That's why Bill Byrne was fired," he says. "We had a suspicion that there was money coming into the league office for merchandising that was not being distributed among the teams. . . . Nobody trusted him after a while." In what appears to be a substantial exaggeration, the *Chicago Sun Times* reported that "the league fired (Byrne) this summer after he allegedly mishandled about $800,000 in league funds."

Byrne disputes the suggestion. "I remember one time a couple of owners forced an audit with me with Haskins and Seals, one of the biggest auditing companies, and they said, 'I hate to break the news to you guys, but you owe Bill about $345,000,'" he says. "They go, 'Ohhh.' It's like one of those things, 'Where is the money going?' That happens when you are not successful—they point their fingers." Some owners later urged him to return to management, Byrne says, but he'd "had it."

Byrne claims that some investors had gotten themselves into serious trouble. "I knew one guy was going to jail," he says. "Then I knew another guy . . . , if the league didn't fold he had no way out. If the league folds, he doesn't have to make that money good. It was over a million dollars." People with big money have big egos, Almstead said after the power shift.

"They don't like to lose money. It's failure and they don't like to fail. They look around for someone to blame. There's the guy who got them into the franchise, so they blame him."

POSTSCRIPT

Byrne wasn't quite through with the WBL. Earlier that year the owners had granted him a franchise in Tampa Bay for his efforts in founding the league, but as the third season approached, Byrne telegrammed a request to sell the franchise to an investor in New England, Joseph Reither. (Byrne denies that he sold the franchise. "I didn't sell it, I gave it away," he says. "I never sold it, no matter what you hear.")

Some owners balked at the transfer, even though eight of the nine had approved Reither's application for a franchise before Byrne became involved. This might seem like a chance to "get even" with Byrne, Geller said (to "stick it to the Riddler," as Tom Davis wrote), but that was shortsighted. Almstead, by then the president of the Dallas Diamonds, and Geller issued a warning. If the transfer didn't go through, they would pull their franchises, two of the strongest. A deal was struck, and Byrne's involvement with the WBL came to an end.

Sherwin Fischer was appointed interim commissioner of the WBL and relocated headquarters to Chicago. "If Fischer had been our commissioner all along, we would have been light years ahead of where we are now," New Orleans Pride owner Claudette Simpson said. "We're still struggling because of early mistakes." The choice of Fischer was "natural," Nevers says; the Hustle was one of the strongest franchises and had captured a certain imagination in Chicago.

The new commissioner's first big challenge was learning which teams would still be around when the third season began in a few months. Earlier that spring, after two franchises folded and two others came close, the board had voted to require each team to show $150,000 in usable assets or else suspend operations. The deadline—"Black Tuesday," Tom Davis called it—was September 30, 1980.

When the fateful day arrived, the casualties were the 1979 champion, Houston Angels; the 1980 champion, New York Stars; the 1979 and 1980 runner-up, Iowa Cornets; and the Milwaukee Express (formerly Does). "This paints a grim picture when the WBL's two best teams fail to survive," a columnist for *Minnesota Basketball* wrote. "What can it say for the rest of the league?"

Perhaps those teams were too busy winning championships to apply themselves to the basics, New Jersey's Milo suggested. "If we don't put people in the seats, we're gone. It's that simple." He was right, Stars player Lynn Arturi believes. "In a way, we placed more emphasis on winning than we did on marketing ourselves. Not that winning wasn't important, but you know, if nobody is coming to see you, who cares?"

In October 1980 Fischer sent an open letter to the league, expressing his hopes for the upcoming season. "Progress is often costly and painful. Usually it's worth it," he wrote. "Let's not forget, we're innovators. . . . We are unique, no longer a curiosity but an important factor in the national professional sports scene. We have a quality product that is producing a new kind of 'Super Star'. A new breed of Heroine."

16

The Super Rookies

People will pay to see me play, to see if I'm over-rated. That's great. If I can be an attraction, that's even better. • **Nancy Lieberman**, *Dallas Times-Herald*, September 24, 1980

They call her "Blaze" for short, and a blaze she is once she gets to wheeling and dealing on a basketball court. . . . She is the Maravich, Dr. J and Abdul-Jabbar of the distaff set, without their million-dollar bank accounts. • **Will Grimsley** on Carol Blazejowski, *Hagerstown Mail*, July 1978

She's the best big player in the country. She's agile and quick. She can shoot from the outside. She has played forward, high post and point guard. She's both a finesse and power player. I don't see anyone coming who can touch her as an inside player. • **Greg Williams** on Inge Nissen, *Dallas Morning News*, June 15, 1980

The WBL's 1980–81 season was expected to be its showcase year. Joining the league would be three players—the super rookies—who were the talk of women's basketball.

NANCY LIEBERMAN

Nancy Lieberman of Old Dominion University was generally considered the best female basketball player in the United States and the principal spokesperson for her sport. "First came Billie Jean King. Then there was Nancy Lopez. In the '70s, they were, pardon the expression, kings of the women's sports movement. Because of them, it became fashionable for women athletes to compete, to win—and to make big bucks," the *San*

Francisco Chronicle wrote in 1980. "Nancy Lieberman hopes to follow them. What King did for tennis and Lopez for golf, she's trying to do in basketball."

As a youth in New York, Lieberman played basketball every day from morning until night, switching to "radar ball" (listening for the sound) when it was too dark to see the basket. In the evenings, she took the subway into Harlem, where she was the only girl and the only white player on a boys' Amateur Athletic Union team called the New York Chuckles.

Over time, Lieberman began playing in summer leagues with other women who later went on to the WBL, including Carol Blazejowski, Gail Marquis, Kathy Mosolino, and Janice Thomas. "They were in Harlem or in the South Bronx or parts of Brooklyn that I wasn't even allowed to go into," Marquis recalls. "We would all come together to play these games, and Nancy would come off the bench with flaming red hair jumping all over everybody."

That hair, and her aggressiveness, earned the teenager the nickname "Fire." While still a senior at Far Rockaway High School, she was named to the 1976 United States Olympic team, admittedly as a role player selected with an eye toward the Moscow games four years down the road.

An Olympian was tempting for hopeful college programs, and Lieberman became the first high school girl to trigger national recruiting efforts, some of which were blatantly illegal. (Offers included a car, a house, and money for points.) She settled on Old Dominion University in Norfolk, Virginia, where she led the school from obscurity to one of the most dominant women's basketball programs in history, also making a name for herself as the preeminent female basketball player of her time.

Lieberman soon developed a reputation as hard to handle. "As for those players [ODU coach Marianne Stanley] inherited, at least one was best approached with a whip and a chair," the *Virginian-Pilot and the Ledger-Star* later wrote. "The fuss over Lieberman was very good for the women's game, and even better for Nancy, a publicity hound. She did not hesitate to make it known that she considered herself bigger than her coach."

In many ways, she was. Few articles were published about women's basketball in the late 1970s that failed to mention Old Dominion's number 10. "She sees the whole floor and throws flashy but fundamentally sound passes," wrote the *New York Times*. "She is an instinctive rebounder and plays elbow-to-the-throat aggressive defense."

The description was literal: Lieberman's elbows were already notorious. At one game in Madison Square Garden a *Times* writer observed Lieberman's "elbows spearing more timid rivals under the baskets" and called her a "one-woman gang." Teammates were not immune. "She had some really sharp elbows," 1976 Olympic teammate Charlotte Lewis laughs. "She hurt a lot of her own players because she was aggressive at all times. That was just her style of play." (Her weapons were unleashed in the WBL, too, Lewis says: Nebraska Wranglers teammates Carol Chason, Holly Warlick, and Susan Taylor "got many an elbow from her.")

It's all true, Lieberman admits. "I would go after you," she says. "That's just the way I had learned to play the game in New York. And I thought that was the way the game should be played. You come across the lane, you're going to get an elbow. You go in for a rebound, you're going to get hit, you're going to get boxed out."

Such aggressiveness and flash were unexpected in female players. "She plays like a man," Dallas sportswriter Anita Seelig said. "She's street tough, having grown up in the streets of New York City, where playing basketball meant pickup games with guys who didn't think girls belonged on the court." Lieberman's game, "in the ultimate compliment, is a man's game," echoed Lesley Visser of the *Boston Globe*. "She can dribble past anybody with either hand, hit the reverse layup, fire the blind-side pass."

The player heard the comparison a lot. Male sportswriters and fans often said to her, "We don't want you to take this wrong, but you play like a guy." Lieberman took it for the compliment it was. "It might not have been ladylike," she says, "but I think my style of play at that point in time changed women's basketball because we hadn't had somebody play that physical consistently."

Quite simply, no women had ever played the game like Lieberman. In many ways, until recently, the women's game had been a completely different world. Lieberman and her ODU teammates were showing fans "the future of women's basketball," wrote the *San Francisco Chronicle*. "Not surprisingly, it looks a lot like the men's version."

Perhaps the ultimate praise for Lieberman's skill came from Abe Lemons, the longtime men's basketball coach at the University of Texas who, columnist Blackie Sherrod wrote, "passes compliments about as often as Loni Anderson calls you at home." Lemons was not a women's basketball fan (he "couldn't give you a used kleenex for all the women's games ever played," Sherrod noted), but he decided to watch the number 2 ranked Texas women's team take on Old Dominion in a televised game. "I ain't familiar with that sport," Lemons said afterward, "but that team had a redhead who could flat *play*. I mean, she could *play!*"

Lieberman also had another skill, almost as crucial to the success of women's basketball: promotion. She was a marketing major, and one of her first lessons had been marketing herself. She was witty, media savvy, and relished her role as a spokesperson. During the summer between graduation and the start of her pro career, she made over fifty promotional appearances.

When the 1980 WBL draft approached, Lieberman's name topped most lists. The Old Dominion senior was probably the most-written-about women's player in the United States, commentator P. G. "Granny" Wethall wrote. "The finest ball handler, either in college or pro and fundamentally very sound. . . . When someone is slightly familiar with women's basketball the one name they remember is Lieberman."

INGE NISSEN

Another rookie expected to take the WBL to a new level was Inge Nissen, Lieberman's teammate at Old Dominion. The "Great Dane" had the height (six feet five inches) and the agility to become a premier college center, earning Most Valuable Player honors in ODU's second straight title. She was "stately with a finishing-school touch," the *New York Times* said.

Nissen had only begun playing at the age of fourteen in her native Denmark, but just two years later she became the youngest player on the Danish National Team. Hoping to join a college team in the United States, she wrote each school on a Top 20 list to see who might be interested in her. Several were, but Nissen doubted the commitment of some programs for whom basic questions like "who's the coach?" seemed beyond them. "Oh, we don't know," she was told. "It was one of those, 'Sure, we'll give you a scholarship—are you a woman? Okay, we'll give it to you.'"

An assistant men's basketball coach at Old Dominion heard about the skilled Danish player while in Europe, and the school was delighted when Nissen agreed to sign on. She shattered more than a dozen school records and became the first woman to break the 1,000- and 2,000-point barriers, improving her game each year. Between her freshman and junior years, for example, free-throw shooting transformed from a weakness (52.3 percent) to a strength (74.7 percent). Nissen punished opponents in the lane with nearly five blocks per game and was a finalist for the Wade Trophy won by her teammate Lieberman.

Nissen was a new element in the women's game, a very tall but very agile center. Her talents were showcased in December 1979, when she faced a taller, more experienced Soviet squad before what was then the largest audience ever to attend a women's basketball game. "Friday night, in ODU's 76–66 loss to the Soviet women, Nissen showed that she is the difference between any chance the United States has of winning a gold medal in Moscow or settling for silver," *Philadelphia Inquirer* sportswriter Mel Greenberg wrote. "Several times the ODU senior brought the crowd at Norfolk to its feet as she muscled by the taller Soviets."

Nissen ended with 21 points and 11 rebounds, a performance so inspirational that ODU coach Marianne Stanley met with Senator John Warner to see if Nissen could get expedited U.S. citizenship for the upcoming Olympics. "It is doubtful that Stanley will succeed," Greenberg predicted, "and that's too bad." (The issue became moot when the United States boycotted the 1980 Olympics.)

CAROL BLAZEJOWSKI

As a young girl, Carol Blazejowski played basketball whenever and wherever she could—indoors, outdoors, it didn't matter. She was a "playground rat," *Sports Illustrated* said in 1981, "weaned at the school of hard picks."

Blazejowski's high school in Crawford, New Jersey, did not offer girls basketball, so she played in Catholic Youth Organization leagues, and when her school finally added a program her senior year (after she threatened to try out for the boys' team), she took her team to the state championship.

In college "the Blaze" became known throughout the country for her uncanny outside shooting, leading Montclair State to the Final Four in 1976. "We were the only non-scholarship Division I school that was ranked in the top twenty," recalls teammate Pat Colasurdo Mayo. "We just had a whole bunch of unselfish players—but when you have someone like Carol Blazejowski on your team, it's easy to be unselfish." Later that year observers were shocked when Blazejowski was not named to the U.S. Olympic team.

On March 1, 1977, the junior made national news by setting the all-time college record—for men or women—at Madison Square Garden with a 52-point performance against rival Queens College. In her senior year, Blaze again broke all previous women's records with a remarkable 38.6 point-per-game scoring average. Over her four years at Montclair State, Blazejowski averaged 31.7 points per game, the all-time high in Division I basketball.

In 1978, Blazejowski was the first recipient of the Wade Trophy honoring the best female basketball player in the nation. She was, one columnist wrote, "so talented that if she were a college she'd probably be put on probation because the NCAA would be sure you can't be that good without cheating." A year later, Blazejowski was the leading scorer on a team that won the World Championships, presaging an emergence of United States dominance in international basketball.

After graduation, the Blaze was drafted by the WBL's New Jersey Gems, who hoped to showcase her to local fans. "I was contacted, and you know, you're always flattered," she says, but the star had other plans. This time there was no question that she would make the 1980 U.S. Olympic roster. "I had been scorned in '76—at least I viewed it that way—so it was take some decent money and play pro or chase your dream," she says. "There was some time spent on the decision-making process." She turned the Gems down.

SIGNING THEM

On June 16, 1980, Lieberman was lounging beside the pool at a celebrity tennis tournament in Las Vegas when she heard herself paged. "Nancy, my name is Dave Almstead," the caller said. "I am the president of the Dallas Diamonds and you are the No. 1 pick of the Women's Professional Basketball League."

Inge Nissen was doing dishes in Virginia when the Chicago Hustle called. "Miss Nissen's secretary," her boyfriend answered. Nissen had been waiting for word because she was worried she might end up in Dallas. (She had not enjoyed some aspects of her recruiting visit there. One comment that especially bothered her was the threat "'If you don't like the contract, we'll just sit you. We won't play you or trade you or anything.' I was like, 'This sounds like great people. I can't wait to come back here and play for you guys.'")

Reaching terms was next—and WBL owners were about to face what Dallas coach Greg Williams called "the Annie Meyers syndrome." In 1979, the New Jersey Gems had signed Ann Meyers for $50,000, and although they didn't have much choice (she had a guaranteed contract with an NBA team for that sum and wouldn't take less from the WBL), it was "going to hurt them," Lieberman warned, "because players like Blazejowski, myself and anybody who comes off that Olympic team are going to feel that they're worth more than $50,000."

If Meyers was worth $50,000, Lieberman declared, then she was worth double that. "I'm different today," Lieberman says, "but at the time, that's how I felt, that's what I believed." She didn't consider herself a world-class negotiator, and taking the position that she was better and younger than Meyers seemed like a good tactic. "Some people might say that's arrogance," she says. "[But] if Mohammed Ali says, 'I'm gonna beat you in three rounds,' [people think] 'that's pretty cool, he predicted what he was going to do.'"

Could the Diamonds—or any team—pay Lieberman's price? "Lieberman can make or break the league," wrote Anita Seelig in the *Dallas Morning News*. "She *is* women's basketball." To Seelig, the team had no choice; it could ill afford a $100,000 salary, but not signing her would be fatal. "If the WBL slams its doors at the Nancy Liebermans, it will live a short life."

Lieberman figured she could quadruple attendance and boost sponsorships. "I'll put fans in the stands and make a winner out of whoever I play with," she said before the draft. "I'll do for the team that drafts me what Magic Johnson did for the Lakers." She gave the Diamonds her demand and waited, upping her market value with promotional appearances and playing in a men's summer pro league.

"Salaries like these are risky in a league that saw some teams run up deficits as large as $300,000 in 1979–80," *Sports Illustrated* writer Roy Johnson warned. Paying them also risked alienating veteran players. "I always had a certain amount of resentment, and it wasn't really their fault," says three-time All-Star Molly Kazmer (then Bolin). "When you're a big star like that, you have agents or lawyers giving you advice that 'this is how it should be, based on the fact that is how they do it in the NBA.' They just never really stepped up to say, 'Yeah, I'm going to help this women's league make it.' It was more like, 'I'm going to be the star and I'm going to make all of the money.'"

Diamonds management had off-court expectations, Lieberman pointed out to critics. "It's not like they're saying, 'okay, Nancy we just want you to play basketball.' No, they want me to take every speaking engagement, go to this shopping center, do this interview, sell this, and then play basketball too. I think I should be paid accordingly. You don't see Nancy Lopez getting elbows in her face do you? I'm not asking for the world."

It didn't look as though Dallas could sign her, balking at her $100,000 demand. ("Do you want that spread over 30 or 40 years?" Almstead asked. "No, just over one," Lieberman replied.) July went by with no contract. And August. And most of September. "It's time for action," the *Morning News* wrote.

Lieberman stayed put in California until she got a call from Dean Meminger, coach of the 1980 WBL champion New York Stars. As recounted in Lieberman's autobiography, Meminger asked when she was going to report to the Diamonds. Not until she heard a better offer, she replied. "Nancy, book a flight and get down there," Meminger urged. "Show those people that you care about the league and want to play. If you have to call your own press conference, then do it. . . . Don't let the public think that you are the bad guy by holding out."

Lieberman signed a contract with the Diamonds on Sept. 23, 1980. The event was announced at a press conference (cleverly scheduled following Dallas Cowboys coach Tom Landry's weekly media session at the same site), and was picked up by newspapers across the country, many of which ran a photograph of the young star adorned with a large cowboy hat.

Her salary was a state secret, so sensitive that the figure was blacked out even on the league's copy of the contract. The final deal was for $100,000, she later disclosed, $65,000 up front, the rest to be paid after the season. The team also furnished her condominium.

With far less fanfare, Inge Nissen simply signed her Chicago Hustle contract and mailed it back; it was "no big deal," she said. Her negotiations with the Hustle also weren't complex: "I gave them a figure. They gave me a figure." That was it. Nissen wasn't opposed to a little hoopla on her signing, as Chicago press assumed; unlike Lieberman, though, she didn't have anyone to help arrange such things.

"I had an agent and he was a wonderful guy," she says sarcastically. Apparently, the agent hadn't appreciated Nissen's request to change parts of his proposed contract. "He signed it and sent it back to me and said, 'Well, obviously we cannot do business, but now you can't do business with anybody else.' I was like, 'Oh, man.'" The agent then "lost" the scrapbook that Nissen's mother kept of her daughter's career "and told me to come and get it if I thought I could," she says. "Sweetheart."

Nissen's contract with the Hustle started at $40,000, with additional performance incentives. (Always good for a quote, Nissen told a reporter that she wanted a big salary because she would like to drive a Cadillac instead of her old beat-up pickup truck. "At least she's honest," Maggie Daly wrote.)

Blazejowski also expected—and got—Annie Meyers–type figures, signing with the Gems for $50,000. "I think that most players understood that a player of Carol's caliber, even back then, well deserved the highest salary," teammate Jill Jeffrey says. "I think it was pretty obvious to the whole country that Carol was the premier player of the league at that point."

PLAYING THEM

Lieberman was "considered the savior-superstar of the Women's Basketball League before she had even signed her first pro contract," the *San Francisco Chronicle* observed, but Coach Williams didn't want expectations to be too high. "I wouldn't lay that off on her," he said. "She's a great player, but I wouldn't label her a savior. No one player can do that."

But Lieberman wanted the label. "I loved it," she says of being called the league's superstar. "I didn't smoke, I didn't drink, I didn't do drugs, I didn't go to the clubs; I was boring as crap. I had one goal, and that was to be the best player. So I'm glad I was put in the position that I was, because I felt that I would handle it the right way for women's basketball."

Fans, opponents, and the media all wanted to see if Lieberman was as good as everyone—including the rookie herself—said she was. Nebraska Wranglers guard Carol Chason remembers looking forward to going at it with the Diamonds star. The night before, though, Chason took ill from dehydration. "I'm throwing up in the dressing room. I'm throwing up on the plane. I'm throwing up in the hotel room. We get to the gym in Dallas and I'm throwing up." She didn't care—no way was she going to miss a chance to play against Nancy Lieberman.

How could opponents stop Lieberman? Former New England Gulls coach Dana Skinner doesn't know; "whatever I was doing as a coach didn't work against her." Chicago Hustle coach Bill Gleason had an idea: "Give her $100,000 and try to sign her." Officials in San Francisco came up with a third approach in a December 28, 1980, game that Lieberman remembers well. "What's the best way to stop somebody?" she says. "Don't let them do anything." Lieberman was whistled for a WBL-record 17 turnovers—11 of them for traveling, not an offense that an experienced player would commit often. "Is that not bizarre that 11 were traveling violations, like I had never played basketball before?" she asks. "If I caught the ball and looked at you, I was called for traveling."

The fact that Lieberman was so physical added to the intensity when playing against her. "On the court, she was mean," Mary Barrineau of the *Dallas Times Herald* wrote in 1982. "She crashed her way to the basket. She dove for the ball. She used her elbows and knees to get opponents out of the way."

Chason came away from their battles black and blue—and gladly returned the favor. "I can't say that I didn't give any back, either, because I was just as physical," she says. Lieberman never did anything inappropriate, in

Chason's view. "I would never consider her a dirty player, that was just part of the game. But you know, she's feisty, she works extremely hard, and she's very, very good."

Lieberman was too a dirty player, Minnesota Fillies center Marie Kocurek says. "We were jogging down court, and she was running beside me in the open court, side-stepping with her feet trying to trip me up. Neither one of us had the ball. When she did that, I said, 'You touch me again and I will knock you down.' " Linnell Jones remembers well a Lieberman elbow to her gut. "I'll never forget that referee standing right there—he saw all of it and didn't say one word. I was right there on her, I was holding her down, and boom, right there in my stomach."

The Diamonds were the highest-drawing road team in the wbl's 1980–81 season, and in January 1981, a Diamonds home game outdrew a home game the same night for the Dallas nba team. Lieberman worked exhaustively to promote the wbl and the Diamonds. "She knew she was an ambassador, she knew that she had a job to do outside of the basketball court," says assistant coach Tom Davis. "Nancy's salary probably was one-quarter player three-quarters publicity."

The team's star attracted the attention even of reporters otherwise indifferent to the league. Famed sportscaster Howard Cosell openly admired her and requested that Lieberman be seated at the dais with him at a dinner in his honor. "Reporters to whom the wbl is merely a rumor await her in each city," wrote Lou Gelfand of the *Minneapolis Tribune*.

Lieberman made news even when she *didn't* play, such as rampant speculation that appeared in sports pages across the country when she was absent from a game in February 1981. It showed how much Lieberman meant to the league, the *Washington Post* noted, "that when she missed a game last month due to a mixup in plane connections, it was bigger news than anything she could have done on the court."

Lieberman's on-court performances were also getting their due, though. The reviews were in, and she was a hit:

St. Louis Post-Dispatch: "Lieberman is one of the wpbl's few legitimate drawing cards and certainly one of its most entertaining players to watch. Her passing game, which forces her teammates to be alert at all times, keeps the audience awake, too. In short, Lieberman is the quintessential athlete—an entertainer who pleases both her coach and the crowd."

Chicago Tribune: "Differences between men's and women's pro basketball are vast. But there is one similar characteristic: the handful of stars a fan will pay to see are equally spectacular. . . . [The crowd] watched a player who is destined to become a legend. Perhaps the first in her own sport."

Dallas Times Herald: "She has excellent court sense, as evidenced by her crisp blindside passes. In the New York summer league, her ballhandling and passing impressed the men. She is almost flawless at spinning and dribbling between her legs and past defenders. It may be her rebounding and defense, though, that set her apart. There are better shooters, but no one is more aggressive on the rebounding—gaining position, jumping with elbows flared—or as intimidating on defense."

St. Paul Pioneer Press and Dispatch: "Nancy Lieberman was a revelation in the second half. . . . She plays the game with a quickness and, more importantly, a cleverness, which is unique to the women's version of basketball. What Nancy Lieberman does is play the game with creativity, a flair which can only be attained on a big-city playground."

The last quote was especially significant because the writer, Patrick Reusse, was one of the most vocal critics of women's basketball at the time. After one Dallas-Minnesota game, he begrudgingly wrote, "Well Nancy, this is tough for a dedicated basketball chauvinist to admit but, it wasn't bad. Finally, a woman who can play the game."

In Dallas, Lieberman was always the player sought out by the camera, while others were relegated to anonymity as part of "Lieberman's team." "I have never been a part of a team where a player had so much say so," says Joanette Boutte, but Lieberman's stature didn't seem an issue for most players. "I really don't think there was any jealousy," teammate Katrina Anderson Sacoco says. "We were grateful because she brought a lot of attention to us. We would laugh sometimes because it would be whatever team we were playing versus 'Lieberman and the Dallas Diamonds.'"

Diamonds coaches were uncertain how teammates would respond to a celebrity in their midst, and an early test came during a van ride back from team physicals. Next to Lieberman sat shy Rosalind Jennings, who seemed a bit in awe of the superstar. "Lieberman kept trying to get Jennings to open up, and finally they were chatting away all the way back to the hotel," assistant coach Tom Davis wrote. "Afterward Ros was so pumped, because here was Nancy Lieberman talking to her. And Glory to God if she wasn't a normal person."

Like Lieberman, Carol Blazejowski lived a different lifestyle than most of her teammates, driving a black Corvette with "Blaze-1" plates. (It was purchased with prize money from a *Superstars* competition. Blazejowski earlier donated it to U.S.A. Basketball to maintain her amateur status, but received it back after the United States boycotted the Olympics.)

"Now that Blazejowski, she was a good basketball player," wbl founder Bill Byrne says fondly. "She never gave anyone any static. She would come and she played. We never read much in the paper about where she wanted this and she wanted that and demanded."

What Blazejowski wanted the most was the ball and a chance to do something with it, but opponents weren't going to let that happen. "You gave her shots, she was going to make it," St. Louis coach Larry Gillman says. "She was a hell of a shooter—*hell* of a shooter." The key, then, was to keep her from getting a look at the basket, which usually meant fouling.

Blazejowski knew what they were doing. "It's like when you are a premier team and everybody is out to get you, there's a target on your back," she says. "When you are a premier scorer in the league and you contribute heavily to the team's point production, you know they're coming at you. That's just inherent to the game." She still blew her stack at times, often drawing a technical foul from whichever unlucky official happened to be nearby. (The Blaze led all players in technicals that season.)

Gary Libman of the *Minneapolis Tribune* recounted the young player's frustrations in one game:

On the bench after scoring 27 points and fouling out of last night's game at the Minneapolis Auditorium, she jumped up, shook a towel and walked down the bench toward the base line, screaming at an official. She wanted a foul called against the Fillies on a play in which Gems guard Tara Heiss was knocked to the ground. A minute later she stood up, waved the towel and shrieked at the officials again to call a foul on the Fillies' Nessie Harris during a rebound battle with New Jersey's Willodean Harris. This time the foul was called.

During the game she also had screamed at an official. "The ball went off her head. It's off her (expletive deleted) head. They're so stupid," she could be heard exclaiming when an out-of-bounds call went against her.

In that entire game, Blazejowski had been allowed only one jump shot. "You can't shoot with people hanging all over you," complained Gems coach Kathy Mosolino. Minnesota coach Terry Kunze subtly confirmed the accusation. "She [Blazejowski] is so smart and so active, she might have had 45 points if we were playing in New Jersey," he said. In spite of smothering defenses, though, Blazejowski still led the WBL in scoring in 1980–81, averaging 29.6 points per game.

In Chicago, Inge Nissen's season didn't go exactly as she hoped. On the court, she was dominant as expected, averaging more than 23 points and 12 rebounds per game, but after winning all nine of its exhibition games and the first four of the regular season, Chicago began to struggle, its record hovering at .500. "We have no consistency, no game plan," Nissen said after a last-minute loss to Nebraska. "Sometimes we work it in low . . . sometimes we shoot from outside." Others, however, questioned whether Nissen was sufficiently motivated.

Off the court, meanwhile, the team was self-destructing as "oldtimers" and new players squared off over personal conflicts and playing time. (One Hustle fan even spat at newcomer Donna Geils, who replaced a popular player in the starting lineup.) Coach Bill Gleason had been a successful high school boys basketball coach, but "he had no clue as to how to deal with women," Nissen says. "If you have a bunch of women who don't really like each other and nobody to control them, you're talking about a terrible atmosphere."

Midway through the season, the Hustle switched to a faster-paced offense, and Nissen began playing more minutes, at times staying on the court for entire games without rest. When the season ended, she was first in the league in blocked shots (3.2 per game, nearly twice as many as any other player), third in rebounding, fifth in scoring, and sixth in free-throw percentage.

"Nissen is the truest of the centers in the WBL," Dennis Latta of the *Albuquerque Journal* wrote in 1981. "She moves to the basket smoothly and does a good job of anticipating on rebounds. There's no argument that she's the best in the U.S."

17

Foul Play

FEBRUARY 9, 1981, EVERLY, IOWA

Craig Kunzmann was surprised to see his wife Linda arrive at the renovation site he was working downtown. His mother had called, Linda said, and Craig's sister Connie was missing. "You'd better be up to see her."

Eleanor Hartmann was upset. She had received a strange phone call from someone with the Nebraska Wranglers who said Connie hadn't shown up to practice, she told Craig. The man wanted to know if she had gone home to Iowa. "What do you think could have happened?"

Craig had a bad feeling. His sister wasn't the type to miss practice. If there was one thing about Connie, she was dependable. She had always been happy-go-lucky, always upbeat, always doing whatever it took to play the game.

Connie Kunzmann was one of the few players with the talent and the attitude and the persistence to stay with the Women's Professional Basketball League from the beginning. Three years earlier, Craig might have been a little skeptical about his sister's decision to try professional basketball, but things had worked out well for her. She had always been able to handle herself, but to miss practice without telling anyone . . .

"She's either pretty sick or something's very wrong," he thought. Could she have been in a car accident? He made some calls to Omaha, but no one knew anything. Someone would let him know if Connie turned up.

The next morning Craig and his younger brother Rick walked into their mother's house. Eleanor had never been an early riser, and she hadn't gotten much sleep the night before. She looked up at them from her bed. "What have you heard?" she asked immediately. Craig steeled himself to tell her the news.

Always a bridesmaid. That's what Connie Kunzmann told her teammates on the Nebraska Wranglers. Twice before, her former team, the Iowa Cornets, had been on the brink of the wbl championship, and this time she wanted it. That kind of attitude—plus 8 rebounds, 10 points, and 3 steals per game—was one reason coach Steve Kirk brought the twenty-four-year-old with him to the Wranglers when the Cornets folded. She was a solid, reliable player who put everything she had into the game.

Connie was "Midwest," says Iowa teammate Mo Eckroth, pleasant and hardworking. "I never really saw her lose her temper. I remember she was just a big—you know, you just saw her throwing hay." The middle child of three born to Ray and Eleanor Kunzmann, Connie came home one day excited to have made the junior high basketball team. Shooting wasn't her strong suit at the time, and she was assigned to be a "guard," a strictly defensive position under Iowa's six-on-six rules.

In high school Connie played on the famed Everly Beefeaters that had won ten state championships in the 1960s and '70s. The Beefeaters had been out of the state tournament the past few years, but Connie's defensive play as a freshman starter (she topped all girls in the state in "interceptions") led them back. "Seems like once she got in high school, she really took off with it as far as a guard goes," Craig recalls. By her senior year, Connie had grown to her full six feet one inch, and the coach moved her to a "forward" (offensive) slot. In this new niche she averaged 34 points a game and was first-team offense all-state.

After graduation, Connie continued her basketball career at Wayne State in Nebraska, transitioning to full-court five on five. "She kind of pitched her tent in that gymnasium," her college coach Chuck Brewer said in 1978. "She put in an awful lot of hours. Whatever you asked for, she always gave you more." Among other things, she set school records with performances such as 40 points and 25 rebounds in a single game.

Connie loved competition, Craig remembers. "If she could play basketball, or if she could play softball some place, it didn't make much difference what the cost was, or what it took. She would go and do it." Pain was irrelevant; a serious knee injury her senior year in college did not keep her out of a game. "Wrap the knee tighter," she told the trainer. "I want to play." Craig Kunzmann wasn't much of a basketball fan, but he wanted to support his sister when she talked about joining a new pro league in the spring of 1978. "I thought, 'Well, women haven't gotten a long ways with their sports and their programs and stuff, and it'd be neat if she could make a go of it and get things started,'" he says, but he was still concerned. "I guess I had cold feet on it, as hard as I hoped that things would go. But, you know, I was just being understanding and hoping that she would be a pioneer."

And she was. During their two seasons, the Iowa Cornets were one of the WBL's most successful franchises, and in the stands for most of their games were Connie's mother and stepfather, Eleanor and Clifford Hartmann. When the Cornets suspended operations before the league's third season, Connie was invited by Kirk to join his new team, the Nebraska Wranglers.

In Omaha, she once again inspired teammates with her positive outlook. "She was team captain, and she didn't even start," says Wranglers teammate Carol Chason. "That's not easy to do." Connie was a team player all the way, Holly Warlick recalls, "a cheerleader on the bench."

The Wranglers were a first-year franchise, but it quickly became apparent that they were the team to beat in the WBL. Connie's role was to provide toughness and energy off the bench, says teammate Charlotte Lewis. "We used to call her Clark Kent. She was the garbage guy. I mean, she was getting points all over the place just from sheer aggressiveness, scrambling. She hit the floor. She didn't care about the burns and stuff like that." The Wranglers had an unusually deep bench, including the league's most dominant post player in Rosie Walker, and midway through the season Connie found her playing time decreasing. Paychecks had also become sporadic, and trade rumors were bouncing around. Connie was depressed. "I'm really sick and tired of being kept in suspense," she wrote. "Getting walked on, told lies to, not getting paid on time and putting up with all this shit that is being thrown at us. I guess I wouldn't be here if I didn't want to. But I'm really confused as to what I want. I want too much or expect too much from myself and my job."

One subject of trade speculation was her roommate Genia Beasley. "I'm sure we can't have no-cut, no-trade contracts and we know anyone can go any time," Connie wrote in January 1981. "It hurts so bad when we all get along so well. Maybe what bothers me more than anything is trying to say goodbye to someone and possibly losing touch. It's happened before. . . . I really feel for Genia." In the end, Beasley was not traded. (Actually, she refused to report, and the trade was nixed). "Things changed overnight," Connie wrote. "Things are back to normal."

In spite of these moments of doubt, Connie's outward enthusiasm never flagged. "She had a great personality. She didn't have the most talent on the team, but she was the hardest worker on the team," says Walker. "She never complained. She always went out there and did her best. She was satisfied."

In early February 1981 Kirk was named to coach the East squad in the WBL's All-Star Game in Albuquerque. Two of his players, Walker and point guard Holly Warlick, were named to the team. The schedule leading up to the All-Star break was tough, and the Wranglers' seventh game in nine days came against their biggest rival, the Dallas Diamonds. Walker pounded in her usual numbers (26 points, 21 rebounds), but the Wranglers' next best performance came from Connie, who hit seven of eight shots from the floor, ending with 19 points and 10 rebounds.

Early in the fourth quarter, with his Wranglers trailing by 12 points, Kirk sent Connie in to guard the Diamonds' Nancy Lieberman. In two minutes, she drew a charging foul against the Dallas star, stole a pass that led to a fast-break basket, and made three quick shots. "She was killing us," Lieberman later told writer Ira Berkow. "Connie played the game of her life." Dallas withstood the rally to come away with the win, but Connie finished with her best game of the season.

The team returned to Omaha, while Kirk and his two All-Stars, Walker and Warlick, headed for New Mexico. That evening, Connie donned her green and yellow Iowa Cornets jacket and drove to Tiger Tom's, a sports bar that had unofficially adopted the team. "That was the place that we could go after games and hang out—both teams, if they wanted to," Lewis says. "We would always invite the other team, and they could relax a little bit before they went back to their hotel and got ready to leave the next day."

Connie's roommates decided to stay in, but they knew their personable teammate would not be short of company. "She always met people and struck up conversations," Beasley said. "When I first met her, I thought, 'No one is that friendly.' But she was. When she left the house, she said, 'I'm going out to have a good time.' Those were her parting words."

At the bar Connie met up with some of the Wranglers and did what she always did: had fun and drank beer. "She loved her beer—believe it," Lewis laughs. "She would drink beer and then come to practice. There ain't no way that I could run like she could. She was just a beer person, and she would tell you that. She was a country girl and she would party."

Lewis noticed that Connie was spending time with a man they had met there before, and when her teammates left, Connie turned down their invitation to go get something to eat. They knew she had her car, and figured she would be all right getting home.

She didn't come home.

Staying out all night did not itself raise an alarm (Chason didn't immediately think, "Oh, no, something happened that night"), but it was unusual. "It just wasn't like her not to come home without letting somebody know," Beasley recalls. When she didn't appear at next day's practice, her teammates were shocked. Connie Kunzmann—"a 110 percent, gung-ho type of player," as teammate Janet Flora says—never missed a workout. "Once she didn't show up for practice, we knew something was wrong, because she was the kind of player that at night would do whatever she wanted to, then come to practice and beat us all in sprints," Chason says.

From New Mexico, the coach called to see how practice had gone. Fine, his assistant reported, "except that Connie Kunzmann didn't show." Kirk was confused. "What do you mean she didn't show? Did she call you?" No, she hadn't. "Well, she'll call you," Kirk predicted. Connie wasn't the kind of player who skipped practice; he knew that from their days in Iowa. The team wasn't sure where Connie was, Kirk told Warlick, one of Connie's roommates. *Strange.*

The next day, she failed to show again—another $50 fine. "Now, I *know* Connie did not go against Mr. Kirk," Lewis said worriedly. This wasn't right. In New Mexico Kirk picked up the phone again. "Did Connie come today?" he asked abruptly when his assistant answered. No. Did she call? No. Did her teammates know anything? They didn't. "As soon as I hang up, your next call is to the police," the coach instructed. "I know this girl, and right now I'm very much alarmed."

Kirk had a sick feeling. "I just knew something was drastically wrong," he recalls. "One day surprised me, and two days—I just knew. This was not a girl who would pick up and go home because she was mad or something." Still, some wondered if she had done just that. "There was a lot of speculation that she just up and left, but her parents didn't think that," Chason says. "We didn't think that, because she loved the game."

At 9 p.m. on Sunday, February 8, 1981, Connie Kunzmann's disappearance was officially reported. The *Omaha World Herald* asked anyone with information to call the missing persons bureau, and the police quickly discovered her yellow Mustang still parked outside Tiger Tom's. For her roommates, the uncertainty was "eerie," says Beasley.

At 4:30 a.m. Tuesday, February 10, 1981, twenty-five-year-old Lance Tibke walked into an Omaha police station and confessed that he had killed Connie Kunzmann. Later that morning, Kirk called Craig Kunzmann in

Iowa. "I'm sorry, but I've got bad news," he said. "Connie's dead. Some guy turned himself in. We're not quite sure of all the details. He says he killed her, that he hit her over the head with a tire iron and stabbed her. And then threw her body into the Missouri River."

Craig was stunned. He had been worried since the first phone call from Nebraska, and now he had the duty of telling his mother the tragic news. He asked his brother Rick to drive down from nearby Spencer, Iowa. As the family talked, they held out hope. Maybe this man was wrong; maybe Connie was still alive when he threw her into the water. But the rest of the world held no such optimism. "Connie Kunzmann, professional basketball player, is dead," the *Washington Post* reported, "a homicide, the cruelest shock yet for a league struggling to survive."

Authorities pieced together the grim details. Three weeks earlier, Connie and some Wranglers teammates had made a promotional appearance at Tiger Tom's, presenting trophies to winners of a local softball tournament and handing out tickets to upcoming games. On the third-place team was Lance Tibke, a security guard at a local nuclear power plant. The two hit it off and spent the evening together.

On the night of February 6, 1981, Tibke stopped at the bar after dropping his fiancée at her home after a movie. There, he ran into Connie again. When Tiger Tom's closed at 1 a.m., he drove her to an isolated spot near Springwell Cemetery a few miles away.

What happened next was not entirely clear. Tibke claimed that Connie became aggressive when he refused to cheat on his fiancée, but police were skeptical. So is Lewis. Connie was determined not to do anything that would interfere with her career, she had told her teammates, and especially not to get pregnant, Lewis says; "no way" would she have demanded sex.

The two fought. "He ended up getting whupped in the process," Lewis says proudly. "She was whupping his butt. When we saw him, he had black eyes and everything. Apparently she was getting the best of him." Reaching for a small pocketknife in the ashtray, Tibke stabbed Connie, then drew a tire iron from under the driver's seat. "I began to pound her and pound her and pound her," he told Ira Berkow in 1982. "She said, 'Stop it, stop it. Please, don't.' But I couldn't stop. I don't know why. She was a nice girl. I didn't have anything against her."

He buried the torn and blood-stained Iowa Cornets jacket in the cemetery, where it was found a week later. From there, he drove to the Missouri

River, backed his truck down a boat ramp, pulled Connie's body out, and waded into the water until it floated away with the current.

"I just remember crying" when the news came, teammate Janet Flora says. "There were a couple of us who couldn't stop." Refusing to speak to the press, the players met privately at 11:00 a.m. Tuesday and issued a statement:

> Connie was more than our teammate. She was a friend to each of us, just as every member of this team is. We play together as a team, as a family. She was a member of our family. Her loss is felt more deeply than one we work with. It is felt as one we love and live with.
>
> We feel that Connie was the type player that is a most valuable part of any team. She was talented, yet maybe not the most outstanding we have. However, Connie provided that intangible that is so important. In any situation, in any game, in any relationship, she gave more than she had to get a positive benefit from it. Each of us knows that anything Connie was assigned to handle, she could more than measure up to.
>
> Never did you hear her complain about her position on the team or in life. She did not accept it, she attempted in every way to make it better. She did it for herself, she did it for those she knew. The word "impossible" was not known to her. It was because of Connie, and the attitude she possessed and passed on to us, that this team has found the success it has.
>
> She can't be replaced on our roster. She can't be replaced in our hearts. Athletes, and people, like Connie do not come along every day. We are deeply hurt that this happened. We are frightened that such incidents even occur in our world. We live in an age when life is threatened even at conception. We hate that Connie was taken from us and her family at this point in her life. Her memory will remain with us forever. Her life will become ours. We will live and play as Connie would have, as Connie would want us to do.

Police tried to search the frozen river, but near-blizzard conditions moved in with thirty-five-mile-per-hour gusts and a wind-chill temperature of nearly 50 degrees below zero. Divers could not enter the icy waters, so searchers could do little more than peer into the river from the banks. A state patrol helicopter had no better luck. Although no body had been found, second-degree murder charges were filed, and Tibke was released from custody after posting a $1,500 cash bond.

Even though the Wranglers were not as close-knit as his Iowa Cornets team, the tragedy still disrupted the team's focus, Kirk says. "It was very difficult for everybody, the fact that she wasn't there, and what happened." All of the players felt bad, he said. "I told them I wanted each player to play more like Connie. . . . Connie was one heck of a person and a hustler. I would like the Wranglers to model their lives after her fine qualities, thus her life on earth would not be in vain."

Some players still thought there was a chance that Connie was not dead. "For a long time we couldn't believe it, because there never was a body," Walker recalls. "That was something to help us go on and play and keep our hope alive, because there never was a body until later." But they also knew it wasn't likely. "It was a hard time," she says. "A real trying time."

The next evening's game in Chicago was postponed ("The Hustle's game with the Nebraska Wranglers was called off for the most grisly of reasons," the *Chicago Tribune* reported), but the team decided to finish out the season. "We're going to play knowing that she'd want us to go on," Beasley said. It was as if Connie were still part of the team, says Chason.

The Wranglers placed Connie Kunzmann on the inactive list and activated Peggy Pope. The team's next game was on the road against San Francisco, and in honor of their missing teammate, Nebraska players wore black patches on their jerseys.

Half a dozen more searches did not turn up a body, and Connie's family was growing desperate. Finally, Craig and two cousins drove down from Iowa. "We weren't satisfied with what was being done and what was going on," he recalls. "It had been a long time since we had found anything out or heard anything down there, so we were just going to go see what we could find out for ourselves." On their way down, Craig's cousin insisted, "If we do come up with something, we want you to get out of here. We'll take care of anything. I don't want you living with what we find for the rest of your life." Craig agreed.

The men sought help from an unusual source. Forty-nine-year-old Greta Alexander of Delavan, Illinois, had acquired extrasensory perception twenty years earlier when she was struck by a bolt of lightning in the bedroom of her house, she said, and over the years she had become one of the country's best known psychics, consulted often by frustrated law enforcement or frantic families seeking help in locating missing loved ones.

Alexander claimed the ability to "become" a victim, and said she had a special gift when bodies of water were involved. Two years earlier she had been credited with guiding an officer by walkie-talkie to the body of a long-sought drowning victim in Iowa. That incident, and others before it, were well publicized, and Connie's family had heard about her. "We had that chance, so we kind of went with it," Craig says.

They called Alexander, who agreed to help their search. From her home in Illinois, Alexander said she would try to guide them by trying to sense Connie. "She would get different vibes or, you know, different feelings," Craig recalls, and the men would follow up on her leads. "Do you see anybody walking around? Do you feel like there's somebody looking at you?"

"There's an officer that has come down and walked past me and stopped and looked at me," Alexander declared. ("Wow, this is really weird," Craig thought.) The men called back for more clues. "All she could tell us was she kept putting her in a place," Craig says.

"I'm caught in a tree," Alexander said. "Would you please help me get free?" The men dutifully looked for trees, which lined the riverbank. Rolling branches around, they called Alexander again. "Do you feel like you're loose now? Are you free?"

"No," she replied. "I'm still in the tree." The search was unsuccessful.

Meanwhile, the Wranglers continued to vie with the Dallas Diamonds for home-court advantage in the upcoming playoffs. On March 28, 1981, they lost to Chicago at the buzzer, and as they waited for the flight home, the coach went to call his assistant to plan the next morning's practice. Lewis still remembers the look on Kirk's face when he returned. "They found her," he said.

Earlier that day, two young boys fishing along the banks of the Missouri had found a body snagged in the limbs of a large tree that had fallen into the river about a mile from the Dodge Park boat dock. The area had been covered with ice during earlier searches. Dental records confirmed that it was Connie Kunzmann, and an autopsy revealed a skull fracture as the cause of death, although she also had several stab wounds.

Her family was saddened by the news, but also relieved in a way that the ordeal was finally over. "You know, there's always that little bit of hope that maybe it wasn't her, maybe she was able to get out, to crawl up on the bank, and somebody would find her or somebody would help her," Craig says. After a few days, that hope had faded, and now the family could have closure. "I think it was kind of a release," he says. "It was a bitter ending, I guess, as far as that goes. It was something that we didn't really want. We were hoping and praying it didn't happen, but it did."

The Wranglers lost their next two games. "It started all over again" after Connie's body was recovered, Beasley says. "You kind of put stuff like that out of your mind and just move on, and it resurfaced."

For the last game of the regular season, the Hartmanns drove down from Iowa and were presented with flowers and a resolution from the Omaha City Council. The WBL announced a new Connie Kunzmann Hustle and Harmony Award for the player who most personified its namesake's work ethic and collegiality. (It went to New Orleans Pride captain Sybil Blalock.) In April 1981 the Wranglers won the WBL Championship.

Lance Tibke pleaded guilty to second-degree murder and was sentenced to the Nebraska state prison "for imprisonment at hard labor, for a period of Forty (40) years." He was paroled on June 25, 1990.

Connie Kunzmann was buried in her hometown of Everly, Iowa, with a smiley face engraved on her tombstone. When Craig Kunzmann thinks back on his little sister, he remembers birthday parties, neighborhood get-togethers, and, of course, "I remember going a lot to her basketball games. I really enjoyed going and watching her play basketball. I guess I'd give my right hand to go see that again, you know."

18

Suspended

There were no intentions to hurt Chicago or the league, but only to draw attention to the gravity of our situation. Unfortunately, we inadvertently did both without helping our situation at all. The players who felt it right to protest that night expected the wrong things to happen. We all somehow didn't consider our own suspensions.
• **Marie "Scooter" DeLorme**, Minnesota Fillies, to Sherwin Fischer, April 2, 1981

BOSTON, JANUARY, 1981
Chris Critelli sipped her beer as she relaxed with some teammates from the New England Gulls. She knew the man who sat down beside her at the table; he was a friend of the coach.
"How much money can you girls get together?" he asked.
Critelli shrugged. "Two nickels to rub together."
"Well, if you can find a couple hundred bucks . . ."
"For what?"
"Well, we can do him in."
Critelli gaped as his meaning sank in. They both knew who "he" was: Gulls owner Joe Reither, whose franchise, and the plight of its players, had been headline news lately. The Gulls captain was no fan of Reither, but the suggestion shocked her naive Canadian conscience. "Um, I don't think we'll have to resort to that," she declined politely. Ultimately, the players would find another way to stand up for themselves.

On Friday, March 20, 1981, a van carrying eight Minnesota Fillies players and coach Terry Kunze pulled up outside the Holiday Inn–Lakeshore in

Chicago for a game the following night. While the others waited in the lobby, Kunze and player–assistant coach Scooter DeLorme headed for the registration desk. Minutes ticked by, and the women began to wonder what was taking so long.

DeLorme was hastily making phone calls. The credit card that Fillies owner Gordon Nevers had given her had been declined, and she couldn't get hold of him. She was able to reach investor Dick Higgins, at which point she handed the phone to the coach. "Gordy gave us a bum credit card," Kunze complained. "They wouldn't let us register. They told us Gordy had tried to pass a bad check there. So here we are, after driving up in a van, sitting in a lobby. Finally, I put the rooms on my personal credit card. It was pretty embarrassing."

Not entirely true, Nevers says — more on that later.

Heading up to their rooms, the players talked about the incident, and later that evening, DeLorme received a phone call. Some of the women wanted a team meeting the next day, and at 2:30 p.m. Saturday, all eight players gathered in a hotel room.

Concerned players got right to the point: Nevers was surely going to fold the team after an upcoming three-game home stand. If the franchise couldn't afford hotel rooms in Chicago, how could it afford remaining road trips to Dallas and San Francisco? DeLorme said she had heard from a reliable source that the trips were already paid for, but others were skeptical. They hadn't been paid regularly in months. By majority vote, the players then made a decision that, former commissioner Sherwin Fischer says, killed the wbl.

At about 7:30 Saturday evening, former Fillies player Tonyus Chavers settled in at her Minneapolis apartment to listen to the game on radio. Instead, when the 7:35 tip-off arrived, she heard a startling announcement: The Minnesota Fillies had just walked off the court. "Those girls got the backbone!" she exclaimed.

Fischer remembers that night well. "We played the Star Spangled Banner, the teams lined up, and just as they lined up, they paraded out to the parking lot, with me in hot pursuit," he says. Still wearing their blue and yellow uniforms, the Fillies filed into their van, followed by Kunze. Someone with the Hustle ordered a barricade erected across the exit, and the coach emerged from the van to talk with Hustle president Larry Cooper.

Kunze knew his players' intentions and should have urged them to play, Nevers believes, but didn't because he was too friendly with the team.

"Consequently, then, all of a sudden it was easier to put me on the bad side as the owner," he says. "You just don't do stuff like that if you are coaching for somebody and somebody is paying your salary. You work for him—you don't work for the players."

Fischer climbed into the van and begged the Fillies to stay. "Come back onto the floor, play the game," he pleaded. "It isn't professional. We'll make sure you get paid." The players weren't buying it. Unless the league paid them today, they weren't playing. Fischer refused. Paying the Fillies would set a precedent, and the league didn't have that kind of money anyway. "They said, 'no ticky, no washy,' and that's how they left it," he says. "That was the demise of the league."

After about ten minutes, the van driver crept toward the blocked exit. "The van stopped," reported the *Chicago Tribune*. "Several players sat with heads in hands. Others just stared. The guard entreated the players, with no luck. Finally, the barricade was removed. 'Girls, please,' the guard yelled as the van left the lot."

None of the Fillies players wanted to call it quits, three-year veteran Donna Wilson said, "but we did feel that we had to put our foot down. We felt doing that in Chicago was the best time. We felt we had been used for too long. I love basketball and I want to play. But we thought this was a way to get back at Gordy. We've been the fools for this long."

Fischer wasn't impressed with their reasoning. "I'm sure they were after Gordy Nevers' hide, but he was twelve hours away by car, and he didn't feel any of the heat from the Hustle fans and players," Fischer grumbled. "It was a disgrace." The players could have filed a formal protest, he said. "But this was all premeditated. This was a conspiracy."

Fillies player Kim Hansen acknowledged that the location was not coincidental. "We decided that Chicago would be a good place for us to show the league what our problems are," she said. "The Chicago team had received a lot of publicity, and it was also where the league was headquartered." DeLorme suggested warning Fischer about their plans before the game, but other players recognized the impact of making an appearance.

After the walkout, fans were allowed onto the court for autographs, and two Hustle squads scrimmaged for half an hour while about a third of the crowd watched. Cooper, who found himself giving refunds to some 1,700 customers, threatened a conspiracy lawsuit, but Fillies players denied the allegation. The strike "was not an act of premeditated conspiracy to defraud the Chicago Hustle," wrote Angela Cotman. The team believed that the league would step in and force Nevers to "honor his commitments or be stripped of his franchise," she said.

The players had simply reached their frustration point with the hotel incident, Hansen said. "It was like everything was falling through for us. We were just really fed up with what was going on. Ever since I joined the team in January, I've been getting only partial pay. I've had just about enough to pay the rent and some of the other utilities, but when it comes to the other bills I've really been scraping."

Nevers says that the hotel incident should never have happened, that he knew the card might not handle the hotel bill and had made arrangements with Chicago officials if that occurred. "Before Terry Kunze left with the team, I said, 'Terry, my cards are maxed. I don't know whether this card will clear the hotel or not, but if by any chance you have any trouble, I have talked with Sherwin or Cooper and they will come down and guarantee the rooms.'"

According to Nevers, he and the coach were having "a little disagreement" about the direction of the team, and Kunze used the credit card problem to exact some revenge. "It was the same old story of me telling them something that wasn't true, and that I had told him the card was good," Never says. "When he went in there, I think he just basically saw an opportunity to make me look bad, even more so, if you will, and said, 'See I told you, he lied again.' That is the gospel truth."

Word of the walkout reached Nevers before the team arrived home. "I was mortified," he says. "I called Sherwin and I said, 'Here is what has happened, as you know. They say they acted against me, but they acted against the league.' I asked the league to suspend them, and he did." Two hours after leaving Chicago, the team called Nevers from a payphone and were told of Fischer's decision. The suspended players were Angela Cotman, Coco Daniels, Scooter DeLorme, Nancy Dunkle, Kim Hansen, Nessie Harris, Anita Ortega, and Donna Wilson.

Kunze insisted that the league couldn't suspend them. "The Minnesota management has had 59 million breaches of contract," he said. "They're at fault, not us. . . . Why doesn't the league reprimand Nevers for not paying us?" Nevers intended to pay, Kunze acknowledged, but was just short of money. "I'm not saying he's a cheat or a crook or anything. Maybe he's a dreamer. He just expects the players to sympathize with his situation even though they can't pay the rent and don't have a nickel to their names."

Fillies players emphasized that they had worked hard up until the walkout. "Perhaps we shouldn't be given a second chance, but I would be interested in knowing how many other players would have gone up to the time we did," Harris told Fischer.

The Fillies not only did the right thing, "they got the idea from us," said Chicago player Althea Gwyn, whose former team, the New England Gulls, had staged a less publicized protest earlier in the season. At the time, the Gulls hadn't been paid for months, and a manufacturer had even asked them to return their uniforms, which hadn't been paid for. (The players refused that request.)

Donna Simms remembers when she and two Gulls teammates were confronted by an angry landlord after their rent check didn't clear. "Our paychecks were bouncing higher than the basketballs," she laughs. "I have a shirt that says 'Property of the New England Gulls,' but doesn't 'property' usually mean it's been paid for?"

Gulls players pooled what little money they had, along with food stamps from former teammates, to buy groceries. The restaurant at a motel where Beverly Crusoe, Krystal Kimrey, and Anita "Sister" Green shared a single room cut off their credit, but a waitress took pity and invited them to her home, where she fed them roast beef sandwiches and cookies. Some players learned to snitch food by sneaking into a local college cafeteria.

Kimrey moved into a house with three other teammates and slept on the couch. Her parents sent money, and other players turned to family and friends. Gerry Booker's parents lived nearby and sometimes fed the players. "We found ways to survive," Gwyn says, but some players were getting only one meal a day.

By January 8, 1981, Chris Critelli felt it was time for action. The Gulls were playing a home game that night against the Minnesota Fillies. "Listen," she said, "as soon as the national anthem is over, we're going into the locker room, and we're going to stay put until all of the gate receipts are given to [coach] Dana Skinner or divvied up amongst us." Some teammates were aghast. "Oh, we can't do that," they protested, but she dug in. "You will never see a dime if you don't stand up for what you need to do." The players agreed, and Critelli told the referees what was coming.

The teams warmed up, lineups were introduced, and then the Gulls turned and ran into the locker room. Owner Joe Reither followed, and the women told him "no pay, no play," Simms says. The owner was having financial problems, he said; among other things, a fire had damaged one of his stores that was uninsured. The women had financial problems of their own, they countered. "I said, 'We're not coming out until gate receipts are in Dana Skinner's hands,'" Critelli recalls. "Sure enough, Dana assured us that he had the gate receipts, not that they were that much. At least if it was $50 each we could go buy food."

Media reports about the team's plight struck a nerve with local residents, and suddenly total strangers arrived at players' doorsteps, casseroles in hand. A beer keg was smashed through Reither's store window. Critelli was presented with the well-wisher's drastic proposal to "take care of" the problem by removing Reither from the picture ("we can do him in").

Reither sought new investors but said the players' public actions had cost him at least one serious prospect. The long-awaited paychecks did not materialize, and then came what the *Boston Globe* called "the final humiliation." At a home game in Portland, Maine, on January 15, 1981, Reither reportedly told Gulls players they would have to pay the referees out of their own pockets if they wanted to play.

The team had pinned its hopes on that game. "That was supposed to be the savior for us," Skinner recalls. "Basically he gave them a little bit of money with the promise that this game up in Portland was a huge event being promoted across the state. He kept telling everybody it was going to sell out, and right after the game he was going to hand money out to everybody and make good on his contractual obligations."

About ten days before the game, Skinner ventured up to Portland to scout the facility, only to discover that the Civic Center personnel had no idea what he was talking about. No game was scheduled. There had been no promotion. Skinner hurriedly booked the court, and a local paper agreed to run a couple of brief notices, but Skinner knew it didn't look good.

The day before the game, Gulls players met with a lawyer, Massachusetts state representative Gerald M. Cohen, who drew up a proposal for them to present the next day. "When the game rolled around, we had pretty much decided as a team that if nobody showed up, that is basically where they were drawing the line," Skinner says. "That this is it."

The players lined up on one side of the court, with Reither, puffing a cigar, on the other. In between was Skinner, carrying messages back and forth. The players wanted Reither to sign an agreement guaranteeing them a share of gate receipts. He refused, unless the women agreed not to become free agents or breach their contracts before February 1. The players refused.

Matters were at a standstill until Reither suddenly agreed to sign their proposal. Although he denied it, the players suspected he had learned what they now heard from Civic Center officials. Gross receipts would be only about $500, leaving the Gulls in a hole even before the officiating crew was paid. "That's when he told us we had to pay the officials out of our own pockets," Lisa Schlesinger said. "And of course we didn't have any money."

It was the last straw for New England's players, who grabbed their belongings and boarded the bus for a long, sullen ride back to Massachusetts. Was the franchise folding? "Ask the girls. They're making all the decisions," Reither said. What did he expect them to do? Critelli asked. "The only reason we are quitting is because this just can't go on. We can't pay our rent, we can't buy food. We've been taken advantage of because we love this game so much."

The owner pointed a finger at the players themselves. Below a photograph of Critelli's open, mostly empty, refrigerator, the *Lawrence Eagle-Tribune* reported a suggestion by Reither that the players' money problems might be due to a lack of frugality on their part. He also accused Gulls players of carrying off two barrels of beer from a concession stand and stealing all but three of the team's wbl basketballs. "I think the North Andover Police ought to get a search warrant and go into their cars and apartments," he said.

On January 20, 1981, Fischer revoked the New England Gulls franchise. Reither's conduct, he wrote, had "resulted in substantial loss of credibility on the part of the league on a national level." The wbl Board of Governors unanimously ratified Fischer's decision. Reither did not emerge unscathed, however. "The owner of New England is paying heavily for what he did," Critelli wrote Fischer later that year. "He and his family are having a miserable time."

The Gulls walk-off received relatively little press, but it was one step beyond a protest by the California Dreams the prior season. Dreams players had been well treated early on—perhaps too well, they realized later, including nice apartments and a plush workout facility—but crowds had not met expectations (attendance at one game was 88), and now paychecks were sporadic. On the road in New Jersey, they suddenly discovered that their plane tickets were one-way—they had no way to get home. "It was like a nightmare," Michelle McKenzie recalls.

The players panicked. They were stranded across the country with no money to buy tickets. "What are we going to do?" Patti Bucklew asked her parents, who had driven from Pennsylvania to watch the game. The crisis ended when the players unexpectedly were handed tickets for a return flight home. Not until years later did Bucklew learn that her parents had bought the tickets for her entire team.

The women returned home, but they were losing faith, McKenzie says, and on February 27, 1980, California's next home game was abruptly called off. "The game was canceled without my authorization, my consent or my knowledge," Dreams owner Larry Kozlicki declared. "It was a unilateral decision by our general manager, Bob Joseph, and he is being terminated from his position effective immediately. We have games to play, and intend on following through with the schedule." The players had arrived at the Convention Center to find it locked, Kozlicki alleged.

The issue wasn't the arena (which confirmed prepayment through the end of the season) but whether the Dreams could field a team. Joseph claimed that only two players were willing to play that night. Actually, it was three, said Nancy Dunkle. Actually, it was five, said Bucklew. No, it was nine, Kozlicki said, the only holdouts being Dunkle and Jane Ellen Cook. The numbers were unclear, but a majority had voted not to play. "The players had rebelled, and we decided we weren't going to play any more games," McKenzie says. "If we weren't going to get paid, then why play? Especially after you got left [in New Jersey]."

The next day, anxious WBL owners discussed the situation. Kozlicki said he could play that night's game against Milwaukee, but he needed an exemption from league rules requiring eight players on the bench. That would be only a temporary solution, Minnesota's Nevers said; showing up with only five or six players would make the game and the league a "travesty." Kozlicki's request was denied. Less than a week later, another home game was cancelled, reportedly because most of the players refused to play, and on March 2, 1980, the league revoked the Dreams franchise after 28 games.

"I couldn't believe it happened twice," says McKenzie, who had also experienced erratic paychecks with the Dayton Rockettes the season before. "Not until the California team did we band together and really stick to our guns as far as, 'Well, no, we're not going to play.' Before then, we were trying to punt. We were trying to make ends meet as far as pulling out savings, trying to at least keep your apartment and keep playing."

Ironically, the Fillies' walkout a year later generated far more ink than media usually gave the WBL. "As the ownership around the league started to run into financial problems, it started hitting the press," says San Francisco Pioneers president Marshall Geller. "All of a sudden, some girls were owed money, they were living out of their cars because the team couldn't pay them. Any decent newspaper is going to pick that up and make it a big issue. It became almost like a self-fulfilling prophecy; pretty soon everybody kept saying this league is not going to make it."

Investors were worried not only about the welfare of the players but also about public perceptions. Pioneers co-owner Alan Alda was supportive of women's athletics, Geller says, but was also conscious of his image, as any celebrity would be. "When it started going bad in the league and the press became really nasty, everybody wanted to duck. Willie Brown [another investor] didn't want to be involved in things that got bad press. Alan Alda called me one day and said, 'You know what? I don't want our girls to suffer like any other girls in the league. If we need to put more money in just to make sure they get paid or anything, you call me.' That was a nice gesture, but do you understand what he was saying?"

The Fillies walkout hurt the league badly, Fischer says, but the players said that wasn't their intention. "I believe in the wbl and what it has done for the development of women's professional basketball," Angela Cotman said. "When the survival of an entire league depends upon the continued existence of other teams, then problems encountered by one team become part of a problem for others."

Fischer rejected a request from Nevers to lift the suspensions, and the Fillies owner vowed to finish out the 1980–81 season with a new squad. "This is not going to kill the league," he said. Several wbl fans wrote Fischer to protest Nevers's plan. One emphatic letter said: "If you permit that management to field a team of 'scabs' and allow those games to be sanctioned by the league, you will reinforce every negative opinion about the wbl. You will prove that it is not in business for the love of basketball, the cause of women, or even the pursuit of money. You will prove that the owners in this league are conspiring to take some quick tax losses for a couple of years, and will use players and coaches who love basketball with no intention of becoming an established organization."

The plan to find replacements proceeded. "Maybe I'm just not very smart and I keep banging my head against the wall," Nevers said. "But someday there's going to be a successful women's basketball league in this country and I'd like to hope I was a part of it." He started with a call to Lynnette Sjoquist, a first-season Fillies player who was now the team's public relations director and loyal supporter.

Sjoquist had been shocked to hear of the walkout. "I am probably a little too Pollyanna to think that anything like that would happen," she says, and her worst memory of the WBL was her disappointment with the striking players. "I just couldn't understand that they weren't seeing the big picture. Wrong or right, I thought the big picture was we had to keep working at this, and we would make it work."

Sjoquist picked up the phone and, even resorting to the ultimate weapon (tears), cajoled several free agents and college seniors into playing. Not all of them were enthusiastic. "I remember that some that I called on were not open to the idea. They felt that the Fillies had wronged those players that weren't getting paid," Sjoquist recalls. "But like I told them, the players were getting every dollar that we had. It wasn't a case of the people in the front office running away with the money."

Others were more receptive. Elsie Ohm, a top player at nearby Mankato State the year before, read of Nevers's intentions in the newspaper and turned to her mother. "I bet I'll be getting a phone call," she predicted. Sure enough, her phone rang the next day. Would Ohm be interested in helping the Fillies finish their season? "What the heck?" she thought. "If I can get permission to leave work, I'm going to do it." She had just started a new job with the *Faribault (MN) Daily News*, but her boss was fine with it; maybe Ohm could contribute some articles about her adventure, he suggested.

Other recruits who played at least one game with the "patchwork" team were Patti Decker, a former Milwaukee Does player from Minnesota; Cheryl Engel, an ex-Fillie; Rachel Gaugert, a senior at the University of Minnesota; Mary Manderfeld, a senior at Minnesota; Susan Meredith, an ex-Fillie; Lynn Peterson, a recent graduate of Mankato State; Cindy Pummill, who had attended the Fillies' training camp; Linda Roberts, a senior at Minnesota; Brenda Savage, a Minnesota graduate; and Sue Wahl-Bye, an ex-Fillie. Two volunteer coaches, Mark DeLap, who worked for a local printing company, and Mel Riley, men's basketball coach at Minneapolis Community College, were rounded up.

Manderfeld played because she wanted the league to survive, she said; although she had no plans to go professional, some of her fellow Gophers might. Roberts said she wanted to show support for women's professional basketball. For Ohm, the franchise was offering her something another WBL team had not the previous summer—"a chance to play basketball and have fun."

Although she was a post player in college, Ohm was assigned the point guard position, which meant getting familiar in a hurry with the smaller

WBL ball. Fillies management let her take home an official basketball, which became her only souvenir of the league ("I actually kept that ball because I thought that might be the only payment I get," she says, "and that's what it was").

The *Daily News* ran humorous pieces about Ohm's brief foray into professional sports. "Real worry came when I realized I was an uncoordinated, out-of-shape ballplayer," she wrote. "And I had to go on that night as a substitute in front of a crowd, the media and a professional team. That wasn't asking too much of my body, was it? Can you imagine the feeling of performing with that pressure when you know you'll get winded running out for the starting lineup?" (Ohm was exercising a bit of creative license. She had actually been playing ball with men at the local YMCA and was still in pretty good shape.)

At the Curtis Hotel in Minneapolis, the Fillies replacements arrived at the same moment that their predecessors and Kunze were holding a press conference elsewhere in the hotel. Burglars shouldn't bother with the Fillies front office, Kunze quipped. "I don't know what you'd be able to get," DeLorme added. "There's a few filing cabinets in there and a typewriter that's probably not paid for. But that's a bad joke."

The new players were handed uniforms and told to bring their own socks. After a single practice, the makeshift team reported for duty at the Minneapolis Auditorium. Not surprisingly, they were routed by the visiting St. Louis Streak, which was already ending its season on an upsurge. "The Streak did a few double takes Monday night after coming out to warm up for their Women's Basketball League game against the Minnesota Fillies," the *St. Louis Post-Dispatch* reported. "Were all those new faces in Fillies uniforms a secret weapon?" No, as the 126–80 score showed, but "the satisfaction for the home team was merely keeping the franchise alive."

Meanwhile, the ex-Fillies watched—and heckled—from the stands, unabashedly cheering for the visitors. "I'm rooting for St. Louis," Hansen declared, "because they're part of the WBL." The Streak were being coached that night by a player, and the women urged her to pull no punches. "We were ragging on her, 'What are you doing? Why are you holding back? You better run them to death!'" Chavers says. "It was so twisted."

The new players disagreed that they were "scabs." "We didn't sign the contracts for them and I don't feel as if I'm crossing a picket line," Wahl-Bye said. "Actually, we're helping them by keeping a franchise alive whether they like it or not." Chavers didn't like it and held a grudge until years later, when Roberts explained why she did it. She knew the league was on its way out, Roberts told her. "If I couldn't be a professional player for two or three years, I could be for one night." Chavers thought about it, and then "I was like, 'Oh, okay.'"

Meanwhile, Nevers resented the sudden—belated, he felt—interest of media "vultures" who finally covered a Fillies game. "One of my people came to me today and said, 'You know, the only time we get any ink is when one of our players gets killed or when our players don't get paid,'" he asserted. (The murder of Nebraska Wranglers player Connie Kunzmann a month earlier had also generated national attention.)

By previous arrangement, the Fillies faced the Streak again the following night, and Kunze urged fans to boycott. "If the crowd at the games could see what's happened the last four months, there wouldn't be a soul at the games," he said. Only one hundred fans showed up for the second game against St. Louis, and the results were the same. "Showing no mercy, the Streak sprinted to a 40–16 first-quarter lead and were never threatened," the *Post-Dispatch* reported.

The last two games of the season were in Dallas and San Francisco; to cut costs, Sjoquist assumed the mantle of player-coach. The Fillies lost to the Diamonds 114–70 and to the Pioneers 122–61. Still, it was fun, says Ohm. "I pretty much knew that we didn't have much of a chance, but I figured that it was my opportunity to be a professional basketball player." Ohm also enjoyed spending time with players she had faced in college. "You know, when you have a rivalry, you usually hate the other person's guts. I just thought it was nice that I got to play with people that I thought I hated and didn't have any respect for, and I ended up liking them."

The Minnesota Fillies finished their season, but the damage was done, according to Fischer. "That walkout was the worst thing that could have happened to us," he said. "If there's anything that will kill the league, it's not paying the players." At a WBL Board of Governors meeting in May 1981, Nevers was found not guilty of provoking the strike.

19

Home Court Disadvantage

CENTERVILLE, IOWA, OCTOBER 11, 1982
Molly Bolin sat silently in the courtroom, watching her ex-husband's lawyer cross-examine her mother on the witness stand.

"Has your daughter ever done cheesecake?" asked the lawyer. Wanda van Benthuysen wasn't sure what he meant, and he handed her Exhibit 10. "Do you know what this is?"

Of course she knew; anyone with even a passing knowledge of the Iowa Cornets knew about The Poster: an 18" x 24" black-and-white shot of the Cornets' pretty blonde guard in a one-piece swimsuit, the most successful promotion in the WBL's three-year history. It was now a featured exhibit in Bolin vs. Bolin—*evidence, according to Molly's ex-husband Dennie, of why he should have custody of their five-year-old son Damien.*

"What is it?" The lawyer held up the poster.

"This is a publicity picture that she worked for," Mrs. van Benthuysen replied.

"Of your daughter?"

"Yes."

"In a bathing suit?"

"Yes."

"With a rather interesting pose?"

"Well," she declared, "not only was her parents but her in-laws was proud of that picture when we saw it."

"Has your daughter ever done cheesecake?" the lawyer demanded again.

"This is not what I would call cheesecake," Molly's mother insisted. "This would be a publicity work."

The lawyer wasn't satisfied. "You still haven't answered my question," he snapped. "Has your daughter ever done cheesecake?"

"Would you explain what you are referring to by cheesecake?" she asked. "That is a new word to me."

"You don't know what it means," the lawyer said cynically. "Hasn't your daughter ever told you about suggestive sexual poses?"

"Well, she's never taught me about sex."

The last few months of "Machine Gun" Molly Bolin's wbl career were not her happiest. Her new team, the San Francisco Pioneers, was not likely to make the playoffs. Relations with her husband, Dennie, who hadn't found a job in California and who had, by his own admission, begun to "drink more than I should have" at times, were deteriorating. A week before the season ended, Molly and Dennie argued until 3:00 in the morning. Soon afterward, Dennie packed up Damien and headed home to Iowa—and so began a two-year legal battle that changed the law there forever.

Monna Lea ("Molly") van Benthuysen and high school sweetheart Dennie Bolin married in 1976, when Molly was eighteen. Dennie, then twenty-one, worked construction while Molly attended nearby Grandview College on a basketball scholarship. When their son Damien was born in 1977, Molly stayed home to take care of him.

She couldn't get the game out of her system, though. "I was going berserk just being a mother, watching soaps and cooking supper," she said. "I realized that while I wasn't really *un*happy, I had to have a career. But then, having been raised to never cross your husband's word, I had to have Dennie's blessing." She got it—which was fortunate, she said, as she probably would have played anyway. The next year, she rejoined the team at Grandview, where teammates showered little Damien with attention when Dennie brought him to practice.

In March 1978 Molly Bolin became the first player to sign a contract in the Women's Professional Basketball League. Over the next three years, she developed into one of the wbl's most successful and popular players. Because Dennie's construction job was seasonal, he was able to tend Damien while Molly pursued her basketball career, and as her fame grew, reporters began to refer teasingly to Dennie as "Molly's husband." The label sometimes bothered him, Dennie said, but he had learned to laugh about it.

"The second season he definitely became Molly's husband and lost his own identity," Molly says now. "That created a lot of problems right there, and the fact that I was always in the press and being asked to do promotions in my free time. We were pioneers, and we were always teetering on the brink of failure. I was so focused on the fact that I was going to do anything I could to make this work, that tunnel vision no doubt contributed to relationship problems."

The whole situation had been hard for Dennie, Molly said in the WBL's third season, "especially since all his friends are supporting their wives like they were brought up to do. I wanted to succeed so bad that it sometimes meant going over his head." His wife's career took some getting used to, Dennie admitted to a Des Moines sportswriter. "I was used to Molly being here when I came home. All of a sudden I'd come home and there was nothing." Still, Dennie was supportive and went to as many of Molly's out-of-town games as he could.

When the Iowa Cornets suspended operations in late 1980, Molly was lured to a Southern California team in a newly formed rival league. The Bolins moved to Los Angeles, but within a few months that league had evaporated. WBL owners were anxious to bring the superstar back into their fold, and in January 1981 Molly signed a lucrative contract with the San Francisco Pioneers.

Dennie was unable to find satisfactory work there, and Molly's basketball salary supported the family. It was more cost effective for the San Francisco team to make extended road trips rather than fly back and forth to games, so Molly was sometimes gone for weeks at a time. The Bolins' relationship deteriorated, and shortly before season's end, Dennie went back to Iowa with Damien, moving in with his parents.

Molly returned after the season, but it was clear that the marriage was over. Dennie's attorney filed a dissolution (divorce) proceeding in June 1981 and drafted an agreement for the parents to share "joint custody" of Damien. Unfortunately, as the Bolins were to learn, the agreement did not explain just what that meant. (An estimated one-third of all divorces in Iowa at the time had similar joint custody arrangements.)

In the ensuing months, Dennie remarried, and conflicts arose regarding arrangements with Damien. Molly decided she needed a lawyer and was referred to a woman who knew something about unconventional career paths. A few years earlier, fifty-four-year-old Ione Shadduck had completed a long journey through Drake University's law school in her spare time as a physical education instructor, devoting five years of part-time and summer school work to earn her law degree. A self-described "radical" feminist, Shadduck also followed basketball, and she immediately recognized the name of her famous caller.

By now, Molly was back in California, leaving Damien with her ex-husband for the summer. When she returned in September to pick him up, Dennie told her—falsely—that he had a court order preventing her from having their son for more than two weeks, but he eventually allowed her to take Damien to Brea, California, where she worked as a renovator. To her dismay, Molly discovered that Damien had a serious dental condition that required surgery and also an untreated eye problem. She arranged for his care, enrolled him in preschool, and told Dennie he could have Damien in Iowa for two weeks before school started.

In July 1982 Molly received a phone call from an Iowa police officer warning her that Dennie was coming to kidnap Damien from his school. The officer teletyped the following to the California State Police:

WE HAVE WORD THAT A SUBJECT FROM OUR CITY IS ENROUTE TO CALIFORNIA, CITY UNKNOWN AT THIS TIME, TO ABDUCT HIS 4 YEAR OLD SON FROM HIS DIVORCED WIFE. SUPPOSEDLY, OUR INFORMATION SHOWS THE ABDUCTION IS TO TAKE PLACE AT A DAY CARE CENTER TODAY, 07–29–82.

Molly hurriedly pulled Damien out of school. Two days before his scheduled arrival date, Dennie flew in from Iowa and went directly to the preschool looking for the child, only to learn that he wasn't there. If Dennie wanted to take Damien back to Iowa, Molly told him, he would have to sign an agreement promising to return him in two weeks. Dennie signed the document but enrolled Damien in school instead. When Molly flew back to Iowa, Dennie hid the child and, without telling her, obtained a restraining order preventing Molly from taking him back to California.

In an emergency hearing, a judge let the order stand (and then, at the end of the hearing, made the startling announcement that his son happened to be Dennie's original divorce lawyer). Molly wanted to visit Damien, but Dennie would agree to only a couple of hours in the basement of his parents' home. "He's going to be worse off if I see him for a couple of hours under those circumstances than if I don't see him at all," Molly told her attorney. "That's just going to mess him up."

As everyone left the courtroom, Molly broke down. "I've had enough of this!" she shouted. She was already infuriated—enough to call him a "chicken shit"—by Dennie's refusal to speak to her the night before at a local festival, and she had called her former father-in-law a similar name when he refused to tell her where her son was. (These incidents showed that Molly had a "problem with temperament," Dennie's lawyer later said: "You just blow your stack and swear and cuss.")

Fisticuffs had already broken out once between Molly's family and Dennie's, and residents of the small community began to take sides. (Molly's mother stopped attending her usual church because of confrontations with some of Dennie's supporters.) Tensions were running high when the trial began with a new judge, the Honorable Richard Vogel, a month later. "Boy, it was not a pretty trial," says Shadduck.

As it progressed, Molly watched Dennie's attorney hold up with disdain the promotional poster that had helped support the family during her playing days with the Iowa Cornets, a poster that had generated valuable publicity for the team, including a feature in *Sports Illustrated*, and made her the subject of a bidding war in her final season. "Are you ashamed of having done that?" he asked. No, Molly replied, "I have never done anything I'm ashamed of."

Part of her job was to promote the Cornets, Molly explained. "In my position as a basketball player, a good part of my value to a team was my marketing value, which did include a lot of publicity pictures. It was all done in promotion," she said. "The team had to survive on that type of thing. I really didn't mind. It was kind of fun. I don't feel like I did anything that was detrimental either to my image or to my family or embarrassing to Dennie." Yes, a photograph of her in a swimsuit had appeared in the *San Francisco Chronicle*, Molly said; one of the Pioneers' owners had submitted it to the paper. She was surprised to see it, but the overall response to it was positive.

The three-time All-Star's basketball career also came under fire, as the lawyer painted it as a disservice to her son. "How about '79, did you spend quite a bit of time on the road?" he quizzed Molly during the trial.

"I don't know what your estimate is on quite a bit of time," she replied. "In comparison to a total year, I would say it was very little time. In comparison to a season, it was half the amount of time."

"Well," the lawyer leafed through Exhibit 3, an Iowa Cornets program, "you spent time in Milwaukee in 1979, didn't you?" The Cornets' first road game that season had been against the Milwaukee Does.

"Yes." Also Cedar Rapids and Des Moines (the Cornets' home courts).

"Spent time in Dallas?"

"Yes."

"Spent time in Washington DC?"

"No," Molly corrected him. "Washington DC and Philadelphia had folded before we played them so we didn't go."

"But it was anticipated that you were going to go?" he said.

"Yes, it was part of the schedule."

"You spent time in St. Louis?" Yes, she acknowledged. And New York. And Chicago. And Houston. And New Jersey. And Minnesota. And New Orleans. And California.

"Okay," Dennie's attorney continued. "So from November the 18th through March the 16th, you spent a lot of time in various and sundry cities throughout the United States?"

"When you say a lot of time, I say in a period of four and a half months, part of the time was spent traveling," Molly replied. "It was part of my job."

Too much so, the lawyer suggested. "What was the attitude at the time you were living together?" he asked Dennie.

"She was wanting to play ball," Dennie said. "She was wanting to pick endorsements, commercials, and she was always—to me she was worried about them more than the family."

"Would it be fair to say she was wrapped up in her chosen profession?"

"Yes." She expected her career to come before his, Dennie complained.

"Did she, in fact, travel all around the country and leave you and the child—"

"Yes."

"—alone? . . ."

It was demeaning to hear the criticisms of her job, Molly recalls now. "In those days they could use a career against you because if you had a career, obviously you weren't a full-time mom, and what kind of a mom were you to be out traveling with a basketball team?"

When Molly was on road trips, Damien stayed with his grandparents a lot, Dennie's mother testified. "What would your reaction have been if it had been Dennie who had been the basketball star as opposed to Molly?" Shadduck asked. It was an intriguing question, as this was the first reported case of a female professional athlete having her career used against her in a custody battle. "I think a man, in a father and mother, have a different role in a—I mean, this would have been his profession," Mrs. Bolin replied uncertainly.

The Bolins had a "role-reversed" marriage, Dennie's expert testified: "Traditionally the husband is the breadwinner and is out doing the work and the wife is at home doing things there, taking care of things," but when the family was in California, Dennie was home with the child, and Molly was supporting the family. Dennie had been the primary caregiver in this role reversal, the expert said, and custody should stay with him.

But wait a minute, Shadduck pointed out—hadn't the Iowa Supreme Court said that mothers should no longer be given preference in child custody just because they happened to be the primary caregiver? "Dennie is not the mother," the expert replied. True, Shadduck said, but wasn't the expert saying that, in this "role reversed" family, Dennie basically played the role of mother and therefore should get custody? "Dennie is not Damien's mother," the expert repeated. "Dennie is Damien's father, so in my opinion that does not play a part."

After three days and sixteen witnesses, the judge took the matter under advisement. A few weeks later, Shadduck opened her mail to find a written ruling: Custody of Damien Bolin was awarded to his father. "We were very shocked," she says. "Well, you had to know Judge Vogel. Then you weren't so shocked." Molly was devastated, and Shadduck tried to console her. "We can appeal this," the lawyer encouraged.

Vogel's ruling acknowledged that the parents' schedules when they were married were somewhat compatible, but he pointed to the Iowa Cornets programs to show Molly's absences from home. The family's relocations at times were also because of her career, he added. Both parents were fit, but the boy had been with Dennie most of the time since the Bolins' separation, he was already enrolled in school, and Moravia was more his "hometown." With red pen in hand, an exasperated Shadduck underscored line after line of the judge's ruling. "No evidence," she scribbled beside one statement. "He's biased," Shadduck concluded.

"Where is justice?" Molly asked a local news writer. "It never even occurred to me that I wouldn't win this. They got into mudslinging and made all these insinuations like I was leading some wild lifestyle in California. That couldn't be more of a lie. I feel like I've been crucified because I played basketball and am single and not living in a small Iowa town."

One insinuation that troubled her involved her relationship with a former Cornets teammate who offered Molly a place to stay in California and helped her find a job after the wbl folded.

Although Dennie's attorney denied that he made any "inferences at all of any improper conduct" between the women, he did raise the subject repeatedly at trial. Did they have a "close association"? he asked. Had they lived together since the divorce? What did Molly's expert think about the roommate's "femininity or masculinity"? Was she a "parent" figure for Damien?

In a typical exchange, the lawyer questioned Molly about the remodeling company she worked for, which was located in Laguna Beach, California:

"Laguna Beach is kind of an art community; isn't it?" he asked.

"I would say so," Molly had agreed.

"It's sort of a gay community, too, isn't it?"

"I really have no idea."

"I see. You don't know whether San Francisco has a gay community either, do you?" the attorney said sarcastically.

"I have heard things to that effect, and I have read things to that effect," she replied.

Molly was disillusioned by her first real exposure to the negative perceptions some people held about female athletes. "In high school, everybody thinks it's great that the girls play basketball. And then I was wife and mother and also played basketball. That was fine. But once I was on my own, I was a jock. It was a real slap in the face to realize what some people will think of you," she said. She was frustrated and angry that she had to defend her sexuality. "What I'm fighting on this is the same old stereotype that is always put on women athletes."

Yes, she was heterosexual, Molly told the reporter. Her former teammate was like a sister to her. "She came along to help me at a time when I became almost suicidal over things in my life. She literally pulled me out of some very rough times. . . . Three teams folded on me, my marriage broke up, now I've lost my son. So many bad things." Without the support of her roommate, she said, "I don't know how I would've made it."

The only legal recourse for Molly was now an appeal to the Iowa Supreme Court, arguing that the judge had unfairly punished her for supporting the family with a job that took her on the road at times. "Even if she were still a professional athlete, she should not be deprived of custody of her child," Shadduck urged the court. "Such a ruling would set a precedent for spouses of all professional athletes and other workers who must spend some time away from home to claim custody of the children because the other parent must work for several days at a time in other places than the hometown."

The Bolin case raised a new issue for the Iowa Supreme Court. What did "joint custody" mean? Only three years earlier, the court had said it meant that parents would share physical custody. Now, it wasn't so sure. The legislature had made changes to state law recently that suggested it did not agree with the court's earlier ruling, but the new laws did not apply to the Bolins' dispute.

The Iowa Supreme Court decided that its earlier decision was wrong. From then on, only one parent would have physical custody of a child. The justices then reviewed the evidence in the Bolins' case to decide who it should be. The answer, they unanimously agreed, was Molly. "The record shows she has maintained a mature, patient and loving concern for Damien's welfare," Justice Mark McCormick wrote for the five-member court. "Her attitude and conduct in attempting to work out the custody problem within the law have been commendable."

The court sent a stern message to all divorcing parents: "Even though the parents are not required to be friends, they owe it to the child to maintain an attitude of civility, act decently toward one another, and communicate openly with each other. One might well question the suitability as custodian of any parent unable to meet these minimum requirements. Problems are likely to develop under any custodial arrangement. The adults must have the maturity to put their personal antagonisms aside and attempt to resolve the problems."

The court concluded that Molly had done just that, and that she would provide Damien with a wholesome and loving home in a nice community. The ruling was reported in the court's official publication, the *Northwestern Reporter*, and has since been cited in more than two dozen other cases, by courts not only in Iowa but also in Minnesota, South Dakota, Wisconsin, and Guam.

When it was over, Molly was grateful to Shadduck. "I probably would have gotten my butt kicked if it hadn't been for my lawyer, who went beyond the call of duty to see justice done," she says. The case remains a highlight of Shadduck's career, the lawyer says. "It was Molly Bolin, it was a case that was mine and I won, and I got my name in the *Northwestern Reporter*. What more could you ask?"

20

Final Buzzer

It was like Mickey Rooney and Judy Garland in a movie: "Hey, let's start a pro-league." • **Mel Greenberg**, *Philadelphia Inquirer*

NEW YORK CITY, APRIL 20, 1981
Sherwin Fischer was looking forward to this. He was about to generate some of the most valuable publicity in the WBL's three-year history, a national television appearance on NBC's Today Show *on the morning of the league's championship game.*

He was supposed to have been here a week ago, but a last-minute page at the airport had alerted him that the death of boxer Joe Louis was preempting the scheduled interview about women's basketball. Now, across the table from Fischer, in front of a huge "Bryant Gumbel" logo, sat the interviewer who would become the show's cohost a year later. Before the show Gumbel had put Fischer at ease; "I'm all in favor of women's basketball," he mentioned while their makeup was being applied.

Cue Gumbel. "Let's turn our attention to basketball," he began. "A lot of basketball fans around the country may know that the Kansas City Kings beat the Phoenix Suns, and that the Milwaukee Bucks lost to the Philadelphia 76ers to move on to the NBA finals in their various conferences. But how many know that the Nebraska Wranglers and the Dallas Diamonds are tied at two games apiece in their best-of-seven series? They are playing it out in the finals of the Women's Pro Basketball League, a best of seven set." (Actually, it was best of five.)

On the screen flashed images from a game in Omaha. As Gumbel spoke,

Dallas's Hattie Browning dribbled down court in her dark blue road uniform, being chased by Nebraska's Josephine Wright in white and red. Browning fed a quick pass to Rosalind Jennings, who sank a jumper from the right side of the key.

"The Wranglers and the Diamonds may be playing their hearts out, but not a lot of people are watching," *Gumbel's voice-over continued. On screen, the Wranglers' Carol Chason passed to a wide-open Holly Warlick on the baseline, and her shot from 15 feet was good.*

"Two games in Dallas this weekend drew over 7,000—"

With her back to her defender, Dallas star Nancy Lieberman spun to her right and tossed a short shot toward the basket. It bounced off, but Lieberman leapt for the rebound and, in midair, flipped the ball one-handed off the backboard and in.

"—but for the most part attendance for games in the Women's Pro Basketball League has been dreadful—"

The camera panned across a mostly empty area behind the Diamonds bench. The buzz of a shot clock sounded, but from the applause—and the irate stomping of Diamonds coach Greg Williams—the home team evidently had scored at the last second.

"—averaging 1,800 a game."

Time for the guest. "The Commissioner of the Women's Pro Basketball League is Sherwin Fischer"—*the camera flashed to a nice-looking man with thick hair and sideburns, dressed in a blue suit with fashionably wide stripes*—"who runs an executive search firm, and became a commissioner when his firm couldn't find a commissioner for the league."

Gumbel turned to him. "Sherwin, let me ask you something: Is your league dying? Is this its last year?"

"No, definitely not," *replied the commissioner.* "We're very much alive."

"Why do you—how can you say 'definitely not' when it's averaging only 1,800 a game?" *Gumbel persisted.*

Fischer hid his irritation. Gumbel was a supporter? "It's shown a 40 percent increase in attendance, which must sound a little bit ridiculous, but the response from the media this year has been so overwhelming," *he stated calmly.* "During this playoff series down in Dallas—I wasn't planning on going down there, but Saturday I did attend the fourth game of the season's final playoff, and watched 76 or 7,800 people cheer the Dallas Diamonds on, only to see Dallas lose in the final seconds."

"OK, but you've got a problem with identity." *Gumbel held up a folded* newspaper. "*I mean, I'm looking at the New York Times this morning. On page 11 at the bottom here*" (*he circled a couple of lines with a pen*) "*this is the space devoted to the Women's Basketball League playoffs. How do you combat this?*"

"*What we actually need right now, and what we are negotiating on right now, is a national TV contract,*" Fischer said. "*In fact, there are six or seven national networks, mostly cable, that we are negotiating it for next season.*"

"*Is that what it will take to save the league?*"

"*I believe, like any other sports league around the country, that none of us could survive without national TV,*" Fischer replied. "*Even in Chicago — there was recently on NBC in Chicago on the Chicago Bears, who are certainly sold out every day, a report that without TV, the Bears would not show a profit.*"

Gumbel posed another question. "*When the NBA is struggling, when golf seems to be struggling, a lot of college sports are struggling, why do you feel at this point in time there's still a market?*"

"*I don't think a lot of people realize that this is the only women's pro team, sport, in the world,*" Fischer said (*forgetting for a moment professional leagues in other countries*). "*There are no other team women's pro sports. Women's basketball is, in my opinion, a new concept, which people have to see to really appreciate.*" Fischer warmed to his subject. "*Just being down in Dallas on Saturday, it was absolutely unbelievable,*" he said. "*The fans were crying. They were so excited they were crying. On Friday night, there were 8,117 people at Moody, and my head official called me and said, 'Sherwin, you have to come down here. You cannot believe the enthusiasm of the fans.' But if they don't come out and see it, they won't appreciate it.*"

"*Sherwin, I hope they do start coming out and seeing it,*" Gumbel said as the interview concluded. "*Otherwise, the Nebraska Wranglers and the Dallas Diamonds will be playing the last games of the WBL. Thanks very much for coming on.*"

Fischer didn't show it, but he felt sandbagged. Gumbel's questions all seemed to focus on the negative. Still, it could have been worse. At least he hadn't asked Fischer about the highly publicized walk-out a month earlier on the commissioner's home turf. "*Thank you,*" he echoed.

The postmortems began even before the third season was over. "Since the birth three years ago of the Women's Pro Basketball League, team owners have been savaging their brainchild with gross mismanagement, questionable financial practices and deceit," wrote Lacy Banks of the *Chicago Sun-*

Times. "Now, in the midst of the league playoffs, death knells are tolling for the bruised and battered league. The symptoms are grave and numerous."

WBL representatives remained optimistic, at least on paper. "I'm bullish on the concept of women's pro basketball," St. Louise Streak owner Vince Gennaro said. "People say we got in too early, but you hear that about any investment. When it's the right time, then it's too late. Somebody has already done it by then." Dallas Diamonds president (and former WBL vice president) Dave Almstead agreed, to a point. "The concept of women's pro basketball will go," he said. "It's sound. But the fruition of the concept will be shaped by the people in it. You're only as strong as your weakest link."

During the playoffs in April 1981, Fischer reported that he was doing some "soul-searching" about his role as interim commissioner. "That job takes a lot of time," he told the *Chicago Tribune*. "I wouldn't mind if I got cooperation from the other owners, but the board of governors doesn't tell me what to do. They throw everything in my lap. I think there should be a full-time commissioner and a marketing staff."

A month later, Almstead replaced Fischer as interim commissioner. "I thought we had done a fine job with such a small staff and we were correcting a lot of administrative mistakes that had been committed in the past," Fischer said. "But the board of governors decided these changes would be in its best interest."

Meanwhile, San Francisco Pioneers owner Marshall Geller was stewing about the WBL's future. On May 21 he submitted a proposal to the league suggesting an immediate assessment of $100,000 per team to be spent on a full-time commissioner and a marketing specialist, along with players from each team to do promotional work. Geller advocated the league take a year off to rebuild, and that each team be required to show resources of at least $500,000 after paying off all outstanding debts.

If the proposal was not accepted, Geller warned, the Pioneers would not play in 1981–82. San Francisco's investors were prepared to continue, Geller says now, if they were convinced that other teams were financially stable. "We had had an owner's meeting for the Pioneers and decided we would put in another half million dollars because we felt that with any new sport and any new league, you need staying power."

Geller believed that if the WBL could show stability for a few years, it would eventually link up with the NBA. Some NBA owners had begun to express interest, he says, such as San Francisco Warriors owner Franklin Mieuli. "Franklin told me, 'If I really knew that this league was going to be around, I would help you guys. I would invest money in the team and I would put you in the arena. We would market for you,'" Geller says. "You've got to give the NBA owners in those days some credit. They were interested, but we just couldn't show the stability."

Geller's motion gathered a majority of five votes. "We're getting back to the position where we should have been all along," Almstead said. "I don't want to price teams out of the league, but at the same time, if we are going to be partners in the league, we must all be equitable financially."

The 1981 player draft, originally scheduled for June 16 in Chicago, did not take place. The league wrote players on July 13, 1981, that the WBL was "in transition," and that the draft would be postponed while it worked to hire a new commissioner, establish a strong financial base and marketing program, and create a grievance committee.

Among other problems for the owners to resolve was that under a settlement of lawsuits filed against them by Philadelphia Fox players, the WBL was prohibited from commencing a 1981–82 season unless $41,000 was paid to the Fox players by October 31, 1981. Individual teams that did not pay their share were barred by court order from participating.

While owners considered these issues, retired AT&T vice president William "Bill" Haarlow submitted a proposal to restructure the WBL. Haarlow was a former All-American basketball player at the University of Chicago and had played professionally with John Wooden on the Indianapolis Kautskys during the 1930s. He identified five "lessons" from professional sports history that, in his view, the WBL had not heeded:

1. A commitment to strong centralized league leadership is required. League leaders must not be intimidated from bold action. There must be a clearly defined #1 executive or executive committee who has power and room to maneuver and the leadership must provide realistic and continual reappraisal of long term growth objectives and strategy.

2. Markets must be selected based on potential. There must be a determination of the criteria that is most likely to influence the league's appeal and the economics of a franchise, i.e., size and growth of market, degree of saturation by other sports, target audience, operating costs, and previous experience with an attitude toward other leagues or teams. The league must avoid expanding into new markets at the expense of the talent pool.

3. There must be a commitment of balanced ownership resources. The League must balance the urgency to close a franchise sale against the commitment by new owners of capital to team and market development. Women's basketball has to confront building primary demand which is a costly marketing proposition that requires knowledgeable and well-funded programs. There should be a five-year building plan and owners with the same perspective and staying power should be attracted.

4. The League must build and sustain the sport as a dynamic entertainment medium. There must be an evaluation of alternative formats and rules to make the sport appealing to the widest range of potential patrons and viewers. For a new sport, the live experience is critical to building viewership for ultimate video revenue.

5. Non-Gate sources of revenue should be built. A commitment must be made to professional league headquarters marketing services, video strategy and negotiation, licensing, and advertiser-sponsor development. This function must be undertaken gradually as the sport develops and grows.

Haarlow offered to serve as commissioner under a three-year contract starting at $65,000, plus 30 percent of broadcasting, merchandising, and sponsorship revenues. If the owners approved the proposal, he would schedule a 1981 college draft at the end of August. "We must build credibility from the start and words alone will not accomplish this," he said.

Geller considered the proposal too broad and open-ended. A new commissioner would not solve the league's underlying problem, he said, "which is the unstable and insolvent status of the majority of the League members." The Pioneers formally withdrew from participation in the WBL. "The question is not only a commissioner," Geller told the other owners, "it is whether there is a market for our product."

On September 24, 1981, Almstead informed the WBL Board of Governors that he was resigning as interim commissioner. "Since I was requested to take over the position at the last league meeting on May 23rd, 1981," he wrote, "the members of the league have been totally inactive, non-functioning and have neglected their responsibilities to the league and to the other franchises in the league as outlined in the league by-laws."

Shortly afterward, Almstead announced publicly that the WBL had ceased operations. "I'm not giving up a sinking ship," he said. "The ship has already sunk." The league had folded, he said, because "greed prevailed over brains. . . . Nobody wanted to come up with certain capital requirements. In general, most of the owners were waiting to see if there were other potential owners who would buy them out." Fischer and Nebraska Wranglers owner Larry Kozlicki disagreed. "This is not the first time Dave has made rash statements," Kozlicki said.

In late October, New Orleans Pride co-owner Claudette Simpson said there would be no new WBL season unless a major new sponsor appeared on the horizon. Fischer and Kozlicki wrote to their fellow owners in November, noting that the league had not held a draft, had no officers, and was without an office, and no game schedule had been prepared. "The league's dilemma is caused by a lack of management, a lack of marketing and a lack of money," the letter said.

"Some teams from time to time have indicated an interest in continuing to operate and playing basketball this year," they wrote. "Most of you, however, have shown no interest at all and have either announced your closing, released your players, given press releases saying that the league is finished or a combination of several of these." The Hustle and Wranglers still wanted to play, the men said, but two teams did not make a league. Did anyone else want to try for a season to begin in February or March 1982?

Gennaro in St. Louis did, but he was skeptical. "I think a discussion of reorganization is long overdue," he replied. "However, I cannot conceive of a reorganization which would permit adequately capitalized teams to participate by February or March 1982." New York, which had earlier suspended operations, wouldn't be ready by 1982 but planned to play in the 1983 season, owner Ed Reisdorf said. New Jersey was giving up; owner Robert Milo just didn't think the present members had the money. "The league will take big $$$," he wrote. "Without new investors the situation is not very good!"

Iowa wasn't in a position to play, but owner George Nissen was willing to attend an owners' meeting. San Francisco was interested in playing, but not necessarily in the WBL. Gordon Nevers hoped to sell the Minnesota Fillies to a Detroit investor. The Dallas survey was returned, the envelope stating it was no longer in business, but franchise president Dave Almstead had recently declared, "If the league plays, I'm Popeye."

The Chicago, Minnesota, and Nebraska owners called a meeting for December 12, 1981, to address a ten-item agenda, including the league's current structure, teams' financial structures, and a "general review, evaluation and discussion of the future, if any, of the WBL." The meeting did not take place, and a formal resolution was circulated to dissolve the WBL, which was signed by a majority of owners in February 1982.

Most players were not formally notified of the WBL's fate. "It's funny, but there never was an official article about the league folding," Sue Peters said. "It just drifted off into thin air." The players "just seemed to know it," Jody Rajcula recalls. "It was like this underground communication that was between players, everyone was trying to look out for everyone. We all had an idea."

The rise and fall of the WBL followed a "script" written by dreamers past, the *San Francisco Chronicle*'s Glenn Dickey said:

> The owner announces that he's willing to lose money for three, four or even five years to establish the team. But he doesn't really mean it, ever. This is, after all, a man who has been very successful in at least one other business, and in his heart, he truly believes that he can be successful where others have failed.
>
> There is great enthusiasm at the start. If it's an established sport (as in the WFL and ABA), the owner is constantly assured that the existing league isn't enough to satisfy the fans' interest, and his team and league will prosper. If it's a new sport, such as indoor soccer, videotape showings are always greeted by great excitement, and the owner is told that his sport is filling a vacuum.
>
> Then, the season starts and reality sets in. The owner discovers a basic fact about fans: that they follow the herd. They will show up in great numbers to see an event they've heard is important, but discounted and even free tickets can't get them out to see something new.
>
> It always costs more money to get the operation going than the owner anticipated. Money doesn't trickle out; it runs out the door.
>
> About a month into the season, the owner gets a call from an office employee who tells him that the printer isn't going to print any more programs until that last bill for $370 is paid. The owner blows up. It isn't that he doesn't have the money; he does. But he's always been in a position where his credit was unquestioned.
>
> The owner's personality changes. Sometimes, he blames the media for a lack of coverage, forgetting that newspapers and television and radio stations are commercial enterprises, too. They use stories that

interest readers and viewers—just as the owner would if he owned the newspaper or station.

Around the office, his employees start to give him a wide berth; he isn't pleasant to be around. At parties, he makes a determined effort to smile and make small talk and avoid talking about his team. But his friends, meaning well, keep asking him: "Do you think you'll be able to break even this year?" Finally, inevitably, somebody asks: "If you had it to do all over again, would you?"

Aaaargh!

So what killed the first women's professional basketball league? Observers cite any number of factors, such as the 1980 Olympic boycott, poor management, disinterested media, and a general lack of interest in women's sports. Each of those factors did indeed play a role, some more than others.

A key fact, though, is that most of the men willing to take a chance on a WBL team did not have the financial ability to withstand the early years of huge losses—$150,000 to $450,000 each season—that all professional leagues go through. "If you study history, in the NBA's first 10 years they were leaving Schenectady in the middle of the night," Geller said in 1981. The same is true for all pro leagues, says Nevers. "Go back to the NFL—any league. They've all got their horror stories."

By the late 1970s NBA franchises were worth millions, but it had taken thirty years of sacrifice by players and owners to reach that stage. Investors who envisioned the WBL as an NBA-in-progress (an image that league officials publicly downplayed but privately enjoyed) were not equipped for the long haul.

The WBL needed owners who could endure the normal bumps of a start-up business, says Geller: "Companies start out. They raise some money. They grow a little. They need to raise some more money. They have to stay in business. They have to develop a new product. They have to do certain marketing things." Women's basketball was no different from any other new business, he says. "You have your good times and your bad times."

Most WBL owners did not have that kind of staying power, but the league didn't have much choice. Multimillionaires were not knocking on its door, and an owner with some resources was better than no owner at all. "There were a handful of good owners, but there were some owners that were in it for a quick buck and you're not going to build a league like that," says New Orleans Pride general manager Steve Brown. "You're going to have to develop it over a decade or more. To think you're going to come in a year or two, invest some money, and turn it around just isn't going to happen."

Some owners believed they had sufficient resources because they expected a better rate of return. League founder Bill Byrne said publicly that it would take three to five years for any team to see a profit, but some investors seemed more optimistic. "While most owners say they are committed to a three-year process of selling the league as an important entertainment function, they are not as convincing as wbl president Bill Byrne would like them to be," wrote the *Dayton Daily News*.

"I give Slick Bill a lot of credit. He was a hell of a salesman and a good man, but you had to take what you got," says Brown, now a consultant to small businesses. "Some of these guys just didn't have the type of capital and thought for whatever reason they could buy a team year one and sell it in two or three years at a big profit, which was just a dream sequence."

Ultimately, the weaker franchises dragged down the stronger ones. "It's pretty lonely out there when you are putting up money and nobody else is ready to put up any money," Geller says. "Bill Byrne—you know, he's an entrepreneur, but he's also a dreamer, and I think he was less than candid about the finances of the league and the other teams."

Adverse publicity generated by the financial problems of weaker franchises created a self-fulfilling prophecy that the league was going to fail, Geller says. The biggest problem he faced as interim commissioner, Sherwin Fischer agrees, "wasn't the owners—it was owners not paying their players." The league's reputation was "going straight downhill" with that kind of press, which drove away potential sponsors.

Ownership instability was compounded by the mistakes of league officials, some observers suggested. In 1980 sportswriter Lacy Banks, a frequent critic of wbl management, compiled a list of Byrne's alleged missteps: "Using league money to maintain ownerless teams; admitting several new owners who were not financially qualified to see a team through a season; breaching player contracts and triggering lawsuits against the league; encouraging premature coast-to-coast expansion that resulted in exorbitant travel expenses that proved decisive in the economic demise of half the league."

"I think Bill Byrne was fine," Cornets owner Nissen says. "He had grandeur and was caught up in what we always do when we have a new product. You have three mistakes: 1) You get over-enthused, 2) You are worried about your competition, and 3) You want to make up all the money you put into it. You need to not get sucked into those kind of things. I think he liked to go too fast—big league, you know." (There will always be criticism of the league or his efforts, Byrne says. "Anything beyond three people you are going to have disagreements or different attitudes, opinions, etc. You know what the old adage is: Everyone has their opinion and also has a bottom.")

Analysis of the wbl's collapse must also take into account Byrne's suggestions that were not followed by owners. "Three things will fold a club," he said before the inaugural game. "No. 1, player pay; No. 2, travel expenses; No. 3, arena costs." The wbl was "on top of all three," he reported. It might have begun on top, but beginning in the second season, all three factors began to diverge.

PLAYER PAY. "I personally believe that the league went under because of two things," says player Patti Bucklew. "One, owners that came in there thinking that they were going to make a quick buck, which wasn't going to happen in that day and age; two, players who got greedy because they thought that they were better than the rest."

Bucklew isn't the only one who places blames on the high salary demands ($50,000 or more) of a few players, mostly in the third season. "You want to talk about resentment," says Wanda Szeremeta. "I have resentment [at the time] because I've been in the league from Day 1 and played for this minimum salary, played for the love of the game, and now all these big-time ball players are coming in and asking for this kind of money. I said, 'That's it, its going to kill us,' and it did."

Other players doubt that higher salaries made that much of an impact. The difference between her teammate Carol Blazejowski's $50,000 salary and the lowest paid player wasn't enough to break the league, says Jill Jeffrey. "We're not talking millions of dollars here."

TRAVEL COSTS. The wbl's rapid growth in season two also draws blame. "We expanded too far, too soon," Fischer says. "It ended up with teams traveling thousands of miles to play before a few hundred fans. We tried to run before we learned how to crawl." Initially, there were no teams west of the Mississippi, and several could bus to games. In 1979–80 the wbl extended to both coasts and to the northern and southern borders, driving up travel costs.

"I think when we started expanding it to the 12 teams on each coast, it did start to get too expensive for the amount of attendance that we were generating," Fillies player and public relations director Lynnette Sjoquist says. An embargo by oil-producing countries was sending gasoline prices—and airfares—through the roof. Add in hotel costs (because teams were supposed to arrive a day early), and the costs were "terrible," Iowa owner Nissen says.

ARENA COSTS. During the WBL's first season, most teams played in modest facilities or traded rent for a piece of the action. The next year, some franchises began renting huge, expensive facilities, such as the Superdome in New Orleans and Madison Square Garden in New York.

"It was the only way to make it," New York Stars co-owner Ed Reisdorf contends. "We believed if we were in Madison Square Garden that the press could no longer ignore us. We were playing double-headers with the [New York] Knicks frequently. We thought it would make the whole league a success, and we were willing. I would have been happier if everyone else would have contributed to it, but they weren't going to do that, and so we bit the bullet and we did it, and it didn't work."

Owners would have been better off staying with smaller facilities, Iowa Cornets general manager Rod Lein believes, and had they done so, the league might even have survived. "If we could start small and grow—that's what I tried to do, but they wouldn't listen to me."

There are two schools of thought about renting plush facilities, in Geller's view. "One of them is by doing it in the Garden, you gain the status that you wanted as a professional sport. I don't argue with that. But the problem is, when you're doing it at Madison Square Garden or Pacific Auditorium in San Francisco or the Forum here in Los Angeles, it didn't offset some of these other places playing in high school gyms because they didn't pay the rent."

Posh facilities did convey a message to some. The WBL "upgraded its credibility" by sharing arenas with NBA teams, the *New York Post* concluded. Playing in the Garden—"you can't get any classier than that," the *San Francisco Chronicle* wrote. Reisdorf worked out a "great deal" with the Garden, he says (only $15,000 per night), and there was an allure to playing in the historic arena. "It was exciting for everybody except when you are writing out the checks."

Basketball Weekly associate editor Clifford Smith wrote at the beginning of the second season, "It may look packed in a smaller arena but let's face it, you play in a minor league arena and you reflect a minor league operation. You play in a place like the Superdome, and you're talking style. Why eat chop meat when there's filet mignon on the table?"

Perhaps because most people can't afford filet mignon, especially if there's too much of it. "I remember going down to play New Orleans at the Superdome, and looking up to the ceiling, and just seeing empty seats for what seemed like forever," recalls New England Gulls coach Dana Skinner. "It just didn't make a lot of sense to me that a start-up league was trying to play in venues like that."

Playing the Stars in the Garden before a Knicks game was a great experience, Washington Metros player Jodi Gault says—"Can't say that the crowd was." A thousand fans in a place as big as the Superdome was like having one fan there, Lynn Arturi felt. "With a thousand fans you can't even shoot," Martha Hastings says. "The baskets looked so weird because there was so much distance behind them."

WBL owners' biggest problem wasn't necessarily the money going out, Milwaukee Does supporter Jan Doleschal believes, but rather the money *not* coming in. "I don't think they were in over their head in what they expected to invest financially, I think they were in over their heads in what they expected to make in revenue," she says. "There was nothing to indicate that this was going to be a success." Owners thought the sport would catch on more quickly than it did, says former Cornets manager Kate McEnroe. "People just thought they could put on the games and people would come."

Attendance was a problem for most teams—"If you're cheating on your wife, don't go to a Pride game," a high school coach reportedly said in New Orleans, "because if anyone knows you they'll see you"—but it did improve each year. In the WBL's third and final season, reported home attendance (which was sometimes inflated) ranged from 1,043 in New England to about 2,400 for Dallas and Chicago. The league average was 1,533. In the 1980–81 playoffs, however, Dallas averaged nearly 4,000 for its two home games against New Jersey and more than 7,000 for the two finals games against Nebraska.

The key to better attendance, most owners felt, was television. "TV, either locally or nationally, is pivotal because it can force-feed our product to people in their homes," Streak owner Gennaro said in 1981. "Our problem has not been getting people to come back once they've seen a game, it's been getting them to come in the first place."

The only franchise with good television was Chicago, which went into its first season under a contract with WGN. "These stations here in Chicago were looking for time to fill in, and they were a strong believer in Title IX and women's professional basketball," Fischer says. "They thought it would be successful, also." And it was. The ratings for Hustle games were twice as high as forecast, and WGN bought the rights to nine more games. The Hustle even outdrew the NBA's Chicago Bulls a couple of times, the station confirmed.

No other team had significant television exposure. Cable stations were only beginning to emerge, and the outlet for sports productions was limited. "Today, hell, they'll buy a flea crawling on a monkey's back," Byrne says, but back then it was a different story.

Had the growth of cable begun a few years earlier, the WBL would have ended up with a television contract, Dallas Diamonds owner Jud Phillips believes. At the time, though, the only way to get time on a network affiliate was to buy it. (Air time for a Diamonds' game would cost $3,000, he says, assuming it was a West Coast game starting after prime time.)

The pro league was a hard sell, and getting harder with each public revelation of shakiness. "The TV people started doing some checking on financial stability and all the other things they would want before they would schedule a whole season of games," Geller says, and they weren't convinced. "You are never going to get anywhere if you present an image to the public that you are living from hand to mouth," he says. "Players are sleeping in cars. Girls are going to the press and telling them they haven't been paid. Arenas are shutting people down unless the league wired them money tomorrow."

From the WBL's earliest days, Byrne had warned owners against letting that kind of dirty laundry get into the press. "I never complained to the media or anything," he says. "If it was positive, we would talk about it; if not, we were in a hurry. Negative things, there's plenty of it out there if you want it, but it really doesn't work, especially in building a league."

If the league hadn't folded, it would finally have landed a national television contract, Fischer says. He had met with the sports network ESPN, which had then been on the air nearly two years, and believed they were close to a deal. "With that TV contract we would have survived," he says. A consultant also reported that a handful of cable stations and one network had agreed to televise some WBL games the following season, and even to pay for the rights. "Get a dose of media exposure," advised the *Press Box*. "Take two TV games and call me in the morning."

The best hope for such exposure, one that WBL officials and owners had counted on from the start, was the 1980 Olympics. "Those Olympics are going to be very important for us," WBL spokesperson Meg Griggs said in 1979. "There will be network television coverage and a lot of attention focused on women's basketball, which should help us—especially if we sign as many of those Olympic players for next season as we expect to."

Marshall Geller devised his own plan to exploit Olympic momentum and lined up the funding. Immediately after the medal ceremony, he would sign Carol Blazejowski or Nancy Lieberman to the first $1 million contract in women's basketball: "We were going to go to the Olympics and right there, in front of whoever was televising it, have either one of those two sign a million-dollar contract, which would have been really startling news in those days for a woman's professional athlete."

The expected Olympic boost never came to pass. On December 24, 1979, the Soviet Union invaded Afghanistan, and talk soon began of boycotting the upcoming Olympics in Moscow. The country's best-known female basketball player, Nancy Lieberman, then a senior at Old Dominion, urged against it. "It's a shame that U.S. athletes have to be used as a political wedge," she said. "I don't think sports and politics mix. It would be a shame if they hold back the American athletes."

But when President Jimmy Carter announced that he did not believe the United States should participate in the Olympics, Lieberman felt she needed to support the decision, and she withdrew from the U.S. National Team. "If President Carter says don't go, I don't go," she said. "I have to put my country before my individual interests." Five days later, the United States Olympic Committee voted to comply with the president's request.

"When President Carter boycotted the Summer Olympics for political reasons, he set back the growth of Women's Professional Basketball at least for two years," wrote *Sportswoman's T.E.A.M. Basketball Digest* publisher P. G. "Granny" Wethall. It killed the WBL, Geller believes. If the U.S. team had won, or even medalled as everyone expected, "funding would have come out of the woodwork for this venture," he says. "I'm not only talking about San Francisco. Even the worst teams could have been sold to somebody who had a couple of bucks and wanted to take the next step, but it never happened."

When it was all over, Fillies owner Nevers says he had no regrets. Pain, maybe, but no regrets. He remembers one evening in the steam room of an athletic club when a local business owner asked how things were going. Fine, Nevers replied. "Well, I'd like to tell you something," the businessman said. "You tried something that none of us had enough guts to try. It didn't work, but your head is up and you're in great spirits, and I take my hat off to you." Although they were too late, the kind words were still a balm to Nevers. "That was probably the one thing I needed to let me know that I wasn't such a bad boy after all."

21

Snapshots of the WBL

BOSTON, NOVEMBER 1980

New England Gulls officials were in a bind. Their team was scheduled to play an exhibition game against the New Orleans Pride, but the Pride were refusing to come unless the Gulls paid their travel expenses. That would cost too much, especially for a preseason game. And, come to think of it, all the fans really cared about was seeing a game. . . .

The Gulls put in some calls, and down came some players from the New Jersey Gems with uniforms in hand. Their job: to impersonate the Pride. It wasn't like fans would know what the players looked like, anyway. Gulls player Martha Hastings laughed when the name of a black Pride player was announced, and lily-white Wanda Szeremeta ran onto the court. "It was just hilarious that they pulled this off," she thought.

NEW ORLEANS SUPERDOME, 1977

Willem "Butch" van Breda Kolff heard a voice yell out at him. It was that pain in the ass again, the guy that won front-row season tickets to the New Orleans Jazz by naming the team and then proceeded to ride the coach relentlessly. Van Breda Kolff signaled for a substitution. "Hey, he's taking you out because you've got too many rebounds!" Great. "The only guy in New Orleans that didn't like me was Steve Brown, then he had to win the goddamn thing, and I had to listen to him every night."

Two years later . . . van Breda Kolff picked up the phone. After nearly thirty years of coaching, he had settled into a job as athletic director at the University of New Orleans, but on the line was a man with an unexpected offer. A professional basketball team—a women's team—was coming to town, and the New Orleans Pride wanted him on the bench.

The coach laughed. You can't afford me, he said. "We can't afford not to have you," the caller countered. "They love you in this city. We need your name."

Van Breda Kolff agreed to meet with the Pride's general manager—and immediately recognized him. "You're the sonofabitch who kept hollering at me every game!" he exclaimed. Yes, he was, Brown admitted. The ultimate heckler now wanted the coach to come to work for him. All right, van Breda Kolff agreed—if Brown didn't try to tell him how to do his job this time. ("I don't know if I forgave him, because I didn't forget him," van Breda Kolff says.)

Molly Bolin was ecstatic. In front of 4,788 screaming fans, her Iowa Cornets had just clinched a playoff spot over division rival Minnesota Fillies, and she had just set a new WBL scoring record with 53 points. Moments later, though, Bolin's elation turned to fear—her mother had collapsed in the stands.

Rushing over with the team doctor, Bolin soon had good news. Mrs. Van Benthuysen had only fainted from excitement. "She hyperventilated and passed out," Bolin (now Kazmer) recalls. "That was pretty scary." The following season, Bolin broke the scoring record again, dislocating her shoulder in the same game. "When I got hurt, they had to carry my mom out," she laughs. "She's very excitable."

Bolin holds the all-time single-game scoring record in women's professional basketball (55 points), the single-season scoring record (1,179), and the highest average score (32.8). And Bolin's defense? "Nonexistent," she admits, "but not from lack of effort." She hadn't played defense in Iowa's six-on-six program and didn't learn much at college, where her main job was to put the ball up. "Molly Bolin could flat out score," says teammate Mo Eckroth. "She couldn't guard my mom, but she could flat out score."

The WBL scoring record would have been even higher if a new owner of the Cornets had gotten his way. "I want Molly Bolin to score one hundred points in a game," Dick Vance told head coach Steve Kirk. The coach shook his head. "Well, if we do, it'll be great marketing," Vance insisted. "You're too defense oriented."

"Listen," Kirk argued, "she got 55 in one game, and that was about as difficult as you can get. My credibility is always on the line because Molly is taking all the shots." Kirk was already running every out-of-bounds play, every set play, every fast-break play for her. "I've done everything possible. There is no way that I can get one hundred points."

Vance persisted. "I think you can," he said. "I'll tell you what: if she gets one hundred points, I'm going to give you $10,000, and I'll give every girl on the team $1,000."

"You could give me $100,000 and give every girl on the team $10,000," Kirk replied. "She can't get a hundred. I would lose the team in doing that, even if I could do it. My goal is to win the championship." The coach went home that night expecting to be fired. Luckily — for Kirk, anyway — Cornets management soon learned that Vance's check had bounced.

• • •

The only other female professional basketball player to break the 1,000-point mark in a single season is the New Jersey Gems' Carol Blazejowski (1,067). During one 53-point performance on March 13, 1981, the Blaze scored 21 straight on free throws.

• • •

Speaking of scoring phenoms, a key player on the 1979–80 champion New York Stars was Pearl "the Earl" Moore, the all-time leading scorer in women's collegiate basketball. After scoring 177 points at Anderson Junior College in South Carolina, Moore transferred to Francis Marion College and added another 3,884, for a total of 4,061 points. In January 1980 Moore sank 1022 of 1191 foul shots during a four-hour free-throw marathon at a Greater New York Auto Show. She would have gone another hour, but she was worried about tiring herself out for that night's game.

• • •

On the road in Chicago, Dallas Diamonds radio broadcaster Eric Nadel was dismayed that a halftime show was to be forty minutes long, complete with marching band and tuba stationed only a few feet away from him. A couple of dogs were then sicced on two tackling dummies, and as Nadel looked down at his stats, he heard four gunshots ring out. He leapt out of his seat, knocking his soft drink the length of the press table. The shots, he was relieved to learn, were part of the dog act.

• • •

The inaugural WBL draft in New York City on July 17, 1978, ended with a final selection by the New York Stars' Larry Kinitsky, who generated laughs by writing the name of sports commentator and former Miss America Phyllis George. "That's Miss America, not All-America," he quipped. The Chicago Hustle also made an interesting pick: Sandy Allen, listed in the *Guinness Book of World Records* as the tallest woman in the world at seven foot seven and a quarter inches. Neither played in the WBL.

• • •

In the WBL's first season, no shot counted for three points, no matter how far a player was from the basket. One player who missed out that year was the Dayton Rockettes' Vivian Greene. While most players could make a lay-up or a short jumper, the *Dayton Daily News* noted, "Greene plays in another area. She doesn't shoot, she launches. When Greene lets go of the basketball [usually from 30 feet, the *News* claimed], a whoosh is heard in the stands."

• • •

Chicago Hustle point guard Rita Easterling holds the WBL's all-time single-game assist record with 21, set in the inaugural game on December 9, 1978.

• • •

The WBL's biggest draft-day bargain might have been a ninth-round selection in 1979. Linda Matthews's high school hadn't offered girls basketball, but she walked on to the team at North Carolina State. Five games into her sophomore year, Matthews was hit by a car. She spent the rest of the season on crutches and then dropped out for a year before returning as a junior. In July 1979 Matthews was drafted by the Philadelphia Fox and became the team's most dominant player, averaging 17.6 points, 5.2 assists, 3.7 rebounds, and 2.8 steals per game. After the Fox folded, she was picked up by the California Dreams and finished out their season with 15 points per game.

Another ninth-round sleeper was Iowa State's Pat Hodgson, a 1979 Iowa pick. She ended up third in scoring (11.4), rebounds (6.2), assists (3.3), and minutes played for the Cornets.

Pat Montgomery, a 1980 WBL All-Star (who was kicked off her team at Utah State in her senior year for celebrating a 38-point performance with a beer), was a seventh rounder in the 1979 draft. She ended up second on the Minnesota Fillies in scoring (18.2) and minutes played, and third in rebounds (7.9).

• • •

The California Dreams' first coach, Mel Sims, taught a disco class in his spare time.

• • •

Five overtime games were played in the WBL's first season—four of them by the Milwaukee Does. One was a "knock-down, drag-out fight" against the New Jersey Gems on March 30, 1979, that barely ended at three overtimes and set several lasting records in women's professional basketball, including most combined points (324) and most points by one team (163). Nearly three hours into the game, Wanda Szeremeta iced a 163–161 victory for the Gems with eight seconds left by sinking two free throws, her 38th and 39th points. Twelve other players also scored in double figures: New Jersey's Gail Tatterson (32), Karen Logan (18), Susan Martin (17), Denise Burdick (14), Debbie Mason (13), Kathy Solano (12), and Maggie Nelson (10), and Milwaukee's Cindy Ellis (38), Brenda Chapman (35), Gerry Booker (21), Deb Prevost (19), and Joanie Smith (17).

• • •

The WBL's biggest upset occurred on January 9, 1981. The New England Gulls were in turmoil at the time. They hadn't been paid in months, and some players were eating only once a day. They now faced the toughest assignment in the league: the Nebraska Wranglers, who were rumbling toward the title.

When they arrived in Omaha, the Gulls gave up their meal money to pay for hotel rooms. That night, just as the league's Goliath seemed sure of another victory—the Wranglers led by 11 points in the fourth quarter—the struggling Gulls suddenly launched a furious comeback. A balanced attack by Althea Gwyn (21 points), Chris Critelli, Jody Rajcula, and Susan Summons (20 each) led New England to the shocking win. "In the locker room afterwards, none of us cared if we didn't get paid," Rajcula recalls. "We just beat the number one team in the league. A team that was falling apart came together as a group of women that were playing the game that we loved, and we beat them."

• • •

When former NBA coach Larry Costello signed on with the Milwaukee Does in 1979, he took his new job seriously, even checking out rival Chicago Hustle's preseason games. "I could smell his breath, he was so close to the bench behind us scouting," Hustle coach Doug Bruno jokes. Bruno knew that Costello would be charting the Hustle's plays and decided to steer him off course. "We're going to run this little deal," he told his players. "If we're going to go on the right side, we're going to call out a number. If we go on the left side, we're going to call out a color. You can use any number and any color, just because I want to mess with Larry."

Hustle point guard Rita Easterling dribbled down the court. "27," she called. The ball went to the right, and the players all made whatever moves they wanted. The next time down, she called out a color and went left. The result wasn't always the same—sometimes a player took the base line or went up for a jump shot—but it was always the same play. "Larry's writing all of this crap down," Bruno laughs. "It was hilarious."

• • •

The Houston Angels did not participate in a mid-season draft that dispersed players from the dissolved Philadelphia and Washington franchises, and a reporter asked coach Don Knodel why he had refused to pick. "Refused to pick?" Knodel exclaimed. "That's a lot of bull. We were in a plane flying back from San Francisco when they decided to have the draft without us. They could have waited." The coaches learned of the draft after they landed.

• • •

Several WBL players and coaches had great nicknames. In addition to Carol "the Blaze" Blazejowski, Carmen "Cheese" Fletcher, Rosalind "Pig" Jennings, Paula "Moose" Mayo, Evelyn "Snoopy" Bender, and Charlene "Toy" McWhorter were the following:

> "Machine Gun" Molly Bolin. A *Washington Post* reporter coined this memorable nickname in 1979. She disliked it initially, but "it certainly fits, because Bolin is an extraordinary and prolific shooter," the *St. Louis Globe-Democrat* wrote after she put on a 47-point clinic against the St. Louis Streak. "Thursday night, she just shot the Streak to death."

Pearl "the Earl" Moore, a clever spin on the nickname of another basketball great, Earl "the Pearl" Monroe.

"Wicked Wanda" Szeremeta, who, the *New Jersey Monthly* wrote, "charges the basket like some crazed matriarch." This moniker was courtesy of a sports information director at Montclair State in Szeremeta's junior year.

Marie "Scooter" DeLorme, so dubbed by her father when she was a baby. (She had a sister Skeeter.)

• • •

The Dallas Diamonds had the number one pick in the 1980 WBL draft. Over dinner the night before, Diamonds coach Greg Williams asked owner Michael Staver to confirm that it was solely his decision. "OK, Greg has the final say," Staver declared. "He is making the call. Who are we drafting tomorrow morning?"

Williams knew the answer. He had called several top college coaches to ask, "It's between Nancy Lieberman or her teammate Inge Nissen. Who would you take if you were in my position?" The response was almost unanimous: Nissen. "Lieberman is a great, great player, no question," nearly all said, "but you're talking six feet five inches versus a five-foot-ten-inch guard, I'd take six-five."

"We're drafting Inge Nissen," Williams said.

At 9 a.m. the next morning, the draft began. The Diamonds had three minutes to make their selection. The coach scribbled on a piece of paper, folded it, and waited for Staver to appear for the announcement. And waited. And waited. Diamonds president Dave Almstead hurried to the coffee shop downstairs, but Staver wasn't there. He ran back to their hotel; again nothing. "You have one minute, Dallas," WBL president Bill Byrne declared. The clock ticked, and Williams glanced again at the door. Where was he? They wanted him to have the honor of making the first pick.

Finally, Staver wandered into the room, stopping to greet people. His owner was a night person, the ultimate party guy, Williams knew, and he'd obviously had a good time in the Big Apple. The coach quickly handed him the note. They were almost out of time. Blurry eyed and half out of it, Staver looked at it in confusion. "Wait a minute, what's this?"

Williams shoved him toward the microphone. "Hurry up—get up there and make the pick before we lose it!" The Diamonds selected Lieberman. Williams had changed his mind overnight.

. . .

The day before the 1980 draft, tempers flared as six owners accused San Francisco Pioneers general manager Marshall Geller of illegally signing South Carolina State's Margaret English, the six-foot-four-inch sister of NBA Hall of Famer Alex English, who had been assessed as a potential first-round pick. English should have been placed in the draft, they insisted. League president Bill Byrne broke a tie vote, upholding the signing but penalizing San Francisco a 1981–82 draft pick.

. . .

On March 24, 1981, Pioneers fans witnessed a classic shootout between Molly Bolin and New Jersey's Carol Blazejowski. By the end of the first quarter, San Francisco led 41–31, and Bolin had 21 points (the most ever scored in a single quarter). The Pioneers won, but 27 second-half points from the Blaze drew the Gems to within four.

. . .

The record for most points by one WBL team in a regulation game is 153, scored by the Chicago Hustle against the Dayton Rockettes on March 8, 1979.

. . .

The WBL's longest known shot was a 55-footer by Minnesota Fillies guard Donna Wilson, a buzzer beater to end the first half of a December 12, 1979, game against the Milwaukee Does.

. . .

Two players who were expected to do big things in the WBL's first season instead were sidelined until the following year. Six-foot-four-inch Shelia "Too Tall" Patterson, who averaged 20 points and 20 rebounds at Federal City College, was the only local player on the Dayton Rockettes. In the team's debut on December 15, 1978, Patterson already had 15 points and 18 rebounds in 25 minutes of play when she was tripped up by an opposing player, tearing ligaments and cartilage in her knee and ending her season. A year later, Patterson played 34 games with the St. Louis Streak.

At a preseason Minnesota Fillies practice in November 1978, 1976 Olympian and All-American Patricia "Trish" Roberts from the University of

Tennessee landed badly on a rebound and tore cartilage in her knee. The injury kept her out of all but a few minutes in four games at the end of the season and in just ten games the following year. In 1980–81, Roberts played 34 games for St. Louis.

. . .

During a game in San Francisco, Houston's Karen Aulenbacher landed face first while diving for a loose ball, and a Pioneers player toppled onto her. "160 pounds came on the back of my head," she remembers. "It looked like someone dropping a watermelon." She was knocked out, blood covering her face, but no ambulance was available, so she was rushed to the hospital by taxi. While she was recuperating in San Francisco for three days, coach Don Knodel, who had a full-time job apart from coaching, stayed with her. When Aulenbacher returned home, she needed a face protector, and Houston Rockets player Rudy Tomjanovich lent her the mask he had worn two years earlier after nearly being killed by a famous punch from Kermit Washington.

. . .

"You girls must be the New Jersey Gems," a man in Dallas drawled at Donna Simms and her teammates. "So, show us your gems." "Why don't you show us your jewels?" Simms replied.

. . .

In St. Louis the Dallas Diamonds were waiting for the coach to bring their van around when a well-dressed man with a chic umbrella happened by. Spying Diamonds guard Vanessa Barnes, it was love at first sight. Hurrying to his car, he drove alongside the van, honking and waving to get Barnes's attention. When the van pulled into a gas station, the man insisted on speaking to her. Finally, assistant coach Tom Davis rolled down his window, and the admirer stuck his face in.

Jotting down his name and phone number, the man slipped it through the window. He then announced that he could outrun, outjump, outshoot, or outplay any of the Diamonds. He preached for the Lord, he said, and would be making a lot of money soon. He would like to make a lot of little basketball players with Barnes, he told her. With the gas tank filled, the Diamonds took off again, leaving the suitor behind. "You sure know how to pick 'em," Barnes's teammates teased.

• • •

At Madison Square Garden before a 1979 game, renowned artist LeRoy Neiman drew sketches of San Francisco Pioneers players.

• • •

During the 1979–80 season, a *New Yorker* columnist attended a New York Stars game with an enthusiastic fan and later recounted some of his friend's observations: "Watch No. 11, Sharon Farrah. . . . She's a tough kid. She looks as if she really wanted to do harm to someone. Best snarl I've ever seen. The other guard is Janice Thomas, No. 10. She's only five feet three, and looks as if she weren't afraid of anything. She can scoot around all night. She can dribble faster than I can talk. And there's No. 6, Gail Marquis, who's my favorite. She scores a lot, and she sure can bound. She's also beautiful. The best thing about her is that she does everything without changing expression. It's hard to be cool when you're getting hit in the stomach with four or five elbows, but she is. . . . Oh, and there are the Young twins. Faye and Kaye, No. 22 and No. 20. I've seen them in two games and one yogurt commercial. Now that I think about it, they're my favorites."

• • •

Ann Meyers had four triple doubles in her single WBL season with New Jersey: 19 points, 10 rebounds, 10 assists (and 9 steals) against Iowa on January 19, 1980; 30 points, 10 assists, and 11 rebounds against New York on February 11, 1980; 17 points, 13 assists, 10 steals (and 8 rebounds) against St. Louis on February 28, 1980; and 29 points, 14 rebounds, 13 assists (and 7 steals) against New York on March 15, 1980.

• • •

Chicago's WBL franchise was originally dubbed the Skyline, until one afternoon when players Karen Logan and Mary Jo Peppler challenged some men at Navy Pier to some two on two. A TV crew filmed it and later joked on air that the men had been hustled.

"That's a good name," Logan decided. "That's what I'd been doing my whole life. When I was growing up, it was prove, prove, prove. Guys would be saying bad things about women, so you'd try to trick them into games and then blast them. And I figured we were in Chicago, and isn't it known for its con artists and dealings? And then there was the idea of disco and dancing, which gets us to the beauty of movement." The name did wrinkle a few brows. "We didn't like that too well," WBL Director of Communications Frank Cunningham said. "I mean, there are a lot of things people could do with a name like that."

• • •

In 1979–80 the Dallas Diamonds did not win a single one of their 18 road games.

• • •

In its three years the WBL had eight players who averaged 40 or more minutes of play per game over an entire season. The all-time iron woman was Anita Ortega, who recorded 1,543 minutes in 36 games for the San Francisco Pioneers in 1979–80. And they weren't easy. She was "making a habit of playing 48 minutes—at an absolutely frantic pace," the *San Francisco Chronicle* wrote. The Pioneers played brutal defense, employing a full-court press in one game for 46 of its 48 minutes.

The other members of the WBL's 40-plus club were Brenda Chapman, Minnesota Fillies and Milwaukee Does (1978–79, 44.5 minutes per game; 1979–80, 40.8); Donna Geils, New Jersey Gems (1979–80, 40.9); Vivian Greene, Dayton Rockettes (1978–79, 42.4); Ann Meyers, New Jersey Gems (1979–80, 41.1); Angela Scott, Dayton Rockettes (1978–79, 41.5); Vonnie Tomich, Dayton Rockettes (1978–79, 40.8); and Donna Wilson, Minnesota Fillies (1978–79, 42.5; 1979–80, 41.0).

• • •

Two popular WBL coaches were suspended by their owners in the second and third seasons. In 1980 the New Jersey Gems' Howie Landa was suspended for "insubordination, conduct unbecoming a coach and holding an unauthorized scrimmage." The coach also supposedly failed to report that Willodean Harris was injured at the workout. Yes, the team held a scrimmage, and yes, the player's knee popped out, Landa said, but the team had a ten-day gap between games and needed to practice. It was just a personality conflict between owner and coach, thinks Wanda Szeremeta, who was appointed player-coach.

On February 17, 1981, WBL commissioner Sherwin Fischer informed New Orleans Pride general manager Claudette Simpson of reports that coach Butch van Breda Kolff "has not worn proper attire at regulation games.

Also he has on other occasions used abusive language and smelled of liquor." Among other things, the coach was accused of "wearing tennis shoes without socks." (Not true, van Breda Kolff says. He didn't bother with socks during practice, but he always wore them at games.) Two days later, the Pride suspended van Breda Kolff. Something he had learned long ago, the coach said, was that owners can do what they want to do. "I just want to know how I keep getting fired when I have more wins than losses."

• • •

The last game of the 1980–81 Chicago Hustle's regular season was played under court order. Shortly before midnight on March 27, 1981, general manager Ed Smythe tried for the second time to terminate head coach Bill Gleason. (Gleason had earlier said that if the owners wanted him out, it would take legal action. "He was actually fired earlier this month, and he totally refused to go," a staffer told the *Chicago Tribune*.)

On the afternoon of March 28, 1981, Gleason's daughter, an attorney, delivered a lawsuit and motion for temporary injunction to the home of Chief Chancery Judge John Hechinger, and less than a minute before tip-off that night, Gleason appeared with a court order prohibiting the Hustle from replacing him as coach. The teams warmed up while Hustle co-owner Larry Cooper, himself a lawyer, reviewed the paperwork. "OK, Bill, you can coach tonight," he conceded. "But that's only because of a court order. I respect court orders." The 3,108 people in the stands for Fan Appreciation Night soundly booed Gleason, but the next day the Hustle agreed to pay his full two-year salary.

• • •

WBL games were usually preceded by an honorary tip-off. Luminaries who tossed up a WBL ball included NBA Hall of Famer Dave Cowens, tennis legends Billie Jean King and Martina Navratilova, Mike Connors (star of *Mannix*), San Francisco mayor (and later U.S. Senator) Dianne Feinstein, Iowa governor Robert Ray, and Illinois deputy assistant governor (and later Seventh Circuit Court of Appeals judge) Ilana Rovner. ("She threw it, all right," the *Chicago Tribune* said. "It went up 30 feet, dusting a cobweb off a light fixture.")

• • •

New Jersey Gems guard Jill Jeffrey was only five feet tall, which often prompted jokes that she was the team's ball girl. As Jeffrey waited to enter the New Orleans Superdome, a prankster teammate told security that she wasn't with the team. "I had my sneakers over my shoulder, I had a bag, but this woman was like, "No, you can't get in here,'" Jeffrey says.

She called out to Gail Marquis to verify her story, but Marquis replied, "Little girl, I don't know you." Finally, Jeffrey sent someone to retrieve Gems coach Kathy Mosolino to vouch for her. When Mosolino was later ejected (something about "obscene gestures to the official"), Jeffrey took over, and as the team left the arena, the woman who had earlier refused her entrance screamed, "You're not only a player, you're the coach!"

Mosolino had played with and against several women she was now coaching, which made it hard at times because she knew the players so well, Marquis says. One day, a frustrated Mosolino confronted them. "Why don't you respect me?" she asked. "You know I respect you, baby," Janice Thomas replied.

. . .

Dean Meminger was annoyed with his San Francisco Pioneers. "You guys are always saying this 'rah-rah' shit, but you never have any kind of effort," he complained. "I don't want to hear this 'rah-rah' shit. You just get out there and play!" The players found his rampage amusing, and soon adopted a new rallying cry, yelling "Rah rah rah shit!" out of each huddle.

One evening, guard Cardie Hicks was singing the Star Spangled Banner, and her mischievous teammates decided to have a little fun. This time when they broke from the huddle, they would stop after the final 'rah.' The unsuspecting Hicks returned to the group, and everyone put their hands together. "We go 'rah rah rah,' and Cardie goes 'SHIT!'" laughs Molly Kazmer (then Bolin). "Her eyes got so big. We screwed her over so bad."

. . .

On November 15, 1979, there were 8,452 fans watching the New York Stars take on the New Orleans Pride in the Superdome. Pride general manager Steve Brown pulled out all the stops to attract the record crowd. On hand were the New Orleans Symphony, the San Diego chicken, and the "Ragin' Cajun," who performed the national anthem with a fiddle. "I found myself up in the rafters of the Superdome by myself with tears pouring down my eyes at halftime, emotionally drained," Brown recalls. The Stars came from behind for the win, 120–114, "but it was a great game and a great event," he says.

. . .

The longest winning streak in the WBL's three years was the 1979–80 New York Stars' fourteen consecutive victories. "We simply have the best team in the league," coach Dean Meminger said. "I'm not being vain when I say that. But we are the best and we can make anybody look bad." The Stars didn't make it easy, though, often having to dig themselves out of holes. "It seems the Stars don't come out until late," the *New York Post* wrote. "And then they just barely shine through." The Stars played in six of the WBL's fourteen overtime games that season.

. . .

The most dramatic elbow thrown in the WBL was a shot to the stomach of Iowa player Doris Draving in the 1978–79 season. "We were out there playing, and all of a sudden Doris goes down. She can't get up," teammate Rhonda Penquite recalls. Blood began trickling from Draving's mouth, and her teammates panicked. "Oh my God, she's killed her! She's got internal bleeding—she's going to die!" What the Cornets didn't realize was that Draving had bitten her tongue (hence the blood).

. . .

The WBL was often chided by the press for its frequent coaching changes. (Milwaukee, for example, had five coaches in their first year.) The league "takes a back seat to nobody when it comes to firing coaches," the *Chicago Tribune* wrote. "Five clubs have tried coaches as frequently as a woman might change dresses while shopping in a boutique," the *Houston Chronicle* said.

The fastest trigger in the WBL was Milwaukee, where head coach Candace Klinzing was fired after a single five-point loss in the WBL's inaugural game. Klinzing had the last laugh, though. She filed suit for breach of contract and settled for $5,000. When the Does lost eight of their nine next games, she rubbed a little more salt in the wound, calling management once a week or so to offer, "Well, if you want me back, I'm still here."

. . .

The New York Stars were the WBL's best trash talkers. "Show me what you know! Let me see the play!" Janice Thomas taunted Chicago Hustle guard Rita Easterling in one game. When Easterling called for the "stack play," Thomas tweaked her again. "Show me the stack!" Meanwhile, Althea Gwyn, who said she was tired of having thirty points dropped on her by Debra Waddy-Rossow, dogged her throughout the game. "What you gonna do?" she pestered. "Where you going? I'm gonna make you work tonight."

• • •

"Little boys have sports idols they can look up to. Why shouldn't little girls have the same thing?" Houston Angels coach Don Knodel asked in 1979. "One of these days you might see a woman basketball player on a bubble gum card." Beginning that year, six wbl players were featured on their own Sportscaster trading cards: Carol Blazejowski, Randi Burdick (marking the wbl's first season), Pat Colasurdo (as the 1979 number one draft pick), Nancy Lieberman, Inge Nissen, and Ann Meyers.

• • •

Iowa Cornets player Charlotte Lewis was so strong, a Chicago sportswriter claimed, that when she spiked a basketball in response to an officiating call, it took six seconds to return to the floor.

• • •

Chicago's Rita Easterling took seven charges in one game.

• • •

Milwaukee center Lynda Gehrke was invited to take part in a local fashion show. As requested, she wore her lime-green and purple Does uniform with the usual knee-highs and tennis shoes. The organizers then slipped her into an expensive mink coat, although the sleeves weren't long enough for the six-foot-two-inch basketball player. ("Keep your hands in the pockets," they told her.) "I'm not a model, for God's sake, I'm an athlete," Gehrke thought, but she gave it her best shot, striding down the runway in her big tennies and fur coat and pirouetting (or something like it) at the end.

• • •

In St. Louis, Linnell Jones became attached to two young children who were in a bad home situation. "I kind of took them under my wing, and I would pick them up for the games," she recalls. "I would take them home after the games. I would take them somewhere to eat. They made me a little wristband. They would bring me letters. Even after I left, they would write me letters. 'Thank you so much for being a part of our lives. You have really helped us. You will always be our friend.' I will never forget those two little kids."

● ● ●

New Jersey Gems owner Robert Milo and New York Stars owner Ed Reisdorf lived on the same block in Chatham, New Jersey. "When their teams play one another, the situation resembles a feud on a country mountain," the *New York Post* reported.

● ● ●

The most widely circulated action shot from a WBL game was a December 1979 Associated Press photograph that ran in newspapers throughout the country. It depicted San Francisco Pioneers player Muisette McKinney tossing in a lay-up—with an opponent's hand splayed squarely across her face. "Houston's Vicky Chapman (right) goes to extremes to stop San Francisco's Muisette McKinney," the *Los Angeles Times* caption read, "but she made a mistake—she didn't cover the other eye."

● ● ●

The Houston Angels had an all-male cheerleading squad, the Guardian Angels. Tryouts were judged by a mostly female panel, who unabashedly applied certain visual criteria. ("He's a cutie for sure," one raved about a broad-shouldered candidate.) Owner Hugh Sweeney insisted that it would not be a "sex show—this is high class," but rumor was that the squad raised eyebrows with "raunchiness in the tone and quality of some cheers," the *Philadelphia Daily News* reported. "Let's just say the Houston cheerleaders were more gymnastic and acrobatic than those of some other teams," Philadelphia player Lynn Arturi said.

● ● ●

One of the WBL's biggest fans was soap opera diva Eileen Fulton, "Lisa" on *As the World Turns* for more than forty years. Fulton helped promote the New York Stars in 1980 and then traveled to Minnesota on her own nickel the following season and sang the national anthem at a Fillies game.

● ● ●

The WBL's oldest coach was Don Kennedy, who coached the New Jersey Gems in 1978–79. He was 71, the coach confirmed, "but at heart, I'm really 131." Kennedy, the *New Jersey Monthly* said, was a "gent who looks for all the world like a harmless old man who dines in private clubs and jokes with pretty young waitresses who think him cute if somewhat batty."

• • •

One of the most dominant players in the WBL's three-year history was post player Althea Gwyn. By the time she was in sixth grade, Gwyn was already six feet tall and excelled in sports. In junior high, though, she joined a gang, and started drinking and getting into street fights. Her wild ways continued into high school, where she was suspended several times until one day she was spied shooting baskets by the school's basketball coach. Gwyn was quickly recruited for the team, and three years later, her impressive rebounding and scoring caught the eye of Lucille Kyvallos of Queens College.

In 1978 Gwyn signed with the WBL's New York Stars and made an immediate impact. Stars player Kaye Young, a young country girl from North Carolina, remembers well her first encounter with her inner-city teammate. "I was afraid of her. She was a real big, strong girl with an Afro, and really intimidating—not just to any other team but to you, too. By the time I finished playing with her, she was one of my favorite people."

Having learned to play on the streets, Gwyn was used to fighting as part of the game and was prone to "frequent temperamental bursts and rough-housing on the court," the *Arlington Heights (IL) Daily Herald* said, but she was usually forgiven because of her "effusive, go-get-'em spirit and her constant toothful grin. While she may be big, bold and bad, and she may play too rough at times, there's something so likeable about her that she's a tough one to reprimand," the paper said.

• • •

One of Nancy Lieberman's favorite teammates on the Dallas Diamonds was Kathy Shoemaker. "She should have been blonde, 'cause she was like a blonde cheerleader," Lieberman laughs. One day the two drove to practice together, and Shoemaker said she would go park the car. Lieberman got out, and the next thing she knew, Shoemaker was standing beside her while the car rolled down the parking lot. "Uh, Kathy. . . ." Lieberman pointed at the car. "Oh, God," Shoemaker exclaimed. "I didn't put the brake on!"

. . .

When Chicago owners received back a proposed contract they had sent Mary Jo Peppler, they found that the player had retyped it—with a few irreverent amendments (shown in italics):

> 7.4 Player's death shall automatically terminate Player and this Contract. *Then who the hell will care about any of this bullshit?*
>
> 9. DRUGS. Player warrants that at no time during the term of this Contract will she use any drugs. Player agrees that the League President shall have the sole power and discretion to suspend, terminate, and/or fine Player for violation of this paragraph, and the President's finding and decision shall be binding and conclusive on all parties. *If player is found to be unjustly accused of such charges, President shall send Player at Season's end to Tahiti, at President's expense, to recuperate from the ensuing mental cruelty cruelly inflicted by President.*

. . .

Rosalind Jennings, an All-Star with the 1980–81 Dallas Diamonds, was discovered during free agent tryouts. Shortly before the season began, though, Dallas coaches noticed that she seemed to have lost her spark. Before practice one day, teammate Nancy Lieberman approached them. She and Jennings had been up late, she said, because Jennings' father was very ill and not expected to live long. Coach Greg Williams took Jennings outside and told her she was probably going to be cut in a couple of days, so it was all right if she wanted to leave early. A few minutes later, Jennings walked back in. "If you want me to leave, you're going to have to cut me," she declared, and then had a phenomenal practice, securing her place on the team.

. . .

Iowa Cornets coach and general manager Rod Lein was tired. With his assistant, Bruce Mason, he and the team's owner, George Nissen, had just walked two and a half miles from a restaurant to their hotel at the end of a long day. The coaches were sapped, but sixty-four-year-old Nissen wanted to chat. As they talked, Lein looked over and saw that his owner was standing on his head. Nissen, a former gymnast, felt that it was good for the brain. "Something about getting blood to it," Lein recalled.

* * *

Perhaps the most . . . intriguing . . . suggestion for how the WBL could improve itself came from University of Texas men's basketball coach Abe Lemons in 1980. "What this league needs is a midget," he declared (referring to the famous 1951 incident when Bill Veeck sent a little person up to bat in a St. Louis Browns game), "or a woman with three legs, or one with a short body and long legs or a long body and short legs. You know, something people can identify with."

* * *

The first All-Star Game in women's professional basketball was held March 14, 1979, in the Felt Forum at Madison Square Garden in New York City. The decision to have an All-Star game came late, and league president Bill Byrne had to scramble to make arrangements. One call was to Empire Sporting Goods. "What do you want?" Byrne's contact asked suspiciously, knowing Byrne was always bumming something.

"Listen, I'll pay for it," Byrne assured him. "I've got an All-Star Game tomorrow night at Madison Square Garden, we're going to tape delay [broadcast] it. I need 24 uniforms, I need numbers, I need East and West—" What? Was he crazy? "Just have them there," Byrne begged. Local soccer player Charlie Curto's mother came down and worked all day and night. "You wouldn't believe it," Byrne says. "We went on the floor that night, we were suited and ready. I think she was following them down court with her needle, but it worked."

The East won 112–99, and Rita Easterling (sporting 17 stitches over one eye from colliding with a television cameraman the week before) was voted MVP. The *New York Post* gave the game a rave review, reporting that fans enjoyed Althea Gwyn, "with inside moves so good she could do justice to the name Dr. G," Debra Waddy-Rossow's "nearly unstoppable" outside shooting, the "shake and bake" dribbling of Janice Thomas, and Vonnie Tomich's "20-foot bombs."

Gwyn was one of only five WBL players to play in the All-Star Game all three seasons, the other four being Molly Bolin, Marie Kocurek, Paula Mayo, and Janice Thomas. Rita Easterling would also have been on the list, but the final rosters of the 1980–81 All-Star squads inexplicably omitted two players who were among the top vote getters under the rules: Easterling and

New Jersey's Tara Heiss. Shortly before the game, Bolin was appointed to the roster by the league, having rejoined the wbl only a few weeks earlier.

One of the briefest appearances in a wbl All-Star Game was by the St. Louis Streak's Adrian Mitchell in 1980, but it wasn't because of her performance. Playing behind the highly touted Ann Meyers, Mitchell didn't expect to play much anyway, but suddenly the opportunity came. Like most players at the time, however, Mitchell did not have a sports bra and instead wore a regular brassiere. Soon after she took the floor, her bra strap broke. "I came right back out, and when I came out, Annie went in," she laughs. "I didn't get in much more after that."

• • •

As part of their conditioning, Iowa Cornets coach Steve Kirk ordered his players on five-mile runs, which was fine for a former track star like Pat Hodgson, but not for others. Debra "D.K." Thomas especially disliked it. When the women pooped out one day, Kirk chastised them. "You guys act like you are so tired. What if a dinosaur or dog or whatever you are scared of came across that hill right now; what would you do?" Others said they would run, but not Thomas. "It would just have to eat me," she declared in all seriousness. "Just let it eat me, because I am not moving!" The whole team burst into laughter.

• • •

The final game between the Chicago Hustle and the Iowa Cornets in the 1978–79 playoffs was a barn burner. Iowa fought back from an 18-point deficit, and "the Hustle family realized what it needs to bring Chicago its long awaited pro sports title," the *Chicago Tribune* wrote. "Titles in the Women's Professional Basketball League will be won by teams with players like Doris Draving. Draving is Iowa's long-armed, high-leaping, agile, smart center. She stands 6–1 and plays like 6–5."

Only because she was cheating, Hustle coach Doug Bruno insisted. Draving was going over Sue Digitale's back every time, he claimed. The referees had finally heard enough, and Bruno was tossed. Behind by 11 points with just over two minutes left, Rita Easterling led a remarkable comeback, hitting three baskets and feeding Liz Galloway on a quick assist.

With one second left in the game, the Hustle were down 118–115, and Janie Fincher was at the line for two foul shots. She sank the first, then planned an intentional miss. The second shot went up, and to Fincher's dismay, "it hit the front of the rim as hard as it can hit it, but it skipped over it, hit the back of the rim, hit the backboard, hit the front of the rim, popped straight up in the air and fell in the goal," she says. "Just a really screwy thing."

Bruno walked more than two miles back to the hotel, blaming himself for being ejected, even though no one else did. (The ejection actually fueled Chicago's comeback, Iowa's coach believed.) "When Bruno returned to the hotel," the *Chicago Sun-Times* reported, "he was greeted with hugs, kisses, handshakes, pats on the back and a few glasses of brew."

At about 4 a.m., the party transformed into an impromptu softball game. Bruno stepped up to the plate while a tipsy Fincher wound up for the pitch—and beaned Bruno in the head. "I felt bad," Fincher swears, "but I was so drunk that I started giggling." It wasn't deliberate, she insisted. "I said, 'My God, no, I wouldn't do that on purpose. If I was going to hit him, I would have thrown overhand.'" Fortunately, the *Tribune* said, "Bruno was beyond feeling pain."

• • •

Anita "Sister" Green, a sparkplug in the Cornets' offense with an aggressive, penetrating style, was hit by a car while crossing Lake Shore Drive in Chicago on the afternoon of their first playoff game. She was knocked into the air, landing on her head, and spent the next few days in the hospital. The day Green was released she wanted to play, and the coach allowed her onto the court with 2:49 left and the game firmly in hand. Green made a diving steal and an assist, but she was not fully recovered from the accident and was unable to play in the final game against Chicago.

• • •

Nearly six thousand fans poured into the University of Houston to watch the 1979 championship game between the Houston Angels and the Iowa Cornets. The Cornets rallied late in the fourth quarter, and then came a moment they had planned for. Back home, Coach Steve Kirk had devised a play in the event they needed a single basket with basically no time left. The team would advance the ball to half court by calling a time-out, and then their most accurate passer would lob it in to Doris Draving under the basket. Kirk held a competition and narrowed the list to Rhonda Penquite and Connie Kunzmann. He chose Penquite.

In the title game, though, Penquite hadn't seen much action, getting cold on the bench from the ice hockey rink beneath it. "Just let Kunzmann do it," she urged Kirk. "She's all warmed up. I'm not warmed up. Don't put me in that position." No, he had to be fair, the coach replied, "I said it would be you, and so it is you." Penquite was furious, but she got ready for the pass, deciding that she'd better put a little extra oomph on it to give Draving a chance. She recalls vividly what happened next: "The ref gives me the ball and I take this breath, and Doris is just looking at me in anticipation because she knows I can throw this ball perfectly. I let it go, and eleven people on the floor and everybody on the bench, their eyes go all the way up and back. It went totally over the backboard." She went back to the bench and sat down. No one said a word. "Some day this will be funny," she told herself. "Some day this will be funny."

• • •

Getting home court advantage in the WBL was sometimes an interesting process. In 1979–80, the Minnesota Fillies had a better record than the New Orleans Pride, but when the California Dreams franchise folded, the Fillies needed an opponent for their last home game, Fan Appreciation Day. The Pride agreed to fill in, in exchange for home court advantage against the Fillies in the upcoming play-offs.

A more intense battle came in the last game of the 1980–81 season between the Dallas Diamonds and Nebraska Wranglers. Before the game, the Diamonds coaches realized that, if Dallas won, the two teams would have identical records, including against each other, and the tiebreaker would be total points scored during the season. To get home court, Dallas needed not only a win, but a big win. Midway through the fourth quarter and with an insurmountable lead, coach Greg Williams ordered a full-court press and then called a time-out with less than a minute to go. "We're going to try to run a 3-point play and get the point spread," he told his players, and it worked. But Nebraska coach Steve Kirk had figured out what they were up to, and a last-second field goal by the Wranglers foiled the Diamonds' plan.

"[Nebraska center] Rosie Walker may be the worst shooter outside two feet in the Women's Basketball League," a Dallas sportswriter said in 1981. "But that's OK. We'll probably never find out." The Wranglers' game plan was simple, he said: "Every 24 seconds, Rosie go short." That's right, Walker says: "I knew my limits. I shot three or four feet from the basket. If you got me any further, I was handicapped."

Midway through the season, the league MVP almost quit. The problem? She couldn't get any sleep because prostitutes were yelling at cars all night long beneath her apartment window. Coach Kirk quickly got her another apartment.

• • •

The final game of the 1980–81 playoffs in Omaha was delayed for nearly half an hour by an unexpectedly large crowd that far exceeded the gym's seating capacity. More than four thousand fans crammed into the facility, including dozens who sat on the basketball court itself behind both baskets. When the play-offs began, *Chicago Sun-Times* writer Lacy Banks announced that the worst-kept secret in the WBL was how to defeat Nebraska: stop Rosie Walker. The best-kept secret, though, was how to stop her.

Epilogue

Someday when we're in our rocking chairs and girls are making $100,000 a year, we'll laugh about these struggling times. • **Bill Byrne**, *Washington Post*, February 25, 1979

CHICAGO, SEPT. 20, 2003

A group of women leaned back in their chairs as they watched film of an old WBL game, taunting each other as if only twenty-five minutes had passed since their playing days together, rather than twenty-five years.

"What kind of move was that?" "Hey, girl, didn't you see me open under there?" "Nah, I couldn't see over Thea's hair." "Oowee—that was some D!" A second generation also followed the action on the screen. "Mom, is that you? Is that what you guys wore?"

In the lobby, heads turned to gawk at more than sixty tall women who gathered for the 25th Anniversary WBL Reunion. ("Are you basketball players?" one curious man finally asked.) The women reminisced, laughed, and took over the hotel's sports bar.

While coaches Doug Bruno and Candace Klinzing looked on, referee John Katzler whistled Sue Digitale for fouling Lynda Gehrke during a reenactment of the first professional women's basketball tip-off. Many photographs were taken, many friendships renewed. The WBL lived again, for one weekend at least.

The WBL was a "gallant attempt," sportscaster Ann Meyers Drysdale has said, a "great shot" in attorney Scott Lang's view. Most telling about those quotes is that twenty-five years earlier, both speakers were more than a little annoyed with the wbl. Meyers spent the entire 1980–81 season holding out in a contract dispute; Lang represented dozens of players who accused the league of taking advantage of them.

Looking back, most of those who were once disappointed now give the historic league its due. "I wouldn't say I regretted it," St. Louis Streak owner Vince Gennaro says. "I would say I had the privilege of being part of something that was very exciting. I took my chance and tried to make something big." The consequences were severe, though. It took years to recover from a personal bankruptcy, he admits, "but I think at this point I'd look back and say I'm really glad I did it."

wbl players "loved it, even if we complained a lot," Tanya Crevier said a year after the league folded. "We enjoyed being part of something that was important for women." It was fun to be a part of, says Vonnie Tomich Raketic, "because no matter whatever league starts after, we were the first, no matter what." When people tell Tomich she was born at the wrong time, she disagrees. "Maybe not. Not everybody can be a pioneer in something."

None of the complaints, or the hardships, or the disputes matter now, says Minnesota Fillies owner Gordon Nevers. "I am proud of all the girls that played for us, every one of them," he declares. "Even the ones I didn't get along with, or didn't get along with me, I don't care—I still had a great deal of respect for them. They are pioneers, and I think they deserve a lot more credit than they have gotten."

It was Bill Byrne's vision—and wbl owners' wallets—that gave players their historic opportunity. "We spent 12 and a half million dollars in three years," Byrne says. "And that was big money then, believe me—that was a lot of money." Organizers truly wanted the wbl to succeed, says Lynn Arturi Chiavaro. "They worked like it was going to take off, and they really believed in it. They all pushed and did everything they could to make this thing go."

When their wbl careers came to a close, so did the dreams of many players. "It was discouraging to have nothing when it all ended," Iowa Cornets star Molly Bolin said in 1982. "I had no job and I had no money. All I had were a lot of good memories. After that, I didn't work out, I didn't watch basketball on television and I didn't even think about it. I was too depressed." Many of her colleagues had given up jobs and put their life's plan on hold, Rhonda Penquite says. "After it was over, then it was like, 'Well, what are we going to do?'"

Lynette Sjoquist felt empty after years of working to promote women's sports. "I ended up being short on cash and short on a career, but I wouldn't have traded it for anything," she says. Arturi knew there was only a small window in her life that she would ever play at that level, and when the WBL folded, she realized sadly that other women would not have that chance.

"I feel sorry for every little girl out there dribbling a basketball today, because she doesn't have the dream of being a professional basketball player," coach Greg Williams said in 1982. It's tough to dream of something that's not there, notes Mo Eckroth, who grew up fantasizing about something she could never have (the NBA) rather than a women's league that didn't exist.

Girls reap so many benefits from sports that "it's hard to think back when there was a time that people didn't think that women and sports belonged together," Donna Orender (then Geils) says. "They are just so important, for so many reasons." That might not be enough to justify a professional league, she acknowledges, "but how great it was for young girls and women of the time to have that kind of opportunity."

Having been one of the first female professional basketball players is something fun for Krystal Kimrey's nieces and nephews to ask about. "Yeah, I was there," she tells them, "but we don't have to go into details about how it really was." Actually, Kimrey has no regrets, she says; after all, she was young and just getting started in the real world.

Joanette Boutte likewise sees her time in the WBL as part of her education. "I look back at it as a painful lesson, but a very necessary lesson. For women who never looked at themselves as one day being able to play something that they enjoy, basketball for money, it was a rude awakening," she says, then quickly amends—"It was an *interesting* awakening."

One part of that awakening was the realization that being a star in college did not guarantee stardom as a professional. "All of a sudden you realize that you're right in there with all the rest of them, that you're not automatically the best anymore, that you're having to fight for it," says Cheryl Engel. "It's a huge growth curve."

That reality was also jarring to Mariah Burton Nelson, who bounced around several WBL teams. "I went home and laid on my bed for about a month afterward," she says. Although Nelson concluded that a lot of men in the WBL were "sexist and homophobic," she now looks back with more tolerant eyes. "I accept it. And I'm actually sort of proud now having been a pioneer, and having participated in that social experiment."

If WBL players have regrets, it is most often that their sacrifices have been erased from history. "It's like we never even existed," says Patti Bucklew. "Nobody even knows about us." It's unfortunate that the WBL was so early, Gennaro says, and the re-emergence of women's professional basketball so late, "that it's not even viewed as the forerunner, because it was too far ahead of it."

Jessie Kenlaw wishes that players in the new millennium had a greater understanding of how things used to be. "The players today have no clue whatsoever of the things we had to go through just to play basketball," she said in 2000. "But it's a different era now. Now it's more like, 'What can you do for me?' as opposed to when we played, when we were just trying to lay a foundation because we loved the game so much." Muffet McGraw echoes that sentiment. "I started out six-on-six, wearing a skirt," she said in 2001, the year that her Notre Dame Fighting Irish won the NCAA title. "These kids, they grew up going to Nike camp, seeing their name in the paper."

When Genia Beasley sees all that today's players have, "it's like, 'You guys have no clue, no clue at all. If I had only been twenty years younger . . . ,'" she says wistfully. "People that have the opportunity to play now have no idea what we went through to play professionally in the United States. It's ridiculous. We did it just because we love playing, not because we were getting paid a heck of a lot."

Attitudes have changed, Carol Blazejowski says. "It's not where it is on the men's level, but a lot of these players now come up through the college ranks with x-amount of pairs of shoes, and don't have to think for themselves and just kind of get catered to," she says. "Back then you played for nothing. You played for pride and love."

Beyond the passion, the WBL impacted many women and men professionally. Greg Williams, who had never coached women before and was working as a salesman when he joined the league, went on to coach women's basketball for more than twenty years, both at the college level and in the WNBA. Doug Bruno, longtime women's basketball head coach at DePaul University, also made his early reputation in the WBL.

Faye Young Miller's WBL experience helped get her definitive *Winning Basketball for Girls* published. Many other WBL veterans continued their basketball careers in the coaching field, including Sybil Blalock, Chris Critelli, Christy Earnhardt McKinney, Eileen Feeney, Valerie Goodwin-Colbert, Sue Hlavacek, Rosalind Jennings, Tanya Johnson, Jessie Kenlaw, Muffet McGraw, Donna Murphy, Inge Nissen, Jody Rajcula, Trish Roberts, Tina Slinker, Susan Summons, and Holly Warlick.

Orender wanted a career in broadcasting and jumped at the chance to do her own radio show in Chicago, the "Hustle Report." When the WBL folded, she went to work for the company that produced the show, which she then parlayed into a position at ABC Sports. That job, in turn, led to her eventual career as senior vice president of television and new media for the PGA Tour. The WBL put her on the career track, Orender says, but more important was the basketball itself. "I loved, loved, loved, the opportunity just to play and compete." Her career came full circle when she was named president of the WNBA in 2005.

Kate McEnroe, public relations director for the WBL and general manager of the Iowa Cornets, got her big break when she pitched a WBL franchise to Bill Daniels, former owner of the American Basketball Association's Utah Stars. "Honey, you couldn't give me a franchise," he told her, "but I am starting this new company called Rainbow Programming." She should come to work for him, Daniels suggested, and when McEnroe later left the WBL, she took him up on the offer. Over the next two decades, McEnroe became president of Rainbow's American Movie Classics and WE: Women's Entertainment cable channels, propelling them to national prominence.

Even adversity sometimes turned into opportunity. Eckroth considers a serious injury while she was with the Iowa Cornets one of the best things that ever happened to her. "I was extremely shy, and when I fractured my leg, I did the play-by-play on the radio for the weeks that I was out," she says. All of a sudden, she opened up. "Nobody knew me. If I screwed up, it didn't matter. I didn't have to be somebody. It was really good for me."

Ironically, it was Kathy DeBoer's years as a pro that inspired her to seek a career in college athletics, which she felt had more balance. "When athletics is professional, it's all about winning and losing; there just isn't anything outside that," she realized. "That was too harsh of a reality for me to face most of the time." Lessons learned in the WBL also helped DeBoer understand the concepts later shared in her book *Gender and Competition: How Men and Women Approach Work and Play Differently*.

The first generation of professional basketball players took unique memories with them. In Minnesota, DeBoer and her roommates Scooter De-Lorme and Marie Kocurek were "the oddest trio there could have ever been, the feminist Yankee against these two southern ladies," DeBoer laughs, but she thinks back fondly of the three of them living together and debating everything.

Camaraderie is mentioned by many WBL players. "The players—even the ones I got in fights with—if I saw them today, I would give them all a hug," says Gail Marquis. For Jill Jeffrey, the WBL meant lifelong friendships and the accomplishment of becoming a professional basketball player at only five feet tall. For others, favorite memories were seeing big city lights for the first time, or playing in New York City's fabled Madison Square Garden. (But catching a cab there was the worst, Earnhardt jokes.)

Sandra Smallwood had never been to the Big Apple when her New Orleans Pride played the New York Stars. The night before the game, she stared, mesmerized, through her hotel room window at snow falling and people on the streets at all hours. The game was a double header at the Garden with the NBA's New York Knicks, and Smallwood was awed to see legendary Knicks players standing nearby while the women's game played out. It was her best game of the season, and she was interviewed by the *New York Times*. "That whole episode was a dream for me," she says.

It was a dream come true for Nancy Lieberman as well. "I was so proud to play for Dallas," she says. "I was so proud to be part of that league. And I really appreciate all the players, and the coaches, and management who were a part of it." So does Holly Warlick. Although Warlick played in the WBL for only one season, the memories in Nebraska have stayed with her. "I wouldn't trade that for the world," she says. "If I could, I'd still be playing. I was in heaven for one year."

Appendix wbl Teams and wbl Player Roster

WBL TEAMS

California Dreams (1979–80)

Chicago Hustle (1978–81)

Dallas Diamonds (1979–81)

Dayton Rockettes (1978–79)

Houston Angels (1978–79)

Iowa Cornets (1978–80)

Milwaukee Does (1978–80)

Minnesota Fillies (1978–81)

Nebraska Wranglers (1980–81)

New England Gulls (1980–81)

New Jersey Gems (1978–81)

New Orleans Pride (1979–81)

New York Stars (1978–80)

Philadelphia Fox (1979–80)

St. Louis Streak (1979–81)

San Francisco Pioneers (1979–81)

Washington Metros (1979–80)

WBL ROSTER

The following players are known to have been on the roster for one or more regular season wbl games.

Alfredda Abernathy, *Alabama State*

Carol Almond, *Appalachian State*

Suzanne Alt, *University of Missouri*

Katrina Anderson-Sacoco, *University of South Carolina*

Sylvia Anderson, *Sam Houston State*

Kathy Andrykowski, *Marquette*

Wanda Ard, *William Carey College*

Lynn Arturi, *Northeastern*

Karen Aulenbacher, *Baylor*

Darlene Bailey, *Cheyney State*

Janice Baker, *Australia*

Vanessa Barnes, *Tuskegee*

Kim Bassinger, *University of Texas*

Genia Beasley, *North Carolina State*

Evelyn Bender, *Jackson State*

Jo-Ellen Bistromowitz, *Montclair State*

Kim Blacklock, *Rutgers*

Sybil Blalock, *Mercer*

Carol Blazejowski, *Montclair State*

Coretta Bloom, *Valdosta State*

Molly Bolin, *Grandview College*

Betty Booker, *Memphis State*

Gerry Booker, *Benedict College*

Joanette Boutte, *Louisiana State*

Mary Bramble, *Western Michigan*

Lisa Brewer, *Northwestern Louisiana State*

Bobbi Brockhage, *Wayne State*

Cindy Brogdon, *University of Tennessee*

Hattie Browning, *University of Texas*

Pam Browning, *University of Kentucky*

Queen Brumfield, *Southeastern Louisiana*

Cindy Bruton, *Tuskegee Institute*

Patty Bubrig, *Nicholls State*

Patti Bucklew, *Slippery Rock*

Kim Bueltel, *Pepperdine*

Denise Burdick, *Immaculata College*

Randi Burdick, *Montclair State*

Carolyn Bush-Roddy, *Wayland Baptist*

Breena Caldwell, *Wayland Baptist*

Belinda Candler, *University of Nevada–Las Vegas*

Peggy Canning, *Jersey City State*

Mary Ellen Carney, *Wayne State*

Dianne Caudle, *Georgia State*

Brenda Chapman, *Western Kentucky University*

Vicky Chapman, *McNeese State*

Carol Chason, *Valdosta State*

Leslie Chavies, *Seton Hall*

Tonyus Chavers, *LeMoyne-Owen College*

Cheryl Clark, *All-American Redheads*

Kerry Clawson, *University of Oregon*

Beverly Coleman

Sheilah Collins, *Rutgers*

Debra Comerie, *William Paterson College*

Theresa Conlin, *University of Michigan*

Jane Ellen Cook, *Louisiana Tech*

Accronetta Cooper, *Claflin College*

Shena Cooper, *Wayland Baptist*

Angela Cotman, *Old Dominion*

Denise Craig, *Shaw (NC) University*

Tanya Crevier, *South Dakota State*

Chris Critelli, *Old Dominion*

Beverly Crusoe, *University of Dayton*

Dale Dalrymple, *Trenton State*

Coretta Daniels, *University of Detroit*

Winsome Davidson, *Howard University*

Paula Dean, *Berry College*

Kathy DeBoer, *Michigan State*

Patti Decker, *St. Cloud State*

Brenda Dennis, *Marshall University*

Marie DeLorme, *College of Charleston*

Sue Digitale, *Cal State, Sacramento*

Gail Dobson, *University of Tennessee*

Doris Draving, *East Stroudsburg*

Tesa Duckworth, *Mississippi College*

Nancy Dunkle, *Cal State, Fullerton*

Gwen Durham, *Valdosta State*

Christy Earnhardt, *North Carolina State*

Rita Easterling, *Mississippi College*

Maureen Eckroth, *University of Utah*

Cindy Ellis, *Illinois State*

Cheryl Engel, *Mankato State*

Margaret English, *South Carolina State*

Sherri Fancher, *University of Tennessee*

Sharon Farrah, *University of Missouri—Columbia*

Eileen Feeney, *Kansas State*

Janie Fincher, *University of Nevada–Las Vegas*

Kathy Fitzgerald, *William Paterson College*

Carmen Fletcher, *St. Johns*

Janet Flora, *Towson State*

Bonnie Foley, *Southern Illinois*

Augusta Forest, *Tougaloo College*

Connie Franklin, *East Tennessee State*

Joan French, *Southwest Missouri State*

Janice Fuller, *University of Nevada–Las Vegas*

Mary Fuller, *Jackson State*

Elizabeth Galloway, *University of Nevada–Las Vegas*

Carolyn Gamble, *Shaw College—Detroit*

Mary Sue Garrity, *St. Joseph's*

Rachel Gaugert, *University of Minnesota*

Jodi Gault, *Slippery Rock*

Peggy Gay, *Eastern Kentucky*

Lynda Gehrke, *University of Colorado*

Donna Chait Geils, *Queens College*

Jean Giarusso, *University of New Hampshire*

Peggie Gillom, *University of Mississippi*

Valerie Goodwin, *Wayland Baptist*

Joslyn Grant, *Santa Monica Jr. College*

Denice Gray, *Indiana State*

Anne Gregory, *Fordham*

Anita Green, *College of Charleston*

Karen Green, *University of Vermont*

Vivian Greene, *Norfolk State*

Drema Greer, *Clemson University*

Venita Griffey, *University of California, Los Angeles*

Denise Griffith, *University of Louisville*

Maria Gross, *LaSalle*

Althea Gwyn, *Queens College*

Melinda Hale, *Slippery Rock*

Barbara Hansen, *Grand Valley State*

Kim Hansen, *Grand Valley State*

Bertha Hardy, *Jackson State*

Lusia Harris, *Delta State*

Nessie Harris, *College of Charleston*

Willodean Harris, *Alabama State*

Martha Hastings, *University of Maryland*

Cindy Haugejorde, *University of Iowa*

Kathy Hawkins, *University of Nebraska*

Mary Jean Hayek, *Montclair State*

Tara Heiss, *University of Maryland*

Cardie Hicks, *Long Beach State*

Vickie Hileman, *Boise State*

Sue Hlavacek, *Cleveland State*

Pat Hodgson, *Iowa State*

Jeri Hoffman, *Southern Illinois—Carbondale*

Ethel Holevas, *William Paterson College*

Glenda Holleyman, *Mississippi College*

Joy Holman, *Benedict College*

Barbara Hostert, *All American Redheads*

Barbara Howard, *Cheyney State*

Connie Howe, *Southern Illinois*

Peggie Jackson, *Concordia State*

Karen Jamison, *University of Kansas*

Jill Jeffrey, *Montclair State*

Rosalind Jennings, *Erskine College*

Jerrianne John, *Wayland Baptist*

Anna Johnson, *Long Beach State*

Gracie Johnson, *Lehman College*

Lydia Johnson, *University of Detroit*

Pat Johnson, *Stephen F. Austin*

Tanya Johnson, *Ferris State*

Belinda Jones, *Louisiana Tech*

Linnell Jones, *Kentucky State*

Sharon Jones, *University of Texas at Arlington*

Kim Jordan, *Ohio State*

Marguerite Keeley, *Wichita State*

Jessie Kenlaw, *Savannah State*

Peggy Kennedy, *Northern Arizona*

Pam Kilday, *Tennessee Tech*

Krystal Kimrey, *University of Maryland*

Marie Kocurek, *Wayland Baptist*

Carol Koopman, *University of Minnesota, Morris*

Nancy Kuhl, *Penn State*

Connie Kunzmann, *Wayne State College*

Faye Lawrence, *Temple University*

Charlotte Lewis, *Illinois State*

Nancy Lieberman, *Old Dominion*

Karen Logan, *Pepperdine; All-American Redheads*

Denise Long, *Union-Whitten (IA) High School*

Carol Jean Loyd, *University of Mississippi*

Cynthia Lundberg, *Eastern Kentucky*

Mary Manderfeld, *University of Minnesota*

Sharon Manning, *Queens College*

Gail Marquis, *Queens College*

Karen Marshall, *Morgan State*

Brenda Martin, *Cal State, Fullerton*

Gwen Martin, *Lane College*

Pam Martin, *University of California, Davis*

Susan Martin, *Immaculata College*

Debra Mason, *Queens College*

Linda Matthews, *North Carolina State*

Dee Dee Mayes, *Ithaca College*

Pat Colasurdo Mayo, *Montclair State*

Paula Mayo, *Grambling State*

Karen Mays, *University of Dayton*

Sharon McClanahan, *Tennessee State*

Muffet McGraw, *St. Joseph's*

Michelle McKenzie, *Federal City*

Pat McKenzie, *Illinois State*

Muisette McKinney, *Cal Poly, Pomona*

Mary Ann McLaughlin, *University of California, Santa Barbara*

Charlene McWhorter, *Albany State*

Mara Melbourne, *Cheyney State*

Susan Meredith, *University of Wisconsin–La Crosse*

Ann Meyers, *University of California, Los Angeles*

Ann Meyers, *University of Dayton*

Maren Michaelson, *University of Minnesota, Morris*

Sandy Miller, *Immaculata College*

Adrian Mitchell, *University of Kansas*

Pat Montgomery, *Utah State*

Pearl Moore, *Francis Marion College*

Diane Morales, *University of Wisconsin–Whitewater*

Mary Morrish, *Ft. Hays State*

Barb Mosher, *Long Beach State*

Dollie Mosley, *Savannah State*

Donna Murphy, *Morehead State*

Mariah Burton Nelson, *Stanford*

Heidi Mae Nestor, *University of California, Los Angeles*

Inge Nissen, *Old Dominion*

Harriet Novarr, *Syracuse University*

Elsie Ohm, *Mankato State*

Anita Ortega, *University of California, Los Angeles*

Katrina Owens, *Fayetteville State*

Sherryl Pate, *Cal State, Los Angeles*

Shelia Patterson, *Federal City*

Felicia Payne, *Dubuque College*

Kathi Penczak, *Union (NJ) College*

Rhonda Penquite, *Oral Roberts University*

Mary Jo Peppler, *Sul Ross State*

Sue Peters, *University of Massachusetts*

Lynn Peterson, *Mankato State*

Gretchen Pinz, *University of Minnesota; All-American Redheads*

Brenda Pitts, *University of Alabama*

Ann Platte, *Western Michigan*

Darla Plice, *Ashland College*

Peggy Pope, *Texas A&M*

Rowanna Pope, *Mississippi College*

Deb Prevost, *Eastern Montana State*

Sandra Prince, *Abilene Christian*

Cindy Pummill, *Concordia University—St. Paul*

Sandra Rainey, *Wheeling (IL) High School*

Joanne (Jody) Rajcula, *Southern Connecticut State*

Candace Rangler, *Central Missouri State*

Albrette Ransom, *Federal City*

Stacey Rhoades, *Cheyney State*

Debbie Ricketts, *Cal State, Fullerton*

Linda Roberts, *University of Minnesota*

Patricia Roberts, *University of Tennessee*

Cindy Rock, *University of Nevada–Reno*

Debra Roelich, *Queens College*

Renee Rutland, *University of Mississippi*

Nancy Rutter, *University of Missouri*

Katrina Sacoco (See Katrina Anderson)

Kathy Sanborn, *University of New Hampshire*

Brenda Savage, *University of Minnesota*

Jennifer Savio, *Kean University*

Mary Scharff, *Immaculata College*

Lisa Schlesinger, *University of Maryland*

Alice Schmidt, *Montclair State*

Mary Schrad, *Briar Cliff*

Angela Scott, *University of Maryland*

Denise Sharps, *Indiana State*

Debbie Sherer, *Urbana College*

Pam Shirley, *Utah State*

Cathy Shoemaker, *University of North Carolina*

Elizabeth Silcott, *Concordia College—Montreal*

Donna Simms, *Queens College*

Lynnette Sjoquist, *Golden Valley Lutheran Jr. College; All-American Redheads*

Jennie Skimbo, *University of Missouri*

Tina Slinker, *Wayland Baptist*

Sandra Smallwood, *Belmont College*

Joanne Smith, *Arizona State*

Karen Smith, *Montclair State*

Kathryn Solano, *Cortland State*

Antoinetta Stachon, *University of Illinois at Chicago Circle*

Deborah Stewart, *University of Maryland*

Lynn Stith, *Cal State, Long Beach*

Rhonda Kite Stunkard, *Oklahoma State*

Susan Summons, *Lamar University*

Kathy Swilley, *William Carey College*

Retha Swindell, *University of Texas at Austin*

Wanda Szeremeta, *Montclair State*

Gail Tatterson, *Salisbury State*

Susan Taylor, *Valdosta State*

Jan Ternyik, *Montclair State*

Debra K. Thomas, *Stephen F. Austin*

Janice Thomas, *Long Island University*

Lisa Thomas, *University of Illinois at Chicago Circle*

Rosie Thompson, *East Carolina State*

Julie Tialavea, *Cal State, Long Beach*

Janet Timperman, *University of Kentucky*

Vonnie Tomich, *Illinois State*

Mary Pat Travnik, *University of Illinois*

Robin Tucker, *Ohio State*

Joan Uhl, *Cal-Poly Pomona*

Joan Van Ness, *Southern Connecticut*

Peggy Vincent, *Northern Kentucky University*

Vicky Voss, *Northwestern*

Leanne Waddell, *Wayland Baptist*

Debra Waddy-Rossow, *University of Nevada–Las Vegas*

Susan Wahl-Bye, *St. Cloud*

Gwen Walker, *University of Arkansas*

Rosie Walker, *Stephen F. Austin*
Holly Warlick, *University of Tennessee*
Cynthia Washington, *Grambling State*
Debbie Washington, *Lemoyne-Owen College*
Suzanne Washington, *University of Oregon*
Gail Wasmus, *Ashland College*
Heidi Wayment, *Biola College*
Nancy Wellen, *Luther College*
Ethel White, *High Point College*
Cindy Williams, *Southeastern Louisiana*

Roberta Williams, *South Carolina State*
Sarah Williams, *Southeastern Louisiana*
Donna Wilson, *Gainesville Jr. College*
Laurie Wilson, *University of California, Santa Barbara*
Josephine Wright, *Middle Tennessee State*
Faye Young, *North Carolina State*
Kaye Young, *North Carolina State*
Chris Zabel-McGoldrick, *St. Joseph's*
Dori Zwieg, *High school/AAU*

Source Notes

When a person is quoted or referenced in the present tense, the source is an interview with him or her. Those references are not included in these notes. For most other sources, the following abbreviations are used. (In the rare instance when identification of the source is incomplete, it usually has been found in a scrapbook in which the full cite was not available.)

ABBREVIATIONS

AHDH	*[Arlington Heights (IL)]* *Daily Herald*	LAT	*Los Angeles Times*
AJ	*Albuquerque Journal*	LBIPT	*Long Beach (CA) Independent Press-Telegram*
BG	*Boston Globe*	LET	*Lawrence (MA) Eagle-Tribune*
CAD	Chicago Area Dailies	MIL.S	*Milwaukee Sentinel*
CD	*Columbus Dispatch*	MINN.S	*Minneapolis Star*
CRG	*Cedar Rapids Gazette*	Minutes	Minutes of WBL Board of Governors meeting
CSM	*Christian Science Monitor*		
CST	*Chicago Sun-Times*	MJ	*Milwaukee Journal*
CT	*Chicago Tribune*	MMF	*Minneapolis Metropolitan Forum*
DDN	*Dayton Daily News*		
DMN	*Dallas Morning News*	MT	*Minneapolis Tribune*
DMR	*Des Moines Register*	NCAA	*NCAA News*
DTH	*Dallas Times Herald*	NJH	*New Jersey Herald*
HC	*Houston Chronicle*	NJM	*New Jersey Monthly*
HP	*Houston Post*		
IS	*Inside Sports*		

NOTP	New Orleans Times-Picayune	RS	Republic Scene
NSL	Newark Star-Ledger	SFC	San Francisco Chronicle
NYDN	New York Daily News	SI	Sports Illustrated
NYP	New York Post	SLGD	St. Louis Globe-Democrat
NYT	New York Times	SLPD	St. Louis Post-Dispatch
OCR	Orange County (CA) Register	SN	Sporting News
OWH	Omaha World Herald	SPPP	St. Paul Pioneer Press
P & S	Physician and Sportsmedicine	STBD	Sportswoman's T.E.A.M. Basketball Digest
PDN	Philadelphia Daily News	TD notes	1981 notes of Tom Davis, unpublished
PEB	Philadelphia Evening Bulletin	WBN	Women's Basketball Newsletter
PI	Philadelphia Inquirer	WP	Washington Post
		WS	Washington Star

PROLOGUE

The opening anecdote is from Bill Byrne. Byrne's background is derived from numerous news articles, including "Pro Basketball Returns with the Minnesota Fillies, MMF, Nov. 13–19, 1978; "WBL Set to Make History," MIL.S, Dec. 8, 1978, and the 1978 WBL media guide.

Information about WBL staffers is from interviews with Byrne and Kate McEnroe, and from "Columbus Joins 11 Cities in New Pro Softball Loop," CD, Jan. 2, 1977, and "Invading a Man's World," Algona Upper Des Moines, Nov. 22, 1979. Discussion of the WBL logo is from interviews with Byrne and Mock.

Much of the pre-WBL chronology is from Karen Logan. The Red Heads article was "All Red, So Help Them Henna," SI, May 6, 1974. Bakunin's efforts are from "Gals' Pro Five Planned," Arizona Republic, July 24, 1974; "Town Gets Professional Team," Plainfield IN Messenger, 1974; "Karen Logan's Goal Is Superstars Win," Eureka Times-Standard, ca. Feb. 1975; "Sideline Slants: Karen Logan Optimistic about Superstar Chances," Eureka Times-Standard, ca. Jan. 1975; "Beating the Obstacles with Amazing Grace," SFC, Jan. 15, 1975; "Karen Logan Looks for a Fast Break," womenSports, Jan. 1976; and articles from unidentified newspapers in Logan's scrapbook, including "Karen Logan Competes in Superstars for Women," ca. 1975; "Logan to Join New Women's Cage Group," Mike Jessie, pre-Jan. 1975 (Redheads challenge); "Karen Logan to Compete in Women's Super Star Competition," Diana Trichilo, Fortuna (CA)-area paper, 1975; "Karen Logan, Fortuna's

Superstar," Fortuna (CA)-area newspaper, ca 1975; "Pink Panthers' Biggest Enemy Is Time," Bob Ruf, ca. Feb. 1975 (no cheap baskets, "we'll probably fold").

Immaculata's historic games are from "Basketball," *womenSports*, Feb. 1975; "Kickers," *womenSports*, June 1975; and "Women's Basketball Draws 11,969, *NYT*, Feb. 23, 1975. H-O-R-S-E is from "Challenge of the Sexes," *womenSports*, Mar. 1976; "Sideline Slants: Karen Logan Set Male Chauvinism Back Step," *Eureka Times-Standard*, undated; and "Challenge of the Sexes," *LAT*, Nov. 18, 1975. U.S. National Team information is from the *Basketball News 1979 Yearbook*.

Frankfort's efforts are from Logan; "New 12-Team Pro League Fulfills Basketball Dreams," *NYT*, Jan. 23, 1977; "Women Form Pro League in Basketball, *WP*, Jan. 20, 1977 ("like my mother"); "Woman's Pro Basketball Career Could Be Just Dribble Away," *Salt Lake Tribune*, ca. Jan. 1977; "Women's Professional Basketball, Anatomy of a Failure," *womenSports*, Dec. 1977 ("barefoot," "waiting game"); "Sideline Slants: Karen Logan Can Pick WBA Quintet," *Eureka-Times Standard*, ca. Jan 1977; "Pro Basketball for Women Due," unidentified UPI article in Logan's scrapbook, Jan. 1977; correspondence, Tim Koelble to Coach, Mar. 3, 1977; "Women's Basketball Goes Big League Soon," *CSM*, Mar. 9, 1977; "New Attempt to Form Pro Loop," *SN*, Feb. 25, 1978. The "I just hope" quote is from "An Uncommon Woman," *Sacramento Union*, Mar. 1, 1978.

The incorporation, first meeting, and organizers' contracts are from the Articles of Incorporation, Organization Agreement, By-Laws, and Organizational Meeting Minutes, all dated Oct. 11, 1977. The WBL's first press release (untitled) was dated Dec. 15, 1977; the *Wall Street Journal* advertisement is from Jan. 27, 1978.

The "cynical" comment is from "Gal's Pro League to Begin This Year," *Greenwood (MS) Commonwealth*, Feb. 19, 1978. Moore's quote is from "WBL to Give Women's Basketball Its Best Shot," *CAD*, Mar. 10, 1978; Flannery's quote is from "For Blaze, Matter," *PDN*, Apr. 5, 1978. Losing players to the Olympics is from "New Attempt to Form Pro Loop," *SN*, Feb. 25, 1978; and "Women's League Lives to Draft Again," *Newsday*, June 13, 1979. The "premature" comment is from "Women's Professional Basketball, Anatomy of a Failure," *womenSports*, Dec. 1977.

The "blemishes" quote is from "Fans Only Dribble In for Fillies," *MINN.S*, Jan. 5, 1979; see also "It's No Longer a Juggling Act," *CST*, Nov. 28, 1978; and "Karen Logan," *Sportswoman*, Dec. 1976. The "passing glance" remark is from "Gal's Pro League to Begin This Year," *Greenwood (MS) Commonwealth*, Feb. 19, 1978. "Backyard" is from "Women Cagers Ready to Play for Pay," *Bellevue (WA) Journal-American*, Feb. 24, 1978.

The need for distance from Frankfort is illustrated by "Women's Pro Basketball Has a History of Hot Air," *PEB*, July 28, 1978; "Women's Pro Basketball on the Way,"

WP, Mar. 21, 1978; and "Women's Pro Basketball League: The New Million-Dollar Baby," *Ms.*, Mar. 1980. "No gag" is from "*WBL* to Give Women's Basketball Its Best Shot," *CAD*, Mar. 10, 1978.

The entry fee and operating expenses are from "Jackson Group Considering Entry in *WBL*," *Biloxi So. Mississippi Sun*, Mar. 23, 1978; and "A Women's Pro Basketball Team for D.C.?" *WS*, May 14, 1978. The number of applicants is from "*WBL* to Give Women's Basketball Its Best Shot," *CAD*, Mar. 10, 1978; and a 1978 *WBL* brochure.

The Mississippi group is from "Jackson Group Considering Entry in *WBL*," *Biloxi So. Mississippi Sun*, Mar. 23, 1978; "*WBL* Shopping Cart Visiting Jackson," *Jackson Clarion-Ledger*, July 7, 1978; "Pros Considering Jackson," *Jackson Clarion-Ledger*, Feb. 16, 1978. Washington's Fetheroff is from "Women's Pro Basketball on the Way," *WP*, Mar. 21, 1978 ("dream"); "Owner of Wiz Bets on Women," *WP*, July 30, 1978 ("hasn't signed"), and Minutes, Oct. 3, 1978.

The Tampa group is from "Is Pro Women's Hoops Coming?" *Tampa Tribune*, Mar. 16, 1978; "Pro Basketball for Women Likely in Area," *Clearwater Sun*, Mar. 29, 1978. The St. Louis investor is from "Pro Basketball Plans Bared," *SLPD*, May 24, 1978; and Minutes, Aug. 24, 1978. The San Francisco group is from an interview with Marshall Geller. Information on potential Seattle and Portland investors is in the *Seattle Post-Intelligencer* articles "Pro Hoop May Hit Home," July 18, 1978, and "Wait 'til Next Year," July 25, 1978, and in "Portland to Have Franchise in Women's Pro Basketball," *Oregonian*, June 15, 1978; "New Team in Town Seeks Coliseum Dates," *Oregon Journal*, June 15, 1978; and "Portland Cage Bid Withdrawn," *Oregonian*, June 21, 1978.

The first six teams and the owners' decision to keep with eight are from Minutes, June 30, 1978, and Aug. 24, 1978; the Dayton transfer is from Minutes, Oct. 3, 1978.

1. THE LIGHTS GO UP

The opening anecdote is from "Hustle Struggling to Beat Sexism," *CT*, Jan. 14, 1979. The Does taking pictures is from Barb Hostert and the photographs. Klinzing's background is from "Does Coach Wants Team on the Run," *MIL.S*, Nov. 7, 1978.

DeLisle's "asked for it" quote is from "And Now . . . the Does!" *MJ*, Dec. 8, 1978; pregame efforts are from "Does Selling the Real Thing—Basketball," *MIL.S*, Dec. 6, 1978. Women buying tickets is from "Does Are Five Days Away from Making History," *MIL.S*, Dec. 4, 1978. Reddy and Neblett are from "Does Selling the Real Thing"; Neblett's background is from "Italian Earthquake Relief Concert," *STBD*, Dec. 12, 1980. "Cow pasture" is from "Women Go Courting Pro Basketball Dollars," *CST*, Dec. 9, 1978. Milwaukee Does Day is from "Does Selling Real Thing." "Are you uneasy" is from "Gals' Basketball Opens His Eyes," *SN*, Dec. 9, 1978.

Background on the starting players is from the Milwaukee Does' 1978–79 program; the inaugural game program; "WBL Set to Make History," *MIL.S*, Dec. 8, 1978; "Does Are Five Days Away from Making History," *MIL.S*, Dec. 4, 1978; "Joanie Still High on WBL," *MJ*, Apr. 12, 1979; "Keeley Tops Scoring List," *(Wichita State University) Sunflower*, Feb. 18, 1977; the 1978–79 Chicago Hustle program and media guide; "Does Hope to Run," *MIL.S*, Dec. 9, 1978; "Hustle's Rita Easterling—the 'All-American' Girl," *CT*, Apr. 17, 1979; "Path to the Hustle Takes Strange Turn," *CT*, Apr. 6, 1979; Chicago Hustle release, July 12, 1979; "Debbie Waddy Russell," *Chicago Defender*, Apr. 11, 1979; and "Women Go Courting Pro Basketball Dollars," *CST*, Dec. 9, 1978. Information on Logan's injury is from an interview with her and several news reports on the Hustle.

Attendance is from the official scorer's report and "Female Pros Make History," *NYT*, Dec. 10, 1978. "Echoes" is from "Women Get Jump on Shot at the Pros," *PI*, Dec. 11, 1978. "Lewis and Clark" is from "Does Hope to Run," *MIL.S*, Dec. 9, 1978; "storybook" is from "Does Are Five Days Away from Making History," *MIL.S*, Dec. 4, 1978. Information on the referees is from Mano and Katzler and from "History in the Making," *Referee*, Feb. 1979.

Smith's first shot is from "7,824 See Hustle Win," *CT*, Dec. 10, 1978, and "Does, Hustle Show Plenty of Talent," *MIL.S*, Dec. 10, 1978. Game details and statistics are from the official play-by-play, stats sheets, and scorer's report. Crevier's ball-handling skills were mentioned by many interviewees and in *WBN*, 1:1.

The ovation is from "Opener Does It for Fans," *MJ*, Dec. 10, 1978, and *WBN*, 1:1. "Decibel level" and DeBoer's "nervous" comment are from "Women Get Jump on Shot at the Pros," *PI*, Dec. 11, 1978. Easterling's praise is from "Does, Hustle Show Plenty of Talent," *MIL.S*, Dec. 10, 1978. The postgame quotes from the *Sentinel* and *Journal* are from the Dec. 10, 1978, articles cited above. Logan's "made history" comment is from "Opener Does It for Fans."

2. CHANCE OF A LIFETIME

The opening stories are from TD notes and Holman. Thomas's job description is from "Women's Pro Basketball League: The New Million-Dollar Baby," *Ms.*, Mar. 1980; Platte's is from an untitled article in the *Grand Rapids Press*, Mar. 16, 1980; Scharff's is from "The Dreams Come True," *OCR*, Oct. 25, 1979. Rath's "144 super seniors" comment is from "New Attempt to Form Pro Loop," *SN*, Feb. 25, 1978.

Information on Hawkins's high school experience is from the 1978–79 Iowa Cornets media guide; Melbourne's is from California Dreams player profiles; Mayo's is from "Women's Pro Basketball a Viable Sport," *HC*, Jan. 28, 1979; Nestor's is from "The Artist Formerly Known as UCLA Star," *Los Angeles Daily News*, Feb. 21, 1998;

Prevost's is from "Fillies bow to Iowa in debut," *MT*, Dec. 16, 1978; Tucker's is from "Cornets Glad Tucker Came into Pro Ball," *DMR*, Apr. 17, 1979.

The description of iron-on uniforms is from Platte; Sjoquist's uniform is from "Playing against Women 'New' for One Fillie," *(Minneapolis) Golden Valley Post*, Dec. 21, 1978; Young's changing in a stall is from "A Sporting Chance: Title IX Opens Doors for Athletes Such as Kaye and Meagan Cowher," *Pittsburgh Post-Gazette*, Oct. 6, 2002.

Fincher's bucket is from an interview with her; Thomas's playing in schoolyards is from "Women's Pro Basketball League: The New Million-Dollar Baby," *Ms.*, Mar. 1980. Bush-Roddy's watching the Redheads is from "Basketball First for Big-D," *DTH*, Oct. 10, 1979; Kennedy's basketball over dolls is from "On the Rebound," *(Des Plaines) Suburban Trib*, June 27, 1979; Cooper's cap with a tassel and Wilson's tryout are from "What's Tall, Wears Eye Shadow, and Can Kill from the Corner?" *Twin Cities Reader*, Dec. 1978; Engel in the gym, Holleyman's trauma, and English's "dolls" are from interviews with them; Peters's brother is from "Living Legends," *Worcester (MA) Telegram and Gazette*, July 27, 2003. Chapman's and Jackson's experiences are from "What's Tall"; Gross's and Smallwood's are from interviews with them.

Lieberman's punctured balls are from "Fame My Way," *Women's Sports and Fitness*, Sep. 1986. Information about the Youngs' and Aulenbacher's parents are from interviews with them. The description of Brumfield's coach is from "Brumfield Nard Turned Late Start to Great Finish," *Baton Rouge Advocate*, June 17, 2002. Kocurek, Ortega, and McKenzie starting to play are from interviews with them. Rainey in a boys' game is from "She Took a Big Gamble—But Made It with Hustle," *AHDH*, Nov. 22, 1978. Hicks and Jones on boys' teams are from interviews with them and from "Hicks Finds the Time to Ruin Metro Debut," *WS*, Nov. 16, 1979.

Accounts of scholarship opportunities for Rajcula, Blazejowski, Andrykowski, Bueltel, Plice, and English are from interviews with them; Novarr's account is from "Gal Cagers Courting Success under Title IX," *NYP*, Dec. 12, 1978; Kite's is from her Stillwater (OK) High School coach's biography; Kenlaw's experience is from "Angels, Times to Remember," *HC*, Aug. 6, 2000.

WBL eligibility rules are from the 1978 brochure "Why the Women's Professional Basketball League?" and Operating Rule 3.1. Colleges represented in the WBL are from league and team rosters. Coates's quote is from "When We Were Queens," *Washington City Paper*, Nov. 6, 1998. Lein as Bolin's coach is from an interview with Lein. The account of Al's Gals is from "Can City Support Team in WBL," *PDN*, Feb. 15, 1979.

The recruiting experiences of Chason, Mayo, Jones, and Davis are from interviews with them; Bucklew's is from an interview with her and "Rockettes' Bucklew Got Her Initial Taste of 'Rock' Jokes While at Slippery Rock," *DDN*, Feb. 28, 1979. Swindell's is from "Hustle Taking Gamble with Swindell," *CST*, June 15, 1979. Roelich's is from "Women Set for Pro Challenge," *NYP*, Dec. 15, 1978.

Tryouts are from TD notes (Dallas/Tennessee) and Chicago Hustle releases, Aug. 16, 1979, and Aug. 26, 1980 (Chicago). Dayton's glitch is from "Rockettes Rocking," *Dayton Journal Herald*, Oct. 21, 1978, and "Rockettes in Quiet Start," *DDN*, Oct. 21, 1978.

The observations of Boutte, Moore, English, Penquite, and Anderson-Sacoco regarding their degrees are from interviews with them; Brumfield's is from "Brumfield Nard Turned Late Start," to Great Finish," *Baton Rouge Advocate*, June 17, 2002; information about Lieberman's degree is from an Old Dominion University news release, May 5, 2000.

The ABAUSA's warning is from "Women's Pro Basketball Has a History of Hot Air," *PEB*, July 28, 1978. Rath's "choice" comment is from "New Attempt to Form Pro Loop," *SN*, Feb. 25, 1978. Gwyn's "just as important" remark is from "Althea Gwyn Is a Tall Drink of Water Trying to Keep Women's Pro Basketball Afloat," *People Weekly*, Mar. 19, 1979; Zwieg's is from "Does 5 Days Away from Making History," *MIL.S*, Dec. 4, 1978. Information on Marquis and Nelson in Europe is from interviews with them; on Nestor in Europe is from "Pride Deals with Pioneers, Puts Two on All-Star Team," *NOTP*, Feb. 6, 1981.

Descriptions of the decisions to play by Duckworth, Gross, Bucklew, DeBoer, Kimrey, Fincher, Clark, Tomich, and Wellen are from interviews with them. The "Dang, Winston" comment is from "Road to the Pros Takes Strange Turns," *CT*, Apr. 4, 1979; Brenda Chapman's remark is from "Fillies Inaugural Friday," *SPPP*, Dec. 10, 1978; Vicky Chapman's is from "Heaven Can Wait," *HP*, Dec. 10, 1978. French's resignation is from "Diamonds Look for New Careers," *DMN*, Jan. 19, 1980. Burdick's is from "Drive, She Said," *Sport*, Feb. 1979, and "Women's Pro Basketball: Guts without Glory," *P & S*, Jan. 1979.

The observations of Szeremeta, Critelli, Bueltel, and Geller are from interviews with them. The "pickpocketing" quote is from "The WBL," *WP*, Feb. 25, 1979.

3. A MAN'S GAME

Connors's quote is from the "Maggie Daly" column, *CT*, Oct. 10, 1979. VBK's quote is from "Butch van Breda Kolff, the Well-Known Feminist," *LAT*, Dec. 9, 1979. "We've got a team!" is from TD notes. The Kocurek-Kunze anecdote is from Kocurek.

The "more emotional" remark is from "Move Over, Bernard King," *NJM*, Feb. 1979. Nadel's quote is from "Nadel Learned to 'Rough It' Doing Diamonds Broadcasts,"

DTH, Apr. 4, 1980; other crying is from "Women Are No Longer Stuck with Half a Court," *CT*, Jan. 27, 1980, and "Easterling Free Throws Clinch Hustle Comeback," *CT*, Apr. 9, 1979.

The Candler incident is from "Bubrig Enjoys Her Role as 6th Angel," *HP*, Jan. 11, 1979. Kunze's "they don't know" comment is from "Minnesota Coach Not Impressed with Team," unidentified Minn. paper, Nov 1979; Kennedy's "hugging" remark is from an undated "Gems Struggle after Good Start," *Asbury Park Press*. The "War" drill is from "There Is No Joy in Iowa," *MT*, Apr. 13, 1980.

The *MINN.s*'s quip about Young is from "Fans Only Dribble In for Fillies," Jan. 5, 1979. Reasons for few women coaches are from "WBL," *SI*, Oct. 15, 1979; "A Passing Fancy, or Just a Gamble," *Philadelphia Journal*, Mar. 31, 1978; and "Women's Pro Basketball League: The New Million-Dollar Baby," *Ms.*, Mar. 1980. Mosolino's theory is from "Jersey Outlasts Streak in Overtime," *SLPD*, Dec. 14, 1980; Brennan's is from "N.J. Thinks It Has Coaching Gem in Kennedy," *Hackensack (NJ) Record*, Sep. 7, 1978. Strathairn's quote is from "A Challenge," *SFC*, Feb. 17, 1981.

Byrne's observation is from "Women's Pro Basketball Pivots toward Success," *American Way*, Feb. 1980. The "deprogram" remark is from "The Meminger Clinic Cares for the Stars," *NYDN*, Mar. 23, 1980; "small details" is from "The Ladies Are Angels," *HC*, Dec. 14, 1978; "libbers" is from "Fast Start for WPBL," *CST*, Dec. 8, 1979.

Reisdorf's "picking a coach" is from "Women's League Lives to Draft Again," *Newsday*, June 13, 1979; landing Meminger is from "Dean the Dream to Coach Stars," *NYP*, June 13, 1979. Lynn Loscutoff's amazement is from an interview with her. "Towel throwing" is from "Hard Sell for the WBL," *RS*, Mar. 1980. Costello's concerns are from an interview with Doug Bruno.

The "Fotomat" remark is from "Hard Sell for the WBL," *RS*, Mar. 1980. Costello's reticence is from "Hustle Regains Fincher, May Lose General Manager," *CT*, Dec. 27, 1979. "Embarrassing" is from "Dean the Dream to Coach Stars," *NYP*, June 13, 1979; coaching as "a science" is from "Stars Hand Pioneers 1st Loss at Home," *SFC*, Dec. 23, 1979; "liberationist" is from "The Meminger Clinic Cares for the Stars," *NYDN*, Mar. 23, 1980.

Kirk's "jocks" remark is from "Meet Supporter of the Cornets," *DMR*, Nov. 29, 1979. Bubrig's "libbers" statement is from "The Ladies Are Angels," *HC*, Dec. 14, 1978. The "gargle" remark is from "Kennedy awaits," *Jersey Journal*, Sep. 7, 1978; Meminger's statement about "students" is from "The Meminger Clinic Cares for the Stars," *NYDN*, Mar. 23, 1980; "He's an ass" is from "The Dean of Women's Basketball," *Women's Sports*, ca 1980. "Softpedaling" is from "Winning Formula," *HC*, Mar. 26, 1979; "X-rated" is from "Angels, Mayo Roll," *HC*, Mar. 28, 1979. The "low-key coach" and no cursing are from "Sparkling Diamonds

Dribble onto Dallas' Court of Sports," DTH, Oct. 10, 1979; Weese's "damn" is from "Diamonds Tarnished," DTH, Nov. 24, 1979.

The dog mess story is from a letter from Diane Zurba dated Dec. 1979 and from remarks by the player involved and a teammate.

VBK's "flowery" language and "bark" are from "Hard Sell for the WBL," RS, Mar. 1980; the "smell so much nicer" remark is from the 1979–80 New Orleans Pride program. Loscutoff's "know it all" is from "Loscutoff Charges; Gulls Owner Denies," BG, Jan. 14, 1981; Knodel's "big ego" is from "Heaven Can Wait," HP, Dec. 10, 1978.

Wilson's quote is from "Women's Pro Basketball a Viable Sport," HC, Jan. 28, 1979; Kirk's "chauvinism" remark is from "WBL Stars Cured Coach's Chauvinism," AJ, Feb. 5, 1981. The "rugby" comment is from "Dreams Fight Off New Jersey as the Refs 'Let It Happen,'" LBIPT, Jan. 15, 1980. Logan's quotes are from "Low-Rent Lives between Jumpers and Drives," WP, Feb. 25, 1979 ("grace"), and "The People (Hustle) vs. Logan," CST, Feb. 8, 1979 ("roller derby").

Nevers's complaint about Houston and "pro ball" and the resolution are from Minutes, Jan. 16, 1979. "Motorcycle gang" is from the "Joe Soucheray" column, MT, Feb. 18, 1979. "Mixed messages" is from a letter from Zebos to Owners, Dec. 19, 1980.

McEnroe's "not the NBA" is from "Invading a Man's World," *Algona Upper Des Moines*, Nov. 22, 1979. Chapman's quote is from "Fans Only Dribble In for Fillies," MINN.S, Jan. 5, 1979; Campbell's is from "Women in $port$," *Miami Herald*, Jan. 27, 1984. Winter's "better shooters" is from "Pollard Could Pass Them All," LAT, Jan. 23, 1980; LaPorte's "prod 'em" is from "Pioneers Hit the Trail," SFC, Nov. 15, 1979.

Teamwork was mentioned by many interviewees. "Quintet" is from "Women Are No Longer Stuck with Half a Court," CT, Jan. 27, 1980. Finney's quotes are from "Pride Considers Move to Kenner," NOTP, Feb. 15, 1981; Sons's statement is from "For Costello in WPBL: Viva la Difference," CST, Nov. 11, 1979. "Time warp" is from "Pride produces basketball out of a forties time warp," NOTP, Feb. 15, 1981. The "no dunks" comment is from "Fillies Have Talent, Tension . . . but Few Fans," MINN.S, Dec. 9, 1979. "Below the basket" is from "Stars Hand Pioneers 1st Loss at Home," SFC, Dec. 23, 1979. Jenkins's and Dickey's SFC columns are "Pioneers Win First at Home," Nov. 30, 1979, and "The Future of Women's Basketball, Dec. 3, 1979.

The "less jaded" comment is from "Hustle Regains Fincher, May Lose General Manager," CT, Dec. 27, 1979; the "egoball" remark is from "Letters to the Green," SFC, Dec. 22, 1979. "Ten women" is from "Hustle Struggling to Beat Sexism," CT, Jan. 14, 1979; the Nadel quote is from "Nadel Learned to 'Rough It' Doing Diamonds Broadcasts," DTH, Apr. 4, 1980. The fraternization stories are from

WBL players. The anecdote about the pregnant draft pick is from her coach; Holleyman's story is based on an interview with her and her signed release.

4. IN THE LOCKER ROOM

The opening quote is from "Hustle Announces Open Locker Room Policy," Chicago Hustle release, Dec. 6, 1978. *Ludtke* is reported at *Ludtke v. Kuhn*, 461 F.Supp. 86 (S.D.N.Y., Sep. 25, 1978). The Cornets locker room was first raised in "Cornets' Training Rules 'Unprofessional,'" DMR, July 18, 1978, and then in "Women's Locker Room Off Limits to Male Reporters," *Mason City Globe-Gazette*, Sep. 28, 1978 ("difference between a girl and a boy").

The men's rights demand is from "Interviewing Women," CRG, Oct. 22, 1978. Holton's quote is from "Iowa Cornets Won't Let Us In," *Cherokee (IA) Daily Times*, Sep. 30, 1978. The WBL release, including quotes from Geraty and Byrne, is the undated "Who's Who in the WBL Locker Room?" Minnesota's policy is from "No Locker-room Lockout," SPPP, Nov. 15, 1978; Chicago's is from "Hustle Announces Open Locker Room Policy," Chicago Hustle release, Dec. 6, 1978.

Mari's locker room quest is from "Locker Room Humor? Not for Male Reporter," unidentified Westchester (NY) newspaper, Jan. 19, 1979. Minnesota's "historic moment" is from "Playing against Women 'New' for One Fillie," *Minneapolis Golden Valley Post*, Dec. 21, 1978; discussion of San Francisco's locker room is from "Pioneers Win First at Home," SFC, Nov. 30, 1979. Fincher's "sock" comment is from "How Goes the Hustle?" CT *Mag.*, Jan. 18, 1981.

The "invasion" statement is from "The Pioneers' Open-Door Policy," SFC, Dec. 20, 1979. The mouse in the locker room is from "Hustle Struggle to Beat Sexism," CT, Jan. 14, 1979; the "athlete's foot" remark is from "Red Ink, Rosy Future," SI, May 14, 1979. Iowa's "interview room" is from "Cornets Promise Excitement, Family Entertainment," unknown newspaper, ca. 1978, in Kate McEnroe's scrapbook. Mayo's quote, and information about the arrangements in New Orleans and Dallas, are from "The Pioneers' Open-Door Policy."

New Jersey's policy is from Szeremeta. Knodel's "striptease" remark is from "The Angels Will Play in Astroarena," *Houston Forward Times*, undated 1978. Wilson's anecdotes are from "Ready to Report from Angels' Dressing Room," HC, Oct. 29, 1978, and "Women's Basketball Makes Debut," HC, Dec. 24, 1978.

5. PLAYING BY THE RULES

Marquis's quote is from an interview with her. The "disco" remark is from "Johnson Fires Streak to 5th Victory in 7 Games," SLPD, Feb. 5, 1981. "Outhomered" is from

"New Jersey Outhustles, Outshoots, Outmuscles the Hustle," CT, Jan. 3, 1981. Skinner's "fair game" comment is from an interview with him.

Rainer's background information is from an undated WBL release, "Supervisor of Officials Named." The board's goal of women referees is from Minutes, Jan. 16, 1979; recruiting Devaney is from New Jersey's Scorer's Report, Feb. 4, 1979. Bruno's "don't know the rules" is from "Hustle Triumphs over Angels, 88–86," HP, Dec. 23, 1978; putting Fincher back in and Fincher being knocked out are from "Pro Is More Than Being Paid," CT, Jan. 15, 1979.

The cost for a protest is from the WBL Playing Rules. The Milwaukee-Iowa protest is from a Milwaukee Does release, Jan. 25, 1979, and "Cornets Open New C.R. Arena with a Victory," DMR, Jan. 27, 1979. The Minnesota-Chicago protest is from "League upholds Hustle Protest," CT, Mar. 20, 1979. Korvas's quotes are from "Korvas Learns to Live with 'Abusive Crowds,' AHDH, Jan. 27, 1981; whether fans went to boo referees is from "WBL Works to Improve Status of Referees," AHDH, Jan. 27, 1981. Description of the drunk fan is from "Pride Halts Dallas, 85–79," DMN, Feb. 8, 1980.

Nucatola's "110 percent" remark, ex-NBA officials, and his changes are from "WBL's Not Petticoat Junction to Nucatola," NOTP, Dec. 16, 1979. "Ludicrous" officiating is from "Pride and Prejudice," NOTP, Mar. 2, 1980; "neither adept nor consistent" is from "Hicks Gets Hot, Pioneers Win as Bolin Debuts," SFC, Jan. 7, 1981. The Dallas foul mix-up is from "Diamonds Even Series with Gems," DTH, Apr. 4, 1981; the Dayton number mix-up is from "Scorebook Error Haunts Rockettes," DDN, Jan. 15, 1979.

The Landa-Brown tussle is from "Pride and Prejudice," NOTP, Mar. 2, 1980. LaPorte's anger is from "LaPorte Blows stack at Ref as Pioneers Lose," SFC, Mar. 30, 1981. The description of the Bruno-Mano incident is from interviews with Bruno, Mano, and several Hustle and Streak players and from WGN game video; the official play-by-play (scoring errors), "Streaks Batter Hustle, Easterling," CST, Jan. 11, 1980 (suspicions); telegram, Bill Byrne to Sherwin Fischer, Mar. 8, 1980, "Faltering Hustle Falls to New York," CT, Jan. 17, 1980; "Hustle Coach Pledges Shakeup after Stars Win," CST, Jan. 20, 1980 (chairs); "Hustle Coach Bruno Attacks Ref in Game," CT, Mar. 8, 1980 ("bang his head"); "Hustle Coach Is Suspended," CT, Mar. 9, 1980; "Assault May Hurt Bruno," CST, Mar. 9, 1980 (Geraty restrained, fans storming court, police); and "WBL Fines Bruno $1,000," CT, Mar. 13, 1980.

Zebos's background is taken from an undated WBL release. The "ladylike" remark is from "Fillies Are Own Worst Enemy," MINN.S, ca. Dec. 1, 1980; excessive fouls are also from Minutes, Jan. 29, 1980.

Mano's payment request is from his note; his list of unpaid officials is from a letter from him to Fischer dated Jan. 4, 1981 ("no holds barred"), and "Refs Claim Back Pay from WPBL," CST, Dec. 14, 1980; Zebos's response is from a letter from him to Fischer, Jan. 10, 1981. The *Referee* exposé is titled "We Can Always Get Somebody," Dec. 1980.

Gennaro's complaint is from a letter from him to Fischer dated Dec. 8, 1980. Technical foul figures are from an undated league list. Mosolino's protests are from "WBL Works to Improve Status of Referees," AHDH, Jan. 27, 1981, "Jersey Outlasts Streak in Overtime," SLPD, Dec. 14, 1980 (shriek), and "Blazejowski Screams Foul as Fillies Topple New Jersey," MT, Jan. 5, 1981 (papers). The "mildly" comment is from "New Jersey Outhustles, Outshoots, Outmuscles the Hustle," CT, Jan. 3, 1981.

That WBL referees did not travel was mentioned often in news articles about the league. Wethall's quote is from "Game of the Week," STBD, 1:1, Dec. 12, 1980. "Friendly whistle" is from "Rita Turns Miss into Hustle Hit," CT, Nov. 17, 1979; information on Iowa's free throws is from "Sox Employee Helps Hustle in Playoffs," CT, Apr. 12, 1979. Other examples are in a letter from Dave Almstead to Fischer, Feb. 23, 1981.

Neutral referees for playoffs and the regular season are from Minutes, May 16, 1979. The "our ball" remark and congratulations are from notes of a phone call from fan Richard Stern to WBL headquarters, Mar. 30, 1981. The free throw chart is from an untitled 1981 league document. Scott's "atrocious" assessment is from "Pride Walks Off, Pioneers Win," SFC, Mar. 30, 1981. Szeremeta's "obscene name" comment is from "Angel Offense Hits Stride in Win over New Jersey," HC, Jan. 5, 1979. Williams's "one way" remark is from "WBL Works to Improve Status of Referees," AHDH, Jan. 27, 1981.

Much has been written on the six-player, half-court game. One summary of the 1970s changes is in "Women Are No Longer Stuck with Half a Court," CT, Jan. 27, 1980. The WBL's 10-minute quarter plans and the change to 12 are from Minutes, Oct. 3, 1978. The "boring" comment is from WBN, 1:1; "just right" is from "Insight, Foresight, Basket! Finalization" by Clifford Smith, printed in the 1979–80 New Orleans Pride program. Nevers' 11-minute suggestion is from a Memorandum to the Board, May 2, 1980.

The original 30-second shot clock is from an early version of the WBL rule book; the change to 24 seconds is from Minutes, Oct. 3, 1978. The promises of 80- and 100-point games are from "WBL to Give Women's Basketball Its Best Shot," CAD, Mar. 10, 1978 (80 points), and "It's the Fillies down the Stretch," SPPP, Oct. 25, 1978 (100 points). The statistic on 100-point games in 1979–80 is from the 1980–81 WBL media guide. The illegal defense rule is from the WBL Playing

Rules. Nicodemus's "clear out" play is from Greg Williams and Lynda Phillip. Bruno's "zone?" comment is from "Hustle Plays Happy to Slow Abernathy and Beat Dallas," CT, Feb. 13, 1980.

Disdain for the NBA 3-pointer is from "Three-Point Play Hasn't Bombed Yet," LAT, Jan. 3, 1980 (gimmick), and "NBA Leaning to 3-Point Goal," NYT, June 13, 1979 (Auerbach). WBL owners' discussion is from Minutes, Oct. 5, 1979. The "rare bird" remark is from "Indoor Games—Thugs, Giants, and Women," *Saturday Review*, Mar. 15, 1980. WBL three-point statistics are from the 1979–80 and 1980–81 media guides. Nevers's proposal to move "in line" is from a Memo to Board, May 2, 1980, and Minutes, June 15, 1980.

Davis at the shot clock is from an interview with him. The "ineptitude" threat is from "Streak Fall Short in Home Debut," SLPD, Nov. 30, 1979. Play-by-play examples are, in order, from Chicago Dec. 14, 1979, Nov. 23 and 16, 1979, Jan. 25 and 19, 1980, Mar. 9, 1980, Jan. 5, 1979, Feb. 8 and 1, 1979; Milwaukee Dec. 30, 1979, Feb. 16, 1980; Minnesota Dec. 13, 1979, Jan. 2, 1979; St. Louis Dec. 6, 1979; Iowa: Nov. 27, 1979; New Jersey Feb. 4, 1979, Nov. 24, 1979; New Orleans Jan. 8, 1981; New York Mar. 4, 1979, Jan. 16, 1980; California Jan. 8, 1980; Dallas, Jan. 9, 1981; San Francisco Jan. 22, 1981, Dec. 4, 1979, Jan. 6, 1980. The "Stats are screwed up" concession is from New Jersey's Dec. 17, 1978, play by play; the Chavers/Crevier mix-up is from Chicago's Feb. 22, 1980, play by play.

The $75 technical foul is from the WBL Playing Rules and Minutes, Oct. 5, 1979; VBK's quote is from "Pride Dust Off Gulls," BG, Dec. 5, 1980; Wohl's prediction is from "Fox Barely Wins," PDN, Nov. 18, 1979. The "big league" comment is from a letter from Zebos to General Managers, Nov. 2, 1980; The "keep them in line" remark is from a letter to Owners, Dec. 14, 1980.

6. WORKING HARD FOR THE MONEY

The opening "luxury" quote is from "Women Set for Pro Challenge," NYP, Dec. 15, 1978. "Basketball Anonymous" is from "Women in the Big Leagues," *Texas Observer*, Apr. 11, 1980. The Cornets blizzard description is from Penquite and Molly Kazmer, "Snow Lag Too Much for Cornets in Loss," DMR, Jan. 15, 1979, and "Red Ink, Rosy Future," SI, May 14, 1979. Kunzmann's quip is from "A Killing in Omaha," IS, Feb. 1982.

The Cornets in New Jersey and the NBA/WBL comparison are from "The WBL," WP, Feb. 25, 1979. Practice times and other jobs are from Tanya Johnson and "Fillies Inaugural Friday," SPPP, Dec. 10, 1978.

The "adaptability" comment is from "Women's Pro Basketball: Guts without Glory," P & S, Jan. 1979. Rutter's quote is from "Red Ink, Rosy Future," SI, May 14,

1979; Lawrence's is from "After Preseason Kinks, Fox' Biggest Hassle Is on the Way," *PI*, Nov. 16, 1979. Lundberg's reaction to her jersey is from an interview with her. DeBoer's comment on "second-class status" is from an untitled article, *Grand Rapids Press*, Mar. 16, 1980; washing uniforms in Dallas is from "Sparkling Diamonds Dribble onto Dallas' Court of Sports," *DTH*, Oct. 10, 1979.

Kocurek's "gorilla" quip is from "For the Fillies, a Year of Frustration, Yet Hope," *MT*, Apr. 1, 1979. Mention of the Hustle's weather conditions is from "Hustle Struggling to Beat Sexism," *CT*, Jan. 14, 1979; Minnesota's snowstorm encounter is from "The Fillies Finish Up," *Twin City Reader*, Apr. 6, 1979. Description of the Corn Dog is from "This Bus Was Headed Somewhere," *Minneapolis Star Tribune*, June 9, 1999 (awe); "No Corn Here—These Gals Mean Business!" *Ankeny Press-Citizen*, Jan. 11, 1979; "The Cornet Legacy," *DMR*, July 28, 1997 (flocking). The police escort is described by George Nissen and Molly Kazmer; see also "Warning Earns a Bolin Poster," *MT*, ca. Mar. 27, 1980.

The Hustle bus breakdown is described in "First Person: My Night on the Hustle," *Chicago Reader*, May 1, 1981 ("take my girlfriend"). The Diamonds getting lost is taken from "Diamonds' Debut Tarnished," *DTH*, Nov. 24, 1979. Bruno's nap is from Easterling. Ortega's "ridiculous" comment is from an untitled and undated article, *SPPP*, in Lynnette Sjoquist's scrapbook. St. Louis's travel arrangements are from "WBL Hits New England," *BG*, Nov. 12, 1980, and "Life in WBL a Bowl of Soup," *SLPD*, Jan. 10, 1980. New York's itinerary is described in "Pioneers Take Charge, Win in OT," *SFC*, Jan. 23, 1980; standbys were also mentioned in "How Goes the Hustle?" *CT Mag.*, Jan. 18, 1981. The Gems' four-in-a-row schedule is from league records and news accounts of the games. The Hustle plane trip is from "Hustle Struggling to Beat Sexism," *CT*, Jan. 14, 1979; the Fillies bus trip is described in "Full of Heart in an Empty House," *SI*, Mar. 10, 1980.

Oranges were required by Operating Rule 11 and were mentioned in numerous interviews, as well as in "Claire: In the Lockeroom," *STBD*, 1:3, Dec. 12, 1980. Wranglers being taped is from Jan Flora. Holevas's experience with the Gems is from "Women's Pro Basketball: Guts without Glory," *P & S*, Jan. 1979. NBA/WBL injuries are from "A Comparison of Men's and Women's Professional Basketball Injuries," *American Journal of Sports Medicine*, 10 (1982): 5. The lack of weights and Bistromowitz's training comment are from "Women's Pro Basketball: Guts without Glory."

The "How cold" remark is from "Fillies Battle Muskies' Problem—Empty Seats," *MINN.S*, Dec. 13, 1979; see also "Dayton Women's Team Finding Pro Basketball Survival Is Rough," *Cleveland Plain Dealer*, Mar. 20, 1979 (no heat at Dayton practices), "The WBL," *WP*, Feb. 25, 1979 (New Jersey fans wearing parkas to games); "Fillies Still Looking for Way to Fill Arena, Coffers," MT, Nov. 30, 1980 (after a game in Iowa and a six-hour bus ride home, the Fillies went straight to a four-hour workout at a gym with no lights, heat, or water). Description of overheating and the fountain is from "WNBA Is Red Hot, But So Was Ladner in Days of Streak," *Biloxi (MS) Sun Herald*, June 26, 1997.

The description of Loews is from "Life in WBL a Bowl of Soup," SLPD, Jan. 10, 1980. Several players, including Katrina Sacoco and Carol Almond, mentioned the *Queen Mary*. Six Cornets players in a room is from "The Lady Is a Hot Shot," SI, Apr. 6, 1981; the Pioneers at Mardi Gras is from Molly Kazmer (then Bolin).

The "unique opportunity" statement is from the 1980–81 Chicago Hustle player handbook, p. 10; in addition to Flora, Tesa Duckworth and Susan Summons also talked about sightseeing on road trips. Hansen's observation about attracting attention is from an untitled article, *Grand Rapids Press*, Mar. 16, 1980. The warning about "pests" is from 1980–81 Chicago Hustle player handbook, pp. 18, 19.

The description of fan involvement is from Fincher and Mitchell, "Hustle's Rita Easterling the 'All-American' Girl," CT, Apr. 17, 1979, and numerous references in Chicago news articles. Fincher's car thief anecdote is supplied by her. The printing of Fillies' addresses is from "Four Area Women Are on Fillies Basketball Team," *Dakota County Tribune*, Dec. 21, 1978.

The "lunatic" quote is from "The WBL," WP, Feb. 25, 1979. Stewart's quote is from "Diamonds, Stewart Look to Next Year," DTH, Mar. 9, 1980. The "Love of the game" remark is from "For Metros, It's Infancy and Poverty," WP, Dec. 7, 1979; see also "Money Metros' No. 1 Problem?" WS, Nov. 30, 1979. Descriptions of clothes locked up, outdoor practices, borrowed tape, and no gas money are from "How Goes the Hustle?" CT *Mag.*, Jan. 18, 1981. The collard greens remark is from Charlene McWhorter. The $100 payment and "life at the top" are from "Happy Holidays, Janie," CT, Dec. 15, 1979. The "carrot" and "pimp" comments are from "For Metros, It's Infancy and Poverty."

McGraw's description of the running car is from "Their Dreams Lasted Only One Season," LAT, Feb. 6, 1998. Fox players' phone and flight problems are from "Fox Thrown to the Wolves," PI, Dec. 21, 1979; the Christmas party and Lawrence's quotes are from "Fox Folds; Players Put on Waivers," PI, Dec. 22, 1979. The Fillies' sleeping and eating arrangements are described in "No Bed of Roses for Suspended Fillies," MINN.S, Mar. 24, 1981. Szeremeta's paycheck anecdote is from an interview with her. The Angels coaches at the "airport" story is from Williams. The description of Wranglers in the locker room is from interviews with the players named.

7. MAKEUP GAME

The "Ludmilla" remarks are from "Basketball Beauty Hustles to the Top," *Parade*, Jan. 18, 1981. The "girl next door" quote is from an untitled article, *New Jersey Daily News*, ca. July 1978.

Bolin's and Fincher's "you don't look like" comments are from interviews with them. Nissen's "shocked" remark is from "Unlikely Twosome," *Chicago Sports Scene*, Jan. 1981. Logan's "masculine" comment is from an untitled article, *Logan (UT) Herald Journal* June 18, 1978. The "good-looking player" quip is from "Hustle Struggling to Beat Sexism," *CT*, Jan. 14, 1979; the "cheerleader" suggestion is from "Pride and Prejudice," *NOTP*, Mar. 2, 1980; the "not so unattractive" quote is from "Heaven Can Wait," *HP*, Dec. 10, 1978.

The "ham hocks" remark is from "'Blaze' Eyes Olympics for 1980," *Hagerstown (MD) Mail*, Apr. 25, 1978. The "how many can be beautiful" question is from "Basketball!" *Mademoiselle*, Mar. 1981. "Not unfeminine" is from "Fans Only Dribble in for Fillies," *MINN.s*, Jan. 5, 1979. The "ladies" quote is from "The Ladies Are Angels," *HC*, Dec. 14, 1978. Duckworth's photo was in "Hustle Struggling to Beat Sexism," *CT*, Jan. 14, 1979.

"Worked miracles" is from "Women's Pro Sports Score with New Image," *Women in Business*, June 1980. Mention of Cook's curves is from an unidentified article in Patti Bucklew's scrapbook; the "jiggle" remark is from "The Hustle: A Spark of Life Stirs in Only Game That's Left in Town," *CT*, Dec. 18, 1978.

The posterior photos were purchased by the author in 2002. The "cute blonde" comment and Bolin's response are from "Machine Gun Molly: An Athlete First," *SFC*, Feb. 27, 1981. The "pigs buy tickets" remark is from "Can a Pro Sports Club Succeed in Westchester?" *NYDN*, July 22, 1979. "What people expect" is from "Basketball!" *Mademoiselle*, Mar. 1981.

The "hair done" quote is from "Pride and Prejudice," *NOTP*, Mar. 2, 1980. *VBK*'s "where are they?" is from an interview with him. Nevers's and Kocurek's "entertainment" debate is from interviews with them.

The "real-good looking girl" remark is from "Hustle Struggling to Beat Sexism," *CT*, Jan. 14, 1979. The GM photographing players is from an interview with a staff member. The "sign her hair" comment is from TD notes.

Janie Fincher was written about often in the *Chicago Tribune* and *Chicago Sun-Times* during the 1978–79 and 1979–80 seasons; *see also* "Hustle Bounces into Pro Picture," *AHDH*, Dec. 3, 1978 (*Playboy* physique). The "fannies" quote is from "Basketball Beauty Hustles to the Top," *Parade*, Jan. 18, 1981. The "breathe deeply" remark is from "Hustle Struggling to Beat Sexism," *CT*, Jan. 14, 1979. "Price of admission" is from "Hustle Woe: Gleason Shows He Can Stomach It," *CST*, Jan. 20, 1981. "Less dull" is from "Fincher Fights Her Sexy Stereotype with Hustle," *CT*, Nov. 16, 1979. The "10" quote is from interviews with Fincher and teammates.

The title "Basketball's Sexiest Shooter" is from "Machine Gun Molly: An Athlete First," *SFC*, Feb. 27, 1981. The poster story is from Kazmer and McEnroe. The "pinup girl" quote is from "Machine Gun Molly Just Doing Her Thing," *CRG*, Jan. 23, 1980, "Farm girl" is from Ted Vincent, *Mudville's Revenge* (New York: Seaview Books, 1981). "People in seats" is from "The Lady Is a Hot Shot," *SI*, Apr. 6, 1981. Critelli's reaction to Fincher's poster and "T&A" are from an interview with her. The "lesbian" stereotype was mentioned in several interviews. "That's their problem" is from "Hustle Star Gives Pro Basketball Her Best Shot," *CST*, June 10, 1979. The "none of your business" quote is from "Basketball Beauty Hustles to the Top," *Parade*, Jan. 18, 1981. The "Screw you" episode and Nelson's experiences are from interviews with those players. The term "dykish" is from a letter from William C. Addison to Gordon Nevers, Dec. 3, 1980.

"Dream" T-shirt is from California Dreams Notes, Nov. 16, 1979. Kozlicki's "makeup" comment is from "Basketball!" *Mademoiselle*, Mar. 1981. Discussing charm school at practice is from "The Dreams Come True," *OCR*, Oct. 25, 1979. The "snap, crackle, and pop" remark is from McKenzie. Meyers's shyness is described in "Maturing Miss Meyers Grows with Sports," *NYT*, Jan. 14, 1979, and "Learning to Speak Out," *OCR*, Feb. 13, 1987. The *Ms.* cartoon appeared in "How to Be Charming While Dribbling," Oct. 1980. The Hustle makeover is described in "First Person: My Night on the Hustle," *Chicago Reader*, May 1, 1981; the Dallas makeover is from Goodwin.

Shroeder's dissertation is "Hoop Meanings: The Media, Professional U.S. Women's Basketball, and the Evolving Discourse of Femininity," Sheila E. Schroeder, diss., Indiana Univ., Feb. 1999, pp. 68, 147; Lucas's is "Courting Controversy: Gender and Power in Iowa Girls' Basketball," Shelley M. Lucas, diss., Univ. of Iowa, Dec. 2001, pp. 160–61, 164, 169 n. 28. The "warm up your winter" slogan is from Cornets promotional material; the "sexist pigs," "sacrifices," and "Molly Dolly" quotes are from "Meet Supporter of the Cornets," *DMR*, Nov. 29, 1979.

The "woman's identity" quote is from Marla Ridenour, "Women's Basketball League —Will Gamble Pay Off?" unidentified Knight-Ridder newspaper, ca July 1978. Dickey's and Geller's comments are from "The Future of Women's Basketball," *SFC*, Dec. 3, 1979. The "lip service" quote is from "The Fillies? If Not Now, When?" *MINN.S*, Apr. 1981.

The *"Female Eunuch"* remark is from "Indoor Games—Thugs, Giants, and Women,"

Saturday Review, Mar. 15, 1980. The "feminists" quote is from *Mudville's Revenge* (New York: Seaview Books, 1981). "Women libbers" is from "Angels May Be City's next champs," HC, Apr. 18, 1979. The Minnesota writer's rebuke is from Robert T. Smith's column, MT, Jan. 16, 1980.

Sims's "women's liberation" remark is from "The Dreams Come True," OCR, Oct. 25, 1979. Coopersmith's quote is from an untitled article, *Philadelphia Journal*, Mar. 31, 1978. "Not sneakers" is from "A Rugged Challenge, But Kocurek Is Game," MINN.S, Oct. 31, 1979. The "perspiring female form" quote is from untitled, DTH, Feb. 10, 1980. King's "pioneers" remark is from "A whole new ball game?" CSM, May 22, 1981. The "esthetically pleasing" comment is from "Where Are the Women's Rights Advocates?" *Sportsline*, Feb. 1980.

Remarks about "flattering" Hustle uniforms are from Karen Logan and several Hustle players and also from "Courting Success," CST, June 11, 1979. The "pulling 'em down" quote is from "Pride and Prejudice," NOTP, Mar. 2, 1980. The comment about "bikini type uniforms" is from "Does Selling the Real Thing—Basketball," MIL.S, Dec. 6, 1978.

The quote about team names being "an affront" is from "Horner's Corner," unidentified Minnesota newspaper, Feb. 6, 1979. The "hustler?" remark is from "Ready to Report from Angels' Dressing Room," HC, Oct. 29, 1978. The "bawdy houses" comment is from "Move Over, Bernard King," NJM, Feb. 1979. "Syrupy" is from "Women in the Big Leagues," *Texas Observer*, Apr. 11, 1980. Nelson's "Honolulu Leis" suggestion is from "Another Shot at a Women's League," SFC, Oct. 16, 1996. Meyer's comment about the WBL is from "Women and Sports," www.lclark.edu/ria/women.html, accessed May 11, 2002.

8. BALL GAMES

Development of the standard basketball is from *Basket Ball for Women*, ed. Senda Berenson (New York: American Sports, 1903), p. 66; "The Evolution of Men's Amateur Basketball Rules and the Effect upon the Game," Thomas Allan Knudson, diss., Springfield College, 1972, chap. 5, Ball (no page number available).

Description of the 1975 H-O-R-S-E game is from Logan. Logan's rationale for a smaller ball is from her 1977 proposal. Adoption by the WBL, including Byrne's research and efforts to find sponsorship, are from Byrne and Logan and from a league article titled "Little Known Facts about Women's Basketball" in the WBL Press Packet for the 1979 All-Star Game. Ryan's praise is from "Women Play by New Rules," *Atlanta Journal and Constitution*, July 2, 1978.

Announcement of the ball is from "Three-Year Contract Signed with Wilson, undated WBL release. The "Viva la difference" quote is from "Jersey Gems Are Different . . . But 'Viva la Difference,'" *Union City Dispatch*, Sep. 7, 1978. The Wilson contract is also from an undated WBL release titled "The WPBL—A Dream to Reality," Minutes, June 20, 1978, and a 1978 WBL Preliminary Marketing Plan.

Logan's concerns about rights to the ball and accounts of its design are from Logan; "Nissen Gambling on Women Cagers," DMT, Mar. 22, 1978; "Women's Pro Basketball Pivots toward Success," *American Way*, Feb. 1980; and the 1981 WBL All-Star Game Program.

The reaction of WBL players and others is from interviews with Byrne, Logan, Carol Almond, Sybil Blalock, Rita Easterling, Marie Kocurek, Donna Murphy, Anita Ortega, Kathy Solano, Butch van Breda Kolff, Holly Warlick, and Ethel White. The statement about warped balls is from "As with Every Birth, Gems Battled Fear and Looked Ahead," *Paterson [NJ] Evening News*, Dec. 19, 1978.

Koelble's remarks on the dunk are from "Now, Presenting Pro Basketball for the Women," *Columbia (MO) Daily Tribune*, June 4, 1978. The 1978 survey is from the *National Association for Girls and Women in Sport Guide—Basketball*, July 1978–July 1979. Pro-dunk comments are from "Women Learn to Play with Big Boys—Watch Out, World!" CT, Nov. 30, 1979, and "Dallas Diamond Star Nancy Lieberman: Women No Plodders," AJ, Feb. 7, 1981.

Information on Hicks dunking is from "Jersey Women No. 1 Pick," NYT, June 13, 1979; "Pioneers Hit the Trail," SFC, Nov. 15, 1979; "At the All Star Game," STBD, 1 (Mar. 1981): 6; "In the Locker Room," SPTB, 1 (June–July 1981): 8; and interviews with Hicks, Molly Kazmer, Marshall Geller, Adrian Mitchell, and Jody Rajcula. The description of Hicks's injury is from "Basketball," SFC, Dec. 12, 1979; "Pioneers Ailing, But Still Rally to Rout Gems," SFC, Dec. 19, 1979; and "The 'Other Magic' Is Back to Give Pioneers a Lift," SFC, Nov. 18, 1980.

Dydek's ability to dunk and her reasons for not doing so are from personal observation at Utah Starz games and practices, and from statements made by Dydek. Leslie's dunk was widely covered, including "Leslie: Expectations Raised by First Women's Pro Dunk," ESPN.com, Aug. 1, 2002, accessed Aug. 2, 2002, and "Leslie Dunks on History," *Orlando Sentinel*, Aug. 1, 2002. Bruno's 1981 comments are from "Lower Rim Would Aid Women's Basketball," CT, Dec. 21, 1980. The 1978 survey is from the *National Association for Girls and Women in Sport Guide—Basketball*, July 1978–July 1979.

The studies cited are "The Effect of a Modified Basketball Size on the Performance of Selected Basketball Skills by Senior High School Girls and College Women," Jean Shirley Cione, master's thesis, Univ. of Illinois, 1962, pp. 3, 42–49, 51 (and an interview with Cione); "Effects of Basketball Size Modifications on the

Performance of Women's Basketball," J. D. McClements, R. D. Bell, J. Fairfax, D. Fry, and R. Wilson (1982), referenced in *New Paths of Sport Learning and Excellence*, ed. J. H. Salmela, J. T. Partington, and T. Orlick, Proceedings of the Fifth World Sport Psychology Congress (Ottawa: Coaching Association of Canada, 1982), p. 54; Jackie Dailey and Bette Harris, summarized in "Reports Published on Small-Ball Studies," NCAA, Jan. 11, 1984, p. 8; "The Women's Smaller Basketball, Its Influence on Performance and Attitude," William S. Husak, Carol C. Poto, and Geoffrey Stein, summarized in "Reports Published on Small-Ball Studies" and published in *Journal of Physical Education, Recreation and Dance*, Nov.–Dec. 1986, p. 20.

Much of the politics surrounding adoption of the smaller ball is from Jill Hutchison and her unpublished 1984 chronology, "The Baby Ball." Jaynes's quote is from "Colleges Adopt Smaller Basketball for Women's Play," *Chronicle of Higher Education*, Apr. 25, 1984; additional information is in "NAGWS Announces Adoption of Smaller Ball," NAGWS press release, Apr. 30, 1984; "The Bouncing Baby Ball Turns 12," NCAA News, Feb. 10, 1997.

Finch's quote is from "Women's Basketball to Use a Smaller Ball Next Year," NCAA, Apr. 18, 1984, p. 12; Garmon's is from "Quotable," *USA Today*, Apr. 20, 1984; Foster's is from "Some Small Talk, Reducing Size of Women's Basketball Spawns Full-Blown Debate," PDN, May 21, 1984.

Other articles debating the change include these from NCAA: "Tests on 'Small Ball' Start to Provide Data," Nov. 21, 1983, p. 11; "Smaller Ball to Be Ready for Next Basketball Season," May 2, 1984, p. 16; "'Intermediate' Basketball on Market," May 9, 1984, p. 12; "Smaller Ball Draws Criticism," May 9, 1984, p. 2; "Letter to the Editor," June 6, 1984, p. 2; and "Smaller Basketball Has Negligible Effect on Women's Scoring," WP, May 8, 1985, p. 7. See also "Basketball," WP, Apr. 18, 1984; "Women to Use Backcourt Rule, Smaller Basketball Next Season," *USA Today*, Apr. 19, 1984; "The Incredible Shrinking Ball," *Women's Sport and Fitness*, Jan./Feb. 1985, p. 76; and "Women Favor Small Ball Change Quickly Gaining Acceptance," *Daily Oklahoman*, Feb. 1985.

Pitts's concerns are from "Smaller Basketball Not Right Size for Women Players," NCAA, Oct. 1, 1984, p. 2; see also "Effects of a Smaller, Lighter Basketball on Skill Performance of Female Basketball Players," Brenda G. Pitts, diss., Univ. of Alabama, 1985, pp. 3, 4, and 27 (describing earlier study). The coaches' quotes are from the 1986 NCAA press guide for women's basketball.

The ongoing player concerns are from conversations with the author.

The WNBA's choice is from "Getting a Grip on the 'Baby Ball,'" *Palm Beach Post*,

July 23, 2002; the international change is from "FIBA Decision Aligns World Play with College," *NCAA*, Jan. 5, 2004.

9. COLOR COMMENTARY

The opening anecdote is from Jones. Information on minorities in the WBL is from "Pioneers Hit the Trail," *SFC*, Nov. 11, 1979; the author's knowledge of the race of most players on WBL rosters; and "A 'Money' Career for Women in Basketball," *Ebony*, Apr. 1980.

Gwyn's quotes are from an interview with her. Many articles discussed race in the NBA, including "Stagnant NBA Wonders If It Should Change to College-Style Game," *CT*, Mar. 26, 1981. Mercurio's quote is from a letter from him to Sherwin Fischer, Dec. 16, 1980. Information on skipping black players and "codes" is from a WBL staffer. White players as window dressing is from three African American players.

Information about the WBL's racial mix in 1980–81 and the speculation about trades in New Orleans is from "Butch and the Simpsons: Both Share Blame for Demise of Pride," *NOTP*, Mar. 20, 1981. Similar allegations in Chicago are from "Diamonds Sparkle vs. Hustle," *CST*, Mar. 15, 1981, and a telephone call with a Hustle player. Information about a black player fomenting racial tension is from an employee of that team.

Sweeney's quote is from Confidential Memorandum, Women's Sports Productions, Ltd. Apr. 1, 1979. The switchblade incident is from an interview with a WBL player who states that she was there.

10. CHANGING THE LINEUPS

Israel's opening quote is from "Women Learn to Play with Big Boys—Watch Out, World!" *CT*, Nov. 30, 1979. The opening story about McWhorter's "trade" is from McWhorter and Bruno; "Hustle Loses, Hopes Deal for McWhorter a Winner," *CST*, Feb. 17, 1980; and a telex from John Geraty to Will Eaton, Feb. 19, 1980.

Comments on Lundberg's trade are from an interview with her. The trade pitch mentioning the player's color and car is from a staffer.

Regarding the Pioneers: Dunkle's criticism, firing rumors, Haugejorde being handed the ball, and whether the problems were with the coach or players are from "One More Loss and a Coach May Be Gone," *SFC*, Dec. 30, 1980; the Draving trade is from "Hustle Suffers First Defeat in OT," *CT*, Dec. 29, 1980, and two memos to all teams from Sherwin Fischer dated Jan. 5 and Jan. 6, 1981. Apologizing is from "Pioneers Finally Get a Win," *SFC*, Dec. 31, 1980. Mayo's retirement is from an interview with her; "Pioneers' Mayo Retires at 23," *SFC*, Jan. 9, 1981; "Changin'

Places," *STBD*, 1 (Mar. 1981): 6; and "Pioneers Trade Dunkle for Minnesota Center," *SFC*, Jan. 27, 1981. The comment about "When God tells me to" is from Glenn Dickey's column, *SFC*, Feb. 2, 1981. Nestor leaving and Ortega trade rumors are from "More Changes by Pioneers; Ortega Next?" *SFC*, Feb. 6, 1981, and "Pride Deals with Pioneers, Outs Two on All-Star Team," *NOTP*, Feb. 6, 1981.

Duckworth's trade is from an interview with her; Hansen's is from a San Francisco Pioneers release, Sep. 3, 1980, and the team's 1980–81 Tryout Camp release; Geils's is from an interview with her (now Donna Orender) and "Geils Fits Marriage into Gems' Schedule," *NSL*, Jan. 29, 1980.

Team turnover is from the 1980–81 WBL media guide (overall); the 1979–80 Fillies media guide and "The Fillies Finish Up," *Twin City Reader*, Apr. 6, 1979 (Minnesota); "Geils, Meyers give Gems hope," *NSL*, Nov. 19, 1979 (New Jersey); "Pride to Open Exhibition Play against Gems Tonight," *NOTP*, Nov. 28, 1980 (New Orleans); and "New-Look Squad Set for Season Opener," *SLPD*, Dec. 7, 1980 (St. Louis).

Alt's quote is from "See Cornets as Aid to Education," *DMT*, Nov. 2, 1978. Information on Geils's shooting is from Ron Linfonte. The list of three-season players is compiled from team and league rosters and box scores.

Details on Fincher's playing minutes are from "Past Hustle Pays Off in Smooth '79 Takeoff," *CST*, Nov. 16, 1979, and "Rita Turns Miss into Hustle Hit," *CT*, Nov. 17, 1979. Fincher being told about the trade is from interviews with her and Bruno. "Say it ain't so," "Mary Pickford," and "grim" are from "Say It Ain't So, Chicago Hustle," *CT*, Dec. 9, 1979; "stupid" is from an undated letter from a fan to Hustle management. Other reaction to Fincher's trade is in "Women Learn to Play with Big Boys—Watch Out, World!" *CST*, Nov. 30, 1979; "'Mistaken' Hustle Puts in Claim for Fincher," *CT*, Dec. 19, 1979, and "Oops—Hustle 'Mistake' of a Deal Has Been Canceled," *CT*, Dec. 20, 1979.

Israel's "heartless" comment is from "Women Learn to Play with Big Boys—Watch Out, World!" *CST*, Nov. 30, 1979." The description of Fincher's posttrade plight is from an interview with her; "Fincher's New Team Waits to Be Paid," *CT*, Dec. 14, 1979; and '"Mistaken' Hustle Puts in Claim for Fincher," *CT*, Dec. 19, 1979. Her return to Chicago is from "Janie's Back!" *CT*, Dec. 20, 1979; "Where's Janie Now?" *CT*, Dec. 22, 1979; and a chronology prepared by the Hustle's public relations director. Information about Fincher's $1,000 is from a letter from her to Hustle management. The "Maybe all this" comment is from "Basketball!" *Mademoiselle*, Mar. 1981.

Ternyik's reason for retiring is from untitled article, *SFC*, Nov. 20, 1980. Earnhardt, Solano, Kimrey, Duckworth, Gault, and Young's retirements are from interviews with them.

11. STANDARDS OF CONDUCT

The opening anecdote is from an interview with Molly Kazmer (formerly Bolin). Nissen's "cornography" vision is from an interview with him and from numerous 1978–79 newspaper articles in the Iowa Women's Archives. Complaints about the team name and Nissen's response are from "These Cornets Play a Bouncy Tune," *DMR*, Dec. 17, 1978; "Fair Play," *DMR*, Dec. 24, 1978; and Nissen.

The quote about "They will be ladies" is from "Cornets Name 1st Coach," *Oelwein (IA) Daily Register*, Mar. 30, 1978; The "don't want her" remark is from "18 Women Willing to Bet on Iowa Pro Cage Team," *DMR*, ca. July 1978. The Rockettes drinking beer is from "Comeback: Rockettes Win in Overtime," *DDN*, Feb, 7, 1979; remarks on Critelli's contests for beer are from "Critelli's Skill Pays Off off Court, Too," *CT*, ca. Mar. 1981. The comments on "whiskey-swigging" women and "Lite beer commercials" are from "Cornets' Training Rules 'Unprofessional,'" *DMR*, July 18, 1978. The remarks on Van Breda Kolff's fondness for brew are from interviews with him, Steve Brown, and several New Orleans players and from "Claire: In the Lockeroom," *STBD*, 1 (Jan. 31, 1981): 5.

The B-A-R hopping comments are from "Does Players Blast Bosses," *MINN.S*, Feb. 1, 1979, and interviews with Klinzing, Hostert, and Lundberg. Discussion of drug use by WBL players and Meminger is from interviews with several WBL players and a staffer. Meminger discussed his drug problems in "Sobering Events Awaken the 'Dream,'" *Milwaukee Journal Sentinel*, Dec. 28, 2003.

12. THE MONEY MEN

The opening anecdotes are from Phillips and McEnroe; "Basketball!" *Mademoiselle*, Mar. 1981; "Diamonds May Have New Life in WBL," *DMN*, Jan. 26, 1980; "Staver Holds Off Decision on Diamonds Franchise," *DTH*, Jan. 29, 1980; "Staver Loves Dallas—and Says It with Diamonds," *DMN*, Jan. 30, 1980; "Staver Hopes to Build Diamonds Monument," *DMN*, Feb. 2, 1980; and "Staver Greets His Biggest Challenge," *DTH*, Feb. 22, 1980.

The effect of the *Wall Street Journal* advertisement is from several sources, including "For Female Basketball, a Big Bounce Forward," *NYT*, July 19, 1978; "The Time Is Ripe," *DDN*, Aug. 13, 1978; and an unidentified news article in Patti Bucklew's scrapbook. Owners' occupations are from numerous articles, including "WBL Hits New England," *BG*, Nov. 12, 1980 (Reither); "Owner of Rockettes in Form," *Dayton Journal-Herald*, Nov. 9, 1978 (Deitelbaum); "Wrangler Owner Says Fun Helps Ease Financial Woes," *OWH*, Apr. 7, 1981 (Kozlicki); "Does Have Come a Long Way, Baby," *MJ*, Sep. 12, 1978; Owner Is Confident Does Will Succeed," *MIL.S*, Sep. 12, 1978 (Peters); and the 1979–80 New Jersey Gems program (Milo).

The comment on the "chocolate Monopoly set" is from "Hard Sell for the WBL," RS, Mar. 1980; the "pork belly" quip is from "Full of Heart in an Empty House," SI, Mar. 10, 1980. Nevers's "coming on strong" is from "Women's Ball Nevers New Venture," *Duluth Herald*, Aug. 11, 1978. Marketing projections are from the league's 1978 Preliminary Marketing Plan.

The "toy," "damn crazy," and "misguided" comments are from "Staver Hopes to Build Diamonds Monument," DMN, Feb. 2, 1980; "precious metal" is from untitled, DTH, Feb. 10, 1980.

Sweeney's background is from "Houston's Hugh Sweeney: The Charlie behind Angels," HP, Dec. 10, 1978. Information on San Francisco's investors is from an interview with Geller; "Women under S.F. Basket," SFC, undated [1979]; an untitled SFC article by Ray Ratto in the WBL's press packet; a Feb. 12, 1980, WBL release; and "A Game Women Play," *Venture*, Aug. 1979.

Reisdorf's "millions" remark is from the "Hard Sell for the WBL," RS, Mar. 1980. Information on the Angels sale is from interviews with Williams and Davis; "Investors to Purchase Angels for $1 Million," HC, Nov. 15, 1979, "Angels purchased by local investors," HC, Feb. 24, 1980; Memo from WBL League Office to All WBL Club Owners, Jan. 8, 1980; and "WPBL Angels' Sale Was Really a Devilish Hoax," CST, Jan. 15, 1980. Information on the $1 million offer for the Hustle is from Fischer and "Women's Self-Perception Crucial to Sports Growth," WP, Mar. 16, 1980.

The "wouldn't take a million" comment is from "Fillies Have Talent, Tension . . . but Few Fans," MINN.S, Dec. 9, 1979. Information about Nevers's losses is from "Loss of Dollars Doesn't Throw Fillies Owner," SPPP, Nov. 14, 1980. His background is from "Full of Heart in an Empty house," SI, Mar. 10, 1980; "Pro Basketball Returns with the Minnesota Fillies, MMF, Nov. 13–19, 1978. The "digging a hole" quote is from "Fillies, Manager Shoot with Optimism," SPPP, ca. Oct. 1978; the other puns are from "It's the Fillies down the Stretch," SPPP, Oct. 25, 1978.

The Hustle stock sale information is from Fischer; the Offering Circular, Feb. 13, 1981; "Chicago Hustle Tries Going Public, Gets Technical Foul in Minnesota," *Wall Street Journal*, Jan. 30, 1981; "Notes: Hustle," CT, Feb. 14, 1981; an advertisement, CT, Mar. 1, 1981; and "Failure of Stock Sale, Heavy Debts May Doom Hustle," CT, Apr. 23, 1981. The bogus check was from Rosie Lee Richard, Mar. 23, 1981.

Brown's inspiration, his meeting with Dr. J., and information about the Simpsons are from Brown, the 1979–80 New Orleans Pride program, and "Red Ink, Rosy Future," SI, May 14, 1979.

Nissen's background is from numerous articles, including "The Man and the Kangaroo," *San Diego Reader*, Aug. 13, 1998. The description of the Iran events is from Nissen and "Nissen Shifts Cornets' Home to Cedar Rapids," DMR, May 4, 1979. Information on Vance and the vacation packages is from "Vance Out as Owner of WBL Cornets," DMR, Mar. 20, 1980. McEnroe's resignation is from an interview with her; "Cornets Charge 'Tampering,' Threaten Diamonds with Suit," DTH, Feb. 23, 1980; and "Diamonds Face Angels, Lawsuit," DMN, Feb. 24, 1980.

13. WRONG LEAGUE

Kindred's quote is from "Disneyball," WP, Sep. 13, 1979. The *Mademoiselle* quote is from "Basketball!" Mar. 1981.

Meyers's background is from an interview with her and numerous articles, including "Meyers Would Try NBA Again," HC, Nov. 29, 1979; "Ann Meyers: The WBL's Gem," CT, Jan. 30, 1980; "Meyers Was There When It All Began," *New Jersey Record*, Mar. 31, 2001; and "Meyers Primed Women's Hoops for Explosion," SLPD, Mar. 30, 2001. Wooden's quote is from "Pioneer Meyers in Hall," *Newsday*, Feb. 9, 1993.

Meyers's explanation for rejecting the WBL is from an interview with her, "Women Aiming Higher," *Street and Smith's Official Yearbook, 1979–80*, p. 63, and "Meyers Would Try NBA Again," HC, Nov. 29, 1979. The "skirt" quip is from "Meyers Superwoman for 3rd Time," *Miami Herald*, Feb. 14, 1983.

Nassi's offer and Meyers's reasons for accepting it are from an interview with her. Information on the Pacers' struggles is from "Central," *Street and Smith's Official Yearbook, 1979–80*, p. 197. Schulman's "gimmick" is from "Wrong League," *Time*, Sep. 17, 1979. "Disneyball" was the title of Dave Kindred's WP column, Sep. 13, 1979. The "If you believe" quip is from "A Long Shot, Yes . . . but a Good One," MINN.S, Sep. 8, 1979.

Reisdorf's quote is from "A Hoop Sideshow?" PDN, Sep. 7, 1979. Brown's telegram is from "People in Sports," MT, Sep. 11, 1979, and "Disneyball," WP, Sep. 13, 1979 (average player).

The "Underalls" comment is from "A Long Shot, Yes . . . but a Good One," MINN.S, Sep. 8, 1979. Information on Long's high school and NBA career are from "A Long Shot"; *Only in Iowa*, Jim Enright (Iowa Girls' High School Athletic Union, 1976); "Girls Basketball Molds Women's Lives," DMR, Mar. 4, 2001; and "The Only Dance in Iowa: A Cultural History of Iowa Six-Player Girls' Basketball," David W. McElwain, diss., Univ. of Kansas, 2001, p. 294. Mieuli's "all girl basketball league" comment is from *Only in Iowa*; a letter from Mieuli to Charles Finley, Sep. 29, 1969; and "Women's Pro Cage League Eyeing December Launch," *Plainview Daily Herald*, May 28, 1978. Long's post-NBA life is from *Only In Iowa*; "Moravia Molly Joins Pro Cage Team," *Ottumwa* (IA *Courier*, June 29,

1978; "Girls Basketball Molds Women's Lives," DMR, Mar. 4, 2001; "Cornets assemble," CRG, ca July 1978.

Bertka's daughter's suggestion is from "Basketball Scout," *womenSports*, Dec. 1975. Eisenberg on Harris is from "Women's Report," *Street and Smith's Official Yearbook 1979–80*, p. 160. Harris's NBA draft selection is from the NBA's 1977 draft list. Blackwell's quip is from "Utah Jazz," *Utah History Encyclopedia*, www.media.utah.edu/UHE/index–frame.html, accessed Dec. 4, 2002.

Meyers's shock is from an interview with her. Talking Meyers out of the tryout is from "Meyers Was There When It All Began," *New Jersey Record*, Mar. 31, 2001. The description of Meyers's tryout and her wanting to stay longer are from "Spunky Meyers Roughed Up by Fillies," SPPP, Jan. 15, 1980, and an interview with her. Kocurek's response is from an interview with her and "'The Star' Falls to the Fillies," MS, Jan. 15, 1980.

Lieberman's "No woman" quote is from "Nancy Lieberman: A New Queen for the Court," SFC, Jan. 9, 1980; her trying out for the NBA is from an untitled article, MT, May 23, 1980. Nevers's quote is from "Can Fillie Coach's Enthusiasm Sell Tickets?" *Rochester Post-Bulletin*, Sep. 25, 1979. Joseph's theory and Dunkle's concern are from "Game's the Same But . . . ," OCR, Sep. 7, 1979. Kindred's quote is from "Disneyball," WP, Sep. 13, 1979.

Meyers's "couldn't afford" quote is from "Pro Basketball Standout Ann Meyers Might Be Energee-Bound," AJ, Oct. 27, 1980; her "opportunity" is from "Meyers Was There When It All Began," *New Jersey Record*, Mar. 31, 2001, and "Wanted: More Sparklers Like Ann Meyers," CSM, Mar. 11, 1980. Meyers's WBL signing is from "Meyers Arrives, Ready to Sign," NJH, Nov. 16, 1979; "Meyers to Get $130,00," PI, Nov. 13, 1979, and the 1979–80 New Orleans Pride program. Reisdorf's quotes are from "NY Is Negative on Ann Meyers," PDN, Oct. 4, 1979.

The description of the negotiation and Meyers as the Gems' "contribution" are from "Meyers a Gem," PDN, Nov. 18, 1979; the "guts" and "I did it" comments are from "Meyers to Get $130,000," PI, Nov. 13, 1979. Missing the press conference is from an interview with Meyers, "Gems' Party Loses Lustre without Ann," NJH, Nov. 15, 1979, and "Meyers Agrees to Gems' 130G," NYP, Nov. 15, 1979.

The "isn't God" quip is from an untitled article, NOTP, Nov. 9, 1979. The salary figures are from "Meyers to Sign 3-year Gem Pact," NJH, Nov. 13, 1979, and Meyers's contract. Szeremeta's reaction to Meyers is from "Better Gems' Attitude Impresses Szeremeta," NSL, Nov. 20, 1979.

The "good PR" quote is from "Last Shot?" DTH, Dec. 8, 1980; the "second-rate" comment is from Ted Vincent, *Mudville's Revenge* (New York: Seaview Books, 1981). Meyers's comment on her intent is from an interview with her. Hustle players' reactions are from "Hustle Players Rap Meyers," CT, Oct. 9, 1979; Mitchell's is from "Like Mother, Like Daughter," CST, Nov. 11, 1979. The "elbow jabs" prediction is from "Women's Pro Basketball League: The New Million-Dollar Baby," *Ms.*, Mar. 1980. Greenberg's "Joe Namath" is from "Meyers Scores 16 as Pro, but Gems Beaten in Debut," PI, Nov. 18, 1979. Signing autographs is from "Meyers Arrives, Ready to Sign," NJH, Nov. 16, 1979.

Meyers as "franchise player" is from an interview with her. The "I'm no superstar" remark is from "Meyers Arrives, Ready to Sign," NJH, Nov. 16, 1979. The CT article is "Follow the Leader," CT, Nov. 19, 1979. The SLPD article is "Nothing Is Streaky about Meyers," SLPD, Feb. 29, 1980. Mobbing Meyers and her 35 percent shooting record are from "Spunky Meyers Roughed Up by Fillies," SPPP, Jan. 15, 1980.

The *Tribune*'s praise is from "Meyers Great, but Hustle the Winner," CT, Dec. 23, 1979; NOTP's is from "Meyers Proves Her Worth to a Losing Pride," NOTP, Nov. 28, 1979; playing "Jesus Christ, Superstar" is from "Women Are No Longer Stuck with Half a Court," CT, Jan. 27, 1980. Information about Drysdale is from an interview with Ron Linfonte, "Gems Outlast Fillies in Overtime, 114–109," NSL, Jan. 6, 1980, and "Gems Romp; Comerie Hurt, Out for Year," NSL, Feb. 10, 1980.

Needing players like Meyers is from "Wanted: More Sparklers Like Ann Meyers," CSM, Mar. 11, 1980. Meyers's stats are from WBL records. The "No one" quote is from "Will the Streak Open at Home in a Blaze of Glory?" SLPD, Dec. 12, 1980. The speculation is from "Ann Meyers, Where Have You Gone?" STBD, Dec. 12, 1980 (renegotiation), and "WBL's Blaze," BG, Nov. 20, 1980 (relocation).

Kozma's demand was in a letter from him to Annie Meyers, Nov. 7, 1980; the arbitration demand was by letter to Milo, Nov. 6, 1980. Meyers's refusal and rocky relationship are from an interview with her. The threat was from Lyndell Carlin Jr. to Sherwin Fischer, Jan. 26, 1981. The "did they care?" comment is from an interview with Meyers. The final arbitration decision is from the Opinion and Award of Impartial Arbitrator, May 27, 1981. The "not bitter" comment is from "Meyers Superwoman for 3rd Time," *Miami Herald*, Feb. 14, 1983.

The "on their bench" quip is from "She's the New Guard in Town," LAT, July 20, 1981; the quote from Riley is from "Nancy Takes a Powder," DMN, July 21, 1981. The jock strap incident is from "An Interview with Nancy Lieberman-Cline," www.fullerman.com/champion/1december/interviewr.htm, accessed Aug. 10, 2002. The "midget" quip is from "Lieberman Joins Boys of Summer," *Ft. Worth Star Telegram*, July 20, 1981; the two players under six feet statistic and the "pound for pound" remark are from "Nancy Shoots for NBA Stars," DMN, July 20, 1981. The Atlanta game and Lieberman's "Moral Majority" quote are from "Nancy Takes a Powder," DMN, July 21, 1981.

14. OUT-OF-BOUNDS

The opening story and Silcott's background in Canada are from *Slipping through the Hoops* (Elitha Peterson Productions, 2001); an interview with Sylvia Sweeney; "A 'Money' Career for Women in Basketball," *Ebony*, Apr. 1980; an e-mail from Linda Rajotte to the author, May 11, 2003; and "Scoring Wiz Sparks Upset of Pioneers," *SFC*, Dec. 31, 1979 (playground skills).

Silcott's preseason absence and return are from the *Ebony* article and "Streak Peaks with Liz the Whiz," *SLPD*, Dec. 7, 1979 ("fun"). "Name her price" and three hundred in attendance are from "Streak's 'Liz the Whiz' Sizzles for 46," *SLPD*, Dec. 14, 1979. The "results are academic" comment is from "Streak Peaks." Silcott's 50-point game is from "Streak's Whiz Is a Wow: 50 Points," *SLPD*, Dec. 20, 1979. "So brilliant" is from "Silcott Dazzles Fillies with 50, Streak Triumphs," *SLGD*, Dec. 20, 1979; see also "Hustle Bitten by One That Got Away," *CST*, Dec. 7, 1979, and "Duel at Kiel: Streak Wins Molly-Liz Show," *SLPD*, Dec. 28, 1979.

Silcott's "gullible" remark is from the *Ebony* article. The term "head-strong" is from a Chicago Hustle release dated Feb. 12, 1980; "head case" is from Molly Kazmer. The Streak's trade thoughts are from "Hustle Loses Fincher as 2 WPBL Teams Fold," *CST*, Dec. 22, 1979. Silcott's trade demand and salary, other teams' lack of interest, "disciplinarian," and Gillman's dilemma are from "Unhappy Silcott Asks for Trade," *SLPD*, Jan. 11, 1980. Fan protests are from "Streak Snapped by Stars, Does," *SLPD*, Jan. 14, 1980, and "Streak Win, and Everyone's Happy," *SLPD*, Jan. 28, 1980. The box score observation is from *SLPD* box scores for the 1979–80 season. The example cited is from "Plice Lifts Streak to a Dream Victory," *SLPD*, Jan. 18, 1980.

Gennaro's comment on the suspension is from "Streak's Silcott Is on Suspension," *SLPD*, Feb. 9, 1980. Information about Silcott speaking to a team official is from "Hustle Wants Doe McWhorter," *CST*, Feb. 9, 1980. Silcott's response is from "Liz Calls Suspension 'Publicity Stunt,'" *SLPD*, Feb. 10, 1980. Silcott's statistics are from a WBL Release dated Feb. 12, 1980. Brewer's no-show and Gennaro's reasons for the trade are from "Lisa Brewer Decides Not to Join Streak," *SLPD*, Feb. 14, 1980. The *SLPD*'s lament was from "Shelia Out, Streak Get Lost in Dream," Feb. 18, 1980.

The "considerable trouble" remark and the LaPorte quote are from "Even the Whiz Can't Put a Hex on Fillies," *San Francisco Examiner*, Feb. 25, 1980. The report of "ball hogging" and taking 15 shots is from "Diamonds Tumble," *DMN*, Mar. 10, 1980. Dickey's quote is from "It Won't Be the Pioneers' Last Hurrah," *SFC*, Mar. 20, 1980.

Information on Silcott's postseason trade is from two WBL documents, "Player Trades—1979–80 Season" and "San Francisco Pioneers Draft Picks—1981," and from an undated San Francisco Pioneers Tryout Camp release. Her becoming a free agent is from a letter from James A. Greenblatt to Sherwin Fischer, Oct. 24, 1980. The description of Silcott's post-WBL life is from "Streak Not Hurting Enough to Woo Liz, But Sign 'Ann Meyers,'" *SLPD*, Dec. 26, 1980, *Slipping through the Hoops*, and Sylvia Sweeney. Other players' undiagnosed medical conditions are from interviews with Jeffrey, Fincher, and a third WBL player.

15. BENCHED

The opening quote is from a letter from Robert J. Milo to Bill Byrne, Sep. 18, 1980.

Information on the Dayton Rockettes collapse is from *DDN* articles dated Jan. 20, 21, 23, 1979, Feb. 8, 9, 10, 12, 13, 1979, Mar. 2, 27, 29, 30, 1979, and Apr. 9, 1979. Events at the Oct. 5, 1979, board meeting are from the Minutes. WBL licensing restrictions are also discussed in Minutes, Jan. 16, 1979, and May 15, 1979.

Cooper and Fischer's exclusion from the May 15, 1979, meeting are from the Minutes. Geraty's resignation is from "Basketball: John Geraty Resigned," *CST*, Feb. 25, 1980, and "How Goes the Hustle?" *CT Mag.*, Jan. 18, 1981.

Wohl's accusations are from "Money Woes," *PDN*, Dec. 22, 1979 ("didn't give a damn"; also $100,000 "funneled"); "Fox Thrown to the Wolves," *PI*, Dec. 21, 1979 ("Howdy Doody", "schlock," "bleeped"); "Fox Folds; Players Put on Waivers," *PI*, Dec. 22, 1979; "Wohl Blames Commissioner for Fox' Demise," *WP*, Dec. 22, 1979; "Rumors, $ Woes Threaten WBL," *NYP*, Jan. 22, 1980; "Hustle Loses Fincher as 2 WPBL Teams Fold," *CST*, Dec. 22, 1979; and "WBL Says Fox Owner Loses Team," *PI*, Dec. 20, 1979. Byrne's responses are from those articles and from "WPBL Angels' Sale Was Really a Devilish Hoax," *CST*, Jan. 15, 1980. Almstead's reply to the *PI* piece is from a letter from him to Frank Dolson, Dec. 29, 1979.

The league's arrangements with Philadelphia are from a letter from David Almstead and Bill Byrne to Eric Kraus, Sep. 28, 1979, *David B. Wohl, Inc. v. Women's Professional Basketball League, Inc., et al.*, Amended Complaint and Jury Demand, Aug. 4, 1980, and related filings, and correspondence from attorney Jerrold V. Moss to Barry Lieberman, Feb. 11, 1980.

Description of the Washington Metros closure is from "First Steps Rocky for WBL Team," *WP*, Nov. 4, 1979; Metros' Officials Report Ownership Transfer," *WS*, Nov. 13, 1979; "Money Metros' No. 1 Problem?" *WS*, Nov. 30, 1979; "Metros Shift to Baltimore Likely," *WS*, Dec. 11, 1979; "Metros Suspend Operations," *WP*, Dec. 21, 1979; "Metros Fold after Only 10 Games," *WS*, Dec. 22, 1979; and "Wohl Blames Commissioner for Fox' Demise," *WP*, Dec. 22, 1979.

The Diamonds folding is from Phillips; "Diamonds' Phillips Forfeits Operation," *DMN*, Jan. 19, 1980; "Diamonds Owner Gives Up," *DTH*, Jan. 19, 1980; and Minutes, Jan. 18, 1980.

Vecsey's "impeaching" comment is from "Nets Bidding for McAdoo," *NYP*, Jan. 22, 1980. The vote of confidence and Byrne's contract reminder are from the Minutes, Jan. 29, 1980. Cooper's quote is from an untitled article, *CST*, Jan. 29, 1980; McCarthy's is from "Staver Officially Owner of Diamonds," *DTH*, Jan. 30, 1980.

The league's arrangement with the new Angels owners is from a letter from Almstead to Gerald Haynes, Feb. 20, 1980; a letter from Earl Elliot to the WBL Board of Governors, Sep. 30, 1980; and TD notes.

The events of the June 15, 1980, board meeting are from the Minutes, and from Byrne, Geller, Nevers, Gennaro, Reisdorf, and Fischer. The financial records are from the league document "Progress Report re: League Office" and "How Long Can WBL Survive?" *Southtown Economist*, Jan. 18, 1981. The "$800,000" quote is from "Referees Blow Whistle on WBL," *OWH*, Dec. 16, 1980. The "big egos" quote is from "Almstead Finds New Dallas Home in President's Chair of Diamonds," *DMN*, July 2, 1980.

The transfer of Byrne's Tampa Bay franchise to New England is from an interview with Scott Lang, Minutes, Oct. 31, 1980, TD notes, and "Tampa Bay Sun Saga Continues," *Tampa Bay Tribune*, Oct. 30, 1980. Simpson's "light years ahead" remark is from "Iowa Free Throw Beats Hustle; Easterling Hurt," *CST*, Jan. 5, 1980. "Black Tuesday" information is from Minutes, May 5, 1980, June 15, 1980, and Sep. 30, 1980; interviews with six team owners; a league resolution dated Sep. 8, 1980; and amendment dated Oct. 1, 1980, and TD notes.

The "grim picture" quote is from *Minnesota Basketball*, Nov. 1980. Milo's "It's that simple" is from an untitled Associated Press article in a WBL public relations file. The final quote is from an Open Letter to Members of the WBL from Fischer, Oct. 31, 1980.

16. THE SUPER ROOKIES

Lieberman's quote is from "Lieberman Fills Tall Order for Diamonds," *DTH*, Sep. 24, 1980. The "Blaze" quote is from "'Blaze' Eyes Olympics in 1980," *Hagerstown (MD) Mail*, ca. July 1978. Williams's quote is from "It Could Be Nissen, Not Lieberman, for Dallas," *DMN*, June 15, 1980.

Many articles in the 1970s described Lieberman as the nation's premier women's basketball player. The "big bucks" quote is from "Nancy Lieberman: A New Queen for the Court," *SFC*, Jan. 9, 1980. Information on "radar ball" and her youthful playing career are available from many sources, including Lieberman's 1992 autobiography, *Lady Magic: The Autobiography of Nancy Lieberman-Cline* (Champaign IL: Sagamore, 1992); "Nancy Lieberman, Queen of the Courts," *BG*, Jan. 25, 1980; and "The Lady in a Court of Knights," *Newsday*, June 4, 1987.

The "Fire" nickname is from "The 'Fire': A Winner in Any League," STBD, Oct. 30, 1980. Information on illegal recruiting is from "Nancy Lieberman: A New Queen for the Court," SFC, and *Basketball News 1979 Yearbook*. The "whip and chair" quote is from "How Stanley, Lady Monarchs and a Sport Grew Up Together," *Virginian-Pilot*, Nov. 11, 2001. "Flashy" is from "Nancy Lieberman Makes a Sales Pitch," NYT, June 14, 1980; "elbows spearing" is from "Dominion Women Triumph at Garden," NYT, Jan. 7, 1979.

The "plays like a man" quote is from "Dallas Hires Williams," DMN, May 14, 1980; "man's game" is from "Nancy Lieberman, Queen of the Courts," BG, Jan. 25, 1980; "the future" is from "Old Dominion Shows USF How It's Played," SFC, Jan. 10, 1980. The Abe Lemons story is from "Lieberman Fills Tall Order for Diamonds," DTH, Sep. 24, 1980.

Promotional appearances and the NBA summer league are from "Queen of Diamonds," *Women's Sports*, Mar. 1981; "Diamonds Sign ODU's Lieberman," DMN, Sep. 24, 1980; "Last Shot?" DTH, Dec. 8, 1980; "Nancy Lieberman Makes a Sales Pitch," NYT, June 14, 1980; and "A Girl Who's Just One of the Guys," SI, July 21, 1980. Wethall's quote is from "WBL All-Star Game Preview," STBD, 1 (Jan. 31, 1981): 5.

Information about Nissen as MVP and ending up at ODU is from "Lieberman Leads Women Stars," AJ, Jan. 30, 1981. The "stately" quote is from "Dominion Women Triumph at Garden," NYT, Jan. 7, 1979. Nissen writing U.S. schools is from an interview with her. Her college statistics are from the 1979–80 ODU media guide. Nissen vs. the Soviets is from "ODU Will Seek Help on Nissen Citizenship," PI, Dec. 18, 1979.

Blazejowski's pre-WBL background is from an interview with her; "The Lady Is a Hot Shot," SI, Apr. 6, 1981 ("rat"); *Lady Hoopsters*, Linda Ford (Half Moon Books, 1999); "My Turn/Blaze's Pioneer Spirit," *Newsday*, May 16, 1999; and "She's Blazing a New Trail," *Newsday*, June 20, 1993. The "probation" comment is from "Coaching Was Never Like This," NYP, Dec. 2, 1978.

The story about Lieberman at the pool is from *Lady Magic: The Autobiography of Nancy Lieberman-Cline* (Champaign IL: Sagamore, 1992). Nissen at the sink is from "Unlikely Twosome," *Chicago Sports Scene*, Jan. 1981. The term "Meyers syndrome" is from "Dallas Hires Williams," DMN, May 14, 1980; "going to hurt" and "double that" are from "Hard Sell for the WBL," RS, Mar. 1980. Seelig's quote is from "Dallas Hires Williams," DMN, May 14, 1980.

The negotiations are from an interview with Lieberman and as described in *Lady Magic: The Autobiography of Nancy Lieberman-Cline* (Champaign IL: Sagamore, 1992) and "Nancy Lieberman Makes a Sales Pitch," NYT, June 14, 1980. The "risky" quote is from "WBL," SI, Oct. 20, 1980. Off-court expectations are from "She's a

Lot Better Than a Lot of Guys in the NBA," *NYDN*, July 6, 1980. Almstead's response to $100,000 is from "Full of Heart in an Empty House," *SI*, Mar. 10, 1980, and "Lieberman Pact Talks Continue," *DMN*, Sep. 12, 1980 ("time for action"), and Lieberman. Meminger's advice is from *Lady Magic*. The press conference and cowboy hat were widely covered, including in "Lieberman Fills Tall Order for Diamonds," *DTH*, Sep. 24, 1980. The redacted salary is from correspondence from Almstead to Sherwin Fischer, Nov. 11, 1980; the final deal is from *Lady Magic*.

Nissen's signing is from an interview with her and "Hustle Gets 'Big Help' in Mail-Top Pick's Contract," *CT*, Sep. 24, 1980, and "Hustle Selects Nissen in Draft," *CST*, June 16, 1980. The terms are from her contract; the "Cadillac" comment is from the "Maggie Daly" column, *CT*, June 20, 1980. Blazejowski's contract is from an interview with her.

The "savior-superstar" remark is from "Pioneers Host Dallas Tonight; Lieberman Out," *SFC*, Dec. 12, 1980. Williams's "savior" quote is from "Lieberman Likes Prospects in Dallas," *DTH*, June 16, 1980. The "Give her $100,000" quip is from "Hustle Victory Fouls Up Lieberman's Efforts," *CST*, Jan. 19, 1981. The turnover story is from the box score and an interview with Lieberman.

The "mean" comment is from "A Queen without a Court," *DTH*, June 27, 1982. Best road attendance is from league records. Cosell's request that Lieberman be seated at the dais is from "Queen of Diamonds," *Women's Sports*, Mar. 1981. The "merely a rumor" quote is from "Case Star Shines at Game, Publicity for Her League," *MT*, Feb. 27, 1981; the "bigger news" incident is from "Lieberman and the WBL Good for Each Other," *WP*, Mar. 22, 1981. The *SLPD*'s quote is from "The 'Doctor' Is In at Kiel," Jan. 15, 1981; the *CT*'s quote is from "Lieberman Fails to Stop Hustle," Jan. 19, 1981; the *DTH*'s quote is from "Last Shot?" Dec. 8, 1980; the *SPPP*'s quote and Reusse's admission are from "Diamonds' Nancy Lieberman Enlivens a Wake," *SPPP*, Feb. 27, 1981.

The van ride is from TD notes. Blaze's lifestyle is from "Blaze Wants 'Fair Chance' at Turnstiles," *STBD*, 1 (Jan. 31, 1981): 5. Blazejowski's yelling and Kunze's comment are from "Blazejowski Screams Foul as Fillies Topple New Jersey," *MT*, Jan. 5, 1981. Her scoring statistics are from league records.

Nissen's statistics and the Hustle's record are from league records. The "no game plan" comment is from "Hustle Beaten by Nebraska in Final Minute," *CT*, Feb. 21, 1981. Nissen's (lack of) motivation is from "Hustle, Gleason Heading to Showdown," *AHDH*, Mar. 21, 1981. Self-destruction is from Nissen and several Hustle teammates, and from "Gleason Hangs On with Hustle," *CST*, Mar. 15, 1981. Geils being spat upon is from "Highland Park Guard Faces Hustle Fans' Boos," *(Chicago) Suburban Sun-Times*, Feb. 27, 1981. Faster-paced offense is from

"Nissen Helps Hustle Run Past Gems," CT, Feb. 24, 1981, and "Hustle vs. San Francisco Pioneers," CT, Mar. 6, 1981. The "truest" comment is from "Nissen, Monarchs Prevail in WBL," AJ, Jan. 30, 1981.

17. FOUL PLAY

The opening story is from Craig Kunzmann. Connie's hope for the title after twice losing is from Carol Chason. Her WBL statistics are from the 1980–81 WBL Media Guide; her pre-WBL playing background is from "Ex-guard to Start for Cornets," *Sioux City Journal*, Dec. 8, 1978, and Clifford Hartmann.

Playing through injury is from Ira Berkow, "A Killing in Omaha," *Inside Sports*, Feb. 1982, as are the quotes from Connie's letters. Accounts of her last game are from Berkow; "Turnovers Wreck Wranglers' Bid," OWH, Feb. 6, 1981; and "Man Confesses Bizarre Slaying of WBL Player," SFC, Feb. 11, 1981. Beasley's "friendly" comment is from Berkow.

The disappearance was reported in "Wrangler Player Reported Missing," OWH, Feb. 10, 1981. Connie's car was mentioned by Berkow and in "Man Confesses Bizarre Slaying of WBL Player," SFC, Feb. 11, 1981. Tibke's confession is from "Ball Player Is Missing; Death Count Readied," OWH, Feb. 10, 1981, and "Wrangler Still Missing; Omaha Man Charged," OWH, Feb. 11, 1981. Kirk's phone call to Craig Kunzmann is from Berkow.

The "cruelest shock" comment is from "A Death Stuns the WBL," WP, Feb. 11, 1981. Details of the homicide are from Berkow; "Ball Player Is Missing"; "Wrangler Still Missing; Omaha Man Charged," OWH, Feb. 11, 1981; and "Police Say Basketball Player May Have Died in Cemetery," OWH, Feb. 18, 1981. The Wranglers' statement is dated Feb. 10, 1981; another was issued on Mar. 4, 1981.

The descriptions of search conditions and the charges filed are from "West Is Best of WBL Stars," SLPD, Feb. 10, 1981; "Police Hunt for Body of Missing WBL Player," PI, Feb. 11, 1981; "Death Report, Storm Delay Sports Program," OWH, Feb. 10, 1981; "Wrangler Still Missing; Omaha Man Charged," OWH, Feb. 11, 1981; and "Police Search Fails to Find Body of Missing Wrangler," OWH, Feb. 12, 1981. Kirk's "not be in vain" statement is from "In the locker room," STBD, 1 (May 1981): 7.

The "most grisly" quote is from "WBL Player Is Murdered," CT, Feb. 11, 1981. Beasley's "she'd want us to" remark is from "Wranglers Praise Role of Connie Kunzmann," OWH, Feb. 12, 1981. Inactive status is from a WBL release, Feb. 12, 1981; black patches are from "Wranglers Praise Role" and "Pioneers Lose, 143–116," SFC, Feb. 12, 1981.

The prior searches are from "Kin Hoping for Relief after Body Identified," OWH, Mar. 29, 1981. Information about Greta Alexander is from "Psychic Has Aided Many Police Cases," SLPD, Apr. 12, 1990; "Psychic Brought Town More Than

Prestige," *Bloomington (IL) Pantagraph*, Sep. 13, 1999; and Arthur Lyons and
Marcello Truzzi, *The Blue Sense: Psychic Detectives and Crimes* (New York:
Mysterious Press, 1991), pp. 69, 81.

The discovery and identification of Connie's body and cause of death are from "Kin
Hoping for Relief after Body Identified," *OWH*, Mar. 29, 1981; "Dental Records
Verify Body Is That of Connie Kunzmann," *OWH*, Mar. 30, 1981. The resolution
and league award are from "WPBL Establishes Kunzmann Award," *OWH*, Apr. 1,
1981, and "Kunzmann Hustle and Harmony Award," *WBL News*, Apr. 14, 1981.
Tibke's sentence and parole are from court files in *The State of Nebraska v. Lance
E. Tibke*, Docket No. 81–1621, and from Nebraska Department of Correctional
Services Inmate Information. Information on the "smiley face" is from Berkow.

18. SUSPENDED

The opening anecdote is from Critelli. The hotel incident and the Fillies' meet-
ing is from correspondence from DeLorme to Fischer, Apr. 2, 1981, and from
Nessie Harris to Fischer, Apr. 3, 1981, and from "Fillies Given WPBL Suspension
Notices," *CT*, Mar. 23, 1981.

Chavers' exclamation is from an interview with her. The barricade and events in
the parking lot are from "Unpaid Minnesota Team Forfeits Game to Hustle,"
CT, Mar. 22, 1981, and Fischer. Wilson's "put our foot down", Fischer's "disgrace,"
and Hansen's remarks about Chicago are from "Nevers Promises Game despite
Fillies Walkout," *MT*, Mar. 23, 1981. DeLorme's wish to warn Fischer is from
correspondence from Angela Cotman to Fischer, Apr. 3, 1981.

The scrimmage and refunds are from "Unpaid Fillies Refuse to Play," *CST*, Mar. 22,
1981; "Hustle Wins When Fillies Walk Out," *AHDH*, Mar. 22, 1981; and "Unpaid
Minnesota Team Forfeits Game to Hustle," *CT*, Mar. 22, 1981. Suspension slips
are from "Fillies Given WPBL Suspension Notices," *CT*, Mar. 23, 1981. Cotman's
explanation of their intent is from correspondence from her to Fischer, Apr.
12, 1982. Fischer's explanation of the suspension is from "Unpaid Minnesota
Team Forfeits Game"; Kunze's response is from "Fillies Given WPBL Suspension
Notices." Harris's remark on the players' effort is from her April 3 correspondence
to Fischer. Gwyn's quote is from "WBL on the Verge of Failure," *CST*, Apr. 5, 1981.

The Gulls' struggles are from Critelli, Lynn Arturi, Althea Gwyn, Krystal Kimrey,
Jim Loscutoff, Jody Rajcula, Dana Skinner, and Donna Simms, and from these
articles: "Fast Breaks, Bounced Checks, and Broken Dreams," *(Boston) Real Paper*,
Mar. 19, 1981; "Gulls Not Soaring Financially, Investors Sought," unidentified
paper, Jan. 15, 1981 (investors); "Loscutoff Charges; Gulls Owner Denies," *BG*,
Jan. 14, 1981; "Time and Credit Are Running Out for Gulls," *LET*, Jan. 16, 1981

(waitress, refrigerator, food stamps); "Reither Accuses Players," *LET*, Jan. 16, 1981 (accusations); "Skinner Home Debut Stormy; Gulls a Team in Turmoil," *Salem (MA) Evening News*, Jan. 9, 1981 (walkout, banks); "Sports Log: Gulls' Future Questionable," *BG*, Jan. 17, 1981 ("final humiliation," "our own pockets"); "Gulls Face Doom as Gate Collapses," *LET*, Jan. 16, 1981 (confrontation, cigar); "How Long Can WBL Survive?" *(Chicago) Southtown Economist*, Jan. 18, 1981 ("pockets," "ask the girls"), and "Gulls Grounded," *SLPD*, Jan. 16, 1981 ("can't buy food"). The revocation is from a letter from Fischer to Reither, Jan. 20, 1981, and Minutes, Jan. 27, 1981. The "paying heavily" quote is from an undated 1981 letter from Critelli to Fischer.

Early plush treatment of Dreams players is from Michelle McKenzie and Vonnie Tomich. Attendance of 88 is from "Dreams Roll before 88," *LBIPT*, Jan. 24, 1980. The incident of being stranded is from McKenzie and Patti Bucklew. The canceled game and revocation are from "No Pay, No Play, Dreams Say," *LBIPT*, Feb. 28, 1980; "Somebody Went to Sleep," *LAT*, Feb. 28, 1980; "Dreams Being Put to Sleep?" *LBIPT*, Mar. 1, 1980; and these Feb. 1980 unidentified articles in McKenzie's and Bucklew's scrapbooks: "Dreams' Nightmare," "Dreams Game Gets Canceled; GM Gets Fired," "Dream Game Called Off due to Legal Problems," and "Women's Basketball League Revokes Dreams' Ownership."

Cotman's quote is from a letter from her to Fischer, Apr. 3, 1981, see also a letter from Cotman to Fischer dated Apr. 12, 1981. Nevers's request to lift the suspensions and Fischer's denial are from Memo to WBL League Office from Minnesota Fillies, Mar. 23, 1981, and Memo, Fischer to Nevers, Mar. 24, 1981. The "not Going to Kill" comment is from "Nevers Promises Game," *MT*, Mar. 23, 1981.

The "scabs" remark is from a letter to Fischer from "A Fan," Mar. 23, 1981; other protests to Fischer were from Lindy McKnight, Mar. 24, 1981, and Nancy Burton, Mar. 28, 1981. Nevers's "someday" comment is from "Fillie Owner Plans to Carry On," *Duluth Herald & News Tribune*, Mar. 23, 1981.

Sjoquist's and Ohm's recollections are from interviews with them. Names of other replacements are from box scores and articles, including "Ex-Fillies Watch New Group Go for Broke," *MT*, Mar. 24, 1981; "Two City Players Are among Fill-ins in Fillies Game," *Rochester [MN] Post-Bulletin*, Mar. 24, 1981; and "Fillies Cried, So 'Mandy' Played Again," *New Ulm (MN) Journal*, Mar. 26, 1981. Manderfeld's and Roberts's reasons for playing are from "Ex-Fillies Watch"; Ohm's reasons and her humorous account are from "Old Cagers Just Dribble Away," *Faribault [MN] Daily News*, Mar. 24, 1981.

DeLorme's "bad joke" remark is from "Kunze Claims He Is Owed $25,000 by WBL Fillies," *MT*, ca. Apr. 1981. The "double takes" quote is from "New Fillies Fizzle as Streak Triumph," SLPD, Mar. 24, 1981. The heckling is from Chavers and "Ex-Fillies Watch New Group Go for Broke," MT, Mar. 24, 1981 (also Wahl-Bye's quote). The "vultures" remark is from "It's the Wrong Time, Wrong Place for Fillies to Score," MT, Mar. 24, 1981; the "any ink" comment is from "She Spoke Up, Got Shipped Out," MINN.S, ca. Feb. 26, 1981. The final games are from "Fillies Lose under New Coach Sjoquist," SPPP, Mar. 29, 1981, and "Earthquake Hits Fillies," SPPP, Apr. 1, 1981. Fischer's "worst thing" remark is from "WBL on the Verge of Failure," CST, Apr. 5, 1981. The not-guilty verdict is from "Failing WBL Lacking a Bell to Toll," CST, May 29, 1981.

19. HOME COURT DISADVANTAGE

The opening scene is from the trial transcript, *In re the Marriage of Dennie Lloyd Bolin and Monna Lea Bolin*, No. CD109–0681, 2:135–36. The quote about Dennie's drinking is from his trial testimony, pp. 77–78. The background of the Bolins' marriage is from *Bolin v. Bolin*, 336 N.W.2d 441 (Iowa 1983), interviews with Molly Kazmer (then Bolin), and numerous references in 1978–80 Iowa news articles.

Molly's "berserk" comment and the remark about Dennie's friends are from "The Lady Is a Hot Shot," SI, Apr. 6, 1981. Damien at college practice is from "A Pro in Search of a League," LAT, Feb. 26, 1983. The "Molly's husband" label and her absences are from "The Men behind Iowa's Successful Women," DMR, June 17, 1979; see also "Cage Frustration over for Moravia's Bolin," *Centerville (IA) Iowegian*, Mar. 29, 1979. Molly rejoining the WBL is from an interview with her and a letter from her to Sherwin Fischer dated Jan. 6, 1981. Dennie being out of work is from *Bolin v. Bolin*; the "breadwinner" quote is from "Machine Gun Molly: An Athlete First," SFC, Feb. 27, 1981.

Post-dissolution events are from *Bolin v. Bolin*, interviews with Kazmer and Ione Shadduck, and trial court documents: Temporary Writ of Injunction Without Bond, Decree of Dissolution of Marriage, Application to Modify Decree of Dissolution of Marriage and Application for Temporary Injunction, Modification of Decree of Dissolution and Ruling on Motion for Rule to Show Cause. The kidnap warning is from a July 29, 1982, teletype introduced as a trial exhibit.

Trial discussions are from the transcript, pp. 42–44 (unnamed source), 71–72 (roommate's "femininity"), 78–80 (wrapped up in career), 87–91 ("I've had enough"), 121–23 ("role-reversed"), 131–32 ("not Damien's mother"), 149 (fisticuffs), 194–95 (promotional photos), 260 (festival), 287–88 (road trips), 290 (not ashamed), 294 ("gay community"), and 302–3 ("blow your stack").

Stereotyping is from "Custody Battle over Molly's Son Rocks Her Home Town," DMR, Dec. 5, 1982; "A Pro in Search of a League," LAT, Feb. 26, 1983 ("slap in the face"); and from Kazmer. The Supreme Court ruling is from the opinion; "Court Cautions Iowans in Bolin Custody Ruling," *DMR*, July 21, 1983; and "Bolin Wins Joint Custody of Son," *Centerville (IA) Iowegian*, July 21, 1983. Other courts citing *Bolin v. Bolin* is from the Westlaw computerized legal research database, West Publishing, accessed June 15, 2003.

20. FINAL BUZZER

The "Mickey Rooney" quote is from Greenberg. The description of the *Today Show* appearance is from Fischer and a videotape of the program. The "death knells" comment is from "WBL on the Verge of Failure," *CST*, Apr. 5, 1981. The "bullish" and "weakest link" remarks are from "Streak, Facing Sanctions, Hope to 'Hang on Longer'" and "WBL Needs TV Exposure to Succeed," both *SLPD*, Apr. 19, 1981. The "soul-searching" comment is from "Former WPBL Chief Plans Rival League," *CT*, Apr. 24, 1981. Fischer's remark about "these changes" is from "Failing WBL Lacking a Bell to Toll," *CST*, May 29, 1981.

Geller's proposal is from a letter to Fischer, May 21, 1981, and his motion to the board, May 23, 1981. The vote is from correspondence from Almstead to Members of the WBL, June 17, 1981; Almstead's "getting back" is from "Money Talks," *DTH*, May 28, 1981.

The planned 1981 draft is from correspondence from Fischer to Lafayette J. Jamison, Apr. 7, 1981. The notice to players was from correspondence from Women's Professional Basketball League, Inc. to WBL Player, July 13, 1981. The deal with Philadelphia players is from the settlement agreement and from correspondence from Joseph Chicco to Fischer, July 31, 1981.

Haarlow's background is from his 1981 résumé; "Floundering WPBL Considers Bill Haarlow for Commissioner," *CST*, July 18, 1981; and *Pioneers of the Hardwood, Indiana and the Birth of Professional Basketball*, Todd Gould (Bloomington: Indiana Univ. Press, 1998), pp. 78–93; his ideas are from Proposal for Restructuring of WBL by Haarlow Management Group, July 8, 1981. Geller's concerns about unstable members are from letters from him to Almstead, Aug. 26, 1981, and to Ownership of the Chicago Hustle, July 31, 1981. "Whether there is a market" is from a letter from Geller to All WBL Team Owners, Aug. 19, 1981.

Almstead's resignation is from a letter to Board of Governors, Sep. 24, 1981. The "sinking ship" and "rash statements" quotes are from "WPBL Still Alive, Says Hustle Owner," *CT*, Sep. 30, 1981; the "greed" comment is from "Women's Pro Basketball Clinging to Life," *CT*, undated. Simpson's dire prediction is from "WBA Season in Peril, a Club Owner Warns," *NYT*, Oct. 29, 1981, and an untitled article,

NOTP, Oct. 28, 1981. Fischer and Kozlicki's "dilemma" statement is from a letter from them to WBL owners, Nov. 12, 1981.

Responses from St. Louis, New York, New Jersey, Iowa, San Francisco, Minnesota, and Dallas are from a Nov. 1981 document titled "WBL Team Summary" and a letter from Fischer to Kozlicki, Nov. 24, 1981. The "Popeye" quip is from "Briefing," *CT*, Nov. 17, 1981. The special meeting is from a Dec. 2, 1981, notice sent by owners of the Chicago, Nebraska, and Minnesota franchises. The resolution dissolving the WBL and owners' signatures are from correspondence from Fischer to WBL Member Teams, Feb. 2, 1982.

Peters's "thin air" comment is from "WBL Had Heart, but No Lifeblood," *BG*, Apr. 4, 1982; Rajcula's quote is from an interview with her. Dickey's "script" statement is from "The Problems of Owning a Pro Team," *SFC*, ca. Apr. 1, 1981.

The "not as convincing" quote is from "It's Like Rassling a Bear," *DDN*, Feb. 2, 1979. Banks's mismanagement claims are from "Hustle Working Two Jobs," *CST*, Oct. 15, 1980. Byrne's "three things" statement is from "WBL Set to Make History," *MIL.S*, Dec. 8, 1978, and "A Women's Pro Basketball Team for D.C.?" *WS*, May 14, 1978.

The "upgraded its credibility" remark is from "Women's Hoop Loop Gearing for 2d Season," *NYP*, Nov. 13, 1979. "Can't get any classier" is from "Pioneers Hit the Trail," *SFC*, Nov. 15, 1979. The "filet mignon" quip is from the 1979–80 New Orleans Pride program. The "cheating on your wife" comment is from "Hard Sell for the WBL," *RS*, Mar. 1980. Attendance figures are from league records. The "force-feed" quote is from "WBL Needs TV Exposure to Succeed," *SLPD*, Apr. 19, 1981. WGN ratings are from "Red Ink, Rosy Future," *SI*, May 14, 1979, and "Elimination of Hustle Costly to New WPBL," *CST*, Apr. 21, 1979. The "dose of media" advice is from "Success Lies Ahead for the WBL," *Westfield (NJ) Press Box*, Feb. 28, 1981.

Griggs's quote is from "The WBL: It's Alive and Growing," *OCR*, Nov. 14, 1979. The "political wedge" comment is from "Nancy Lieberman: A New Queen for the Court," *SFC*, Jan. 9, 1980; "I don't go" is from "Lieberman Vows to Obey Boycott," *DMN*, Mar. 27, 1980. Wethall's quote is from "A Letter from the Publisher," *STBD*, 1:4. The closing anecdote is from Nevers.

21. SNAPSHOTS OF THE WBL

The New Orleans impersonation is from Hastings and Szeremeta. VBK and Brown's history is from interviews with them and from the 1979–80 New Orleans Pride Program. Bolin's record and her mother fainting are from Molly Kazmer and "Bolin Scores WBL Record 53," *DMR*, Mar. 28, 1979. Bolin's statistics are from league records. Vance's 100-point plan is from Kirk.

Moore's record is from "Streak's 'Pearl the Earl' Is Not Used to Losing," *SLPD*, Sep. 18, 1980; her free throws are from "She Just Didn't Stop Shooting," *BG*, Feb. 1, 1980.

Nadel's gunshots are from "Nadel Learned to 'Rough It' Doing Diamonds Broadcasts," *DTH*, Apr. 4, 1980. Long-distance Greene is from "Viv Greene Sits, Then Hits as Rockettes Stone Hustle," *DDN*, Jan. 22, 1979. Easterling's 21 assists are from league records.

Linda Matthews's story is from "Once Uncertain, Matthews Has Become Fox' Leader," *PI*, Nov. 30, 1979, and "Dreams Can Smile after Gorgeous Win," *LBIPT*, Jan. 25, 1980; her stats are from the 1980–81 WBL Media Guide. The Pat Hodgson information is from the WBL 1979 draft list and 1980–81 Media Guide; Pat Montgomery's information is from those sources and "She'll Have a Beer Now," *MINN.S*, Nov. 1979.

Disco Sims is from "The Dreams Come True," *OCR*, Oct. 25, 1978. WBL overtime games are from the 1979–80 WBL Media Guide and league records. The description of the "knock-down, drag-out" game is from "Gems Subdue Does in 3 OT," *NSL*, Mar. 31, 1979. The Gulls-Wranglers upset is from Rajcula and Dana Skinner and from "New England Learns to Win at the Expense of Wranglers," *OWH*, Jan. 10, 1981. The Costello anecdote is from Doug Bruno. Houston being left out of the draft is from "Hustle Stars Anxious for Reply in All-Star Game," *CST*, Jan. 28, 1980.

Nicknames are from "The WBL," Feb. 25, 1979 (Machine Gun Molly), "Bolin, Comets Rinse Out Streak," *SLGD*, Feb. 8, 1980, and "Move Over, Bernard King," *NJM*, Feb. 1979 ("crazed matriarch").

The Dallas 1980–81 draft story is from Williams and TD notes. The Bolin-Blaze shootout is from "Bolin Beats the Blaze; Pioneers Win," *SFC*, 3/26/81. The WBL points record is from league records. Wilson's 55-footer is from an untitled article, *Twin Cities Courier*, Dec. 13, 1979. Patterson's injury and statistics are from "Blastoff!" *DDN*, Dec. 16, 1978, and "Rockettes Lose Patterson for the Season," *DDN*, Dec. 21, 1978; Roberts' are from the "Joe Soucheray" column, *MT*, Feb. 2, 1979, and the 1979–80 and 1980–81 WBL Media Guides.

Aulenbacher's mask is from an interview with her. The "show us your gems" comment is from Simms. The description of Barnes's admirer is from TD notes. Neiman's sketches are from Marshall Geller. The Stars' descriptions are from "Watching the Stars," *New Yorker*, Feb. 18, 1980. Meyers's triple doubles are from "Gems Capitalize on Missed Fouls by Iowa, 111–95," *NSL*, Jan. 20, 1980, "Gems End Season Losing 6th to Stars," *NSL*, Mar. 16, 1980, and box scores. "The name Skyline" is from "Skyline Acquires Two Shooting Stars," *CT*, June 20, 1978, and "Gals Pro Basketball Moving into Arenas," *Amusement Business*, July 15, 1978; the discussion of "Hustle" is from Logan and "Hustle Struggling to Beat Sexism," CT, Jan. 14, 1979; Cunningham's quote is from "Wait 'til Next Year," *Seattle Post-Intelligencer*, July 25, 1978.

Dallas's 1979–80 road record is from league records. Information on players with 40-minute games is from league records. Ortega's "frantic pace" is from "Scoring Wiz Sparks Upset of Pioneers," SFC, Dec. 31, 1979; the 46-minute press is from "Pioneers Eye Diamonds," SFC, Dec. 2, 1979; see also "Tired Pioneers Hang On, Top Angels, 79–75," SFC, Dec. 21, 1979; "Stars Hand Pioneers 1st Loss at Home," SFC, Dec. 23, 1979; and "Pioneers Hold On as Ortega Scores 38," SFC, Dec. 28, 1979.

Landa's suspension is from "Gems Suspend Landa Indefinitely," NSL, Mar. 13, 1980, and Wanda Szeremeta. VBK's suspension is from a letter from Sherwin Fischer to Claudette Simpson, Feb. 17, 1981, and a WBL press release, Mar. 17, 1981. "Without socks" is from "Butch and the Simpsons: Both Share Blame for Demise of Pride," NOTP, Mar. 20, 1981; VBK's quote is from "Butch Is 'Suspended' by Pride," NOTP, Mar. 17, 1981; see also "Changin' Places," STBD, 1 (May 1981): 7.

Gleason's court fight is from CST: "Hustle Attempts to Fire Gleason," Mar. 28, 1981; "Gleason Thwarts Firing, Hustle Wins," Mar. 29, 1981; "Hustle Buys Out Gleason's Contract," Mar. 30, 1981; CT: "'Fired' Earlier This Month, Gleason Still Hustle Coach," Mar. 15, 1981; "Gleason Fired as Hustle Coach," Mar. 28, 1981; "Court Order Keeps Hustle Coach on Job," Mar. 29, 1981; "Hustle Coach Agrees to Quit after 'Amicable' Negotiations," Mar. 30, 1981; and AHDH: "Hustle, Gleason Heading to showdown," Mar. 21, 1981, "Gleason Gets Court Help to Remain Hustle Coach," Mar. 29, 1981; "Gleason Leaves Hustle Position," Mar. 30, 1981.

Honorary tip-offs are from news accounts of the games. "Cobwebs" is from "No Joke: Hustle a Big Winner," CST, Dec. 15, 1978. Jeffrey as ball girl is from Marquis and her. Thomas's "respect you" is from Marquis. The "Rah rah rah" episode is from Molly Kazmer. The New Orleans crowd is from Brown, league records, and "Record Crowd No Big Help to Pride," NOTP, Nov. 16, 1979. The Stars' streak and overtime games are from league records and "Pioneers Take Charge, Win in OT," SFC, Jan. 23, 1980. Meminger's quote is from "Hustle Coach Pledges Shakeup after Stars Win," CST, Jan. 20, 1980; "the stars don't come out" comment is from "Stars down Philly," NYP, Dec. 12, 1979.

Draving's tongue incident is from Rhonda Penquite. Milwaukee's coaches are from "Rockettes, WBL Have Growing Pains," DDN, Jan. 26, 1979. Coaching turnover is from "The Way the Coach Bounces," SI, Dec. 25, 1978–Jan. 1, 1979 (speed record); "Surviving This Far WPBL Milestone," CT, Feb. 11, 1979 ("back seat"); "Winning Formula," HC, Mar. 26, 1979 ("boutique"). Klinzing's settlement is from an interview with her, the check, and a letter from her attorney to the Does' attorney.

New York's trash talking is from "Hustle Gets Psyched Out," CST, Mar. 18, 1979.

Blaze's statistics are from league records; her 21 free throws are from a Chicago Hustle news release, Mar. 14, 1981. Bubble gum cards are from "Winning Formula," *HC*, Mar. 26, 1979; the Sportscasters are from Beckett's *Basketball Card Price Guide* No. 8 (2000).

Lewis's spike is from "Method of Compensation for Fincher Clouded," *CST*, Nov. 30, 1979. Easterling's charges are from "Easterling Puts Hustle in First Place," *CST*, Feb. 9, 1979. Gehrke in sneakers and fur is from an interview with her. Jones's attachment to two youngsters is from an interview with her. The "feud" quote is from "Ann Meyers Debuts in Garden with Gems," *NYP*, Feb. 15, 1980. The "other eye" caption is from a photograph in sect. 3, p. 1 of *LAT*, Dec. 22, 1979. The description of the "Guardian Angels" is from "Rah, Rah, Rah, Sis Boom Bah?" *Woodlands [TX] Villager*, Nov. 29, 1978, and "2 Bits, 4 Bits, 6 Bits, a Dollar, 12 Selected to Holler," *HP*, Dec. 3, 1978 ("cutie," "sex show"). The cheerleaders' "raunchiness" and Arturi's quote are from "Fox Tryout," *PDN*, Oct. 30, 1979.

Eileen Fulton is from Pat Lindquist's column, *(Minneapolis) Skyway News*, Jan. 15, 1981, and several articles in Lynnette Sjoquist's scrapbook. "Gent" Don Kennedy is from "Move Over, Bernard King," *NJM*, Feb. 1979. The "at heart" quote is from "N. J. Thinks It Has Coaching Gem in Kennedy," *New Jersey Record*, Sep. 7, 1978. Gwyn's background is from "Women's Pro Basketball League: The New Million-Dollar Baby," *Ms.*, Mar. 1980, and interviews with Gwyn, Kaye Young, and numerous other players who mentioned her dominance. "Rough-housing" is from "Gwyn Gives Hustle Muscle," *AHDH*, Apr. 4, 1981.

Lieberman's rolling car is from an interview with her. Peppler's amended contract is from a copy of it. Jennings's tryout is from Tom Davis and *Diamonds Tip-Off Newsletter* 5 (fan favorite). Nissen on his head is from "Are Fans Interested? Cornets to Find Out Today," *DMR*, Dec. 17, 1978. Lemons's suggestion is from "Last Shot?" *DTH*, Dec. 8, 1980. All-Star Game scrambling is from Bill Byrne; Easterling's award is from *WBL* records; the rave review is from "East Women Outgun West," *NYP*, Mar. 15, 1979.

The three-time All-Stars are from rosters; the two omitted players are from *WBL* records of All-Star voting (final tally), and a *WBL* Memo to All Players, Jan. 22, 1981 (rules). Thomas's "eat me" is from Charlotte Lewis. Mitchell's bra strap incident is from an interview with her.

The quote about Draving is from "Hustle's Title Hopes Fall Short," *CT*, Apr. 15, 1979. The exciting finale is from "Hustle's Title Hopes Fall Short," Fincher, game video, and "Cornets Rally Past Chicago to Win Crown," *DMR*, Apr. 15, 1979. The "brew" quote is from an untitled article, *CST*, Apr. 16, 1979. The softball game, including "feeling no pain," are from "Fincher Fights Her Sexy Stereotype with Hustle," CT, Nov. 16, 1979, and Fincher.

Green's accident is from "Togetherness Helps Cornets," DMR, Apr. 11, 1979, and "Cornets outHustled; Green Hit by Auto," DMT, Apr. 11, 1979. The 1979 final game attendance is from league records. Penquite's toss is from an interview with her. The Fillies-Pride home-court deal is from "Pride Beaten in Finale," NOTP, Mar. 17, 1980, and "It's Costly and on New Court, but Fillies Still Playing," MT, Mar. 26, 1980. The Dallas-Nebraska home-court battle is from Williams and Davis.

The final Omaha crowd is from Larry Kozlicki, a video of the game, and the box score. The "worst shooter" and "go short" quotes are from "Diamonds Drop Chance," DTH, Apr. 21, 1981. Walker's problem with prostitutes is from Kirk. Banks's "secret" is from "Hustle Needs Stop Sign for Wranglers' Walker," CST, Apr. 4, 1981.

22. EPILOGUE

The WBL Reunion stories are from the author's personal observation. The "gallant attempt" is from "Women's League Taking a Shot," *Newsday*, Oct. 31, 1996, p. A78. Crevier's quote is from "A Killing in Omaha," IS, Feb. 1982. Bolin's is from "Women Bide Their Time on Court While Sport Looks for Support," PI, Nov. 28, 1982. Williams's quote is from "A Queen without a Court," DTH, Jun. 27, 1982. Nelson's "went home" quote is from "Success Lies Ahead for the WBL," *Westfield (NJ) Press Box*, Feb. 28, 1981. Kenlaw's "no clue" comment is from "Angels, Times to Remember," HC, Aug. 6, 2000. McGraw's "name in the paper" remark is from "Big Women on Campus," *Newsday*, Feb. 13, 2001.

Index